Structure in
Nature
Is a Strategy
for
Design

The MIT Press   Cambridge,
Massachusetts, and
London, England

Structure in Nature Is a Strategy for Design

Peter Pearce

Many of the systems described in this book constitute proprietary inventions. Their practical applications are the subject of patents and patent applications and include, but are not limited to, the Universal Node System, the Min-a-Max Building System, and Curved Space Structures derived from the saddle polyhedra and continuous surface systems.

This book was set in VIP Helvetica light and bold by DEKR Corporation, printed on Mohawk Vellum Book by Murray Printing Company, and bound in the United States of America.

Fifth printing, 1990

Library of Congress Cataloging in Publication Data

Pearce, Peter.
 Structure in nature is
 a strategy for design.

 Bibliography: p.
 1. Architectural design.
 2. Nature (Aesthetics).
3. Form (Aesthetics).   I. Title.
NA2750.P4   729   77-26866
ISBN 0-262-16064-1

To Sally and George
for their trust

To Celia and Aleta
for their inspiration

To Susan
for her sustenance

I
**Structure in
Nature
and Design
1**

III

A
Theory of
Structure
137

Preface and Acknowledgments

The birth—or, it may be, the efflorescence into my conscious awareness—of the work presented in this book dates back to 1958 when I was a senior at the Institute of Design in Chicago. At that time I attempted to design a paperboard dwelling system in which significantly varied structural configurations could be assembled from a minimum number of types of mass-produced components. This project was a brief design effort involving a couple of scale models, which were unsuccessful in both their modular and their structural effectiveness. The general problem seemed to me even then to be extremely important; however, the course of my life was such that the idea slipped back into my unconscious for a number of years.

As time passed, and I became inspired by the work of Charles Eames, Konrad Wachsmann, Buckminster Fuller, and D'Arcy Wentworth Thompson, the problem gradually reemerged; and it became the basis of a serious and extensive investigation in 1965 when I was awarded a research fellowship by the Graham Foundation for a study of "Structurally Autonomous, Geometrically Adaptable Cellular Systems." At that time, I knew virtually nothing about geometry, and in particular about polyhedra and the related ideas which are the primary subject of this book. It was uphill from there.

The main themes of this book are: a systematic and, I hope, a comprehensive study of three-dimensional spatial systems; a theory of their interrelationships; and the possibilities for the application of such systems—or at least some of them—to structural and architectural design. I imagine that the book will find its greatest use amongst designers and architects. Yet the work presents a novel application of concepts usually only met with in the sciences; furthermore, a good part of it is devoted to concrete visualizations—by way of photographs of models —of structures dealt with more abstractly by scientists, who usually speak a mathematical parlance accessible only to initiates. Whether my variations on the theme of space-filling will have some application in the physical sciences I cannot say. Yet perhaps the visualizations contained herein may hold some interest for mathematicians, biologists, physicists, chemists, and, especially, crystallographers.

The form of the presentation in this book stems from a strong empirical bias; hence, geometry is approached in a deliberately concrete way. By virtue of this approach, readers without mathematical backgrounds should be able to follow the development of the subject. At the same time, I hope that my presentation will withstand the scrutiny of readers trained in mathematics and science.

I have attempted to create a book that is self-contained, so that the development of ideas can be followed without the use of outside references. However, numerous references are given for the serious student of morphology and geometry.

Although they have expanded into more comprehensive systems, most of the concepts presented in this book were described in preliminary form in a report to the Graham Foundation in the fall of 1966, entitled "Synestructics, the Study of Universal Structure." Since "practical application" has been an important emphasis in my work, and since many proprietary inventions have evolved as part of this work, a company was founded in 1970, called Synestructics, Inc., to pursue the "reduction to practice" of such inventions.

Although Synestructics, Inc., is no longer in operation, the company was able to bring to market in the 1970s a line of "geometrical" educational toys, games, and playground equipment, based upon ideas outlined in this book. In the 1980s, a new company was formed, called Pearce Structures, Inc. This company has succeeded in applying the new vocabulary for architecture presented in this book to a large number of built projects in the building environment. Both small and very large space frame structures have been built by Pearce Structures during the 1980s, relying on the principles of morphology and structure presented in this book. Reporting further on this work with applied architectural systems is beyond the scope of this book.

I owe thanks to many people who, during the course of my investigations and the preparation of this book, offered their encouragement, inspiration, and technical assistance. I would first like to thank the Graham Foundation and its former director, John Entenza, for awarding me a fellowship in 1965 for the initial research and a grant in 1968 to prepare some further material towards the completion of this book. Konrad Wachsmann, Buckminster Fuller, and Charles Eames provided both inspiration and direct encouragement, and for this I am most grateful. Most recently the completion of this book was supported by a grant from the National Endowment for the Arts in Washington, D.C.

I would like to thank Alan Schoen for his enthusiastic interest in my work, for his lively and inspired conversation, and for his helpful clarification of certain mathematical concepts. I am indebted to both Arthur Loeb and Edwin Schlossberg, not only for their continuing interest in my work, but also for their critical review of and constructive suggestions for the original manuscript; and to Arthur Loeb and Gyorgy Kepes for bringing my work to the attention of the MIT Press. For their collective assistance in model building, illustration, photography, and other technical areas, I would also like to thank Robert Brooks, Roger Conrad, Toby Cowan, Robert Fuller, Mark Jurey, and Steve Selkowitz. I would also like to thank the many individuals and institutions—listed in the Photo and Picture Credits—who supplied the beautiful photographs of structure in nature which appear in Chapter 2. Special gratitude is also due to Keto Soosaar for his enthusiastic appreciation of my work, and for his encouragement resulting from our ongoing discussions of the implications and validity of specific structural system applications. I also owe him thanks for his contribution of the Curved Space structural analysis as reported in Chapter 14.

Finally, and most importantly, I would like to thank my wife, Susan, who not only built hundreds of models of all kinds, did a large percentage of the inking of the drawings, and helped me with the photography, but also typed the manuscript and contributed extensively to its preparation and editing. Without her dedication and extensive help, the completion of this book would plainly not have been possible.

Introduction

Systems for Diversity

Man's successful fit into the built environment depends on the possibilities for change and adaptation within a context of conservative resource use. Such possibilities are a function of diversity and efficiency of form, and such diversity of form can enhance man's relationship to his environment. Technological man's pervasive reliance upon standardized undifferentiated form minimizes the possibility for diversity.

The work presented in this book attempts to provide a basis for a rapprochement between the principle of standardization and the need for diversity and change in environmental structures. When properly used, the principle of component standardization is a system of great production and distribution efficiency; it can also be a system which conserves natural resources. In a fundamental way, standardization is a principle of modularity. We need to develop a building strategy with which diversity and change can be accomplished by modular systems which are efficient in their use of natural material and energy resources.

Systems can be envisaged which consist of some minimum inventory of component types which can be alternatively combined to yield a great diversity of efficient structural form. We call these *minimum inventory/maximum diversity* systems.

By such a "system" I mean *a minimized* inventory of component types (a kit of parts) *along with* rubrics whereby the components may be combined. In the best systems, as we shall see, the rubrics lead not to constriction, but to a *maximization* of different, though generically related, structural forms. We will uncover such rubrics by considering the properties of space—of form itself. One characteristic of successful systems will be that the rubrics—the rules of assemblage—and the physical components themselves will be seen to be organically related: the rules will be seen to grow out of the parts, the parts out of the rules. How different from so much of contemporary architecture's divorce of material and method!

In [I.1] I show a geometric scheme that exemplifies the minimum inventory / maximum diversity concept. Four geometric modules, A, B, C, and D, combine into basic (cellular) units, which in turn form endless varieties by combination and permutation. Although this demonstration is only diagrammatic, it begins to illustrate the range of diversity that can be generated from a kit of standardized components.

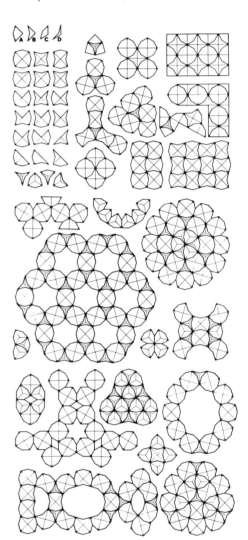

I.1 A minimum inventory/maximum diversity system.

Structure in Nature

In an attempt to understand the concept of minimum inventory/maximum diversity systems we are drawn to nature. Consider the vast number of substances formed by the combinations and permutations of a relatively small number of chemical elements. There are innumerable other examples in nature of form and structure which are generated from the combinations of physically as well as chemically different components.

The snowflake is a most graphic example in nature of the minimum inventory / maximum diversity principle. In fact, it may be considered an archetype of physicogeometric expression. All planar snow crystals are found to have star-like forms with six corners (or subsets thereof). More specifically, they have the symmetry of a regular hexagon. However, within this six-fold form, no two snowflakes have ever been known to be exactly alike. Figure [I.2] shows 37 different snowflakes (Bentley and Humphreys, 1962). The form ranges from very simple and delicate stellate structures through complex filigree-like configurations to bold and relatively massive hexagonal plates. Not only are they all six-sided, but only certain angular relationships occur in these symmetrically branching structures. It is interesting to note that each individual snowflake exhibits a high degree of differentiation within its own form. This variety of pattern which occurs across the face of each individual crystal further emphasizes the minimum inventory/maximum diversity principle.

The molecular structure of the snowflake is the building system by which this infinite diversity is generated. This building system consists of certain physical, geometrical, and chemical constraints (rubrics) which govern the form options. The variety of the snowflake results from a least-energy interaction of its "kit of parts" with the environmental conditions of temperature, humidity, wind velocity, and atmospheric pressure under which it is formed.

I.2 Snowflakes exhibit great diversity of form, governed by certain physical, geometrical, and chemical constraints.

Crystal structures, in general, demonstrate diversity of form as a function of the least-energy internal arrangements of their atomic arrays. In biological structures, the DNA molecule suggests a minimum inventory/maximum diversity principle—although a complex one, with less dependence on physicogeometric constraints than on biochemical interactions. Forms in nature are always generated by structures in nature, and a characteristic range of diversity and differentiation is exhibited within the combinatorial limits of a particular formative process.

In the present work we are concerned primarily with these aspects of structure in nature which manifest themselves in terms of physicogeometric phenomena (built form), since architectural structure operates by definition in this realm. A large part of the form determinants of crystal structures can be characterized as physicogeometric phenomena. Because of this, the relationship of crystals to building structures is more apparent than is the case with biological structures.

An integral part of the concept of minimum inventory/maximum diversity systems is the principle of conservation of resources. The formative processes in natural structure are characteristically governed by least-energy responses. Perhaps the simplest expression of this is found in the principle of closest packing, a principle which even in its most elementary form is common in both the animate and inanimate worlds.

Closest packing is a structural arrangement of inherent geometric stability that finds expression in the three-dimensional arrangement of polyhedral cells in biological systems as well as in the dense arrangement of spherical atoms in the structure of certain metals. If the centers of closest packed equal spheres are joined, a three-dimensional arrangement of equilateral triangles is formed. If the centers of closest packed polyhedral cells in a biological structure are joined through shared faces, a triangulated configuration will also result.

It can be readily seen that the principle of closest packing is equivalent to that of triangulation, and it is well known that triangulated frameworks exhibit inherent geometric stability. Such properties enable framework structures to be built without moment joints, insuring axially loaded members; and this in turn results in high strength-per-weight minimum-energy structures. Planar and domical structures have taken advantage of triangulation for a number of years; the first truly three-dimensional triangulated structures were probably Alexander Graham Bell's tetrahedral kites and space frames. The principle of closest packing/triangulation is one of remarkable universality. It operates independently of scale or materials, with the same energetically conservative effect. Whether at the molecular level, the cellular level, or at the man-made structural level, its inherent stability always establishes a condition of minimum potential energy.

Form as a Diagram of Forces

That nature creates forms and structures according to the requirements of minimum energy is perhaps the most pervasive theme throughout D'Arcy Wentworth Thompson's beautiful work, *On Growth and Form.* Thompson describes how nature, as a response to the action of force, creates a great diversity of forms from an inventory of basic principles. "In short, the form of an object is a diagram of forces; in this sense, at least, that from it we can judge of or deduce the forces that are acting or have acted upon it; in this strict and particular sense, it is a diagram." (Thompson I:16). We can assume that in this creation of form, nature's responses to force action tend to fulfill the conditions of minimum energy.

Form as a diagram of forces is an important governing idea in the application of the minimum inventory/maximum diversity principle to building system design. If a building system can be considered analogous to a molecular structure which is highly responsive to varied actions of force, it may offer the real possibility of generating building forms responsive to the human needs and natural requirements of diversity, adaptation, change, and the conservative use of natural resources. In order to facilitate a design strategy I have attempted an elaboration on the concept of force.

A force may be considered as any factor which may act from within or from without to determine any given form. The form of any structure is determined by the interaction of two fundamental classes of forces: (1) *intrinsic forces,* and (2) *extrinsic forces.* Intrinsic forces are those governing factors which are inherent in any particular structural system; that is, the internal properties of a system which govern its possible arrangements and its potential performance. In the case of our archetypal snow crystals, the intrinsic force system would be its molecular structure which governs the nature or character of its infinitely varied patterns.

Extrinsic forces are those governing influences which are external to any particular structural system. They are the inventory of factors, largely environmental, which give direction to the form options allowed by the inherent combinatorial or form-giving properties of a given structural system. The extrinsic forces in our snowflake example would be those specific environmental factors of temperature, humidity, wind velocity, and atmospheric pressure which interact with the molecular structure to synthesize form.

All forms in nature are determined by the interaction of intrinsic with extrinsic forces. The snowflake typifies all crystalline orderings. The possible external shape options that a given crystal may take are controlled by the internal symmetry of the atomic arrangement; that is, by the system with which the atoms themselves are arranged. The particular local form of a given crystal is determined by the interaction of external environmental factors (e.g., temperature, humidity, etc.) with the inherent principles governing the atomic arrangements. A given crystalline substance may take a variety of shapes; but certain limits to form, usually expressed as angular relationships, are governed by the inherent form-giving properties (the intrinsic force system) of the atomic arrangement [I.3].

I.3 External form dictated by the allowable packings of internal modular elements.

The interaction of intrinsic and extrinsic forces to produce form in nature are relatively comprehensible for the case of inanimate crystals, as the interactions tend to be dominated by physicogeometric phenomena. The process is much more complex and elusive as one examines biological form and structure. The division between intrinsic and extrinsic forces is not always clear and tends to be hierarchical. That is, at one scale a force may be considered extrinsic, but in a larger context, the same force may become intrinsic. This hierarchical phenomenon exists for both inanimate and animate structures. For example, a given molecular structure may constitute an intrinsic force system that controls the options of possible crystalline cell shapes when they are in association with other cells, and the environment formed by the contiguous cells is the extrinsic force that determines which particular option a cell shape may take. The interaction of the extrinsic environmental force with the intrinsic molecular force determines the shapes of the cells in an array. This array of cell shapes then becomes an intrinsic force system that controls the possible shape options of a larger form that reflects still another level of extrinsic force [I.4]. Each successive level of structure is the environment (extrinsic force system) for the preceding level (intrinsic force system). This process can apparently progress ad infinitum.

In the creation of the man-made environment extrinsic forces can be considered the design goals—the various criteria, be they whimsical, philosophical, esthetic, or performance-oriented, that may be imposed upon the designed form. Intrinsic forces in the design of the man-made environment can be considered the "state-of-the-art" technologies and the limitations of their use governed by the level of skill and perceptions available and by the dogma of habit and bias that may prevail.

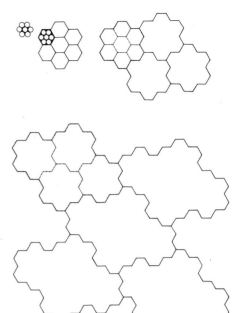

I.4 A hierarchy of intrinsic and extrinsic forces. The hexagonal shape represents an extrinsic response at the lowest level; at higher levels of organization, the hexagonal cell can itself be viewed as an intrinsic determinant of the larger form.

In the present design context, the intrinsic force systems available do not appear to be capable of anything approaching an optimum response to the complexity of extrinsic forces now evident in the manmade environment. The minimum inventory/maximum diversity principle is an attempt to develop a design strategy which embodies an intrinsic force system capable of effective responses to the environmental circumstances which now prevail and will continue to prevail in the future. Such environmental circumstances suggest the following summary of the concept of extrinsic forces as it relates specifically to the design of building systems.

The influences which are external to the inherent properties of a form-giving (building) system constitute a set of extrinsic forces and are the criteria for the creation of building form. These extrinsic forces include: (a) prevailing environmental conditions of temperature, wind, humidity, earth-sun geometry, and their variations;* (b) limitations of resources including energy and materials; (c) topographical conditions; (d) geological conditions; (e) building function including the change of its use over time; (f) relationship to the community; and (g) emotional ambience.

*For a brilliant discussion of the response of different building forms to the stresses of environmental variation and how to optimize form to minimize the need for supportive maintenance energy, see Knowles.

The anticipation of effective building form as a response to these extrinsic forces suggests the following summary of intrinsic forces: a given building system embodies a set of intrinsic forces which determines the inherent properties of the system. These inherent properties include the building system's ability to: (a) conform to arrangements of minimum potential energy, i.e., structural efficiency relative to use of materials; (b) provide diversity of form in order to respond (adapt) optimally to the actions of an array of extrinsic forces; (c) accommodate change in response to the inevitable long term variations of certain extrinsic forces; (d) define a minimum inventory of component types in order to simplify and economize the production and use of the system; (e) take advantage of materials that are consistent with an optimum response to the actions of extrinsic forces and to the economical production of the system's components; and (f) make use of production methods that allow components to be produced economically.

Although the development of sophisticated means by which to analyze extrinsic forces relevant to building design is extremely important (see Knowles), our present concern is the development of a sophisticated and responsive intrinsic force system. Successful design solutions are not possible without the appropriate interaction of intrinsic and extrinsic forces. The field of environmental design has been preoccupied with considerations of design criteria (extrinsic forces) to the neglect of the inherent properties of systems (intrinsic forces) and their implications for creating adaptive form. The present work assumes that the ability to respond effectively to the actions and stresses of extrinsic forces has as a prerequisite an understanding of a theory of intrinsic forces, and that intrinsic force systems do not inherently follow from criteria derived from an analysis of extrinsic forces.

Any environment for human use organizes and distributes energy in various forms. Crystalline material, gases, and liquids are all juxtaposed in a system which exists in three-dimensional space. It matters little what a given spatial complex may look like, be it formally "geometric" or be it amorphously "organic"—its structure is still a matter of physical and geometric relationships. It must work in three-dimensional physical space.

Structure in nature suggests that there must be some fundamental principles and laws, an intrinsic force system, which can form the basis for the design of minimum inventory/maximum diversity building systems. It must be possible to understand the fundamental and comprehensive phenomena which govern the adaptive form-giving potential of modular systems in three-dimensional physical space. Since modularity implies order and order implies symmetry, the intelligibility of a theory of modular structure will depend on an understanding of the extent to which principles of symmetry govern modular order in three-dimensional space. In addition to an understanding of the general nature of modular structure, specific physical characteristics of particular modular arrangements must be evaluated with respect to their structural efficiency in terms of energy utilization.

An Integrative Morphology

Whether they are atoms, spheres, cells, linear members, or surfaces, the components of a physical system have specific size, weight, and shape. The possible ways in which such physical components can fit together into alternative structures are governed by physicogeometrical laws of symmetry. Although such laws can be described mathematically by the abstract relationship of points and lines in space, our present concern calls for a morphological approach in which the elements of modular structures are represented in terms of built form.

Since our concern is a system from which useful building forms can be assembled, we must look at the fundamental principles governing spatial differentiation and enclosure in three dimensions. Any volume which encloses space or which differentiates two or more regions of space can be formed by a collection of surface modules, i.e., polygons. Since any polygon can be defined by a closed framework, i.e., a circuit of edges, any volume can be minimally described as a framework. For example, a cube is composed of six square faces, each of which can be defined by a four-sided frame. The entire cube can be defined by and assembled from twelve linear components or branches. I could go on to give innumerable examples of both finite systems like the cube, or infinite systems like a packing of cubes, all of which can be defined as some kind of modular framework or network.

The requirement of providing for diversity of form suggests that a comprehensive inventory of orderly and fundamental spatial alternatives represented by both finite and infinite networks would be useful, particularly since the state-of-the-art building design approaches exhibit an intrinsic force system dominated by an orthogonal spatial bias.

There can be no doubt that cube oriented geometry is extremely important and relevant to architectural design; however, it has serious modular limitations with respect to the generation of diversity of form, and as a structural framework it has inferior strength-to-weight properties when compared to triangulated systems. The inclusion of orthogonal geometry as an element in a broader view of spatial relationships in three-dimensional structures, rather than as the dominant principle, is bound to increase the inventory of options.

Even children of kindergarten age know that cubes can be packed together to fill space. At this early age a fundamental spatial bias is imposed which is pervasive in Western culture. Virtually all examples of architecture consisting of aggregates of volumetric units, i.e., rooms, demonstrate this bias. It is fairly rare that we actually see true cubes, but how many buildings have been built in which rooms are not defined or enclosed by four vertical and two horizontal surfaces, all disposed at 90° to one another? Most of our cities utilize some form of rectangular grid for the plan of their streets. Cartesian coordinates are a boon to mensuration, it is true, but does it follow (particularly in the age of the computer, when calculations in nonorthogonal coordinates take hardly more time than those in rectangular coordinates) that designers must constrain their forms to the shape of the coordinates upon which they are erected?

As we shall see, reliance upon the 90° angle as a basis for organizing space imposes extremely limited means to reach our goal of maximum diversity and minimum inventory. A cursory observation of natural structures shows that cubes rarely occur. This alone suggests that a careful study of other alternatives is advisable.

As an inventory of form options is assembled consisting of simple finite polyhedra, through polyhedral symmetrical space-filling systems, to a broader class of infinite periodic three-dimensional networks, and beyond, it becomes increasingly clear that the fulfillment of the minimum inventory/maximum diversity principle depends upon the possibility of understanding the interrelatedness of an inventory of alternatives.

The possible common relationship among such alternatives has been explored and developed into an integrative morphological strategy. It is an integrative strategy because it enables entire inventories of systems to be generated as combinations and permutations of common sets of elements, and it is a morphological strategy because it is primarily a concrete physical embodiment of the inherent principles of symmetry and geometry which govern modular order in three-dimensional space rather than an abstract mathematical description of such principles. With this morphological approach, three-dimensional ordering principles in nature can be understood in a direct empirical and sensorially apprehended way. As morphological embodiments of inherent modular principles, such a strategy not only constitutes intrinsic force systems, but can be both physical model systems and architectural building systems as well.

Rather than attempt to set up "architectural" criteria for the discovery of such new spatial possibilities, it is far more useful to establish as our goal a knowledge of all the possibilities for the orderly subdivision, modulation, structuring, and enclosing of space.

We have to be prepared to pursue a course of study which may, at times, seem remote indeed from the creation of improved environments for human use. Yet in the end this path will prove to have been the best, for conclusions drawn from a partial study of space or from a study of space guided by popular experience or assumed technical and engineering limitations cannot uncover fundamental and radical improvements.

Structure in Nature and Design

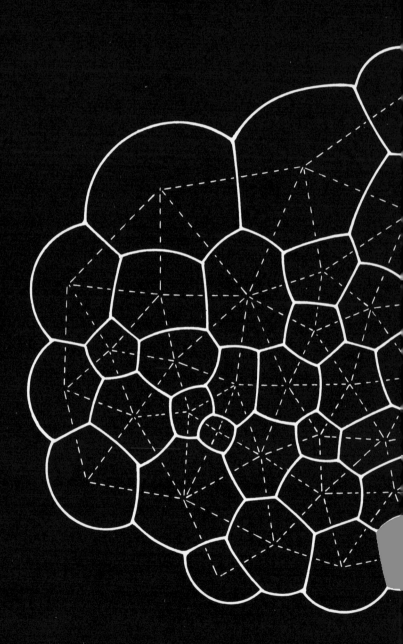

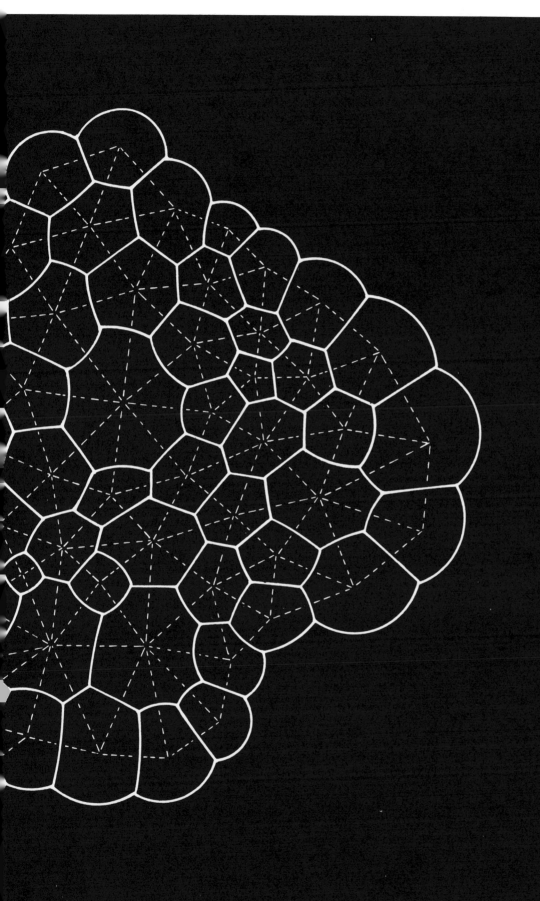

1 Geometry as Structure

The Platonic Solids.
Triangulation and Geometric Stability

Plato was apparently the first person to attempt a geometrical description of structure in nature. He also explored the possibility of developing an inventory of basic geometric shapes (in this case, right triangles) which could be recombined to form the five regular polyhedra* [1.1]. Plato's *Timaeus* contains a detailed account for constructing four of the regular solids from two types of triangles, identifying the four solids with the four elements: the tetrahedron represented fire; the cube, earth; the octahedron, air; and the icosahedron, water. Apparently it did not disturb Plato that the pentagonal dodecahedron could not be formed with his basic triangles. The dodecahedron became for him the shape which envelops the entire universe. These five regular polyhedra became known as the Platonic solids (Benfy and Fikes 1966; Burke 1966). The five Platonic solids are the only convex polyhedra that are bounded by identical regular polygonal faces in which all vertices are equivalent.

The triangle is the only polygon that is stable (rigid) by virtue of its geometry. This can be readily demonstrated by the construction of a triangular frame joined at its vertices with hingeable connectors.

*A *polygon* is a finite connected set of line segments which are joined to each other at their ends such that a closed circuit is formed consisting of edges (sides) and corners (vertices). If the vertices are all coplanar a plane polygon is formed; if not, a skew polygon is formed. A polygon is equilateral if its sides are all equal, and equiangular if the interior angles formed at each vertex are all equal. A plane polygon is considered regular if it is both equilateral and equiangular.
A *polyhedron* is a volume bounded by plane surfaces. It may be considered a finite connected set of plane polygons forming a closed volumetric figure, such that each side of every polygon is shared with one other polygon, and that the sides of these polygons intersect at their ends in groups of three or more to form the vertices of the polyhedron. The polygons are the faces and their sides the edges of a polyhedron. A polyhedron is regular if its faces are identical (congruent) regular polygons and equal, and all of its vertices are equivalent, i.e., all its vertices are surrounded alike.

Such a triangular frame remains rigid—in contrast to polygons of more than three sides, any of which will readily collapse when assembled with hinged joints. Of the Platonic polyhedra only the tetrahedra, octahedra, and icosahedra are composed of triangles, and are, therefore, the only figures of the five that are stable by virtue of their geometry. Again, if we construct all five figures with struts as edges joined at their vertices by hingeable connectors, we see that the cube and dodecahedra collapse, while the other three figures remain rigid. This demonstration has far-reaching significance for the study of structure: triangulation imparts strength to structures even before the physics of materials is taken into account—it provides a head start to, and a guarantee of, structural rigidity.

Although Plato's insights anticipated the concept of modular structures built up from elementary constituent parts, his choices in the pairing of polyhedra with the four basic elements suggests that he may not have been aware of the physical implications of triangulation. It is curious that he would have the unstable cube representing the earth, and the stable octahedron representing air. In any case, the inherent stability of triangulated polyhedra was a principle that he did not elucidate.

Plato's triangles represent an attempt to establish a fundamental morphological system which could account for the variety of forms in nature. It was, albeit primitive, a minimum inventory / maximum diversity system, perhaps the first vision of a geometrically based intrinsic force system.

1.1 The regular polyhedra of Plato (the "Platonic solids"): tetrahedron (a), octahedron (b), hexahedron (c), icosahedron (d), and dodecahedron (e).

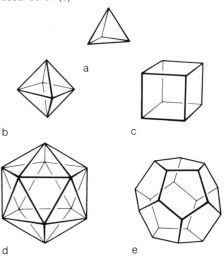

a

b

c

d

e

2

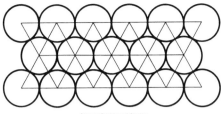

Closest Packing of Circles

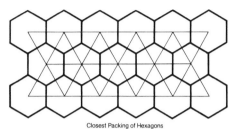

Closest Packing of Hexagons

1.2 Triangulation of two-dimensional closest packed arrays.

1.3 Figures formed by closest packed equal spheres.

a. Cuboctahedron

b. Regular Hexagon

c. Tetrahedron

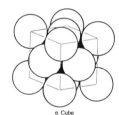

e. Cube

d. Octahedron

Triangulation and Closest Packing

The repeated or iterated pattern of triangles is a pervasive geometrical arrangement in the physical world. It is related to *closest packing* and can range in scale from structures easily seen with the unaided eye, e.g., the bee's honeycomb, to those requiring powerful magnification, e.g., the association of cells in tissues or closest packed atoms in certain crystals. If circles are tightly packed, as densely as possible, and their centers joined, triangles are formed. When the centers of packed hexagons are joined, an array of triangles also results [1.2].

In a three-dimensional array of closest packed (as densely as possible) equal spheres, each sphere is exactly surrounded by twelve others. The centers of the outer spheres are the 12 vertices of a polyhedron known as the cuboctahedron [1.3a]. In the plane, six spheres always surround a seventh, forming a regular hexagon [1.3b]. If three spheres are packed together in a plane as tightly as possible and their centers joined, an equilateral triangle is formed. If a fourth sphere is placed upon the group of three spheres, the four vertices of the regular tetrahedron are established [1.3c].

If six equal spheres are tightly packed, an octahedron is formed [1.3d]. If eight spheres are positioned so as to form the corners of a cube, an unstable condition is created. That is to say, when the sphere centers are joined in this configuration squares are formed, which have no geometrical stability. It takes a minimum of 14 closest packed spheres to form a stable cube [1.3e]. Connecting all centers here, of course, makes evident the diagonal bracing across the cube's six faces.

Consider a stacking of cylinders of equal diameter. As cylinders are stacked upon each other, their natural tendency is to arrange themselves in a triangular order. The end view of such an arrangement looks like the packing of equal circles. This is simply the arrangement which requires the least effort to maintain—it is a minimum-energy configuration. In any case where we analyze the particular physical forces—of surface tension, gravitation, or whatever—that lead to a stable state of some physical system, we find triangulated solutions (i.e., triangulated arrangements) to be associated with the minimum-energy state, or, what is often the same thing, the minimum-resource state.

When packing many circles together, it is most economical (more circles can be placed in a given area) to impose "triangular" packing. In the limit of very many circles, all of a common size, approximately 7% more circles may be placed in a given area of plane surface if their centers can be connected to form equilateral triangles rather than squares [1.4]*

*See Loeb (1966b) for another look at the same question.

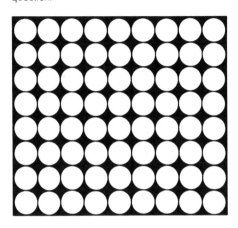

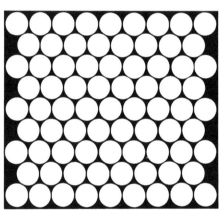

1.4 Comparison of square and triangular packings of equal circles in a given area.

Partitioning and Tessellation.
Networks and Dual Networks

It is well known that, of all plane figures, the circle encloses the greatest area of surface for a given circumference, or alternatively, encloses a given area with the smallest circumference. Likewise, of any three-dimensional shape the sphere matches the greatest volume to the least surface area. Do the circle and the sphere remain the most economical possibilities when we are concerned with the many-celled partitioning of space?

Consider the partitioning formed by closest packed circles: although each circle by itself is very economical (i.e., it encloses maximum area for its given perimeter) small concave triangles are formed between circles. Now, concave triangles match the *least* area with the *greatest* circumference. Consequently we can say that, considering the entire plane, circle packing is not the most economical system. However, let us allow the circles to change their shape such that they fill up the concave triangles, forming hexagons [1.5]. This becomes the most economical method for partitioning a surface into equal units of area.

It is worth reiterating what is here meant by "economical partitioning." That partitioning is economical which divides up a space into cells of maximum size for a given amount of wall material. In the example just discussed, we have seen how simple geometrical reasoning has led us to a hexagonal tessellation of the plane in which there is no "dead" space between cells; all is either enclosed, usable space or wall. Furthermore, though the foregoing demonstration is not to be considered a rigorous proof, it suggests that our hexagonal cells match minimum structure (the overall length of the walls) to maximum usable area.

In addition to being the most economical partitioning of the plane, hexagonal tessellation is also the simplest. That is, a given plane surface cannot be continuously divided without at least three edges meeting at each point. If only two edges meet at a point the plane cannot be continuously divided. It has been shown (Courant and Robbins, pp. 354–361) that if three points are to be interconnected by means of a network whose total length is to be a minimum, they must be joined by three line segments meeting at an intermediate point at 120° angles, with the condition that in the triangle defined by the three points there are no angles greater than 120 degrees. Furthermore, connecting an arbitrary number of random points in the plane in such a way as to minimize the total distance between the points results in a series of line segments meeting in threes at 120° angles within the area defined by the point array [1.6].

The packing of hexagons reveals the fundamental relationship of the triangular order of close packed circles with the requirements of minimal partitioning. Since the general sense of the closest packing of circles is that of associated finite units, i.e., a packing of circular disks or cylinders, and since it is not comprised of straight line-segments joined at vertices, it is usually not considered a network. On the other hand, a packing of hexagons may readily be considered a network since a network can be considered to be a connected set of straight line segments (edges) joined to each other at their ends to form vertices, such that two-dimensional or three-dimensional space is subdivided or partitioned. From any network we can construct a *reciprocal* or *dual* network. A dual network may be constructed on a surface by joining the center of each polygonal cell in a given network with the centers of all of its neighboring cells through their common edges. In the case of the hexagon system, the reciprocal network is an array of triangles [1.2]. When the hexagons are all exactly regular, the triangular network will be composed entirely of regular triangles meeting in groups of six at each vertex. Such a network which is equilateral, equiangular, and in which all vertices are equal, may be considered a regular network.

Sphere packings represent the three-dimensional generalization of circle packings in the plane. The triangular order of sphere packings gives rise to a three-dimensional network of equilateral triangles forming the faces of tetrahedra and octahedra in a space filling array.* Is there a three-dimensional analog to the hexagon packing? Is there a polyhedron which will uniformly partition three-dimensional space with less total surface area per unit of enclosed volume than any other shape? The answer is affirmative but is more subtle than that for the two-dimensional case.

*"Space filling" means the combining of like or complementary bodies in a three-dimensional packing continuously repeated, in such a way that there is no unoccupied space.

1.6 A "minimum-length" connection of random points in a plane.

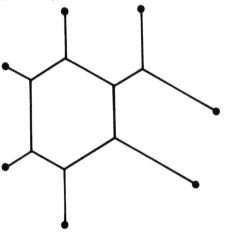

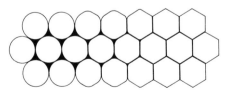

1.5 Changing closest packed circles into closest packed hexagons.

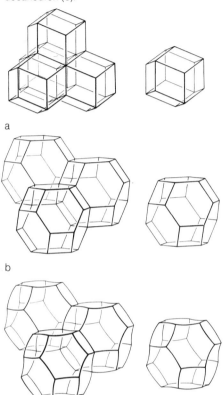

1.7 Rhombic dodecahedron (a), truncated octahedron (b), and the Kelvin minimal tetrakaidecahedron (c).

a

b

c

Filling the Voids: The Kelvin Figure

Just as the closest packed circles left concave spaces between them, so does an array of closest packed spheres. As we might suspect, these concave shapes have high surface area per unit volume and consequently depreciate the minimal-surface advantage of the spheres. If the spheres are swollen to fill in these concave voids, a polyhedron results with 12 identical rhombic faces. It is known as the rhombic dodecahedron [1.7a].

Since in an array of closest packed spheres, each sphere is alike surrounded by 12 others, it is not so surprising that this polyhedron would have exactly 12 faces. A dual network for space filling polyhedra may be found by constructing edges which join the centers of every polyhedron in the space filling array with the centers of all its neighboring polyhedra which share common faces. Doing this we would find that the network which is dual to the space filling array of rhombic dodecahedra is the space filling array of tetrahedra and octahedra in which 12 edges meet at the vertices that fall at the centers of the original rhombic dodecahedra.

Can we say that the rhombic dodecahedron is the shape with the least surface area per unit of volume that will uniformly partition space? Is it the three-dimensional generalization of the hexagon? The answer is no, except in some special circumstances. We must look further.

Lord Kelvin (1887) showed that there is one shape made up of plane surfaces that will uniformly partition space with less surface area than the rhombic dodecahedron. This shape is called the truncated octahedron, a polyhedron bounded by six square faces and eight regular hexagonal faces, a total of 14 faces. The standard plane faced version of this shape [1.7b] has approximately 1% less surface area for a given volume than the rhombic dodecahedron. Kelvin also proposed a "minimal tetrakaidecahedron"* [1.7c], in which a very slight saddle curvature is given to the hexagon faces of the truncated octahedron; the result is approximately 0.103% less surface for a given volume than for the truncated octahedron (Lifshitz).

*Tetrakaidecahedron means fourteen-hedra: a polyhedron with 14 faces. Tetra = four and deca = ten. Tetrakaideca = tetra plus (kai) deca = fourteen.

The closest packing of truncated octahedra can be considered to be a *denser* packing than that of the rhombic dodecahedron because in a space filling array each truncated octahedron is surrounded by 14 others corresponding to its 14 faces, while the rhombic dodecahedron is surrounded by only 12 like cells.

Space filling truncated octahedra give rise to a dual network consisting of congruent isosceles-triangle-faced tetrahedra known as tetragonal disphenoids (Coxeter 1963). This network consists of edges of two different lengths, 14 meeting at each vertex (in the ratio of 1:3). Like the packing of tetrahedra and octahedra, this system constitutes a very efficient, fully triangulated structural framework.

Space filling truncated octahedra is thus evidently a minimum-energy system. As such, it must be considered to be the generalization to three dimensions of the hexagon. Nevertheless, we find that the rhombic dodecahedron, as well as the truncated octahedron, appears as the basis of the solution to certain minimal problems in nature; and thus we are hard put to identify one or the other as the most general solution.

The rhombic dodecahedron and the truncated octahedron exhibit similar geometric characteristics when they are viewed in cellular arrays. With both systems, there are always three shared faces (partitions) meeting on an edge. For the rhombic dodecahedron these shared faces meet at angles of 120°, while for the truncated octahedron they meet at 125°16', 109°28', and 125°16'. In space filling array, the rhombic dodecahedron has two classes of vertices: four edges meeting at a vertex at 109°28' angles and eight edges meeting at a vertex at angles of 70°32', in the ratio of two 4-connected vertices for every 8-connected vertex.* The space filling truncated octahedron has only one type of vertex, which is 4-connected, with alternating angles of 90° and 120°. Looking at the individual polyhedra, we find that the rhombic dodecahedron has eight 3-connected vertices (that is to say, eight with three edges surrounding each vertex) and six 4-connected vertices, a total of 14, and the truncated octahedron has 24 3-connected vertices.

*In this book, an "n-connected vertex" will be taken to be one at which n edges meet.

Many-Celled Soap Bubble Arrays

Where equal tensions exist in all the faces of a cellular array, the array equilibrates into an arrangement in which all shared faces meet at angles of 120° and all vertices are joined alike by four edges meeting at angles of 109°28'. This is exhibited in the random array of soap bubbles shown in [1.8].*

In soap-film behavior, nature has provided us with a most elegant demonstration of minimal principles. When studying a soap-film array, such as that shown in [1.8], we quickly note that neither pure rhombic dodecahedra nor pure truncated octahedra appear. The Kelvin minimal tetrakaidecahedron has been proposed as the archetypal soap-bubble cell. With the minimal tetrakaidecahedron Kelvin enlarged the class of truncated octahedra to include those whose faces are saddle-shaped hexagons bounded by plane arcs. The square faces of the truncated octahedra remain plane, but are necessarily also bounded by the same arc edges. This transforms the truncated octahedron to the minimal tetrakaidecahedron and satisfies the requirement in space filling array that three interfaces meet on a ccmmon edge at 120° angles and that four face edges meet at a common point at 109°28' angles. The minimal tetrakaidecahedron, like the truncated octahedron, has a fully triangulated dual network (tetragonal disphenoidal network).

*Such relationships were first recorded by Plateau in 1873 while experimenting with soap films. See Smith (1954), Courant and Robbins, and Thompson II, Chapter VII.

Since the minimal tetrakaidecahedron has slightly less surface area than the truncated octahedron, it presumably is the minimum-energy shape for an array of equivolume soap bubbles.

Although the Kelvin tetrakaidecahedron is the mathematically ideal minimal-energy equivolume cell shape, it rarely occurs in nature, for the simple reason that nature rarely partitions equally. The few known cases where it has been observed shows it in fairly distorted form. Matzke (1946) conducted experiments to create equivolume soap bubble arrays. He was unable to actually form the Kelvin minimal tetrakaidecahedron, but in a sample of 600 bubbles was able to show that, as an average, the polyhedra had 13.70 faces, very close to the 14. He also observed that a majority of the faces that appeared were pentagons. It is interesting to note that the tetrakaidecahedron has an average of 5.14 edges per face. Figure [1.9] shows camera lucida drawings made from bubble froths in Matzke's experiments. The predominance of five-sided faces is evident, as is the recourse to 3-connected vertices to the exclusion of all others.

It must be stressed, therefore, that even for equivolume arrays, the minimal tetrakaidecahedron can be considered only a theoretical ideal solution.*

*With soap bubble arrays of two different volumes, Matzke found an average of 13.53 faces and again observed that the majority of faces were pentagons. Some rare examples of the Kelvin figure were reported for leaf tissues by Macior and Matzke.

1.8 Soap bubbles.

1.9 Camera-lucida drawings of soap bubble cells (Matzke). The number of faces is given for each figure.

11

12

12

13

13

13

13

14

14

14

14

14

15

15

15

15

16

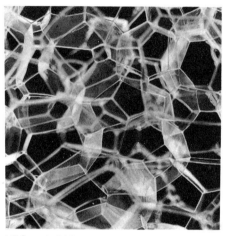
16

Simple Bubble Arrays. The Law of Closest Packing and Triangulation.

For any soap bubble array, either random or uniform, at least we can say that the cells will be organized according to a triangular order. More specifically, in a two-dimensional froth, cells meet in threes around each vertex and consequently always define triangles, and in a three-dimensional soap froth, the cells meet in fours around each vertex and always define tetrahedra. In soap froth there is *never* any exception to this rule.

A single soap bubble floating freely in space is spherical. This is the state of minimum potential energy. When in association with other cells, it becomes more economical for the sphere to change into a polyhedron.

Let us now, following Thompson, consider the conjoining of bubbles that rest upon a plane surface. A single bubble is a simple hemisphere [1.10a]. When two bubbles of equal volume are combined they join forming a vertical planar interface between them [1.10b]. When viewed from above, the spherical surfaces and the interface form two vertices of three edges each where they contact the horizontal plane upon which they rest. Each of the two vertices is surrounded alike by one straight edge and two arc edges. The surface areas of the two hemispheres are a minimum when the tangents of these arc edges meet the straight edge such that they are all surrounded by 120° angles. If there is a difference in the size of two bubbles they will meet so that they still satisfy the 120° angle requirement; in such a case, therefore, all three edges at each vertex will be curved.

If three hemispherical bubbles are combined, it is found that they arrange themselves with three planar interfaces all meeting at 120° angles [1.10c]. The three edges meeting at each point are preserved. When four hemispherical bubbles combine, they also only create intersections in which three edges meet at a point [1.10d]. It is impossible to form a group of four hemispherical bubbles in such a way that they surround a common point in the manner shown in [1.10e]. Such a "square" array is an unstable condition, for the surface area is not at a minimum in this arrangement. The intersection created by four cells on a surface [1.10d] is called the polar furrow (Thompson II:487). This furrow, as we shall see, serves as a useful clue for the identification of closest packing in a variety of contexts.

We may continue adding hemispherical bubbles to our structure, and not once will an intersection appear in which there are other than three edges meeting at a point [1.10f–h]. If the bubbles are all of approximately equal volume all the polygonal circuits that are formed will be very close in shape to hexagons, except those at the periphery of the array. If there are great differences in the sizes of adjacent bubbles in a random array, shapes other than hexagons will appear: pentagons, heptagons, even octagons or more multisided circuits [1.11]. Nevertheless, there will still be no exception to the rule of three edges meeting at a point, and in sufficiently large arrays the shapes will tend to average out to ones of six sides. In all cases, the dual network will be triangular, although not necessarily equilateral.

In three-dimensional arrays of bubbles the rule appears to change to the extent that there are always four edges meeting at each vertex at angles of 109°28′. In actuality, the view of three edges meeting at a point at 120° is simply a *plan* (cross sectional) view of the three partition faces meeting on a common *edge* at 120° angles.*

*This is easily demonstrated with a wire frame tetrahedron dipped in soap. (See Thompson II:497.)

a.

b.

c.

d.

e.

f.

g.

h.

1.10 Simple planar combinations of hemispherical soap bubbles viewed from above. The "square" array (e) is unstable.

1.11 Triangulation of a planar array of random bubbles viewed from above.

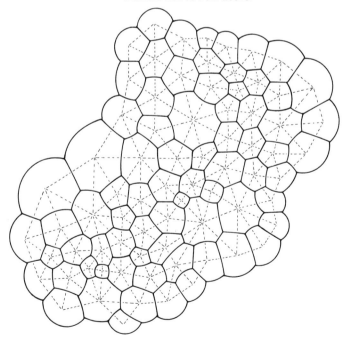

A Law of Closest Packing and Triangulation can be proposed: when compact arrays of volumetric (morphological) units (bubbles, cells, atoms, etc.) are formed by any external or internal attractive forces, they tend to have the greatest possible numbers of neighboring units while equalizing as nearly as possible the distances between their centers. The network which joins the centers of all nearest neighbors is always triangulated (usually in multiples of tetrahedra) and tends towards uniform edge lengths. Also, when such volumetric units consist (momentarily or permanently) of relatively fluid interfaces they tend to take the shape of polyhedra cells of minimum surface area relative to their volumes with faces meeting edges at angles of 120° and edges meeting vertices at angles of 109°28'. These angles are imposed by the forces of surface tension and satisfy the conditions of minimum potential energy.*

With its dual network of equilateral triangles, the rhombic-dodecahedral packing might be taken to be the minimum-energy system for a bubble array insofar as the distances between rhombic dodecahedron centers are all exactly the same. This arrangement, equivalent to the twelve-around-one packing of closest packed spheres, might seem to be the most compact arrangement. But we have seen that the truncated octahedron packs with 14 neighbors, and, as such, is a denser or more compact arrangement than the sphere or rhombic-dodecahedral packing.

*Loeb, inspired by Laves and Fuller, has proposed a similar idea for the structure of crystals: "Crystal structures tend to assume configurations in which a maximum number of identical atoms or ions are equidistant from each other; if more than a single type of atom or ion are present, then each atom or ion tends to be equidistant from as many as possible of each type of atom or ion. It is a simple extension of the fact that a stable system of three identical interacting particles will arrange itself in an equilateral triangle, that four such particles will occupy the corners of a regular tetrahedron, etc." (Loeb 1967b).

The dual network of the truncated octahedron consists of edges which differ in length by 15%. A homogeneous array of identical tetragonal disphenoids results. The tetrahedron is the simplest of all possible polyhedra and is the *strongest* per unit of invested energy. The reciprocal net of the rhombic-dodecahedral array contains both tetrahedra and octahedra. This reflects the fact that both 4-connected and 8-connected vertices appear in the rhombic-dodecahedral array. An octahedron, although a highly efficient structure, may be considered to be somewhat less strong than a tetrahedron—even one that is slightly distorted, as in the case of the isosceles-faced tetragonal disphenoid.

A simple explanation for the rare occurrence of Kelvin's ideal minimal tetrakaidecahedron might be that nature seeks a compromise solution which tends to have the higher density of packing of truncated-octahedra along with the uniform distances of the rhombic-dodecahedral packing. It may be that if some means could be found to measure the distances between the centers of the adjacent equivolume bubbles of Matzke's study, it would be found that these distances differed by less than 15%, and tended to approach the ideal of a uniform distance between cells. The average of 13.70 faces that Matzke observed may constitute a compromise between maximum density and minimum difference in center-to-center distances. This may provide even less total surface area per unit of volume than does the Kelvin figure.

Although it would be difficult to verify, such a hypothesis suggests that an efficient physical construct does not always conform to an ideal mathematical solution. In the study of three-dimensional physical structure, we see that nature frequently utilizes apparent *distortions* of ideal mathematical forms because the distortions are more economical from an energy standpoint.

Closest Packed Unequal Spheres. Coordination Polyhedra and Polyhedral Domains

Frank and Kasper (1958, 1959) have described the structures of complex metal alloys in terms of the packing of spheres in which the allowance of small variations of sphere diameters permits denser packings than the characteristic twelve-around-one packing of equal spheres. Such packings are not homogeneous but combine, for different alloys, in various combinations of 12, 14, 15, and 16 spheres packed around any given sphere. The networks that define the centers of these sphere packing structures consist *exclusively* of space filling arrangements of tetrahedra. They are not all regular but differences in edge lengths are minimized as in the case of the more uniform tetragonal-disphenoidal packing.

The number of spheres surrounding any given sphere is called the *coordination* (or coordination number) Z. If in these sphere packings with coordinations of 12, 14, 15, or 16, the spheres are "expanded" to fill all the unoccupied space, polyhedra result with 12, 14, 15, and 16 faces, respectively. Such polyhedra are known as coordination polyhedra. Any given sphere packing will have a corresponding set of space filling coordination polyhedra.

The dual network to any such space filling system will correspond exactly to the network derived from connecting the centers of spheres in the closest packed array represented by the space filling array of coordination polyhedra. Since both of these networks are equivalent, the number of edges meeting at each vertex will exactly correspond to the coordination number of the sphere or polyhedron representing said vertex. Therefore the number of edges meeting at a given vertex is also known as the vertex coordination Z.

Since the coordination polyhedron represents the environment, or discrete region of space, associated with a given sphere in a closest packed array, or associated with a given vertex of a connected network, such a polyhedron may also be called the domain (or polyhedral domain) of the sphere, or likewise the domain (or polyhedral domain) of the vertex. In the case of the domain of the vertex, the polyhedral domain will have the same number of faces as there are edges joining the vertex found at its center. The network formed by the space filling array of such polyhedral domains is exactly reciprocal to the network connecting the vertices which it represents. For example, the rhombic dodecahedron is both the coordination polyhedron and the polyhedral domain for closest packed equal spheres, and for the network generated by the space filling of tetrahedra and octahedra. The network generated by the space filling array of rhombic dodecahedra is reciprocal to that of the space filling of tetrahedra and octahedra.

Since there are 12 spheres around every sphere in the closest packed array, 12 faces on the rhombic dodecahedron, and 12 edges meeting at each vertex in the network of space filling tetrahedra and octahedra, the coordination number for the sphere, the domain, and network is 12. The reader is reminded that "connected" also refers to the number of edges meeting at a vertex.

a
b
c
d

1.12 Coordination polyhedra corresponding to sphere packings of Z = 12, dodecahedron (a); 14, tetrakaidecahedron (b); 15, pentakaidecahedron (c); and 16, hexakaidecahedron (d).

The coordination polyhedra corresponding to the sphere packings of Z = 12, 14, 15, and 16 are bounded by pentagons and hexagons and their vertices are all 3-connected. They are respectively a dodecahedron bounded by 12 pentagons, a tetrakaidecahedron bounded by two hexagons and 12 pentagons, a pentakaidecahedron bounded by three hexagons and 12 pentagons, and an hexakaidecahedron bounded by four hexagons and 12 pentagons [1.12]. Although Frank and Kasper do not discuss these polyhedra in their articles, they are described in another context by K. W. Allen. We will also take them up in some detail later in this book. Owing to the predominance of pentagons, the 4-connected networks formed by various packing combinations of these four polyhedra have a remarkable resemblance to soap-bubble arrays, which, as we have already noted, also exhibit an overwhelming number of pentagons. If slight warpage of the faces is permitted, all four of the polyhedra just described can be constructed so that in any space filling array all vertices are not only 4-connected but are also equally surrounded by 109°28' angles. Also, the partitioning faces will then meet on common edges in groups of three at 120° angles.

In the 28 different actual and hypothetical structures classified by Frank and Kasper, it is shown that the average coordination is 13.35, remarkably close to the 13.53 average number of faces of Matzke's unequal soap bubbles, and to his 13.70 average number of faces for equivolume bubbles. These complex alloy structures studied by Frank and Kasper seem to follow the law of closest packing and triangulation.*

*Bernal (1959) has proposed a random triangulated configuration for the molecular structure of liquids which, although not necessarily describable as a dense arrangement of spheres, consists of space filling tetrahedra in which the distance between neighboring atoms tends toward a minimum. Bernal's approach shows definite similarities to those others discussed here.

The Soap-Bubble Array as Archetype

A remarkable series of papers by Lewis, Marvin, and Matzke has discussed soap bubbles, compression of lead shot, the cells of various plants, and human fat cells. A generally consistent behavior is exhibited in these diverse realms. The forms of the systems are manifestations of the least-energy principle. All of the systems tend to conform to the law of closest packing and triangulation, although there are many other forces at work, particularly in biological systems where growth rates and sequences control morphological development. Smith compared soap-film-froth behavior to the microstructure of metals and their grain shapes. (Smith 1948, 1952, 1953, W. M. Williams and Smith 1952). In "The Shape of Things" Smith says,

"It seems at first astonishing that the cells of things as different as a metal and a soap froth can be almost indistinguishable in shape, but this is easily understood when it is realized that the interfaces between crystals are themselves essentially liquid like. The atoms in the boundary between two crystal grains are subjected to the opposing fields of both lattices. Since both cannot be satisfied simultaneously, a layer of atoms (probably not more than three or four atom diameters thick) is unable to crystallize. This fluid interface, which must be continuous, has associated with it a high surface tension, which makes it tend to shrink in exactly the same way as a soap film. Only a crystal growing freely without contact with others can have the highly symmetrical polyhedral shape that is usually thought to typify a crystal."

Soap bubble packing, then, can be taken as the *model* or *type* of all systems—biological, physical, chemical—in which there is an economical association of cellular modules. And, at this point we may conclude that triangulation and closest packing are truly equivalent and that closest packing is at the heart of those principles that operate regardless of scale.

2 Closest Packing in Nature

Hexagons, Hierarchies, and Scale Independence

Perhaps the most familiar example of closest packing, and certainly the most sublime, is the honeycomb of the bee [2.1]. This system, in plan one of regular hexagons, contains the greatest amount of honey with the least amount of beeswax (Toth 1964a), and is the structure which requires the least energy for the bees to construct.

The bee's cell appears to be a simple hexagonal prism; however, because the honeycomb consists of two sets of contiguous cells, positioned back to back, it takes on a more complicated form. The back-to-back cells are staggered in such a way that the centers of the set of cells on one side are positioned exactly over half of the three-rayed intersections of cell walls of the set of cells on the other side. This can be seen by looking at [2.2] with care. This arrangement corresponds to a packing of two layers of rhombic dodecahedra (or of two layers of closest packed spheres). The bees' cell is simply a rhombic dodecahedron with one end opened up to form a flat hexagon, and as such it is a 10-faced polyhedron bounded by three rhomboidal faces from the rhombic dodecahedron which form the "bottom" of the cell, six trapezoidal faces which form the six sides of the cell, and one hexagonal face which is the cell opening [2.3].*

The order manifest in the structure of bees' or wasps' nests appears, though perhaps in lesser degree, throughout biological morphology, and we find it to be common in crystal structure. The very ubiquitousness of such energy-efficient solutions is important, because the development of a general morphological system rests on the possibility of discovering fundamental relationships among the broadest range of possible structures. As we examine various natural structures and the reasons for them, we will be constantly reminded that closest packing is simply a reflection of nature's tendency to coordinate extrinsic and intrinsic forces in the most energy-economic way.

*For a detailed discussion of the structure and formation of the honeycomb, see Thompson II: 525.

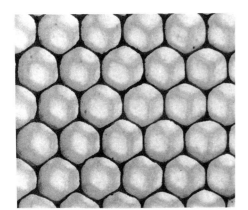

2.1 Bees' honeycomb.

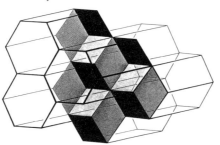

2.2 Honeycomb cell structure.

2.3 Single honeycomb cell, showing rhombic dodecahedron within.

We perceive the possibility of hierarchic structure when we realize that closest packing is independent of absolute specific size. A large number of naturally occurring substances and systems—organic, inorganic, animate, or inanimate—will prove to be closest packed when viewed at the appropriate level of magnification. But, what is more important, within the same substance similar packings or structures (hierarchies) will appear at grossly different scales. In many instances, a closest packed microstructure will determine the options that a closest packed macrostructure may take. We can think again of intrinsic and extrinsic forces, in which one force may become the other as we pass through different hierarchies of scale.

Natural structures are (for the most part) three-dimensional, while photographs and compilations of them, as in this book, are usually two-dimensional representations, such as in the cross sectional views of a cellular structure. These "two-dimensional samples" of three-dimensional structures tend to be dominated by three-rayed vertices, which, as was pointed out in Chapter 1, are often cross-sectional representations of three partition faces meeting on a common edge at equal angles of 120°. The reader is also reminded that in three dimensions the condition of three faces meeting on a common edge at 120° is a consequence of four edges meeting at a common vertex at 109°28′.

Weibel describes a schematic model of the arrangement of alveoli around the alveolar duct of the human lung [2.4]. This structure calls to mind a hexagonal honeycomb wrapped around a cylindrical surface with hexagonal openings facing inward. This alveolar system exhibits a hierarchical structure; the cell walls of the alveoli are composed of very fine capillary networks which are also hexagonally structured. A schematic sketch of this capillary network [2.5] structure shows the juncture of three cell walls. The continuity of the three-rayed hexagonal network of the capillary structure is maintained at this intersection of three cell-wall surfaces.

2.4 Alveoli in the human lung (Weibel).

2.5 Three-rayed, hexagonal capillary network of alveoli (Weibel).

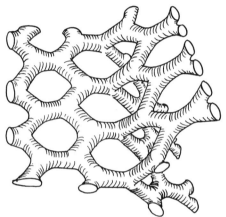

Differential Growth, Edge Effects, and Other Interactions

Although the basis of various two-dimensional networks is the hexagonal cell, in biological systems particularly, we must take into account growth sequences, sequential solidification of various parts, and "edge effects"; all these greatly influence final form. The dragonfly's wing is a very good illustration of this [2.6].

"The wing is traversed by a few strong "veins" or ribs, more or less parallel to one another, between which finer veins make a meshwork of "cells", these lesser veins being all much of a muchness and exerting tensions insignificant compared with those of the greater veins. Where (a) two ribs run so near together that only one row of cells lies between, these cells are quadrangular in form, their thin partitions meeting the ribs at right angles on either side. Where (b) two rows of cells are intercalated between a pair of ribs, one row fits into the other by angles of 120°, the result of co-equal tensions; but both meet the ribs at right angles, as in the former case. Where (c) the cell rows are numerous, all their angles in common tend to be co-equal angles of 120°, and the cells resolve, consequently, into a hexagonal network." (Thompson II:476–477)

2.6 Dragonfly wing.

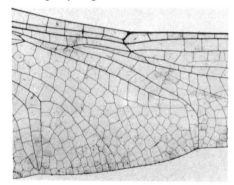

The cracking and drying of mud also proceeds in a "hexagonal" manner, complete with polar furrows [2.7].

On cracked surfaces, such as on ceramic glaze, mud, etc., where the cracks do *not* form simultaneously, 3-connected vertices still appear; however, some areas tend to meet in a 90° configuration (later cracks being perpendicular to earlier ones), rather than in the 120° configuration growing out of situations where tensions or forces are the same in all directions (*isotropic* force or growth). Given a condition of surface isotropy, geometrical considerations alone limit the possibilities, and consequently tend to produce the simplest of all nets, the three-rayed hexagonal pattern. Many writers have remarked on this. Smith (1954) states that "if this limitation is maintained—that three edges must always meet at a point while varying polygon types are permitted—then in any sufficiently large net the *average* polygon will be a hexagon."*

*Smith goes on to show that if V is the number of vertices, P the number of polygons, and E the number of edges in any arbitrary finite sample of an infinite plane net, then V + P = E + 1. If n is the number of sides of the *average* polygon in an infinite plane random net, then V/P = (n − 2)/2. Readers curious as to how an infinite net can have a finite number of elements may examine the stratagem employed by Coxeter (1963, p. 58).

2.7 Cracked mud.

There are numerous structures in which a *final* stage obscures the overall determinant of a particular form. The pinecone is one such case. Seen *before* it has "opened" up into an array of radiating branches, it clearly exhibits the closest packing of morphological units [2.8].

2.8 Pinecone

Although the closest packed organization of the watermelon can be readily seen with the naked eye, it is not likely that we would associate it with our hexagonal structures if we were not acquainted with the concept of the polar furrow [2.9].

2.9 Watermelon

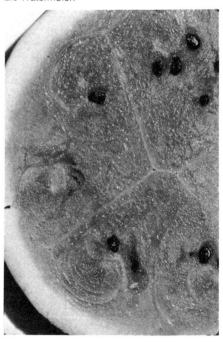

That nature's method of closest packing is independent of scale may be inferred from the preceding illustrations. Mud-crack cells [2.7] are of the order of meters to decimeters wide; the watermelon [2.9] and pinecones [2.8] span decimeters to centimeters; the dragonfly-wing and honeycomb cells bring us down to millimeters; while the alveoli and alveolar networks [2.4, 2.5] occupy microns only. Thus we have already spanned a range of scale of six orders of magnitude. The same structure appears in the region of fractions of a micron, as in [2.10] which shows an electron micrograph of a cross section through the exocrine cells of the pancreas of a mouse. These cells are typical of mammalian ultrastructure. The light grey areas in the photograph are the nuclei of the cells, and we can see cell boundaries that meet in three-rayed intersections. When such cells are formed they tend to compress against each other as more cells divide and crowd (closest pack) into the available space.

A Catalog of Natural Forms

The foregoing examples of hexagons in plane forms, hierarchies, and scale independence do not of course prove that nature *must* act in these ways. Indeed, as in empirical science generally, we can *never* prove that observed behavior is universal, for we can only infer from particular cases; and, if nature has not quite an infinite stock of possibilities, it at least always has one more than the total number we have investigated. Nonetheless, equipped only with a reasonable faith in nature's overall consistency, we can accept induction from particular cases as a reliable guide toward the truth. In this spirit I offer the following catalog of natural forms. Its essence is visual, and its excitement, I think, lies in the exhibited variations on the hexagonal theme. Perhaps the theme will inspire some readers to investigate areas not cataloged here, while the variations will inspire others to seek (or design) similarly satisfying forms.

Metals and Crystals

[2.11] *Heated aluminum sheet.* The surface of a heated aluminum sheet shows, at the early stages of melting, a network not unlike those exhibited by a two-dimensional array of soap bubbles. It not only consistently follows the rule of three edges meeting at a point, but there is a strong tendency for each point to be surrounded by 120° angles.

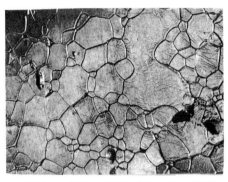

2.11 Surface of a heated aluminum sheet (2.5X, Smith).

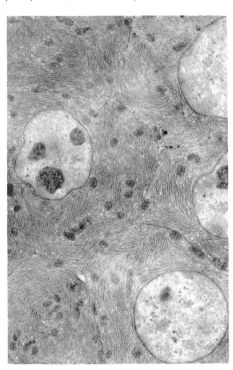

2.10 Ultrastructure of exocrine cells of mouse pancreas (3,700X, Rhodin).

[2.12] *Aluminum-tin alloy*. A dark polyhedral network is formed by the tin surrounding the light cells (crystals) of aluminum. This photograph is virtually indistinguishable from a soap bubble froth seen with the unaided eye. This is even true to the extent that the vertices are typically surrounded by four edges (four cells) meeting at approximately 109°. "The individual grains in a piece of metal or the bubbles in a soap froth must satisfy two conditions—they must be in juxtaposition so as to fill space and their interfaces must conform to the laws of surface tension" (W. M. Williams and Smith).

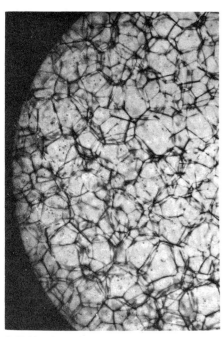

2.12 Aluminum-tin alloy. X-ray microradiograph (15X, Smith and Williams).

[2.13] *Etched aluminum surface*. The etched surface of aluminum typically reveals grain boundaries in which three edges meet at each intersection at approximately 120° angles.

2.13 Etched surface of aluminum (25X, Smith).

[2.14] *Grain boundaries in niobium*. The grain boundaries of a section through niobium metal, revealed through etching, show a similar pattern to that of the heated aluminum sheet. In both these cases, there appears to be a lack of uniformity, but careful study reveals very few, if any, exceptions to the three-rayed vertex surrounded by angles of 120°. The etched niobium metal sample shows a cross section through space filling polyhedra. Each metal grain is a polyhedral crystal which meshes with its neighbors in a closest packed array. The interface between adjacent crystals where regions of different crystallographic orientation meet is called a dislocation in the crystal lattice. The intrinsic forces within the crystal grain confront the extrinsic forces which arise from the environment of neighboring crystals.

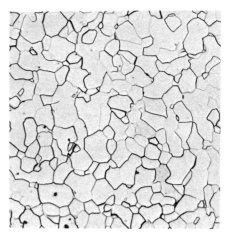

2.14 Grain boundaries in niobium metal (125X, Smith).

[2.15] *Field ion microscope photograph of platinum*. A dramatic verification of the concept of closest packing as a basic structural principle of nature is achieved with the use of the field ion microscope developed by Müller (1957, 1960). In this photo of platinum, closest packed arrays of individual atoms can be seen.

2.15 Field ion microscope image of platinum (600,000X, Müller).

[2.16] *Sphere packing models of metal structure*. The field ion micrograph reveals various symmetrical collections of atoms which follow patterns determined by the possible combinations of planar regions of three-dimensional closest packed atoms. With an array of equal cork balls closest packed with their centers positioned on the vertices of a packing of tetragonal disphenoids, Müller has demonstrated the correspondence of sphere packing models to the actual crystal structure. The sequence reproduced here shows that the pattern exhibited by tungsten is the result of the geometry of the atomic packing.

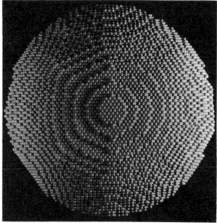

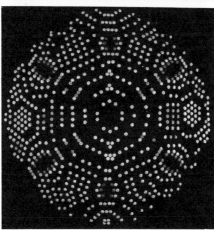

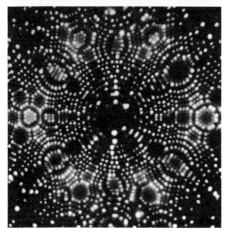

2.16 Sphere packing models of metal structure: cork ball model, same model with certain balls coded with fluorescent paint, and field ion micrograph of tungsten (600,000X, Müller).

[2.17] *A crystal of reticulated cerussite*. This mineral forms an impressively uniform network structure which appears to be dominated by 60° angles. It is what one might imagine a snow crystal would be like if it happened to take a three-dimensional form rather than its familiar flat hexagonal shape.

The external forms of many crystals are well-known polyhedra, such as cubes, octahedra, and rhombic dodecahedra. The various possible options are determined by the internal structure of the atomic arrays. Likewise are the patterns revealed in the field ion micrographs determined by the internal structure of each crystal.

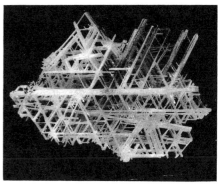

2.17 A crystal of reticulated cerussite (Smithsonian Institution).

Plant Forms

[2.18] *Leaf structure*. As in the analagous growth of the dragonfly's wing, growth *sequences* in such a leaf structure govern the final pattern.

2.18 A typical leaf structure.

[2.19] *Poppy seeds*. The poppy seed exhibits a characteristic dimpled surface which consists of raised edges forming a three-rayed network. Such a pattern is formed by the collapse of a smooth outer shell upon an inner shell due to a loss of moisture. When the outer shell contracts, its surface area remains substantially unchanged and consequently ridges are formed to take up the excess surface. When it is realized that surface tension plays a role in shrinkage, it is clear that the forces which act upon the poppy seed are not altogether different from those which act in the determination of soap-film formations (Thompson II:564).

2.19 Poppy seeds (5X, Jírovec).

[2.20] *Reed*. A cross section of a reed shows a fairly uniform array of cells in conjunction with a finer froth where transitions are made to differing regions within the structure (epithelial and epidermal cells).

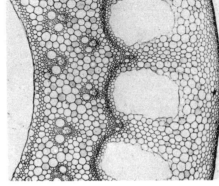

2.20 Cross section of a reed (25X, Jírovec).

[2.21] *Cork cells*. Microscopic cellular structure was first observed by Hooke in the seventeenth century. In his early studies with the microscope he found cork to consist of densely packed chambers somewhat resembling the bees' honeycomb. This was the beginning of the study of cells and cell shape. A modern microscopic view of cork shows the ubiquitous hexagonal cellular structure.

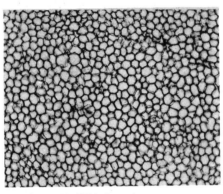

2.21 Cork cells (35X, Jírovec).

[2.22] *Philodendron*. In enlarged view, the upper surface of the leaf of the philodendron appears to consist of highly irregular cell shapes. It is an example of how far away a structure may get from the appearance of the hexagon cell, yet still satisfy its basic characteristics. This structure is most remarkable, indeed; the wiggly lines forming the cell boundaries still manage to meet in three-rayed 120° vertices. Here the average "polygon" still appears to be six-sided. Although the distribution of vertices appears to be quite random, the structure is still highly ordered. The dual network of such an arrangement is still fully triangulated; but because of the extremely asymmetric shapes of the cells, the dual network would require curvature of some of its edges. It is difficult to say precisely what forces cause this leaf surface to be structured in this manner, but it is clear that the structure is a variant of close packing.

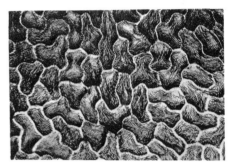

2.22 Upper surface of philodendron leaf (50X, Jírovec).

[2.23] *Mushroom*. The underside of the *Boletus* mushroom consists of a system of closest packed tubules.

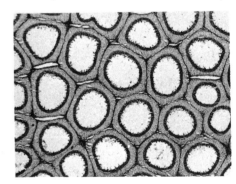

2.23 Underside of a mushroom (35X, Jírovec).

[2.24] *An aquatic herb*. The structure of the aquatic herb "mare's tail" is still another demonstration of hierarchical closest packing of cells. Not only is there a progressive concentric decrease, then increase, in relative cell size, but a peripheral structure appears as a gross framework of modulated cells in which not only the cells, but the framework of which they are the elements, meet at three-rayed intersections. Many such plants consist, not of spherical cells, but of columnar forms that are hexagonal in section yet are still three-dimensional polyhedral cells whose edges still tend to meet four around each vertex in a space-filling array.

2.24 Structure of an aquatic herb ("mare's tail," 70X, Jírovec).

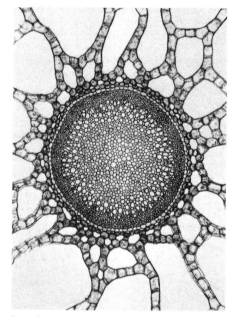

[2.25] *Redwood root*. A cross section of the root of redwood consists of a nearly uniform concentric froth pattern.

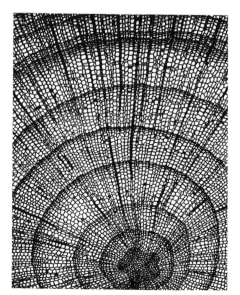

2.25 Cross section of redwood root (Kepes).

[2.26] *The rush* Juncus; *formation of stellate cells*. A curious case that illustrates the duality of triangular networks and closest packed polyhedral cells can be seen in a microphotograph of a cross section of the cells in the pith of the rush *Juncus*. As we have seen, spherical cells that are forced to grow against each other fill all unoccupied space to create polyhedra. The triangulated cell structure of *Juncus* indicates that some other process has taken place. Thompson has suggested a formative process for *Juncus* in which cells, rather than filling all the unoccupied space, tend to collapse except where the original contact was made. (Thompson II:547) This has the effect of creating air voids which surround "stellate" cells in the pith. When these stellate cells are hooked together they form the triangulated network. A diagram of this process is shown in the figure. The possibility that all the cells of the pith would be of equal size is unlikely. Consequently the stellate cells may have varying numbers of rays; and, recalling the arguments of Lewis (1925), I believe these probably tend to average closer to 14 than 12 as suggested by Thompson.

2.26 Pith cells of the rush, *Juncus* (200X, Jírovec) and a diagram showing formation of stellate cells upon the collapse of closest packed hexagons.

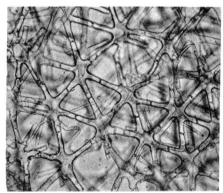

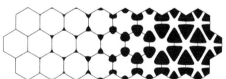

[2.27] *Diatoms*. Diatoms, tiny marine algae with silicon dioxide skeletons, frequently consist of concentric or radiating hexagonal patterns with a uniformity approaching that of the bees' honeycomb. The forces acting within and without are relatively symmetrical and the resulting forms, although infinitely varied, are almost always quite symmetrical. Diatoms take many different kinds of shapes, including squares, triangles, and longitudinal forms. Though they do not all show hexagonal structures in their silicon dioxide skeletons, the triangular form shown in [2.27b] is structured with nearly regular hexagons.

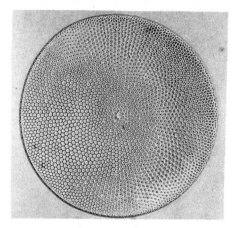

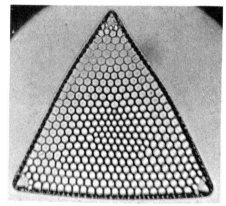

2.27 A circular diatom (400X), and a triangular diatom (300X) (Jírovec).

[2.28] *Pollen grains*. The scanning electron microscope here again reveals the three-rayed network. Such patterns of the surfaces of the pollen grains are determined, for the most part, by the genetic programming of the plant.

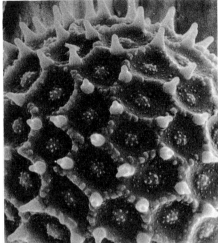

a

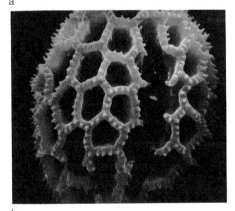

b

2.28 Pollen grain of Morning Glory (a, 700X), and thrift pollen (b, 400X) (copyright 1969, Patrick Echlin and Cambridge Scientific Instruments).

Animal Forms and Viruses

[2.29] *Coral*. A transverse section of a fossilized colony of reef-forming corals again graphically demonstrates closest packing in a natural structure.

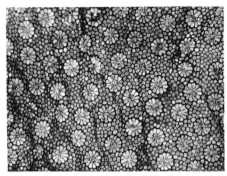

2.29 Section of coral (5X, Jírovec).

[2.30, 2.31] *Giraffe and reptile skin*. An amusing example of a naturally occurring three-rayed hexagonal network is to be found in the pattern of the giraffe skin. The extremely uniform reptile skin is a packing of circles in which small triangles appear at the interstices.

2.30 Giraffe skin.

2.31 Reptile skin (Brodatz).

[2.32] *Radiolaria*. The Radiolaria, numbering at least 4,000 species, each with its own characteristic arrangement of spicules and pseudopodia, are all often spherical in form; as "variations on the sphere," they are of great interest in the present study. Many, although not all, of the radiolarian skeletons have straightforward hexagonal structuring on their surfaces [2.32].

In 1887, Haeckel in his "Challenger Monograph on Radiolaria" illustrated some 3,508 species of Radiolaria.

Close inspection of the three-rayed networks of the Radiolaria (as well as of pollen grains) reveals that not all of the polygons are six-sided. Some polygons have fewer than six sides and occasional polygons of more than six sides are evident. It can be shown that it is impossible with a system of hexagons, regular or irregular, to create a *closed* space (e.g., to completely cover the surface of a sphere) in which all intersections of the surface net are three-connected.

2.32 Spherical radiolarian skeletons (a), froth of radiolarian vesicles (b), and triangulated radiolarian skeletons (c) (Haeckel).

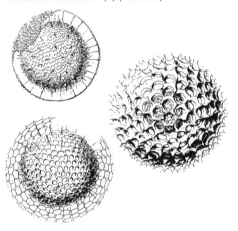

a

The radiolarian skeletons consist of connected arrays of tiny tubular struts forming diverse and complex structural shells. These siliceous skeletons are built up upon protoplasmic bodies usually consisting of collections of component vesicles which are physically equivalent to cells although they are not cells in the usual sense. The vesicles are, in essence, constituent modules for the larger cell. They frequently form a froth of closest packed units spherically distributed (often in concentric spheres) in a closed structure [2.32b]. The hexagonally structured skeletons are formed as the inorganic material is deposited at the intersections of close packed vesicles. It is important to stress that the hexagonal skeletons are *incomplete* structures since their *physical efficiency* is achieved in cooperation with other components of the organism (the close packed vesicles). The mistake should not be made that these hexagonal radiolarian *skeletons* are of themselves good models for the design of physical structures. They are stable (triangulated) only by virtue of their association with the rest of the organism to which they belong. There are a few species of Radiolaria in which there are actually employed fully triangulated spherical skeletons [2.32c].

I do not know to what processes of growth these triangulated radiolarian structures can be attributed. They are essentially duals of the hexagonal skeletons whose formation has been reasonably well explained.* We can be sure that the radiolarian skeletons are nature's most economical structural solution to some given set of conditions. The similarity of these structures to Fuller's geodesic domes cannot but strike one. According to Makowski (in Davies), the French structural innovator Le Ricolais had in 1940 proposed spherical-shell structures based upon the design of the triangulated networks of the Radiolaria. With this proposal, Le Ricolais anticipated Fuller's independent invention and reduction to practice of the geodesic dome which dates from approximately 1948 (Marks).

*Thompson explains in great detail the process of formation of many of the radiolarian forms. However, nowhere does he discuss the triangulated spherical skeletons.

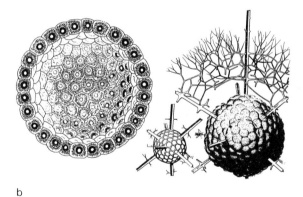

b

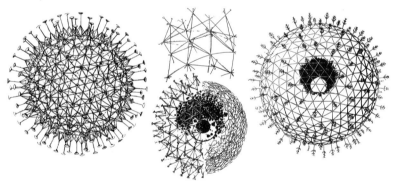

c

[2.33] *Volvox*. A polyhedral structure is seen in Volvox, a freshwater colonial protozoan. Volvox is a spherically organized colony of several hundred to several thousand zooids which occupy the periphery of a gelatinous colonial envelope. The zooids are each enclosed in gelatinous sheaths which are closest packed, forming the familiar three-rayed network on the surface of a sphere. Each zooid is linked to its neighbors by protoplasmic strands which form a triangulated dual network to the three-connected network formed by the closest packed zooid cells.

2.33 Volvox (courtesy of American Museum of Natural History).

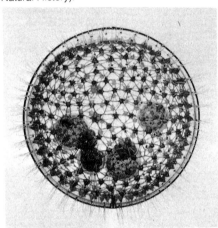

[2.34, 2.35] *Insect eyes*. The surface structure of the compound eye of the bumblebee has nearly regular hexagonal faceting upon a segment of a spherical surface. The scanning electron microscope reveals the closest packed character of the lens elements of the fly's compound eye.

The retinal structure of the moth presents a curious example of a hierarchical morphology. In the cross-sectional structure, circular units are arranged in almost perfect equilateral-triangular order, and are surrounded by a "froth" of tiny hexagons. The cells of this froth fit as a substructure to the relatively gross hexagonal network of the circular units.

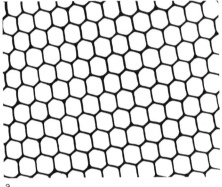

a

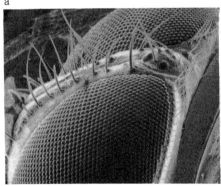

b

2.34 Surface of bumblebee eye (a, 95X, Jirovec), and lens elements of fly's compound eye (b, Marti).

2.35 Retinal structure of moth's eye (150X, Carlson, Steeves, Vandeberg, and Robbins).

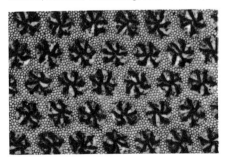

[2.36] *Peritrophic membrane*. The peritrophic membrane which lines the midgut of insects is shown here in an electron microscope photo. The network exhibited by this membrane is equivalent to the packing of triangles and hexagons, which is frequently referred to as the kagome' net after the practice of Japanese basket construction. It has a remarkable, almost exact, likeness to the reptile skin [2.31].

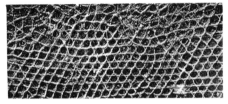

2.36 Peritrophic membrane of cockroach (45,500X, Mercer).

[2.37] *Insect flight muscle filaments*. The filaments in an insect flight muscle, when seen in cross section, show a uniform pattern of triangulation. These filaments are longitudinal and not unlike the steel filaments in a suspension bridge cable, which also has a closest packed structure. When parallel bundles of filaments or wires are "tensed" they are compressed against each other. Under such forces they assume closest packing.

2.37 Insect flight muscle filaments (200,000X, Huxley).

[2.38] *Adenovirus*. Here can be seen an electron-microscope photograph of adenovirus, and also a photograph of a sphere packing model of the same form which reveals more clearly a 20-sided icosahedral configuration. Because the icosahedron gives rise to the most symmetrical distribution of points (or anything) on the sphere, it is reasonable that these spherical virus particles would have icosahedral symmetry.* One can assume that the virus takes this configuration in order to satisfy requirements of minimum energy and that because of the high symmetry, there must be relatively symmetrical intrinsic and extrinsic forces acting in the formation of the virus.

*It is impossible to create a convex polyhedron with more than 20 equilateral triangles and consequently the icosahedron is the generating figure for the most symmetrical possible class of polyhedra. The subdivision of the sphere based upon the icosahedron gives rise to the most uniform cases of triangulated spherical structures. It has been this property of the icosahedron that Fuller has so aptly taken advantage of in the design of his domes. See Stuart (1955).

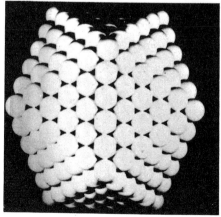

2.38 Adenovirus, and model (Horne and Wildy).

Biological structures with the regularity of crystal architecture only rarely occur. The virus structures show ordered patterns approaching the uniformity of crystals.

I have shown diverse examples that, for a variety of causes, exemplify patterns characteristic of close packing behavior. We cannot say that all of the patterns shown are fully explainable only in terms of closest packing, or a law of triangulation, or even in terms of the forces of surface tension. I have simply attempted to note the occurrence of closely related, if not analogous or equivalent, patterns that do occur in nature. The differences in scale, environment, and substance do not noticeably alter the principles that I have been describing. There can be little doubt that we are dealing with some very fundamental relationships which in any case satisfy minimal principles consistently employed by nature.

3 Some Principles of Built Structure

In Chapter 1 we saw that the triangle is the only polygon that is stable by virtue of its geometry and, passing to three dimensions, that only fully triangulated polyhedra are geometrically stable (p. 3). We now proceed to a fuller study of the consequences of the triangulation of real structures in three dimensions.

It is clear, then, that a built cube, or any other nontriangulated structure, will require rigid (i.e., nonrotating) joints if it is to be itself rigid, while a triangulated construction can get along with hinged (i.e., rotating) joints without collapsing. Now the difference in the effect of rigid and hinged joints is this: the former can transmit (in fact they generate) bending forces* (couples or moments) as well as axial forces, while the latter can transmit only axial forces [3.1]. This is important when we pass over from abstract geometry into the physical world, because nearly all materials can resist far more stress when it is applied axially (tension or compression) than when it is applied transversely (bending).** The same strut is more effective when it is loaded as a column than when it is loaded as a beam [3.2].

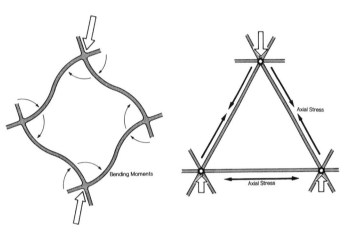

3.1 Loading a square and a triangular frame.

3.2 Applying stresses axially (tension or compression) and transversely (bending).

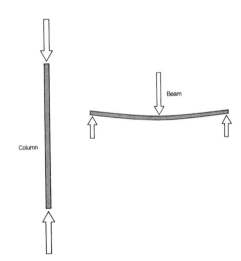

*In materials science applied forces are called stresses, and the subsequent responses of materials are called strains. I will have no occasion to talk about strains directly in this book, and will use "force" and "stress" interchangeably. The reader may have already noted that, following the common parlance of designers, I sometimes use "force" in a wider sense than a physicist or engineer would, giving it the sense of "influence" merely, as in "environmental forces." In all cases, the meaning intended will be clear from the context.

**In this chapter we will not consider torsion (twisting) or shear (the sliding of one portion of a material over adjacent parts), although the latter can be considered a byproduct of bending.

By coupling the fortunate inadequacy of hinged joints to the geometrical stability, we can allow our built forms to take advantage of their struts' high axial strength, and avoid having to rely on their poor resistance to bending.* However, because nontriangulated structures *require* couple-inducing joints, such built forms must perforce respond to moments; they must, and do, distort easily under load.

*A not inconsequential advantage of many-celled triangulated structures, arising from their propensity to distribute stress axially, is their ability to share stress applied to one vertex over a large number of cells. This property could be illustrated by elaborating on the experiments of p. 3. The property is fully exploited by the space frames discussed later in this chapter.

3.3 Loaded cubic (a) and octahedral (b) frames.

a   b

The Loaded Frames

This interaction between purely geometric stability, the properties of joints, and the axial and transverse strengths of materials is illustrated in the experiment with loaded frames that I will now describe. Without an appreciation of this interaction the experiment might appear to be simplistic; with it, as we will see, the experiment is the bridge between abstraction and a concrete functional geometry.

The questions before us are these: How will a nontriangulated (but, by virtue of its joints, rigid) frame compare to a triangulated one under load? Given that each is constructed of the same type and amount of material, which will collapse soonest? Will there be a difference in their behavior on the way to collapse?

The comparison of nontriangulated and triangulated frames is facilitated by the relationship of the square-faced cube to the triangular-faced octahedron. Both polyhedra are comprised of 12 edges. Therefore, when a frame of each figure is constructed of strut members of the same material, diameter, cross-sectional shape and area, and length, they may be considered to be equal in terms of the amount of material they use, or in terms of resource investment. In short, they would weigh and cost the same. Therefore, it is possible, by loading each of these equal weight structures, to directly compare the performance in terms of strength to weight of nontriangulated and triangulated frameworks.

A cube was assembled out of twelve ⅛" diameter polyethylene struts each 4¾" long; these were joined at its eight corners by means of rigid metal connectors. An octahedron was also assembled with twelve of the same struts joined at each of its six corners with a wire connection that functioned more or less as a multidirectional hinged joint. A plastic container, to contain lead shot, was placed on a plastic panel resting on the upper face of each structure. The plastic panel was rigid, so that it did not deflect when loaded, and all loads were transmitted through it to the supporting vertices.

The first sequence in [3.3] shows the gradual collapse of the loaded cube and the second sequence shows the gradual collapse of the loaded octahedron. The cube collapsed totally under a load of 774 balls of lead shot (1,180 grams) and the octahedron collapsed totally under a load of 1,488 balls (2,269 grams). The octahedron in this experiment is nearly twice as strong with the same amount of material, even though it was constructed with flexible joints.

The octahedron, when loaded with the 774 balls of lead shot that caused the cube to collapse, showed little or no sign of distortion due to bending moments. Bending moments are induced by the rigid joints; it is these moments that give rise to the "S" curves in the struts of the loaded cube. By contrast, the octahedron exhibits no such bending moments. Instead, a simple arc is induced by the axial stress in the members as they reach their compressive limits.

We see from [3.3], that the horizontal members of the octahedral frame do not bend. This is because they are loaded in tension; the hinging joints do not allow the bending of the oblique members to be shared with the horizontal members. If the joints were rigid, the bending could be shared by all members, thus increasing the total load capacity of the triangulated framework. Before the point where bending begins, however, it makes no structural difference whether the joints are hinged or rigid. The foregoing experiments were very simple, almost simplistic, but they do demonstrate the structural advantages of triangulated frameworks. One could go on from here to make increasingly complex and sophisticated experiments which might include other variables such as volume and surface area as well as different methods of joining the struts. All the same, the inherent advantage of triangulated structures in terms of strength to weight is clearly established.

Space Frames

Alexander Graham Bell discovered in his search for lightweight structures suitable for flight a framework built up from equilateral triangles. This system consists of regular tetrahedra and regular octahedra. Bell used such structures, not only for his beautiful kites, but also as the basis of a windbreak and an observation tower [3.4]. Bell's essay of 1903 testifies to his awareness of the superior strength per unit weight properties of triangulated structures. Buckminster Fuller, Robert Le Ricolais, and others in recent years have designed structures which utilize this system pioneered by Bell (see McHale 1962; Makowski 1966a).

Bell's kite is an early (though still very useful) example of what has come to be called *space frame* structure. Space frames are called for when large areas must be spanned; these structures combine lightness and enhanced resistance to bending. They can be recognized by their use of a single, or at most a small number, of strut lengths, joined by means of standardized connections. Because of their high resistance to bending, *planar* space frames have been typically used for roofs. Although they are just as applicable, they have been rarely used for walls or vertical supports, presumably due to architectural design constraints (extrinsic forces), rather than due to the inherent properties of space frames (intrinsic forces). Fuller's geodesic domes and other *curved* space frames do away, so to speak, with walls and roofs entirely, replacing vertical-compression elements (walls) and bending elements (roofs) by warped surfaces capable of distributing stresses "isotropically" throughout the structure. Let us consider the span-to-depth ratio of a space frame. This is the ratio of the distance between vertical supporting structures (the *span*) and the *depth* or *thickness* of the frame [3.5]. A 30:1 ratio is generally considered to be the upper limit (Salvadori and Heller, p. 126).

Looking at the tetrahedral/octahedral space frame in plan, we note that it fits into a triangular grid. Because of this, it does not *appear* to be as adaptable to rectilinear structures as certain other systems. The 90° bias of structural designers and architects has prevented a more frequent use of this and other structures based upon 60° or 120° grids. The tetrahedral/octahedral space frame can fit into a square grid, but if this is done with a single layer, the octahedra are cut into square pyramids and are not completely stable. This requires the addition of a long diagonal brace on the square face of the half-octahedron, or the use of rigid joints, both of which stratagems can reduce the simplicity and increase the weight of the system.

a

3.4 Alexander Graham Bell's windbreak (a) and tower (b) (National Geographic Society).

In the 1959 Fuller exhibit at the Museum of Modern Art in New York, a tetrahedral/octahedral space frame with a depth of approximately 3½ feet was cantilevered 60 feet. Thus, if supported at two ends, such a system would have a 35:1 span-to-depth ratio. Even this is not a good indication of the potential of space frames. Out of the bias toward 90° geometry, we usually think of supporting space frames at only two (or four) opposite sides. But because space frames are based upon a 60° (or 120°) geometry, they can be conveniently supported on three (or six) sides. This alters the idea of span-to-depth ratio, and suggests that ratios greater than 35:1 might be obtainable.*

*For surveys of space frame systems and their applications see Makowski (1965), Wachsman, and Borrego.

3.5 Space frame span-to-depth ratio.

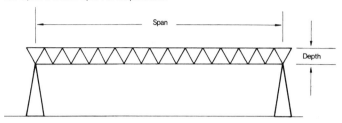

b

Local Instability in Planar and Domical Space Frames

As discussed in Chapter 1, any convex polyhedron bounded by plane polygons other than triangles suffers from geometrical instability. We can give a polyhedron *overall stability against distributed loads* —i.e., stability against any load that can be resisted by a large part of the figure via distribution through the structural members of which it is made—by triangulating all of its faces. However, the structure will still suffer from *local* instability. This instability arises within the now triangulated, but still planar, faces, because any vertex that is within the boundaries of, and coplanar to, a given face is not rigid with respect to forces directed perpendicular to the face.

There are two ways to deal with this condition. Both stem from the fact that resistance to a load directed normal to a structure is proportional to the thickness of the structure in the direction of the load. Or, what amounts to the same thing, resistance to compression is greater than resistance to bending. Both formulations can be illustrated with a piece of paper. As a sheet, it has virtually no resistance to an applied load. However, if it is folded accordion-style, it becomes rigid [3.6].

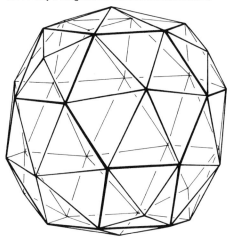

So the first way of dealing with local instability is to replace the "monolayer" faces by space frames. Thus we have still planar, but now thickened (and triangulated), faces.

The second solution is to build up our surface space frame incrementally, by placing the vertices of the triangulating subdivisions above or below the polygon planes so that a periodically convex or concave surface is created. This approach is more economical than the first one, but it introduces additional faceting over the parent polyhedron. Figure [3.7] shows a faceted figure—a fully triangulated truncated octahedron which has become, in effect, a simple dome.

3.7 A fully triangulated truncated octahedron.

One might say that the whole trick to designing successful domes is an awareness of the two methods of dealing with local loads.* The idea of span-to-depth ratio still applies; but in the case of domes we must formulate it by comparing the diameter of the dome to the number of modular increments (polygons) of which it is made. If this ratio of circumference to number of modules gets too high, those regions on the dome's surface surrounding single vertices become nearly flat, and thus lose their resistance to concentrated loads. This may be shown schematically by means of polygons inscribed in semicircles [3.8]. For distributed loads, the semicircle's strength is reflected in the very low span-to-depth ratio that, for such loading, is taken as the diameter over the height, or 2:1. However, this says nothing about the semicircle's resistance to concentrated loads. But if the semicircle is divided into two modular increments, it will have a high resistance to a load concentrated at the vertex. Increasing the modular frequency gives us more places (vertices) where concentrated loads may be resisted, but, at the same time, because of the increasing planarity in the neighborhoods of vertices, the strength at each vertex is decreasing.

*A moment's reflection will show that a structure cannot be made fully stable, i.e., it cannot be fully triangulated, unless it is closed. Spheres and their polyhedral approximations are closed, even when free; whereas domes cannot be considered closed unless they are tied to the ground. The effect of closure upon stability will come up again later in this book.

3.6 Folding a sheet increases its resistance to bending.

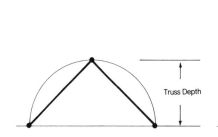
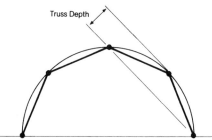

3.8 The hemisphere as a truss. Increasing the modular incrementation of the truss decreases the ability of vertices to resist concentrated loads.

Fuller's geodesic domes have been known to span over 100 ft. with no surface depth at all, short of the diameter of the tubular metal struts; a balanced response to the conflicting demand for local and overall stability. However, with the 200-foot Kaiser dome, faceting was not sufficient to resist the local loads, so the thickened-face space frame solution had to be added [3.9]. Even so, the Kaiser dome required a space frame only one foot deep—a 200:1 "span-to-depth" ratio! Fuller combined the advantage of the sphere (resistance to distributed loads) with that of the tetrahedral/octahedral space frame (resistance to local loads), by wrapping the double layer space frame around the sphere.

Planarity invites bending moments, and is a generally poor way in which to build. Generally, any curved, and particularly any doubly curved, surface will have higher strength per unit of invested resources than a planar system built of an equivalent amount of the same material. This is a primary reason for the use of curved surfaces or their polyhedral approximations wherever flatness is not absolutely required. In either case, plane or curved, we can assume that triangulation provides the optimum structural framework.

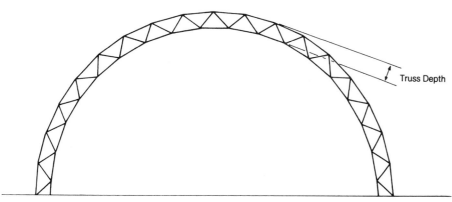

Truss Depth

3.9 Wrapping a space frame around a hemisphere solves the problem of concentrated loads.

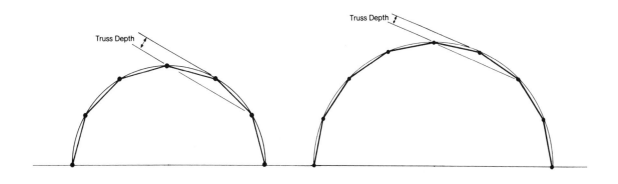

Truss Depth

Truss Depth

4

Ordering Principles and Geometry

In this and the following chapter we will study the geometrical basis of the orderly subdivision of space. If we can inventory all possible ways in which space can be organized, we will come to know the intrinsic forces that determine the geometric options in three-dimensional space and, hence, can develop a comprehensive morphological system. We will begin by examining tessellations (tilings) of the plane and proceed from this to a description of polyhedra.

Tessellations of the Plane

A plane tessellation is an infinite set of polygons fitting together to cover the whole plane just once, so that every side of each polygon belongs also to one other polygon (Coxeter 1963). As we shall see later, the plane tessellation is a special case of an infinite polyhedron.

Regular Tessellations

A regular tessellation is a pattern of congruent regular polygons filling the whole plane, on which all vertices of the tessellation are surrounded alike (uniform).

There are only three possible regular tessellations. They are the tessellations of triangles, of squares, and of hexagons. There are no other cases. This can be simply explained by pointing out that in order to subdivide the plane with polygons, the angles around each vertex must sum to 360°. In the case of regular tessellations this means that only polygons can be used that have face angles that can be whole-number subdivisions of 360°. The triangle, with face angles of 60°, divides 360° into 6 parts; therefore, a tessellation of triangles has six polygons meeting at each vertex. A square, with angles of 90°, divides into 360° into 4 parts; therefore, a tessellation of squares will have four polygons meeting at each vertex. A pentagon has face angles of 108° which cannot be divided into 360° by a whole number, and is therefore not capable of tessellating. A hexagon has 120° face angles, which divides 360° into 3 parts; therefore, a tessellation of hexagons will have three polygons meeting at each vertex. Less than three polygons meeting at a vertex cannot subdivide the plane. Therefore, any polygon with face angles greater than 120° will not be capable of forming a tessellation.

4.1 Regular and semiregular tessellations of the plane.

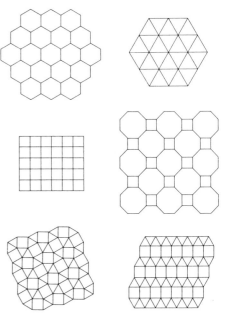

Semiregular Tessellations

There is a second class of planar partitioning known as semiregular tessellations. This class requires that all polygons be regular, and that all vertices be congruent, but permits the use of more than one kind of polygon. In this case the 360° around each vertex can be matched by the summed face angles of more than one type of polygon. There are only eight possible cases of semiregular plane tessellations. They consist of various combinations of triangles, squares, hexagons, octagons, and dodecagons (12 sides). One of these, consisting of triangles and hexagons, can be assembled in right- or left-handed form. Such figures (called enantiomorphs) are mirror images of one another. The regular and semiregular tessellations are illustrated in [4.1].

Tessellations with Regular Polygons

When some of these conditions of order are relaxed an entirely new range of possibilities emerges. If, for example, we only impose the requirement that the entire plane be filled exclusively with regular polygons, but do not require that all vertices be surrounded by equal angles, we find that we can construct a new class of tessellations in which an infinite number of patterns are possible. It is surprising to find, however, that there are still very few types of polygons that we may use. In fact we may use no more than those that appear in the semiregular tessellations. The reason, of course, is the same as before—each vertex must still be surrounded by exactly 360°, and therefore polygons may be combined around any vertex only when their face angles sum to 360°. Some examples of this infinite class of tessellation are shown in [4.2].

4.2 Tessellations with regular polygons.

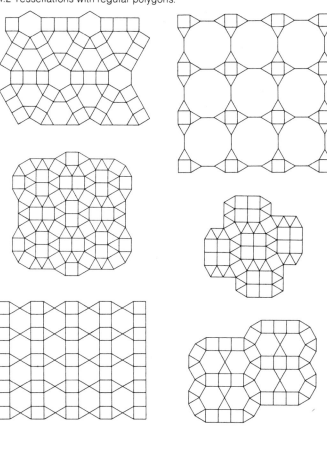

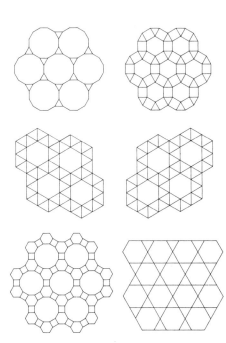

Tessellations and Symmetry

Though I defer until the following chapter a systematic study of the relationship between symmetry and space filling, before we proceed further we will need a working appreciation of the ideas of rotational and mirror symmetry. The rotational symmetry of any figure is determined by counting the number of times it repeats or reproduces itself in one revolution about an axis. Only four kinds of rotational symmetry are possible in the uniform subdivision of space: 2-fold, 3-fold, 4-fold, and 6-fold [4.3].

A polygon has mirror symmetry when one side is the reflection of the other side about a common line which bisects the polygon. (This is also known as bilateral symmetry.) It is possible to uniformly subdivide space with figures having only mirror symmetry and with figures having no symmetry at all [4.4]. Though the drawings give two-dimensional examples, we shall later see that the same laws of symmetry hold in three dimensions, and that any given three-dimensional uniform structure will consist of various combinations of the four rotational symmetries, the mirror symmetry, and/or no symmetry.

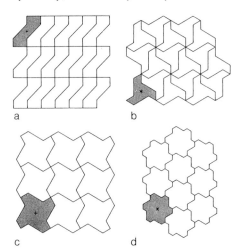

4.3 Tessellations of polygons with n-fold symmetries: 2-fold (a), 3-fold (b), 4-fold (c), and 6-fold (d).

4.4 Tessellations of polygons with mirror symmetry (a) and no symmetry (b).

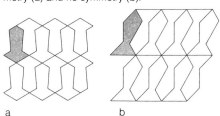

We have seen that the regular pentagon will not serve as a tile in the regular tessellation of the plane. Another way of saying this is that figures cannot repeat themselves on 5-fold axes of symmetry. There is a distorted pentagon which will tile the plane, but it has only mirror symmetry [4.5].

4.5 A mirror-symmetric pentagon that fills the plane.

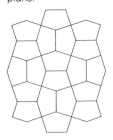

Open Patterns with Regular Polygons

If we eliminate the requirements that all of the plane be filled and that all vertices be congruent, but simply consider *periodic* subdivisions of the plane, with regular polygons, a third class of possibilities emerges. With the removal of the need to fill all spaces with polygons, it is no longer necessary that we use polygons with face angles that can be combined to give 360°. We will still have 360° at each vertex; it is just that a vertex does not have to be entirely surrounded by regular polygons. Such a condition gives rise to "open spaces" of non-regular polygons, many of which are concave. In this class, polygons of 5, 9, 10, and 20 sides may be used. Some examples are shown in [4.6]*

*These examples were the results of some empirical studies conducted by the author with 2nd year architecture students at the University of Southern California.

4.6 Open patterns with regular polygons.

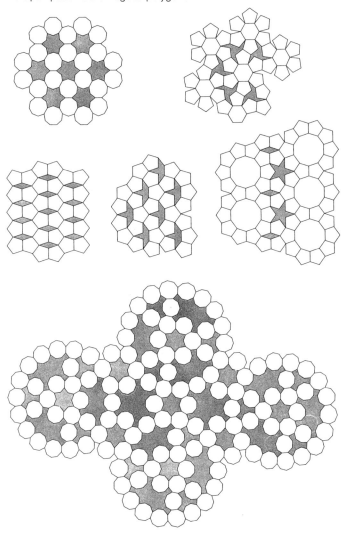

Concentric Patterns with Regular Pentagons

Although the pentagon does not tessellate the plane, it has the curious property that it generates infinite concentrically repeating open patterns [4.7a]. Such concentric open patterns have only one axis of rotational symmetry, about the center of the central pentagon—the only one which shares all of its edges with other pentagons. This kind of pattern is quite different from an infinite tessellation of regular hexagons where all cells are symmetrically equivalent, i.e., the environment around each cell is like that around every other. A variety of concentric patterns can be assembled with pentagons and / or decagons [4.7b]. Because the decagon has twice as many sides as a pentagon, their symmetry properties are similar. We observe there are two great classes of regular figures: first, pentagons, septagons, decagons, etc., that give rise to concentric packing systems; and second, triangles, squares, hexagons, nonagons, etc., that repeat in the plane in true crystallographic fashion—that is, with no unique center of symmetry.

Only those regular polygons with numbers of sides that are divisible by 2, 3, 4, and 6 are capable of infinite repetition in the plane, i.e., only those regular polygons having multiples of 2, 3, 4, or 6-fold symmetry can be the basis of a periodic open pattern. Here I am considering the general case, in which it is not required that *all* the space be filled with regular polygons—only that the polygons could be fit together to generate a repetitive pattern. We can further surmise that any regular polygon which *is not* divisible by 2, 3, 4, or 6 will be capable of generating concentric patterns with a center of symmetry. From this it is apparent that any regular polygon that *is* divisible by 5 can generate concentric patterns with a unique axis of symmetry for the infinite array.

Periodic structures generated as *open* patterns of regular polygons is a subject that, to my knowledge, has been little studied and has only been briefly investigated here.

Dual Tessellations

The concept of the reciprocal or dual network was important to our discussion of closest packed systems. As we shall see, it is also fundamental to the understanding of the properties of all periodic spatial systems. We have already noted the duality of triangular networks and hexagonal networks. A dual network is formed by joining the centers of each polygon to all neighboring polygons through the shared edges. Only one of the regular and semiregular plane tessellations is dual to itself—namely, the square grid. The dual network always forms polygons which are the domains of the vertices; i.e., polygonal domains will have the same number of edges as there are edges meeting at the vertex it encloses.* Any network of a plane tessellation with congruent vertices will have a unique plane-filling domain formed by its dual network. In the case of the array of squares, there are four edges meeting at each vertex at 90°. When the centers of each square face are joined with edges to the centers of all neighboring squares, another array of squares is generated. The polygonal domain of the vertex is a square. Since the tessellations of triangles and hexagons are dual to each other, they form the polygonal domains of each other's networks. In the case of the semiregular tessellations, the dual networks form congruent polygons, but none are regular. Each polygonal domain is capable of repeating itself to fill the plane. Of the eight cases only one has rotational symmetry (2-fold), one has no symmetry and six have mirror symmetry [4.8].

*These two-dimensional polygonal domains are analogous to the three-dimensional polyhedral domains discussed in Chapter 1, pp. 8–9.

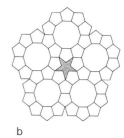

a   b

4.7 Concentric repeating patterns with regular pentagons (a), and regular pentagons / regular decagons (b).

4.8 Dual networks of regular and semiregular tessellations.

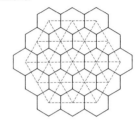

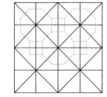

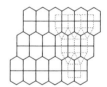

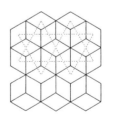
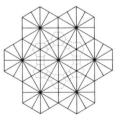

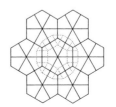

Polyhedra and Their Duals

As mentioned earlier, in the plane it is necessary that all vertices be surrounded by polygons whose face angles sum to 360°. In a finite polyhedron it is necessary that all vertices be surrounded by polygons whose face angles sum to less than 360°; thus a three-dimensional convex figure is formed. When all of the vertices of such a polyhedron share a common sphere it may be considered to be a finite tessellation of the sphere.*

*An example of a fundamental space relationship that can be expressed algebraically is Euler's theorem for polyhedra. It states that for any polyhedron that is singly connected with nonintersecting faces, the number of faces (P), the number of vertices (V), and the number of edges (E), satisfy the equation $P + V = E + 2$. This concisely states the fact that there is always a consistent relationship among the inventory of components of any finite modular structure. For example, the tetrahedron has 4 faces plus 4 vertices which equal its 6 edges plus 2. The octahedron has 8 faces plus 6 vertices which equal 12 edges plus 2, etc. In two dimensions the equation changes slightly. In any finite arbitrary sample of an infinite plane tessellation, the number of polygons, the number of vertices, and the number of edges satisfy $P + V = E + 1$ (see footnote, p. 12). In any random or symmetrical array of packed polygons this relationship holds.

Regular Polyhedra and Their Duals

The first important class of polyhedra are those that are convex and regular. They are composed of regular and equal polygonal faces with all of their vertices equivalently surrounded. There are only five possible cases, the so called Platonic solids, discussed in Chapter 1 (see [1.1]).

Just as it is possible to generate dual networks for the plane tessellations, it is possible to generate polyhedral duals. The dual polyhedron is formed in a manner analogous to that described for the plane tessellation. However, for polyhedra the reciprocation process is somewhat more complicated: a point perpendicularly above the center of each face of a given polyhedron is joined with new edges to similar points above all neighboring faces such that the new edges that connect these points intersect the edges of the original polyhedron, thus forming the edges of a new *dual* polyhedron [4.9]. This pair of dual polyhedra must enclose a common sphere that is tangent to both, at the points where their respective edges intersect. It is usually true that the respective edges of dual polyhedra perpendicularly bisect each other.

It follows from this process of reciprocation that any given polyhedron and its dual will have the same number of edges, and the inventories of faces and vertices will be exactly reversed.

We saw that of the plane tessellations the only self-dual was the array of squares. There is one polyhedron that is a self-dual. It is the regular tetrahedron, which is the only figure to have the same number of vertices as faces. The cube and the regular octahedron are dual. They each have twelve edges, and the cube has six faces and eight vertices, while the octahedron has eight faces and six vertices. The pentagonal dodecahedron and icosahedron are dual. They each have thirty edges. While the dodecahedron has twelve faces and twenty vertices, the icosahedron has twenty faces and twelve vertices. Like the regular plane tessellations, the duals of regular polyhedra are also regular polyhedra, which is a unique property of these regular figures. The duality of the regular polyhedra is shown in [4.9].

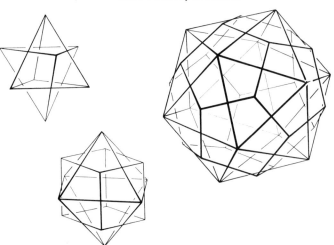

4.9 Dual regular polyhedra.

Semiregular Polyhedra and Their Duals

The existence of the semiregular plane tessellations suggests an equivalent class of polyhedra. The semiregular polyhedra, like their two-dimensional counterparts, require that all polygons be regular but not equal, and that all vertices be equivalently surrounded.

A set of thirteen semiregular figures are usually referred to as the Archimedean solids, since Archimedes was supposedly the first to have studied them. Archimedes' book on the subject has been lost. Kepler made the first complete investigation of all possible semiregular polyhedra.

The thirteen Archimedean polyhedra consist of various combinations of triangles, squares, pentagons, hexagons, octagons, and decagons. Recall that neither the pentagon nor decagon appear in the plane tessellations, and note that the dodecagon, which does appear in the plane tessellations, does not appear in any of these polyhedra. No single polyhedron is constructed of all six types of polygons. Ten of these Archimedean figures utilize only two kinds of polygons, and the remaining three utilize three kinds of polygons. These thirteen polyhedra are shown in [4.10].

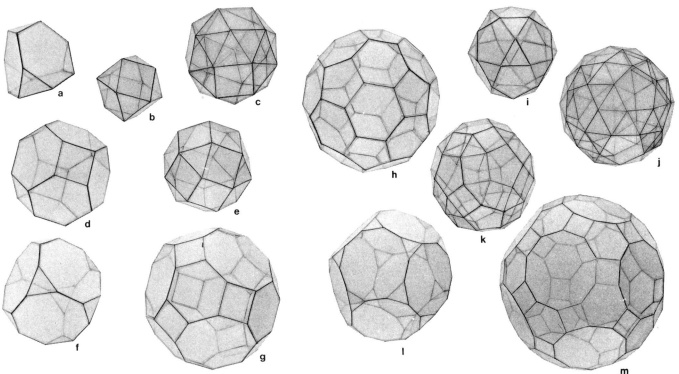

4.10   The thirteen Archimedean polyhedra:
   a   Truncated tetrahedron
   b   Cuboctahedron
   c   Snub cuboctahedron
   d   Truncated octahedron
   e   Rhombicuboctahedron
   f   Truncated cube
   g   Truncated cuboctahedron
   h   Truncated icosahedron
   i   Icosidodecahedron
   j   Snub icosidodecahedron
   k   Rhombicosidodecahedron
   l   Truncated dodecahedron
   m   Truncated icosidodecahedron

For each of the convex regular and semi-regular polyhedra, all vertices fall on a common sphere. That is, the vertices of any one of these polyhedra are always equidistant from a common center. All of the Archimedean polyhedra can be derived from the five Platonic figures by truncations (cutting off) of vertices and / or edges. The obvious examples are the truncated tetrahedron, truncated octahedron, truncated cube, truncated dodecahedron, and the truncated icosahedron. The cuboctahedron can be simply derived from the truncation of the cube or octahedron, etc. Careful examination will reveal that all the Archimedean polyhedra can be generated by means of such truncations.

The duals of the Archimedean polyhedra exhibit many similarities to the duals of the semiregular tessellations. No dual to an Archimedean polyhedron is composed of regular polygons or even necessarily of polygons of equal edge, but all of its faces are congruent. The inventory of faces consists of three-, four-, and five-sided polygons which appear with the following symmetries: two with 2-fold symmetry (rhombic faces), nine with mirror symmetry, and two with no symmetry. Seven of the thirteen dual polyhedra are bounded by congruent triangles and for this reason some have more than passing interest for our study. All thirteen of the dual polyhedra are shown and named in [4.11].

The two figures with rhombic faces, the rhombic dodecahedron and the rhombic triacontahedron, are particularly significant as they are the only duals which have equal edge lengths. We recall from our study of cell aggregates that the rhombic dodecahedron is an often-met-with space filling polyhedron.

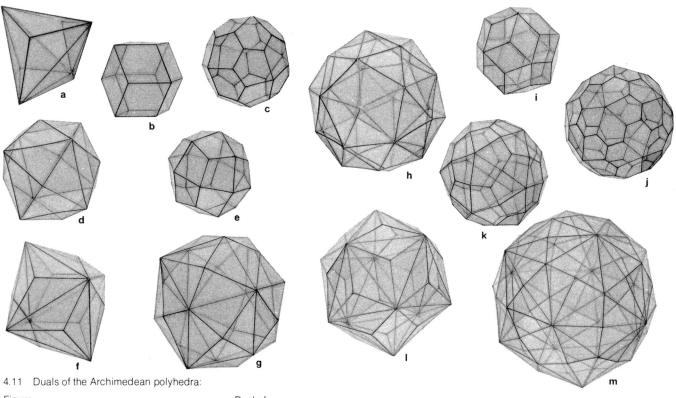

4.11   Duals of the Archimedean polyhedra:

Figure		Dual of
a	Triakis tetrahedron	Truncated tetrahedron
b	Rhombic dodecahedron	Cuboctahedron
c	Pentagonal icositetrahedron	Snub cuboctahedron
d	Tetrakis hexahedron	Truncated octahedron
e	Trapezoidal icositetrahedron	Rhombicuboctahedron
f	Triakis octahedron	Truncated cube
g	Hexakis octahedron	Truncated cuboctahedron
h	Pentakis dodecahedron	Truncated icosahedron
i	Rhombic triacontahedron	Icosidodecahedron
j	Pentagonal hexecontahedron	Snub icosidodecahedron
k	Trapezoidal hexecontahedron	Rhombicosidodecahedron
l	Triakis icosahedron	Truncated dodecahedron
m	Hexakis icosahedron	Truncated icosidodecahedron

Unlike the semiregular tessellations, there are two infinite groups consisting of the prisms and antiprisms, in addition to the Archimedean figures. The prisms and antiprisms correspond to the infinite number of possible polygons. A semiregular prism is made up of two parallel regular polygons of any number of sides, connected in equatorial fashion by square faces [4.12]. The antiprisms are like the prisms except that the equatorial polygons are equilateral triangles [4.13]. Two of the regular polyhedra fall into one each of these categories. The cube is a square prism, and the octahedron is a triangular antiprism. The duals of prisms are called the *dipyramids* (double pyramids), whose faces are congruent isosceles triangles [4.14]. The duals of the antiprisms are called *trapezohedra* and are double pyramid-like figures bounded by congruent trapezia [4.15].

Before we can proceed further, I must define the *dihedral angle*. The dihedral angle is the angle formed between the planes of two adjacent polygons, the angle taken in a plane perpendicular to the common edge [4.16]. All of the dihedral angles for each of the regular polyhedra are equal. However, of the semiregular polyhedra, only the cuboctahedron and the icosidodecahedron have equal dihedral angles. There are nine Archimedean figures which have two dihedral angles and two which have three. The dihedral angle will become quite an important concept as we consider the problem of space filling polyhedra.*

*For a complete atlas of specifications including angular data for regular and semiregular polyhedra see Cundy and Rollett.

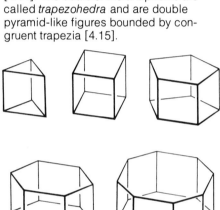

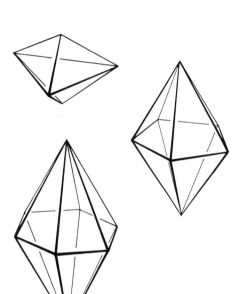

4.12 Semiregular prisms.

4.13 Semiregular antiprisms.

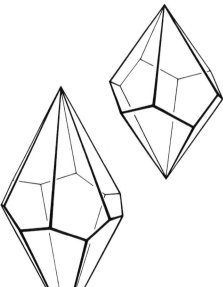

4.14 Dipyramids, the duals of prisms.

4.15 Trapezohedra, the duals of antiprisms.

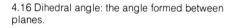

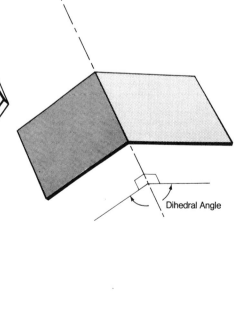

4.16 Dihedral angle: the angle formed between planes.

Dihedral Angle

Compound, Quasiregular, and Stellated Polyhedra

When the cube and octahedron are interlinked with their edges bisecting each other at right angles, a *compound* polyhedron is formed. The 14 apices of this compound polyhedron are the 14 vertices of the rhombic dodecahedron. The edges of the compound figure form the long and short diagonals of the rhombic faces of the dodecahedron [4.17]. When the pentagonal (regular) dodecahedron and icosahedron are interlinked in similar fashion, the resulting 32 apices are the vertices of the rhombic triacontahedron and its edges form the long and short diagonals of the rhombic faces of the triacontahedron [4.18].

Two tetrahedra (remember, the tetrahedron is self-dual) can be interlinked to form a compound called by Kepler the *stella octangula*. Its eight apices are the vertices of a cube and its edges are the diagonals of the cube faces [4.19].

It is illuminating to consider the polyhedra which form the centers or *nuclei* of the foregoing three compounds. The stella octangula can be formed by placing eight regular tetrahedra on the faces of a regular octahedron. The cube-and-octahedron compound has a cuboctahedron as its nucleus. The compound can be formed when six square pyramids and eight triangular pyramids are placed on the faces of the cuboctahedron (assuming, of course, that the proper face angles are used for the triangular faces of the pyramids). The icosahedron-and-dodecahedron has as its nucleus the icosidodecahedron. The compound can be formed by placing twenty triangular pyramids and twelve pentagonal pyramids on the faces of the icosidodecahedron, again assuming that the proper angles are used. These three polyhedra, the octahedron, the cuboctahedron, and icosidodecahedron, are sometimes known as the *quasiregular* polyhedra.

Such a polyhedron has all of its dihedral angles equal, its vertices are congruent, and its faces are of two kinds, each face of one kind being entirely surrounded by the faces of the other kind. All three cases have four-connected vertices and they are the only examples of regular and semiregular figures to have plane equatorial polygons. The octahedron is quasiregular only when its triangular faces are treated as two subsets of four each, such that three of one set always surround one of the other set.

The duals of these quasiregular polyhedra are the figures generated by the compounds for which they form nuclei. The cube is dual to the octahedron; the rhombic dodecahedron is dual to the cuboctahedron; and the rhombic triacontahedron is dual to the icosidodecahedron.

We have so far limited our discussion of regular and semiregular polyhedra to convex figures composed of convex regular plane polygons. There is a very large class of nonconvex uniform polyhedra. They are loosely referred to as stellated polyhedra. A detailed account of these figures can be found in "Uniform Polyhedra" (Coxeter, Lonquet-Higgins, and Miller 1954), where, in addition to the regular and semiregular convex polyhedra, fifty-seven other polyhedra are described.* Among these are four stellated forms known as the Kepler-Poinsot polyhedra, which are those that have regular faces. However, because their faces and edges intersect, these forms are generally far more complex than the simple convex polyhedra. Although they are composed of plane polygons, because of the intersections multifaceted polyhedra are formed with both convex and concave regions. This is characteristic of all of the stellated polyhedra.

The intersection of faces reflects a relatively more abstract concept of space than we have heretofore discussed, simply because it is physically impossible to achieve without actually cutting up the polygons into irregular parts. In the formal classification of these stellated forms, the intersecting polygons form new edges and vertices which are not counted in the inventory of properties. Although these stellated forms have some morphological interest, they are of minor importance in the present study. They will contribute little to our theory of spatial modularity.

*See also Coxeter et al., 1938, for a discussion of a special family of stellated polyhedra derived from the icosahedron.

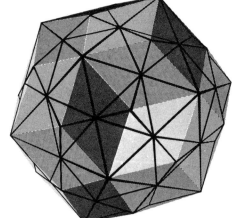

4.17 Rhombic dodecahedron formed as a compound of the cube and octahedron.

4.18 Rhombic triacontahedron formed as a compound of the pentagonal dodecahedron and the icosahedron.

4.19 Cube formed as a compound of two tetrahedra.

Convex Polyhedra Composed of Regular Polygons

So far we have seen that by restricting ourselves to regular, convex plane polygons and a uniformity of vertices for any given figure, the class of possible types of polyhedra that can be formed is very limited: the five Platonic, the thirteen Archimedean polyhedra, and the two infinite families of prisms and antiprisms. If we relax the requirement of uniformity short of the use of regular plane polygons (as we did with the plane tessellations), does this give rise to another set of possible polyhedra?

We saw that there is no apparent limit to the number of different tessellation patterns which can be assembled with the five regular polygons that qualify as tiles. However, in the case of convex polyhedra there are a surprisingly small number of possibilities. Johnson (1966) has proposed that in addition to the regular and semiregular polyhedra there are just 92 others. It is remarkable to realize that the only kinds of faces that a regular-faced solid (beyond prisms and antiprisms) may have are triangles, squares, pentagons, hexagons, octagons, and decagons. The most surprising thing of all is that the list of allowable polygons is precisely the same as that for the regular and semiregular polyhedra. This is another example of a minumum inventory of components that will yield diversity of form.

It is possible with an inventory of six regular polygons to assemble exactly 120 convex polyhedra, including the appropriate finite set of prisms and antiprisms. Of these 120, there are only 10 convex polyhedra that can be made which have congruent regular faces. In addition to the five Platonic polyhedra, there are five others all bounded by equilateral triangles, although it is only in the Platonic figures that all vertices are equidistant from a common center. Of these ten polyhedra, all but the cube and the dodecahedron have triangular faces. We have already noted a special interest in triangulated polyhedra, because of their effectiveness as physical structures, and we can now enumerate all eight cases of convex *deltahedra* (polyhedra bounded by equilateral triangles). The convex deltahedra are as follows: tetrahedron—four faces; triangular dipyramid—six faces; octahedron—eight; pentagonal dipyramid—ten; snub disphenoid— twelve; triaugmented triangular prism— fourteen; gyroelongated square dipyramid—sixteen; and icosahedron— twenty faces. These are shown in [4.20]. The names of the twelve-, fourteen-, and sixteen-hedra are due to Johnson (1966).

We have now a prototypical array of geometric structures that reveals a richness and diversity within the constraints of an extraordinary order. It seems at times almost unbelievable, for example, that there can be only five convex regular polyhedra. This may seem to be a frustrating limitation. However, I hope to show that it is rather a beautiful and useful phenomenon. Without knowledge of these geometric structures and their relationships, the possibility of developing a comprehensive morphological system for modular structures is nil.

a   b   c

d   e

f

4.20   The convex deltahedra:
  a   Tetrahedron (4-hedron)
  b   Triangular dipyramid (6-hedron)
  c   Octahedron (8-hedron)
  d   Pentagonal dipyramid (10-hedron)
  e   12-hedron
  f   14-hedron
  g   16-hedron
  h   Icosahedron (20-hedron)

g   h

5 Symmetry and Space Filling

With this underlying background in plane tessellations and finite polyhedra, we must now move to a subject which, if it is not the most exciting in all geometry, is certainly of the highest importance in our search for a theory of modularity: the concept of space filling polyhedra, which ultimately leads us to the general properties of three-dimensional periodic space. By space filling is meant the packing together of closed three-dimensional bodies in an unbounded or infinite array such that all the space is occupied without intersections of contiguous cells. The obvious question comes to the fore: with an inventory of finite polyhedra on hand, which, if any, will pack together to fill all space?

The question has even more importance than may be immediately apparent as it must be noted from the outset that there is no limit to the number of possible space filling polyhedra. This is to emphasize that the discovery of previously unknown space filling polyhedra is of no particular significance in itself. Space filling polyhedra (old or new) only have significance in the degree to which they relate to some ordering principle. Whether such ordering principles are derived from mathematical criteria or physical constraints or both is immaterial, so long as the determining parameters are well defined. The real significance of the space filling polyhedra is therefore related to the significance of the ordering principles themselves.

For the moment we are content to examine space filling possibilities within the constraints that have evolved through the historical search for ordering principles in nature and in mathematics. Hence the Platonic and Archimedean polyhedra are considered. Later in this examination some new possibilities are proposed based on parameters which have developed from the goals of the present work.

Symmetry Classes

The cube is the only Platonic polyhedron that will repeat to fill all space. It is the most symmetrical variation on the infinite class of three-dimensional figures known as parallelepipeds. The parallelepipeds are prisms whose bases and sides are parallelograms; they are, therefore, six-faced polyhedra. Any parallelepiped will fill space by the congruent repetition of itself [5.1]. The subdivision of space by means of congruent parallelepipeds may be characterized in terms of six symmetry classes or systems. These classes form six of the seven crystal systems of crystallography. The seven crystal classes rely upon various combinations of 2-fold, 3-fold, 4-fold, 6-fold or no rotational symmetry; together, they provide a descriptive scheme of space partitioning. As already mentioned, the cube is the most symmetrical case; that is, it has the greatest number of symmetry axes of any parallelepiped or parallelohedron. A cube has three axes of 4-fold symmetry, four axes of 3-fold symmetry, and six axes of 2-fold symmetry [5.2a]. This is a consequence not only of the fact that a cube's face and dihedral angles are all equal to 90°, but also of the fact that all of its edges are equal.

It will be noted that only the cube is metrically determinate in these seven symmetry classes; i.e., it is the only parallelepiped in which there is a unique set of dimensional relationships that cannot be varied without destroying some aspect of its symmetry. The six parallelepiped classes can be generated by making a series of systematic changes in the edge lengths and face angles of the cube while preserving only parallelism. Three sets of parallel planes are defined by the faces of any parallelepiped.

5.1 Any parallelepiped will fill space by repetition.

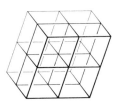

The next most symmetrical parallelepiped class after the cube is the tetragonal system. A tetragonal parallelepiped, like the cube, is also a square prism. All of its face angles are 90°. It differs from the cube in only one regard—its height will be either greater or less than its base but not equal to its base. The tetragonal system has one axis of 4-fold symmetry and four axes of 2-fold symmetry [5.2b].

In the orthorhombic system all face angles are still 90°, but the base has two unequal sides making it a rectangle rather than a square; and the height is yet a third length. The orthorhombic system has only three 2-fold axes of symmetry [5.2c].

The monoclinic system is nonrectangular on one set of planes, with the other two sets of planes rectangular. It has only one 2-fold axis of symmetry [5.2d]. Although the trigonal system has no 90° angles, all of its edges are equal and all of its six faces are congruent. This gives rise to one 3-fold axis of symmetry making it slightly more symmetrical than the monoclinic [5.2e]. The triclinic system has no symmetry. It has no 90° angles, and only those edges, and therefore faces, which are parallel are equal [5.2f].

The hexagonal system is based upon the right hexagonal prism. This prism has six right parallelograms for sides and two regular hexagons parallel to each other on opposite ends. It is not a parallelepiped, but is a parallelohedron because only its sides are parallelograms rather than its bases and sides. The hexagonal system has one 6-fold axis and six 2-fold axes of symmetry [5.2g]. It is considered the most symmetrical system after the cube.*

*We can rank the various symmetry classes by considering the total number of symmetry axes of each class: 1. Cubic—13 axes; 2. Hexagonal—7 axes; 3. Tetragonal—5 axes; 4. Orthorhombic—3 axes; 5. Trigonal—1 axis; 6. Monoclinic—1 axis; 7. Triclinic—no symmetry axes.

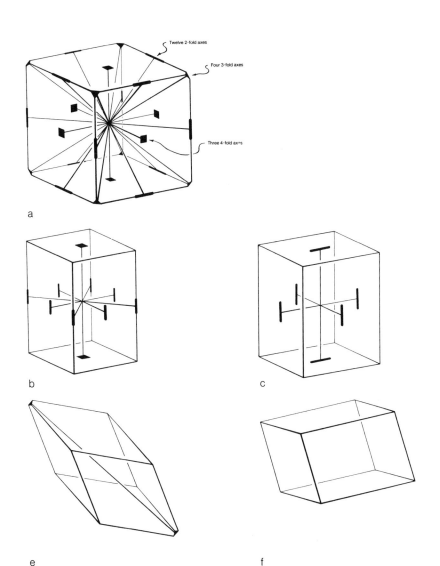

Twelve 2-fold axes

Four 3-fold axes

Three 4-fold axes

a

b

c

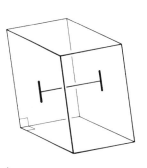

d

e

f

g

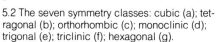

5.2 The seven symmetry classes: cubic (a); tetragonal (b); orthorhombic (c); monoclinic (d); trigonal (e); triclinic (f); hexagonal (g).

Lattices and Unit Cells

In 1848 Bravais showed that there was a maximum of fourteen space lattices or groups of points differing by symmetry and geometry whose translational repetition in space maintained the symmetrical arrangements of the points of a unit cell. Bravais perceived that these fourteen space lattices corresponded to seven crystal symmetry classes.*

In these seven crystal symmetry classes, the parallelepiped (or hex prism)** is the *unit cell* or elementary repeat unit. In crystallography, a unit cell is defined as the basic repeating unit or module that, by simple *translation*, will define the infinite structure. *Translation* is a fundamental *symmetry operation* in which a given unit is repeated by sliding it along an axis or set of axes. Such axes are usually the set described by the edges of a given parallelepiped defined by the unit cell.

When points are placed at the corners of a given unit cell, a *primitive* lattice is formed. These points are called *lattice sites*. These lattice sites are symmetrically equivalent in the sense that they have identical surroundings or environments, i.e., each lattice site is equivalent to every other lattice site. For four of the seven primitive lattices, we can add additional points to face centers and cell body centers so that more lattices can be formed in which all the points are symmetrically equivalent.

*It was determined by Federov (1880) and independently by Schoenflies (1891) that with the 14 Bravais lattices it was possible to generate by means of various symmetry operations "space groups" constituting only 230 possible symmetrical ways of arranging points in space. It is these 230 space groups that form the heart of the analysis of crystals. For complete descriptions of Bravais lattice and a review of crystallography in general see Chalmers et al.; Burke; Hurlbut; and F. C. Phillips.

**The unit cell of the hexagonal system is usually considered to be a right rhombic prism which is ⅓ of the hexagonal prism and itself a parallelepiped.

5.3 Cubic lattices: simple cubic, sc (a); body centered cubic, bcc (b); face centered cubic, fcc (c).

In the cubic system, there can be an additional lattice site placed at the center of the unit cell, thus forming the body centered cubic lattice (bcc). Or, lattice sites can be placed forming the face centered cubic lattices (fcc) [5.3].

In the tetragonal system, in addition to the primitive lattice, it is only possible to have a body centered lattice. However, in the orthorhombic system three other lattices are possible in addition to the primitive. Body centered and face centered lattices are augmented by a lattice with sites added only on two opposite and parallel faces of the unit cell. The system is usually designated C-face centered orthorhombic or simply orthorhombic-C. In the monoclinic system, only a similar C-face centered lattice appears, bringing the total number of lattices up to fourteen [5.4].

Despite the fact that the unit cells and lattices are usually illustrated as parallelepipeds or parallelohedra with edges, from a crystallographer's point of view it is only the lattice sites that are of concern. There is usually no consideration of the nature of the connections between the lattice sites. Because of this the concept of the lattice as understood by crystallographers is somewhat abstract; nevertheless, we will find that the foregoing identification of the seven crystal classes will have its role to play in our development of a morphological system for the organization of physical components in space.* The three cubic lattices—primitive, bcc, and fcc—are the most significant Bravais lattices in the sense that when each lattice point is connected to each of its nearest neighbors with edges, important fundamental three-dimensional networks result. Of the fourteen Bravais lattices, these cubic systems will be given the greatest emphasis in the remainder of this book.

*For a discussion of the relationships between point arrays and connected networks (a polyhedron can be considered a connected network), see Hilbert and Cohn-Vossen's Chapter II.

5.4 Tetragonal, trigonal, orthorhombic, monoclinic, triclinic, and hexagonal lattices.

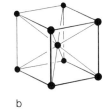

a   b   c

Space Filling Polyhedra

We have seen that of the regular polyhedra, only the cube will fill space. Among the Archimedean polyhedra and the infinite family of prisms and antiprisms, we find that there are exactly three space fillers: the truncated octahedron, the hexagonal prism, and the triangular prism.

We are already familiar with the packings of the truncated octahedron from our discussion of the geometry of closest packed cells [1.7b]. Recall that it is the space filling polyhedron with the least interface area. As we have already noted, in space filling array all of its vertices are identical, with four edges meeting at each point.

The space filling triangular and hexagonal prisms are generated from the plane tessellations of triangles and hexagons [5.5].

Of the thirteen Archimedean duals, only the rhombic dodecahedron will fill all space. It was mentioned along with the truncated octahedron in our discussion of naturally occurring cellular structures [1.7a]. Among the duals of the prisms and antiprisms (dipyramids and trapezohedra), there are no space fillers. Of the class of 92 finite polyhedra bounded by regular polygons, there are also no known space fillers.

Both the rhombic dodecahedron and truncated octahedron have full cubic symmetry [5.6]. The hexagonal prism has one axis of 6-fold symmetry and six axes of 2-fold symmetry. The triangular prism has one axis of 3-fold symmetry and three axes of 2-fold symmetry. Within this set of five space filling polyhedra—cube, truncated octahedron, hexagonal prism, triangular prism, and rhombic dodecahedron— we find only 2-fold, 3-fold, 4-fold, and 6-fold symmetry axes.

Symmetry is not the only factor that allows us to discover candidates for space filling. Another factor is the complementarity of adjacent dihedral angles. In a space filling array of polyhedra the dihedral angles formed by faces meeting around a common edge must sum to 360°. This is equivalent to the requirement of 360° around each vertex of a plane tessellation.

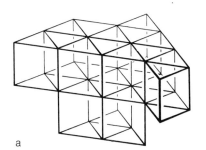

a

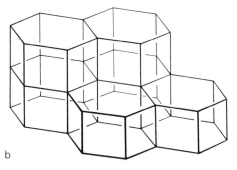

b

5.5 Space filling triangular (a) and hexagonal (b) prisms.

5.6 The rhombic dodecahedron and truncated octahedron have full cubic symmetry.

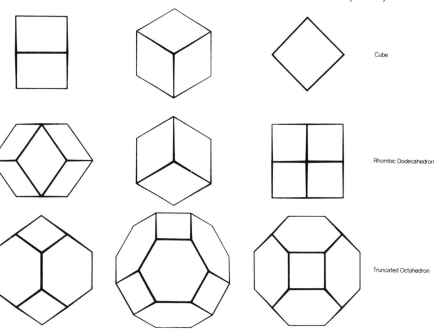

Cube

Rhombic Dodecahedron

Truncated Octahedron

2-fold axis   3-fold axis   4-fold axis

The Tetrahedron and Octahedron and Space Filling

There is no mystery concerning the cube as a space filler, but it is useful to examine the properties of the other four regular polyhedra to see if there are clear reasons why they will *not* fill space.

Because the octahedron is the dual of the cube, it has the same symmetry. However, it will not fill space. Although the symmetry is there, its dihedral angle of 109° 28' makes it impossible for the octahedron to *pack* with itself to occupy all of space. We have already noted, however, that octahedra will combine with tetrahedra to form a fully triangulated network, which in turn describes a space filling array of these polyhedra. This structure is the dual network of the packing of rhombic dodecahedra and it is the lattice which positions equal spheres in closed packed array. In fact, this structure is an fcc lattice [5.3, 5.10a].

Octahedra and tetrahedra will fill space when packed in the ratio of 1:2. This is easily shown by placing tetrahedra on two opposite faces of an octahedron. The result is a space filling parallelepiped with six rhombic faces with angles of 120° and 60° [5.7]. It should be noted that the tetrahedron's faces are parallel to half of the faces of the octahedron, and this explains the ability to form a multiple space filling system. The dihedral angle of the tetrahedron is 70°32', which is compatible with the 109°28' dihedral angle of the octahedron: combining two tetrahedra and two octahedra around a common edge accounts for 360°.

The tetrahedron is less symmetrical than the octahedron (or cube). It has four axes of 3-fold symmetry and three axes of 2-fold symmetry [5.8]. Because they are symmetrically equivalent, either the cube or the octahedron may be used to identify figures with similar symmetry, i.e., the same figure may be designated as having octahedral or cubic symmetry. Because the cube is the space filler, and presumably because it is more familiar, the term cubic symmetry is more generally used.

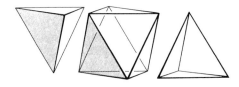

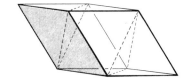

The Icosahedron and Dodecahedron and Space Filling

The icosahedron and the dodecahedron are dual to each other so they have the same symmetry. The icosahedron is the most symmetrical of all possible polyhedra. It is mathematically and physically impossible to describe or construct a polyhedron of higher symmetry. The icosahedron has twenty equilateral triangular faces. There is no convex polyhedron with more than twenty identical regular faces. A triangular face may be divided into six congruent right triangles. When this is done on each face of the icosahedron, a polyhedron can be derived which has 120 congruent faces. This is the greatest number of identical modules which can be used to form a closed polyhedron. The icosahedron becomes, therefore, the most symmetrical system for the subdivision of a spherical surface into modular units. As I pointed out in Chapter 2 it is this property of high symmetry that Fuller has exploited with his geodesic domes and which many virus structures take advantage of. However, this high symmetry makes it impossible to fill space with an icosahedron.*

*Coxeter, DuVal, and Petrie have shown that the icosahedron can generate 59 stellated forms due to its high symmetry. No other polyhedron can generate that many derivative forms.

5.7 Two tetrahedra and one octahedron combine to form a space filling parallelipiped.

5.8 Symmetry axes of the regular tetrahedron: four 3-fold axes and three 2-fold axes.

The icosahedron has the following axes of symmetry: six 5-fold axes, ten 3-fold axes, and fifteen 2-fold axes [5.9]. Since the dodecahedron is the dual of the icosahedron, it has the same symmetry. We note that these two figures have six axes of 5-fold symmetry. It has already been shown in the discussion of plane tessellations that regular pentagons cannot be combined to fill the plane. Only figures with 2-fold, 3-fold, 4-fold, and 6-fold symmetry can subdivide space. In spite of the fact that the pentagonal dodecahedron appears as if it might fill space, it will not quite do it. Its face angles are 108° (very close to the tetrahedral angles of 109°28′), and its dihedral angles are 116°34′ (which is close to the 120° angle found in plane tessellations). The fact that the icosahedron and dodecahedron have elements of 2-fold and 3-fold symmetry suggests that they may have some capability of spatial periodicity, if not complete space filling. Such questions are explored later, along with distortions of these two figures, made in order to accomplish at least approximate space filling.

Regular and Semiregular Polyhedra as Multiple Space Fillers

A multiple space filling system is one in which there is more than one kind of polyhedron. As we have just seen, among the five Platonic polyhedra, the only multiple space filling system is one composed of tetrahedra and octahedra. However, there are also multiple space filling systems which utilize, in various combinations, both the regular and semiregular polyhedra.

The first requirement of multiple space filling is that different polyhedra must have matching parallel faces in common. With this in mind, it becomes readily apparent that the semiregular duals do not qualify, as no two figures have the same faces in common. Of the thirteen Archimedean figures, six are derived from the icosahedron and consequently have full icosahedral symmetry which disqualifies them, even from multiple space filling systems. Of the remaining seven, one—the truncated tetrahedron—has tetrahedral symmetry and the other six—cuboctahedron, truncated octahedron, truncated cube, rhombicuboctahedron, truncated cuboctahedron, and snub cuboctahedron—have full cubic symmetry. Of these six, the snub cuboctahedron has *extra* faces which are not parallel to the faces of any of the others. It is, therefore, disqualified.

Of the Archimedean and Platonic figures, then, there are altogether nine polyhedra that qualify as candidates for multiple space filling systems. In the larger class of semiregular polyhedra, which includes the prisms as well as the Archimedean figures, a look at the semiregular plane tessellations reveals which of the prisms will qualify for multiple space filling. We have already seen that triangles, squares, hexagons, octagons, and dodecagons are the only polygons that can combine in various arrangements to form plane tessellations [4.1]. Any polygon can be used for the ends of a right prism, and if all the sides are taken to be squares, we have a collection of semiregular polyhedra. (The cube, of course, is regular.)

From this, it follows that triangular, hexagonal, octagonal, and dodecagonal prisms qualify as candidates for multiple space filling systems. Further, the eight semiregular tessellations can be considered multiple space filling systems which combine up to three different cell shapes, e.g., cube, hexagonal prism, and dodecagonal prism. Recall that the semiregular tessellations have all their vertices congruent and that if this requirement is waived, there can be an infinite number of plane tessellations composed of regular polygons. The same principle holds with the space filling prisms, i.e., there is an infinite number of multiple systems once the requirement of congruent vertices is abandoned. In the interest of simplicity we will only consider the uniform cases on the assumption that the most interesting nonuniform permutations are derived from them.

We can classify multiple space filling systems according to how many different types of polyhedra the systems require. A space filling system consisting of one type of polyhedron is called a *unary* space filling system. Multiple systems consisting of two, three, and four types of polyhedra are called *binary, ternary,* and *quaternary* space filling systems, respectively.*

*I have discovered no system composed exclusively of regular and semiregular figures that utilizes more than four types of polyhedra.

5.9 Symmetry of the icosahedron and its dual, the pentagonal dodecahedron.

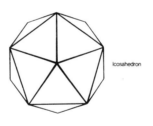

icosahedron

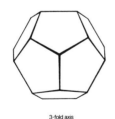
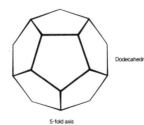

Dodecahedron

2-fold axis   3-fold axis   5-fold axis

In addition to the eight multiple-prism (from the semiregular tessellations) space filling systems, there are eleven more space filling possibilities utilizing the Platonic and Archimedean polyhedra. These eleven are shown in [5.10].*
These range from the binary tetrahedral / octahedral system to the quaternary system composed of the rhombicuboctahedron, octagonal prism, truncated cube, and cube. Unlike the multiple prism packings, these systems do not give rise to infinite numbers of space filling permutations. There is a simple reason for this. Only the cube, out of the nine polyhedra in this class, can be repeated to form a larger version of itself. In the case of the prism forms (including the cube again) of the five qualifying polyhedra, both the cube (square prism) and the triangular prism will repeat to form larger versions of themselves, and the triangular prism can also be placed to form hexagonal prisms.

In summary, the five qualifying prisms give rise to an infinite number of possible space filling permutations. This is consistent with the general nature of the prism class of semiregular figures since there are an infinite number of finite prisms. The Archimedean polyhedra compose a finite class, and we find that their high symmetry limits the inventory of space filling possibilities.

In order to set limits on the number of space filling prism systems, the requirement was established that all vertices in the array must be congruent. Now, in the case of the finite set of eleven multiple space filling systems which are composed of various combinations of the Platonic and Archimedean polyhedra, all vertices are congruent. Thus, all of the space filling systems we have so far mentioned (which total 23 cases) consisting of regular and semiregular polyhedra, including the unary systems and the prism family, can be considered to be uniform structures since in each system all vertices are equally surrounded by the same number of edges. This uniformity has important consequences for the reciprocal space filling arrangements (dual nets) of these 23 space filling systems.

*Andreini was the first to enumerate these.

5.10 Space filling by combinations of Platonic and Archimedean polyhedra.

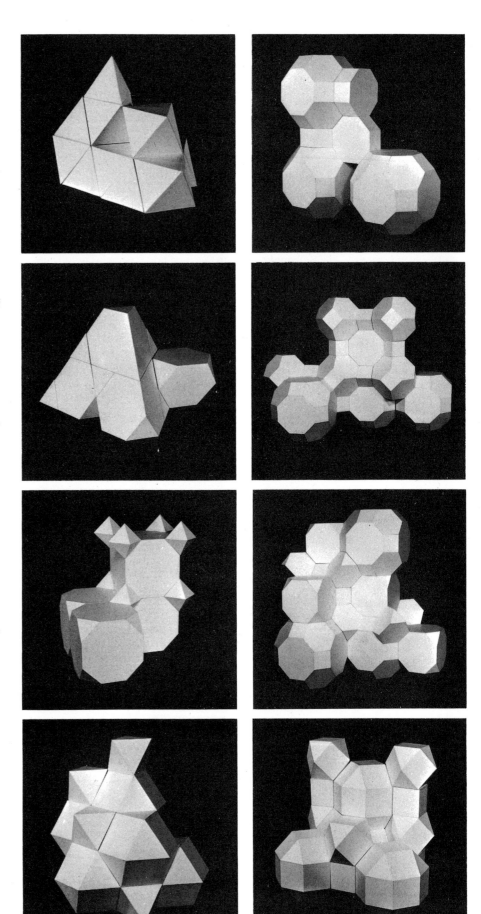

Dual Space Filling

The concept of the dual network or reciprocal space filling has been defined in Chapter 1. In review, it is formed by connecting the centers of each polyhedron in a space filling array to all neighbors with which it shares a common face. It follows from the definition that if all vertices in a space filling array are congruent (uniform), the dual network will form a unary space filling system composed of a single kind of polyhedron. Such a polyhedron has also been described as a domain of a vertex in Chapter 1 (pp. 8–9). If there is more than one kind of vertex in a space filling structure, its dual space filling will be composed of as many different kinds of polyhedra as there are different kinds of vertices.

The 23 space filling systems with congruent vertices give rise to 23 unary space filling systems. However, three of these original 23 uniform systems have dual space filling systems which are also comprised of regular or semiregular polyhedra. While the dual of a single cube is an octahedron, the space filling of cubes is a self-dual and is the only such case.

The triangular prism and the hexagonal prism space filling systems are dual to each other. Therefore, only 20 new polyhedra are formed with the dual space filling systems. Actually one of these is already familiar as the domain of the dual network of the tetrahedral / octahedral system: namely the rhombic dodecahedron, the only Archimedean dual polyhedron that will fill space. It is both a finite dual polyhedron and the domain of an infinite dual space filling system. Subtracting the rhombic dodecahedron then, there are still 19 space filling polyhedra which have not been discussed. These are illustrated in [5.11].

Table 5.1 lists all 23 space filling systems, unary and multiple, consisting of regular and semiregular polyhedra, and the polyhedra of their dual space filling systems.

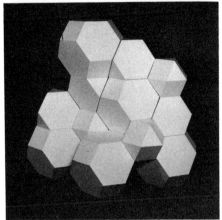

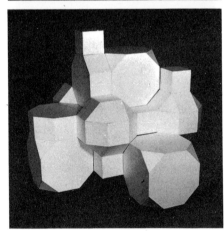

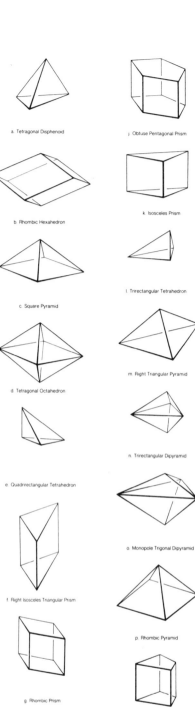

a. Tetragonal Disphenoid

b. Rhombic Hexahedron

c. Square Pyramid

d. Tetragonal Octahedron

e. Quadrirectangular Tetrahedron

f. Right Isosceles Triangular Prism

g. Rhombic Prism

h. Acute Pentagonal Prism

i. Birectangular Pentagonal Prism

j. Obtuse Pentagonal Prism

k. Isosceles Prism

l. Trirectangular Tetrahedron

m. Right Triangular Pyramid

n. Trirectangular Dipyramid

o. Monopole Trigonal Dipyramid

p. Rhombic Pyramid

q. Birectangular Quadrilateral Prism

r. Right Triangular Prism

s. Right Square Pyramid

5.11 Polyhedra of dual space filling systems.

Table 5.1
Space Filling Systems
Composed of Regular
and Semiregular
Polyhedra

Space Filling System	Space Filling Ratio	Vertex Coord.	Polyhedron of Dual Space Filling System	
1 Cube		6	Cube	
2 Truncated octahedron		4	Tetragonal disphenoid [5.11a]	
3 Triangular prism		8	Hexagonal prism	
4 Hexagonal prism		5	Triangular prism	
 5 Tetrahedron	2	12	Rhombic dodecahedron	
Octahedron	1			
 6 Tetrahedron	1	6	Rhombic hexahedron [5.11b]	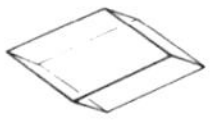
Truncated tetrahedron	1			
 7 Octahedron	1	5	Square pyramid [5.11c]	
Truncated cube	1			
 8 Octahedron	1	8	Tetragonal octahedron [5.11d]	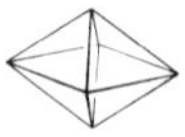
Cuboctahedron	1			
 9 Truncated cuboctahedron	1	4	Quadrirectangular tetrahedron [5.11e]	
Octagonal prism	3			
10 Octagonal prism	1	5	Right isosceles triangular prism [5.11f]	
Cube	1			
11 Triangular prism	2	6	Rhombic prism [5.11g]	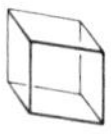
Hexagonal prism	1			
12 Triangular prism	8	7	Acute pentagonal prism [5.11h]	
Hexagonal prism	1			

Table 5.1
Continued

	Space Filling System	Space Filling Ratio	Vertex Coord.	Polyhedron of Dual Space Filling System	
13	Triangular prism	2	7	Birectangular pentagonal prism [5.11i]	
	Cube	1			
14	Triangular prism	2	7	Obtuse pentagonal prism [5.11j]	
	Cube	1			
15	Triangular prism	2	5	Isosceles prism [5.11k]	
	Twelve-prism	1			
16	Truncated cuboctahedron	1	4	Trirectangular tetrahedron [5.11l]	
	Truncated octahedron	1			
	Cube	3			
17	Truncated cuboctahedron	1	4	Right triangular pyramid [5.11m]	
	Truncated cube	1			
	Truncated tetrahedron	2			
18	Rhombicuboctahedron	1	6	Trirectangular dipyramid [5.11n]	
	Cuboctahedron	1			
	Cube	3			
19	Rhombicuboctahedron	1	6	Monopole trigonal dipyramid [5.11o]	
	Cube	1			
	Tetrahedron	2			
20	Truncated octahedron	1	5	Rhombic pyramid [5.11p]	
	Cuboctahedron	1			
	Truncated tetrahedron	2			
21	Hexagonal prism	1	6	Birectangular quadrilateral prism [5.11q]	
	Triangular prism	2			
	Cube	3			
22	Hexagonal prism	2	5	Right triangular prism [5.11r]	
	Twelve-prism	1			
	Cube	3			
23	Rhombicuboctahedron	1	5	Right square pyramid [5.11s]	
	Truncated cube	1			
	Octagonal prism	3			
	Cube	3			

Space Filling Systems Derived from the Rhombic Dodecahedron

There are a few special cases derived from the rhombic dodecahedron which are of some interest. The dual of the cuboctahedron is the rhombic dodecahedron. The cuboctahedron has four regular hexagonal equatorial planes passing through its center. These planes are parallel to the faces of the regular tetrahedron. It is possible on any one given plane to twist the upper and lower halves of the cuboctahedron 60° with respect to one another. The result is a new polyhedron with less symmetry than the cuboctahedron although it still has six square and eight triangular faces. Johnson (1966) has proposed that it be called the triangular *orthobicupola*. This figure has the symmetry of a triangular prism; one 3-fold axis and three 2-fold axes of symmetry. The dual of this triangular orthobicupola is a twelve-faced figure much like the rhombic dodecahedron. It is bounded by six rhombic faces from the rhombic dodecahedron and six trapezoid faces and is called the trapezorhombic dodecahedron [5.12]. Like the rhombic dodecahedron this figure will fill space. Its dual net is an array of tetrahedra and octahedra, arranged somewhat differently than the fcc scheme. Each octahedron has a tetrahedron on its face in the fcc lattice while with this alternative system planar arrays of octahedra surrounded by tetrahedra are stacked so that each octahedron is exactly above another octahedron in a face-to-face arrangement.*

It should be also noted that just as the cuboctahedron will form a binary packing system with octahedra in the ratio of 1:1, so will the triangular orthobicupola.

*This configuration describes the centers of spheres in a special case of closest packing described in the next chapter and called hexagonal closest packing (see pp. 54–61 and [6.1]).

There is another unary space filling system derived from the rhombic dodecahedron. It is called the elongated dodecahedron, and is formed by "fissioning" four of the six 4-connected vertices of the rhombic dodecahedron which share a common plane. Four new parallel edges reconnect the fissioned vertices. A polyhedron is formed bounded by eight rhombic faces and four irregular hexagonal faces with 2-fold symmetry [5.13]. The figure as a whole has four 2-fold axes and one 4-fold axis of symmetry. Its dual net is an array of distorted tetrahedra and octahedra.

Although the rhombic dodecahedron does not appear in any multiple space filling system, it can be used to generate some systems that combine the regular tetrahedron and / or the cube with three different truncated forms.

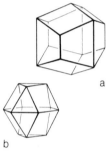

a

b

5.12 Trapezorhombic dodecahedron (a); triangular orthobicupola or twist cuboctahedron (b).

5.13 Forming the elongated dodecahedron by fissioning of rhombic dodecahedron vertices.

Rhombic Dodecahedron   Elongated Dodecahedron

Unlike the regular and semiregular polyhedra formed with regular faces, the rhombic dodecahedron has two kinds of vertices: six 4-connected and eight 3-connected vertices. Because of this it can be truncated in three different ways. If only the 4-connected vertices are truncated, a figure results which is bounded by twelve hexagons (2-fold symmetry) and six squares. If only the triangular 3-connected vertices are truncated, a figure results which is bounded by twelve hexagons (2-fold symmetry) and eight equilateral triangles. If all vertices are truncated, a figure results which is bounded by twelve octagons (2-fold symmetry), six squares, and eight equilateral triangles, for a total of 26 faces [5.14].

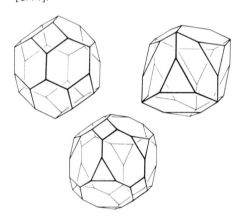

5.14 Truncations of the rhombic dodecahedron.

All three of the foregoing truncated polyhedra form multiple space filling systems in combination with regular tetrahedra placed on triangular faces and cubes placed on square faces. There is one multiple system for each truncated form [5.15]. In the fully truncated figure, if the corners of the square and triangles are allowed to touch, the rhombicuboctahedron is formed. It also has 26 faces, twelve parallel to the rhombic dodecahedron faces, six parallel to the cube faces and eight parallel to the octahedron faces; hence the name *rhombicuboctahedron* [5.16].

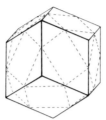

5.15 Multiple space filling systems of truncated rhombic dodecahedra (a), tetrahedra (b), and cubes (c).

5.16 The rhombic dodecahedron and the rhombicuboctahedron.

This rhombicuboctahedron can itself be truncated. Since it is a uniform structure, all vertices would be truncated alike. Two related polyhedra can be derived with 50 faces each. First, when the rhombicuboctahedron's vertices are truncated so that the edges of its faces are bisected, a figure results which is bounded by 6 squares, 8 triangles, 12 rhombuses, and 24 rectangles. Second, when the rhombicuboctahedron's vertices are truncated so that the edges of its faces are divided into three segments, a figure results which is bounded by 6 octagons (4-fold or 8-fold), 8 hexagons (3-fold or 6-fold), 12 octagons (2-fold), and 24 rectangles. These 50-faced polyhedra are shown in [5.17].

These two polyhedra each give rise to quaternary space filling systems. The first figure will fill space in combination with cuboctahedra, regular octahedra, and triangular prisms, and the second figure will fill space in combination with truncated cubes, truncated tetrahedra, and triangular prisms.

5.17 Two 50-faced truncated rhombicuboctahedra (pentacontahedra).

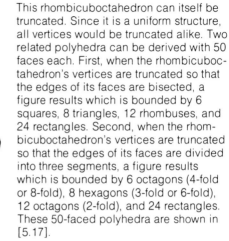

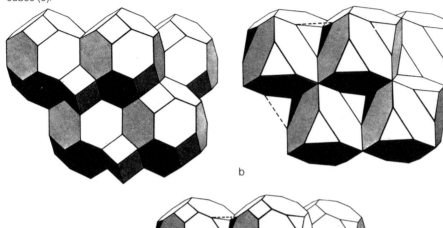

b

c

Connected Networks

Up to this point, we have been assembling space filling structures by combining polygons and polyhedra. Characteristic of all the regular and semiregular systems that we have found is the uniformity of vertices in each case. We now turn to the characteristics of vertices as a guide to the identification of space filling systems. By specifying the number of edges meeting at each vertex and the angles at which they meet, we are in fact identifying the underlying structural networks that define the various polyhedra of which a given space filling system is composed.

The concept of the vertex as the basic unit of structure in space filling systems suggests the generalized notion of uniformly connected three-dimensional infinite periodic networks, in which no reference to polyhedra need be made.*

A review of Table 5.1 shows that there are no space filling systems which have vertices at which fewer than four edges meet. However, there are many examples of uniformly connected three-dimensional networks which have only three edges meeting at each vertex. As for the plane tessellations, it is impossible to have a network with fewer than three edges meeting at a point. In two dimensions this is the pattern of hexagons, but when we move off the plane and into space, many new possibilities arise. Three examples are shown of three-dimensional connected networks [5.18] in which each vertex is surrounded by three edges meeting at 120° angles in a common plane. Since many different systems can be created using the same kind of vertex it is necessary to describe both the vertex coordination and the orientation of the vertices with respect to one another, if a structure is to be fully described. Such networks form polygonal circuits; however, they are usually nonplanar.

*This is a subject that has been extensively delineated by Wells in three books and a series of papers. (See the Bibliography for citations.) It is also a subject that has been examined in depth by Schoen (1967, 1970).

Figure [5.18a] shows a 3-connected network that defines only one polygon—a skew decagon. It is called the Laves network, after its discoverer. It is the network which, with a given strut length, will occupy the greatest volume; it is the network of least density. Figure [5.18b] shows a 3-connected network which defines a skew decagon circuit, as well as a skew dodecagon circuit. Note that in the 3-connected network of [5.18c] plane hexagons are formed as well as skew octagons and skew dodecagons. In addition to 3-connected networks, many networks of higher coordination can be realized. Two examples of 4-connected networks are shown. In one instance [5.19a] four edges meet at angles of 90° in a common plane, as they do in the plane tessellation of squares. However, in this system no squares are formed. As with the three-connected nets, new possibilities are opened up by moving off the plane and into three-dimensional space. This system is characterized by skewed hexagonal circuits.

Another 4-connected net is one in which the edges are coequally surrounded by 109°28′ angles [5.19b]. These are the angles formed by joining the center of a tetrahedron to its four vertices. We have seen that this angle is ubiquitous among the minimal-surface cellular structures found in nature. It is also the bond angle of carbon atoms in the diamond structure. In fact, this particular network can be considered a model of the diamond with a carbon atom positioned at each vertex. This diamond network will prove to be of fundamental importance in the development of our morphological system in subsequent chapters.

Uniformly connected nets are more difficult to enumerate and classify than space filling systems, as there is apparently no limit to the possibilities. Schoen has imposed the limitation of homogeneity, which he defines as the symmetrical equivalence of edges and vertices (Schoen 1967, 1970; Coxeter and Moser). Such a criterion eliminates many possibilities and leaves us with a finite class of systems.

Schoen (private communication) has found that there are more than twenty examples (aside from the regular plane tessellations) of the most simple kind of homogeneous net, i.e., one which is both (a) *locally joined* (each vertex is joined by an edge only to nearest neighbor vertices) and also (b) *locally centered* (each vertex lies at the center of the set of vertices to which it is joined by an edge). If either restriction (a) or (b) is dropped, the number of homogeneous nets is found to be infinite (Schoen 1970, pp. 51 and 86).

Many of the space filling systems of Table 5.1, although uniform, are not homogeneous as all edges are not equivalent. In the examples we have just given, both of the 4-connected nets qualify but only one of the 3-connected nets qualifies [5.18a].

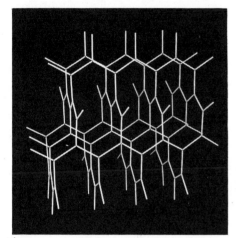

a

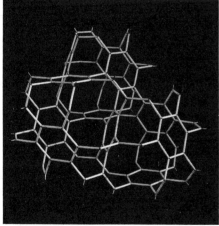

b

The Intelligibility of Three-Dimensional Space

In this and the preceding chapter, we have seen a diverse collection of structures for the organization of three-dimensional space that are alternatives to the cube and to the 90° angle. We have seen clues that indicate that there may be some simple relationships between these various systems. Duality and truncation, taken together, allow us to discover underlying relationships, and symmetry serves as a basis for classification. Uniformity limits the members of an otherwise infinite set, and thus insures the intelligibility of periodically divided three-dimensional space.

Our next goal is to transform this unfamiliar information into a useful design strategy. It will be necessary to discover a morphological system in which *all* of the alternatives for the modular organization of space can be seen in terms of their relationship to each other and to a larger unifying scheme. A basic modular unit must be defined in terms of some kind of totality. A given system in an array of possibilities must be understood as a subset of the whole.

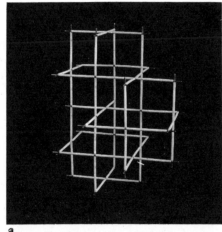

a

c

5.18 Three-dimensional connected networks with three edges meeting at each vertex.

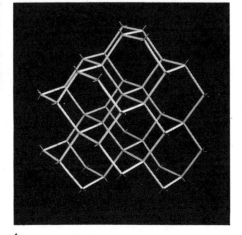

b

5.19 Three-dimensional connected networks with four edges meeting at each vertex.

II A Theory of Spatial Order

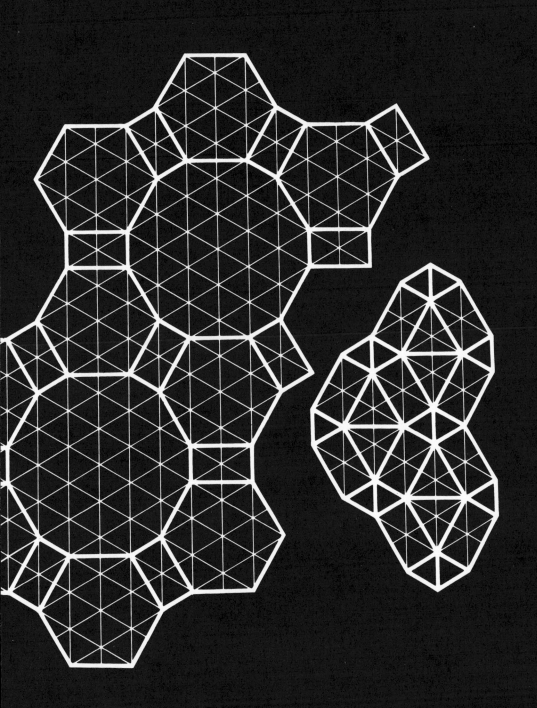

6 Toward a Morphological System

Morphological Units: Mathematics Concretely Embodied

We have now completed a discussion of certain principles of physical structure and a survey of the elementary packing and symmetry properties of three-dimensional space. It is now time to move toward a scheme for integrating the array of spatial possibilities into a morphological system of modular structure. What we will be looking for is a system wherein the underlying morphology is transparently evident in the built form, and where the built form follows, if not undeviatingly, at least in some symmetrical, visually "readable" way, the underlying coordinate system. In other words, the mathematics of the given system or form must be concretely embodied in the physical components from which it is assembled, rather than approachable through the remoteness of abstraction. One means toward this end is the concept of a *morphological unit*—a physical component that, as a subunit of a larger system or class of systems, either determines or is determined by (or both) the larger system or class of systems. Stated more simply, it is one of a small number of the constituent modules from which a built form is assembled.

Spheres as Morphological Units

Many investigators have shown that certain polyhedral shapes may be accounted for by assemblies of closest packed spheres. William Barlow's classic papers remain, even today, the most comprehensive account of this subject.* He showed that there are two different modes for the closest packing of spheres, and that it is possible to assemble cubes from spheres in closest packed array. Prior to his work it was thought that cubes could not be assembled from closest packed spheres, but only from spheres packed on a cubic grid. In the present context the question is: can the closest packing of spheres *generate* (and hence provide a system of classification for) all those polyhedra, regular and semiregular, which appear in the inventory of space filling systems that was summarized in Table 5.1?

The two ways to closest pack equal spheres are called cubic closest packing and hexagonal closest packing; these are manifestations of two fundamental symmetry classes in the theory of periodic structures. In both systems, the spheres are arranged in equilateral triangular order and each sphere is surrounded alike by twelve others.

In a planar closest packing of spheres, each sphere is surrounded by six others. If a second layer of spheres is added, the spheres are positioned vertically above the spaces between the spheres of the first layer. The spheres of the second layer may occupy positions above only every other space, so there are, in effect, two choices for their position [6–1]. However, it is not until the third layer is positioned that these choices have any significance. When the third layer of spheres is added, the spheres may be positioned such that they are directly above the spheres of the first layer or such that they are directly above the spaces of the first layer that were not covered by the second layer.

*See Barlow (1883, 1883a, 1884, 1897). Much earlier, Kepler (1611) tried to explain the shapes of snowflakes in terms of sphere packing; Hooke (1665) applied the theory to various microscopic bodies. Burke (1966, p. 41) mentions Huygens' attempts, c. 1670, to relate crystal structure to underlying form; while in 1813 Wollaston made the connection explicit (Knight 1968, pp. 37–49). Barlow's work follows directly upon Wollaston's. The entire exercise was repeated, this time for built as well as natural forms, by Fuller only as late as the 1940s (Marks 1960, p. 134).

If the spheres in every third layer (of a repeating array of closest packed spheres) are positioned vertically above the *spheres* of the first layer, the resulting arrangement is called hexagonal closest packing. This is because the vertices of hexagonal prisms can be defined by the positions of certain sphere centers in the array.

On the other hand, if the spheres in every third layer are positioned vertically above the *spaces* of the first layer that are not covered by the second layer, the resulting arrangement is called cubic closest packing. This is because the vertices of cubes can be defined by the positions of certain spheres in the array.

We have seen that our inventory of space filling possibilities is comprised of polyhedra with either cubic or hexagonal symmetry.* The symmetry of these polyhedra corresponds exactly to the symmetry of the two forms of sphere packing—cubic and hexagonal.

*Tetrahedral symmetry is a special case of cubic, and triangular symmetry is a special case of hexagonal symmetry.

Four spheres can be packed so that these centers fall at the vertices of the regular tetrahedron, and six spheres can be packed so as to give the vertices of the regular octahedron. We saw in Chapter 1 that a minimum of fourteen closest packed spheres are required to define the vertices of the cube [1.3]. In like manner, it is possible to accumulate spheres in closest packed arrays so as to account for the vertices of *all* of the regular and semiregular polyhedra that appear in unary or multiple space filling systems.

An assembly of closest packed spheres can be easily terminated in such a way that polyhedral sets of planar arrays of spheres are formed which are parallel to and correspond to the faces describing many different polyhedra. Following the crystallographers' usage, I call these planes *cleavage planes*. The cubic closest packed spheres have three sets of cleavage planes; these sets account for all of the faces of polyhedra with tetrahedral or cubic symmetry. The hexagonal closest packed spheres also have three sets of cleavage planes along which lie the faces of polyhedra with hexagonal (or partly hexagonal, e.g., the triangular prism) symmetry.

6.1 The two options in the closest packing of equal spheres.

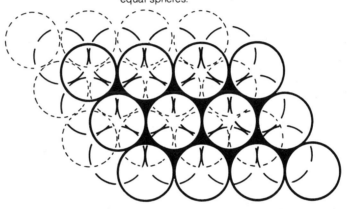

Cubic Close Packing

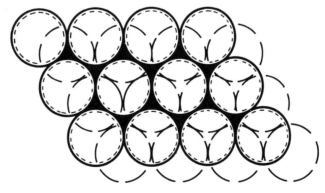

Hexagonal Close Packing

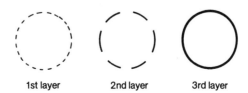

1st layer   2nd layer   3rd layer

The illustrations in Table 6.1 show how polyhedra can be "generated" by accumulations of closest packed spheres. The *minimum* number of spheres necessary to generate all the vertices for each polyhedron is given in the table. In addition, the total number of spheres on the outer shell or layer is noted. In four cases, the minimum number and outer-layer number are the same, as all spheres are on the surface. As shown, the first eleven polyhedra are derived by cubic closest packing and the next six are derived by hexagonal closest packing.

In order to generate the edges of the polyhedra, the centers of neighboring spheres at the corners in each assembly must be joined. With some of the semiregular polyhedra this gives rise to edges of more than one length. This is true of the truncated cube, the rhombicuboctahedron, and the truncated cuboctahedron, and all of the prisms. Due to these differences of edge length, these polyhedra are not, strictly speaking, semiregular. However, the truncated cube, rhombicuboctahedron, and truncated cuboctahedron are truncated polyhedra in a very precise sense. For example, the 43-sphere rhombicuboctahedron is simply a cuboctahedron with three spheres on an edge (42 spheres on the outer layer) in which a sphere has been removed from each of its twelve corners—92 minus 12 equals 80 spheres on the outer layer (No. 9, Cubic System, Table 6.1).*

*With much larger accumulations of spheres it is possible to form semiregular polyhedra that are very nearly equilateral. For example, if a cuboctahedron is assembled from spheres such that there are 11 spheres on each edge, when it is properly truncated an approximately equilateral rhombicuboctahedron results.

There are three polyhedra (Nos. 7, 9, 10, Cubic System, Table 6.1) in this collection that have octagonal faces; but in each case the octagon has sides of two different lengths. These octagons are formed by the removal of a sphere from each corner of a square composed of sixteen spheres. [6.2]. When the remaining sphere centers are connected to form the polygon, *both* nearest neighbors and next-nearest neighbors must be joined. This accounts for the two edge lengths. The resulting octagons have only 4-fold symmetry, not the 8-fold symmetry of the regular figure.

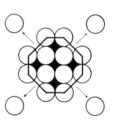

6.2 Octagon formed by the removal of corner members in a square array of spheres.

This additional edge length gives rise to rectangular faces on the rhombicuboctahedron (No. 8, Cubic System, Table 6.1) and truncated cuboctahedron (No. 9), as well as on the octagonal prism. If multiple space filling is to be required of these slightly modified semiregular polyhedra, it is necessary to introduce a *tetragonal prism* (No. 11) bounded by four of these same rectangular faces with squares at each end. This figure has the symmetry of the tetragonal crystal system discussed in Chapter 5. It replaces the cube that appears in the space filling system Nos. 16 and 18 of Table 5.1, and is optional in Nos. 1 and 10. The tetragonal prism is not used as a substitute for the cube in Nos. 19, 21, 22, and 23 of Table 5.1. The tetragonal prism is generated by a minimum of nine spheres.

All prisms, except the octagonal prism and the previously discussed tetragonal prism, result from hexagonal closest packing. The polyhedra resulting from cubic closest packing give rise to two edge lengths. However, the hexagonal prism is composed of sets of *three* different edge lengths. Whereas in the hexagonal system every member of the third layer is exactly above a corresponding member of the first layer of spheres, in the cubic system it is the fourth layer that is thus coincident to the first.

The hexagonally packed prisms all have as their *altitude* the distance between the center of one sphere to the center of a sphere two layers directly above or below. The layers of spheres are arranged in triangular order and form the cleavage planes for the triangular, hexagonal, and dodecagonal faces. The other two edges are the distances between nearest neighbors and next-nearest neighbors in this plane.

Table 6.1
Regular and Semi-regular Polyhedra as Accumulations of Closest Packed Spheres

	Polyhedron	Minimum No. of Spheres	No. of Spheres on Outer Shell		Polyhedron	Minimum No. of Spheres	No. of Spheres on Outer Shell
Cubic System							
	1. Tetrahedron	4	4		9. Truncated Cuboctahedron	135	80
	2. Cube	14	14		10. Octagonal Prism	33	28
	3. Octahedron	6	6		11. Tetragonal Prism	9	8
	4. Truncated Tetrahedron	16	16	**Hexagonal System**			
	5. Cuboctahedron	13	12		1. Triangular Prism (A)	7	6
	6. Truncated Octahedron	38	32		2. Triangular Prism (B)	11	8
	7. Truncated Cube	62	48		3. Hexagonal Prism (A)	17	14
	8. Rhombicubocta-hedron	43	30		4. Hexagonal Prism (B)	38	32
					5. Dodecagonal Prism	89	68
					6. Orthorhombic Prism	13	9

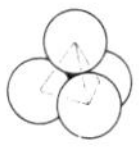

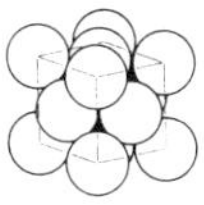

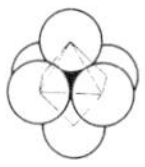

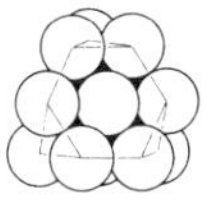

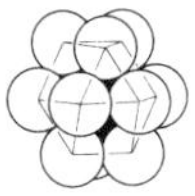

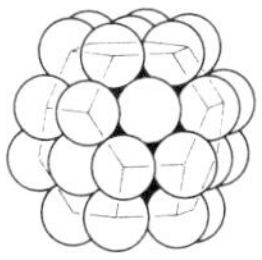

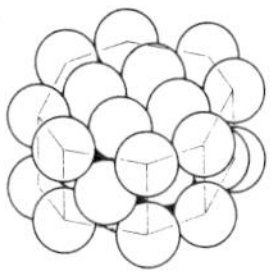

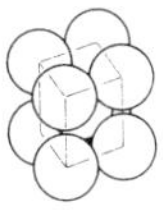

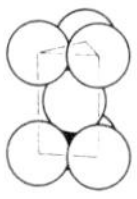

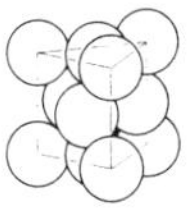

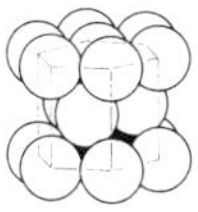

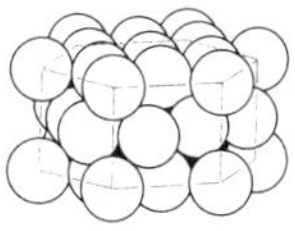

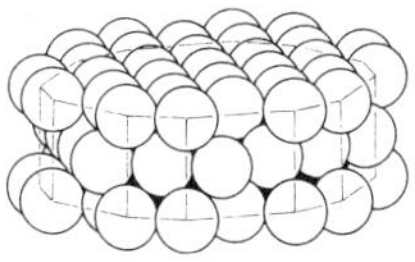

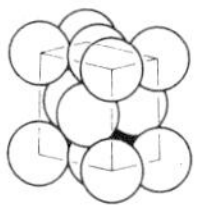

The dodecagon face (see No. 5, Hexagonal System, Table 6.1) is formed when a sphere is removed from each corner of a hexagon composed of a planar array of 37 spheres (four on each edge). This process is shown schematically in [6.3]. The resulting dodecagon has, of course, only hexagonal rather than full 12-fold symmetry. A set of polyhedra that can be used to construct the space filling systems of Table 5.1 must include two forms of triangular and hexagonal prisms (Nos. 1-4, Hexagonal System, Table 6.1) and an *orthorhombic prism* (No. 6). It is characteristic of the hexagonal closest packed system that these prisms, when viewed from above, will be seen to fall along an equilateral triangular grid. The orthorhombic prism is a substitute for the cube which normally appears in the multiple-prism space filling systems.

6.3 Dodecagon formed by the removal of corner members of a hexagonal array of spheres.

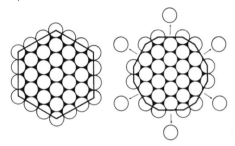

Figure [6.4a] shows the manner in which the so-called A (Alpha) and B (Beta) prisms, the orthorhombic prism, and the dodecagonal prism make it possible to achieve all of the hexagonal prism space filling systems (seen here in a plan on a triangular grid). Because the prism space filling systems correspond directly to the two-dimensional tessellations, it is sufficient to show the two-dimensional nets. It is necessary to superimpose the octagon/square system on a regular square grid, each vertex of which is the projection of the center of a sphere in cubic closest packing [6.4b]. Although the cubic closest packed spheres yield a fully triangulated grid, a secondary square grid is also formed by the projection of equators of octahedra in the array. We noted earlier that when the center of each sphere in a closest packed array is joined with edges to all neighboring spheres, the edges define the space filling of tetrahedra and octahedra consisting entirely of equilateral triangles. In cubic closest packing, the octahedra are lined up so that their square equators combine to form three series of intersecting square grids parallel to the faces of a cube.

6.4 Hexagonal system of multiple space filling prisms on a triangular grid (a); octagonal prism/cube space filling on a square grid (b).

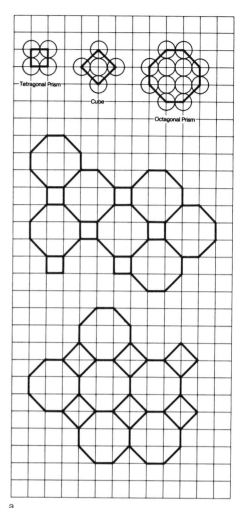

a

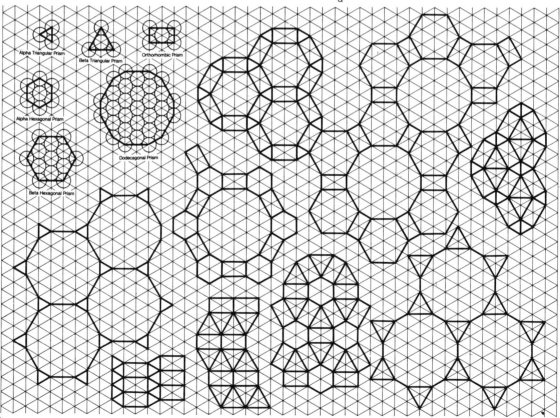

b

In hexagonal closest packing, no square grid is formed because of the manner in which the octahedra are stacked one upon the other. These space filling systems must be oriented to the triangular net. This explains the necessity of the orthorhombic prism, which is a replacement for the square prism (cube), in those space filling systems which conventionally incorporate triangular, hexagonal, and/or dodecagonal prisms in combination with the cube.

The fact that all of these polyhedra can be classified in terms of closest packed spheres is remarkable, even granting that subtle metric problems remain. All of the symmetry properties of the polyhedra are preserved, except for the octagonal prism and dodecagonal prism, which here have lower symmetry than their semiregular counterparts. The closest packing of spheres serves to show the interrelatedness of the various systems. It demonstrates an array of orderly permutations of a simple overall system.

Since all the vertices of tetrahedra and octahedra in a space filling array correspond to centers of closest packed spheres, any of the vertices of the polyhedra classified in Table 6.1 can also be defined by the vertices in the tetrahedral / octahedral space filling. Because of the usefulness of triangulated structures, this becomes a tantalizing bit of knowledge.

Figure [6.5] shows closest packed spheres generating the truncated octahedron and a corresponding similarly oriented model showing the tetrahedral/ octahedral network of equilateral triangles, which also generates the truncated octahedron. Figure [6.6] shows a similar set of spheres generating the truncated cuboctahedron.

a

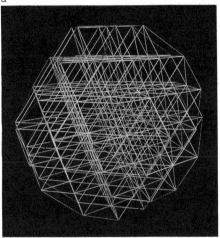

b

6.6 A closest packing of spheres (a), and a tetrahedral/octahedral network, both of which generate the truncated cuboctahedron (b).

a

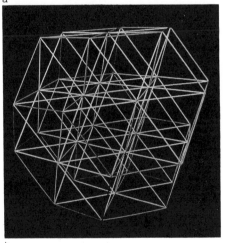

b

6.5 A closest packing of spheres (a), and a tetrahedral/octahedral network, both of which generate the truncated octahedron (b).

In Table 6.1 only the minimum number of generating spheres has been given for each polyhedron. It is possible, of course, to closest pack spheres to form any of these same polyhedra with large numbers of spheres along each edge. Fuller has shown this with his concentric sphere packing (Marks). For example, exactly twelve spheres will pack concentrically around a center sphere forming the vertices of the cuboctahedron (No. 5, Cubic System, Table 6.1; see also [1.3a]. Additional concentric layers of spheres may be indefinitely packed around this same nucleus resulting in larger and larger cuboctahedra [6.7]*

*Fuller has shown that the number of spheres on each successive layer is given by $10n^2 + 2$, where n is the number of the layer (or the number of intervals between spheres on a given edge, as this will always correspond to the number of the layer). Fuller refers to this modular incrementation as the *frequency* of the system.

6.7 Generating cuboctahedra by the concentric closest packing of spheres (after Fuller).

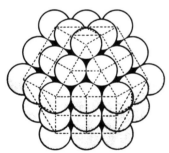

One Frequency

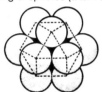

Two Frequency

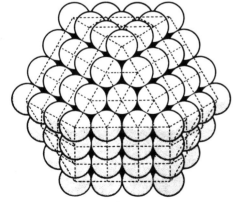

Three Frequency

The cuboctahedron is the only polyhedron of the regular and semiregular figures that can be formed from a concentric packing of spheres. This concentric structure also yields a modified cuboctahedron which is twisted 60° on one equatorial plane [6.8]. This configuration arises out of hexagonal closest packing, and defines a shape of less symmetry than the cuboctahedron defined by cubic closest packed spheres. It is the triangular orthobicupola of [5.12].

6.8 The triangular orthobicupola is a hexagonal closest packed structure.

Just as the rhombic dodecahedron is the domain of the cubic closest packing, the trapezorhombic dodecahedron is the domain of hexagonal closest packing.

Other polyhedra can be built up in various ways—the tetrahedron, for example, grows by addition of additional layers of packed spheres to one face only. This is shown in [6.9].

That larger polyhedra can be built up from equal spheres means that tetrahedra and octahedra may also be accumulated to yield larger and larger polyhedra. The implications of this, when combined with the inherent triangulation of these systems, are examined later in the book. An appreciation of the packing properties of tetrahedra and octahedra is the basis of a spatial sensibility which enables optimum use of the principle of triangulation for architectural structures.

The dual space filling systems are absent from Table 6.1. All of these systems can be classified according to the closest packing of spheres; however, this does not prove to be very convenient. For example, it takes a minimum of 93 spheres to form the vertices of the rhombic dodecahedron, and even at that, the rhombic faces are not well illustrated. In general, the sphere packing system is cumbersome, if not altogether ineffective, for classifying the polyhedra of the dual nets. This is particularly true of the cubic system.

6.9 Enlarging the tetrahedron by adding layers of spheres to one face.

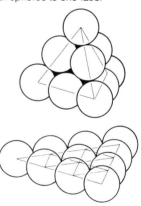

Although our concern has been the classification of those regular and semiregular polyhedra which are components of space filling systems, the icosahedron has some interesting properties in relation to sphere packing that should not go unnoticed. Fuller has pointed out that if the center sphere of a 13-sphere cuboctahedral array is allowed to "shrink" in diameter, the twelve outer spheres shift into a new contracted position to form the twelve vertices of the icosahedron. This constitutes the most symmetrical distribution of spheres closest packed around a common center point [6.10a].

However, this system is not capable of repeating itself in concentric layers as is the cuboctahedron packing. Single shells of spheres can be formed with any arbitrarily large number of spheres along each edge of the icosahedron, but they cannot form concentric contiguous layers of spheres. If all spheres are equal, twenty planar triangular arrays are formed corresponding to the twenty triangular faces of the icosahedron [6.10b,c].*

*A variation of the equation that accounts for the number of spheres in the outer shell of the cuboctahedron also accounts for the number of spheres on the outer icosahedral shell. This may be written as $10(m-1)^2 + 2$, where m is here the number of spheres along each edge of the icosahedron. This packing principle of the icosahedron is closely related to the structure of the Fuller (1969a) geodesic domes and, as Horne and others have observed, to the structure of certain viruses (Horne 1963a; Horne and Wildy).

Limitations of Spheres as Morphological Units

The sphere packing approach is quite an effective morphological accounting system, but it does have limitations. Although we know that the centers of spheres can be joined to form an equilateral triangular network, the sphere itself has no finite characteristic symmetry that can be related to the discrete geometric relationships and finite symmetries that our polyhedron exhibit. It has an infinite number of symmetry axes of infinite-fold rotational symmetry; it is simply *too* symmetrical. In fact, as far as periodic arrangements in three-dimensional space are concerned, the sphere itself can be considered an amorphous (shapeless) element. The interconnections that join the sphere centers to define the edges of various polyhedra classified by sphere packings are after all, only imaginary constructions. Even though their positions and direction are determined by the manner in which spheres *must* associate in closest packing, there is still much interpreting to do.

6.10 Twelve spheres packed around a point form the icosahedron (a); and twenty planar triangular arrays of spheres around a point form the 20 faces of the icosahedron shell (b, c).

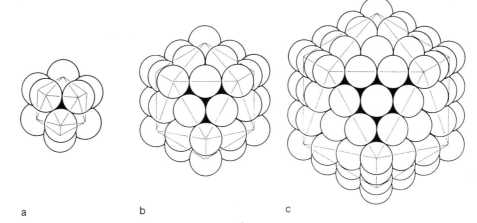

a   b   c

6.11 The rhombic dodecahedron as a morphological unit: cubic closest packing.

Tetrahedron

Truncated Tetrahedron

Rhombicuboctahedron

Octahedron

Cube

Truncated Cube

Tetragonal Prism

Truncated Octahedron

Cuboctahedron

Octagonal Prism

Truncated Cuboctahedron

6.12 The trapezorhombic dodecahedron as a morphological unit: hexagonal closest packing.

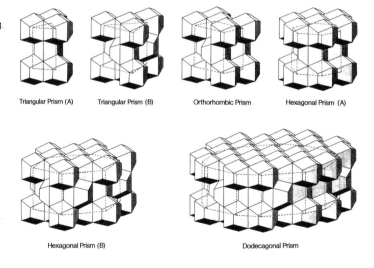

Triangular Prism (A)

Triangular Prism (B)

Orthorhombic Prism

Hexagonal Prism (A)

Hexagonal Prism (B)

Dodecagonal Prism

Polyhedra as Morphological Units

If we are to have a morphological basis for modular structure, we must be able to account specifically for all of the components—the interconnections as well as the vertices. Our morphological units in and of themselves must account for specific angular relationships, which the spheres do not provide in any direct way. We must find an atomic or morphological unit which is defined inherently in terms of its relationships to the whole, so that its very shape predicts the manner of its association with other like forms.

Because the rhombic dodecahedron is the domain of the sphere in closest packed array, it may be considered as an alternative morphological unit.

But, to cover all cases arising from sphere packing, it must be paired with the trapezorhombic dodecahedron. Then, the first figure will serve as the morphological unit for structures based upon cubic closest packing; and the second (which is the dual of the triangular orthobicupola), for systems based upon hexagonal closest packing [6.11, 6.12]. With this we see that relatively subtle differances of geometric relationships, e.g., cubic vs. hexagonal closest packing, can be differentiated (perhaps even predicted) by the inherent limitations given by the shape of particular morphological units.

The sites of the fcc lattice correspond to the centers of spheres in cubic closest packing (see p. 40). Therefore, the rhombic dodecahedron is also the domain of the fcc lattice. Similarly, the truncated octahedron is the domain of the bcc lattice. We have also seen that the dual net of space filling truncated octahedra is the space filling of tetragonal disphenoids which forms a fully triangulated net with vertex coordination of fourteen. Remember that the crystallographic lattices are not concerned with the interconnections of points in space, but only with relative point locations defined in terms of symmetry. The tetragonal disphenoid array is formed when both nearest and next nearest neighbors are connected from each point in the bcc lattice, which explains how these structures are related.

The truncated octahedron can also be considered a morphological unit. We have seen that twelve spheres (or rhombic dodecahedra) can be packed around a center sphere (or rhombic dodecahedron), forming the twelve vertices of the cuboctahedron. The truncated octahedron exhibits similar behavior. If truncated octahedra are placed on the fourteen faces of a nuclear truncated octahedron, their centers form the fourteen vertices of the rhombic dodecahedron. Concentric layers may be added and each new layer reveals still a larger rhombic dodecahedron.*

The rhombic dodecahedron is itself a dual space filling polyhedron. This suggests that truncated octahedron packings may be able to account, at least to some degree, for some of the other dual space filling polyhedra. A few dual space fillings can be accounted for by packings of truncated octahedra; however, the bulk of these polyhedra are difficult to organize with the truncated octahedron as the morphological unit.

The regular tetrahedron, octahedron, and cube can also be formed by combining truncated octahedra; however, the truncated octahedron does not serve very well as an accounting system for the more complex figures. For example, it takes 80 truncated octahedra to define a single larger truncated octahedron, whereas it takes only 38 spheres to define the same figure.

Space filling polyhedra are morphological units of more specific geometric content than spheres. For example, the rhombic dodecahedron and the trapezorhombic dodecahedron of themselves reveal the differences between cubic closest packing and hexagonal closest packing. The rhombic dodecahedron has full cubic symmetry, while the trapezorhombic dodecahedron has only one axis of 3-fold symmetry and three axes of 2-fold symmetry. The truncated octahedron also has full cubic symmetry; but its faces have no planes in common with the rhombic dodecahedron and, therefore, its packing arrangement is different.

*The number of truncated octahedra on each layer is given by the equation $12n^2 + 2$, where n is the number of the layer. The first layer has 14 truncated octahedra, the second has 50, the third has 110, etc. This equation was reported by J. W. Marvin (1939a).

Since, as morphological units, the rhombic dodecahedron and truncated octahedron can generate a variety of different polyhedra in the cubic system, perhaps a morphological unit could be derived which would combine the properties of both figures. Such a combination may provide a basis for a more integrative morphological system. If we are to pursue this line of thought, it will be necessary (at least temporarily) to abandon the hexagonal system, i.e., trapezorhombic dodecahedron packings. With the hexagonal system set aside, is it possible to develop a universal morphological system which can account for all of the figures which comprise the various space filling polyhedra of the cubic system?

The space filling nets of both the truncated octahedron and rhombic dodecahedron are fully triangulated. For the former, the dual net consists of congruent isosceles triangles, and for the latter, it consists of congruent equilateral triangles. The fact that both of the polyhedra have cubic symmetry suggests that the dual nets might be related in some simple way to each other.

To review the symmetry involved: cubic symmetry is that of three axes of 4-fold symmetry, four axes of 3-fold symmetry, and six axes of 2-fold symmetry. In the space filling net of tetrahedra and octahedra, each vertex has a coordination of twelve corresponding to the twelve faces of the rhombic dodecahedron which forms the dual net. This rhombic dodecahedron is a domain in the sense that as the space filling dual of the tetrahedral/octahedral system, it accounts for the discrete geometrical and symmetrical arrangements which define the typical vertex. The edges of the network emanating from the center of the rhombic dodecahedron pass through the centers of each face and are perpendicular to the faces [6.13]. These edges are equivalent to the six axes of 2-fold rotational symmetry of the cube.

6.13 The rhombic dodecahedron is the domain of the 12-connected tetrahedral/octahedral network.

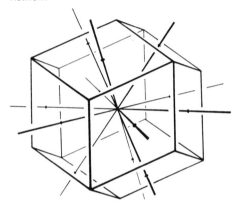

The truncated octahedron is the domain of the tetragonal disphenoidal space filling network. Each vertex in this structure is alike joined by fourteen edges. When these fourteen edges emanate from the center of the truncated octahedron, six pass perpendicularly through the centers of the six square faces and eight pass perpendicularly through the centers of the eight hexagonal faces [6.14]. The six edges are directed along the three 4-fold axes of the cube and the eight edges are directed along the four 3-fold axes of the cube.

6.14 The truncated octahedron is the domain of the 14-connected tetragonal disphenoid network.

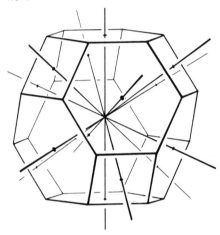

Thus, there are three sets of *planes* which are perpendicular to the three sets of symmetry axes of the cube. These three sets are called cube, octahedron, and dodecahedron planes. They are parallel to the faces of the cube, octahedron, and rhombic dodecahedron, respectively [6.15]. The cleavage planes of the cubic closest packing of spheres correspond to these planes. It is significant that for all of the polyhedra of tetrahedral or cubic symmetry which compose space filling systems, the faces are parallel to one or more of the three sets of cubic planes and this includes all of the dual space fillers. The rhombic dodecahedron's faces are parallel to only one set of planes, while the truncated octahedron has faces parallel to the cube planes, as well as to the octahedron planes. Among the semiregular polyhedra, only the rhombicuboctahedron and the truncated cuboctahedron incorporate all three planes. Neither of these polyhedra will fill space alone, and, therefore, it is impossible to form a space filling morphological unit which combines all three planes.

6.15 The cubic planes: cube (a), octahedron (b), and dodecahedron planes (c).

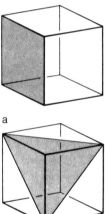

a

b

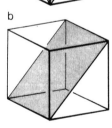

c

Morphological Networks

We have seen that the edges of the tetrahedral / octahedral network plus the tetragonal disphenoidal network include all of the symmetry axes of the cube. Since we cannot represent these directions with a single space filling morphological unit, perhaps a more versatile and visceral morphological scheme could be derived by way of a *morphological network*. It may be possible to form a network which can incorporate all three types of cubic axes in one system, perhaps a *universal cubic network* in which the elements of position and direction can be concretized as built form. If we consider all of the thirteen symmetry axes of the cube passing through the center of the cube, a vertex is formed in which 26 edges meet [6.16]. Of the 26 edges originating from this vertex, six are directed toward the centers of the cube faces, eight are directed toward the corners of the cube, and twelve are directed toward the midpoints of the edges. The same 26 directions may be derived from the octahedron because of its duality with the cube. If the 26 edges originate from the center of the octahedron, six are directed toward the vertices, eight are directed toward the faces, and, as in the cube, twelve are directed toward the midpoints of the edges [6.17].

Both the rhombicuboctahedron and the truncated cuboctahedron have 26 faces which are perpendicular to the directions of the aforementioned 26 edges. When the edges originate from the center of either of these polyhedra they are directed towards the centers of each face. These are the only semiregular polyhedra in which this is true. These two polyhedra are the only ones which incorporate all three sets of cubic planes; it is not surprising, then, that they have this relationship to the 26 edges. We may consider either of these polyhedra to be the domain of a 26-connected network; however, we have already noted that neither of these polyhedra can fill space alone. This suggests that it is not possible to form a uniform network in which *every* node is equally joined by 26 edges. It will be shown later that for every 26-connected vertex, exactly three 6-connected vertices are required.

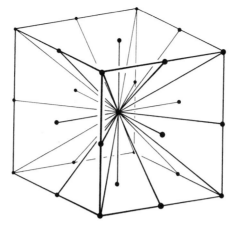

6.16 Twenty-six edges originating from the center of the cube (symmetry axes of the cube).

6.17 Twenty-six edges originating from the center of the octahedron (symmetry axes of cube = symmetry axes of octahedron).

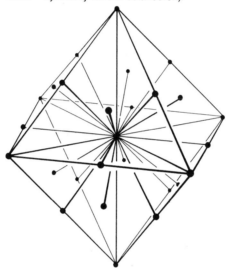

Abstraction and Built Form: The Morphological Node and Branches

The concept of symmetry axes is relatively abstract. In the rest of this chapter I will expand on the concretization of this concept, so as to reduce the abstraction of symmetry to catalogable, *buildable* form. The notions of "vertex" and "edge" are also abstract, although to a lesser degree than that of symmetry axes. It is easy enough to visualize hard spheres or polyhedra as physical units or modules. The idea of vertex and edge needs to be given in a similarly concrete form. If we are to define vertices and edges in terms of specific physical form, we must find *edge* and *vertex* morphological units that embody the appropriate geometry and symmetry.

We have seen that the domain of the 26-connected vertex is either the rhombicuboctahedron or the truncated cuboctahedron. Perhaps one of these could be viewed as a *vertex* with a set of complementary edges with cross-sectional shapes that would match faces on the polyhedral domain. At this point, it will be useful to adopt some new terminology. Vertices, actually built as specific physical entities, shall be designated as *nodes,* and built physical edges shall be called *branches.*

A framework consisting of 26 cubes placed around a central cube can be used to generate a rhombicuboctahedron of proportions particularly well suited for use as our *morphological node*. Figure [6.18a] shows such an array of cubes in which the octahedron planes are placed in the eight corner cubes. Dodecahedron planes are placed in the twelve cubes which lie between pairs of corner cubes, and the six cubes at the centers of each side contain simple cube planes. Thus the rhombicuboctahedron is bounded by six square faces, eight triangular faces, and twelve rectangular faces. Because of the rectangular faces it does not strictly qualify as a semiregular polyhedron, but the *individual faces* and the rotation axes to which they are perpendicular have the same n-fold rotational symmetries. That is, the rectangular faces have 2-fold rotational symmetry and they are perpendicular to the six axes of 2-fold symmetry; the triangular faces have 3-fold rotational symmetry and are perpendicular to the four axes of 3-fold symmetry, and the square faces with 4-fold symmetry are perpendicular to the three axes of 4-fold symmetry.

The specially proportioned rhombicuboctahedron is then the ideal form for our morphological node.* Its square, triangular, and rectangular faces serve to identify the character of the morphological *branches* that must meet at this node. Because there are three sets of symmetry axes there must be three different branches. The rhombicuboctahedron accounts for these three branches with its three faces and dictates that the branches have cross-sectional shapes which correspond in symmetry to the axes they represent. Therefore, the branches will have rectangular, triangular and square cross sections corresponding to 2-, 3-, and 4-fold symmetry axes respectively [6.18b].

A most interesting fact may now be noted. The branch of triangular cross-section must be twisted along its symmetry axis exactly 60° so that when two rhombicuboctahedral morphological nodes are joined by a 3-fold branch they are properly oriented to each other. If a nontwisted 3-fold branch is used the nodes become cubically disoriented. Here we have a manifestation of a subtle and fundamental difference between cubic symmetry and hexagonal symmetry. With the nontwisted branch it is possible, in combination with the twisted triangular branch, to build certain hexagonal structures.

*Although the truncated cuboctahedron has 26 faces, all of these faces do not reflect the symmetry of the rotation axes to which they are normal. For example, it has hexagonal faces perpendicular to the 3-fold octahedral axis and octagon faces perpendicular to the 4-fold axes.

The Physical Model System

In order to facilitate the empirical exploration and assembly of various modular networks, I have developed a model system. It is based on the foregoing morphological node and is shown in [6.19].* The model system consists of a molded plastic node and extruded plastic branches. The node is our specially proportioned rhombicuboctahedron with 26 spokes emanating from its faces: six square spokes, eight triangular spokes, and twelve rectangular spokes. There is a set of three branch types corresponding in cross-sectional shape to the spokes on the node. The branches are hollow and are designed so they will just friction-fit around the proper spoke. The node, including its spokes, of [6.19] is 1.25 inches in diameter.

*This system is protected by U.S. Patent 3600825 "Synthesized Natural Geometric Structures" and six additional patents in Canada, France, Germany, Great Britain, Italy, and Japan.

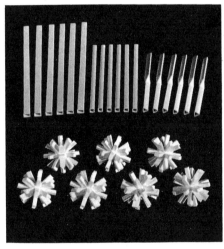

6.19 Morphological node connectors and branches.

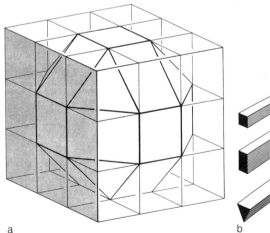

a   b

6.18 Cubic planes generate rhombicuboctahedral envelope of morphological node (a); cross sections of morphological branches having 4-, 2-, and 3-fold symmetry (b).

Since the spokes on the node and the branches are shaped according to the symmetry of the rotation axes they represent, when networks are assembled, no matter how randomly, the nodes always remain properly oriented with respect to one another.

In order to achieve the twist in the three-fold branch mentioned above, it is necessary to provide a three-fold splice which incorporates the 60° twist. When two short lengths are joined to each end of the splice, a properly twisted 3-fold branch results. This twist can also be an integral part of a one-piece molded branch.

This physical model system embodies principles of symmetry which govern modular order in three-dimensional space, and it makes such principles accessible to direct sensory experience. This system is a sophisticated "Tinker Toy" with which we can study modular systems as physicogeometrical constructions rather than analytical, algebraic abstractions.

The Universal Network and the Universal Node System

I have already hinted at the possibility of a universal cubic network (p. 65). We now move toward the realization of that ideal with the just-described universal cubic node. In the interest of brevity I shall refer to this as the Universal Node.®* The Universal Node connector, with its 26 spokes, has full cubic symmetry. Figure [6.20] shows three views of the node along each of the symmetry axes. In order to fully realize a universal cubic network it is necessary to establish not only the characteristic node and the cross sections of the corresponding branches but the relative *lengths* of the branches as well.

*The term Universal Node is a registered trade mark of Peace Structures, Inc.

This model system is available from Pearce Structures, Inc. Chatsworth, California 91311.

A convenient notation for identifying the three branches can be borrowed from crystallography in which points, vector directions and crystal planes are established in terms of an x, y, z (rectangular) coordinate system. Set eight cubes as octants surrounding the origin x = y = z = 0 of a coordinate system. Because only signs change in the various octants of the coordinate system, and not the distances to corresponding points, it is only necessary to consider the octant in which all the values are positive, i.e., the upper right top quadrant. The coordinates are those of the point toward which a given vector is directed from the origin. The cube edges emanating from the origin (the lower left rear corner of the cube) have the following coordinates: x = +1, y = 0, z = 0; x = 0, y = +1, z = 0; and x = 0, y = 0, z = +1 [6.21a]. The coordinates of these *points* may be abbreviated as 100, 010, 001, keeping in mind that the numbers are always in x,y,z order. The *direction indices* or the vector *directions* to these points (i.e., the set of three vector components that will carry one from the origin to the points) are enclosed in square brackets: [100], [010], [001]. The *Miller indices* of any *plane* have the coordinates of the direction to which the plane is perpendicular. To distinguish them from vector directions, the Miller indices of a plane are placed in curved brackets. The planes (faces) perpendicular to the [100], [010], and [110] directions would be indicated as: (100), (010), and (001).

6.20 Symmetry axes of the Universal Node connector.

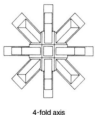
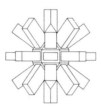
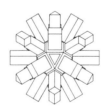

4-fold axis   2-fold axis   3-fold axis

6.21 Various points x, y, z on the cube in the first octant of a rectangular coordinate system. The direction indices of these points are denoted by [x y z]. Shown are the cube edges (a), face diagonals (b), and body diagonal (c).

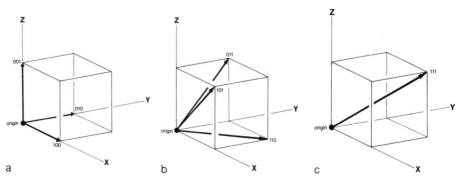

a   b   c

The direction indices of the octant face diagonals starting from the origin are [110], [101], and [011] (see [6.21b]). There is only one body diagonal emanating from the origin into the first octant; its direction indices are [111] (see [6.21c]). Only the signs change when we write the direction indices for the edge, face and body directions for the other octants. When all of the sign combinations and permutations are combined with all possible triplets of 0 and 1, all 26 directions of the Universal Node connector will have been accounted for.

Because, up to sign changes, there are only three unique sets of coordinate combinations, we may refer to each set simply as the [100], [110], and [111] directions. We will henceforth designate our three branches accordingly: cube edge direction, [100] branch; cube face diagonal direction [110] branch; and cube body diagonal direction, [111] branch.

The edge length ratios of the branches are obtained by means of the Pythagorean theorem. If the cube edge is A units long, then the face diagonal is $A\sqrt{2}$ units long, and the body diagonal $A\sqrt{3}$ units. We will see that various multiples of these ratios account for all of the edges that appear in the space filling inventory of the cubic system in Table 5.1. It is important to note, however, that these are ratios of the distance between nodal *centers* and not to the actual lengths of the branches, which, due to the necessary bulk of the nodes, will be somewhat shorter depending on the radii of the nodes.

We can now proceed to the development of a universal network that combines the tetrahedral/octahedral space filling net with the tetragonal disphenoidal space filling net. The tetragonal disphenoidal network can be derived from the tetrahedral/octahedral network and vice versa. In this respect, it is useful to consider the relationship of the tetrahedral/octahedral network (composed of [110] branches) superimposed on its dual rhombic dodecahedral network (composed of [111] branches).

When they are in their proper dual relationship, the nodes of the rhombic dodecahedral array fall at the centers of every tetrahedron and octahedron with the nodes of the tetrahedral/octahedral array at the centers of the rhombic dodecahedra. These nodes may be connected to each other in such a way that a superimposition of tetrahedral/octahedral and tetragonal disphenoidal arrays are formed. This gives rise to a network consisting of both 26- and 14-connected nodes and the inadvertent appearance of 4-connected nodes where [100] and [110] branches cross each other. A model of this network is seen in [6.22]. The model is seen to be in the form of a truncated octahedron.

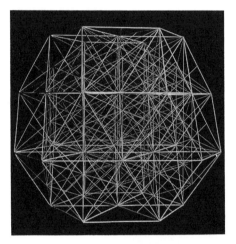

The 26-connected nodes are formed at the 12-connected nodes of the tetrahedral/octahedral array where the 14 additional branches of the tetragonal disphenoid network meet. The additional 14-connected nodes of the 26-, 14-, and 4-connected network are at the centers of the rhombic dodecahedra. We may add 12 more [110] branches to these 14-connected nodes so that they are also 26-connected. When this is done the 4-connected nodes become 6-connected as the new [110] branches cross the intersection of the original [100] and [110] branches. It is impossible to form a network consisting entirely of 26-connected nodes. For every 26-connected node, there must be three 6-connected nodes. This network is shown in [6.23] and [6.24]. The important thing is that both the 4- and 6-connected nodes are subsets of the Universal Node. In the former, the branches are attached to two spokes in the appropriate [100] directions and two spokes in the appropriate [110] directions [6.25], while in the latter, the branches are still attached to two spokes in the [100] directions but now have four [110] directions [6.26].

6.22 Tetrahedral/octahedral and tetragonal disphenoid arrays combine to form a network of 26/14/4-connected nodes.

6.23 The universal network. Note the 26- and 6-connected nodes here and in the following figure.

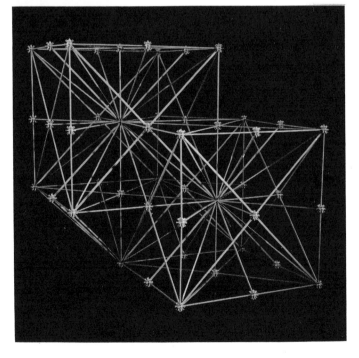

6.24 Detail of the universal network.

6.25 Four-connected subset of Universal Node connector with two [110] and two [100] branches.

6.26 Six-connected subset of Universal Node connector with four [110] and two [100] branches.

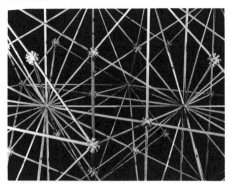

6.27 Twelve-connected subset of Universal Node connector with all 12 [110] branches.

6.28 Fourteen-connected subset of Universal Node connector with all 6 [100] branches and all eight [111] branches.

We see from this construction that the respective typical nodes of the tetrahedral/octahedral [6.27] and tetragonal disphenoidal [6.28] systems are also subsets of the Universal Node connector. Further examination shows that the characteristic vertices of all of the polyhedral space filling systems consisting of regular and semiregular polyhedra of the cubic system are subsets of the Universal Node. The vertices of all the individual polyhedra which compose these space filling systems may therefore also be considered subsets of the Universal Node connector. All of the edges of these space filling nets or individual polyhedra are various combinations of [100] and [110] branches. What is even more remarkable is that *all* of the space filling nets which are dual to the systems composed of regular and semiregular polyhedra may be assembled from Universal Node connectors and various combinations of [100], [110], and [111] branches. Note that [111] branches only appear in the dual nets.

The network consisting of 26- and 6-connected nodes [6.23] and [6.24] can be considered to be the universal cubic network in which all of the cubic space filling systems and their dual nets exist simultaneously in a single construct. Any given space filling network is then a subset of this universal network. The interrelatedness of all these systems is manifested in a minimum inventory of morphological component types which can be assembled into a vast array of diverse structures. Not only do the various plane faced polyhedral systems appear as subsets of the universal network, but a very large class of uniform and semiuniform* periodic networks not composed of plane faced polyhedra are also included.

*To review, uniform refers to infinite periodic networks in which all nodes are of one kind (congruent). Semiuniform refers to infinite periodic networks which have *infinite* sets of congruent nodes of more than one type.

When all of the nodes of the universal network are considered as an array of points, the sites of the primitive cubic lattice are defined. When only the 26-connected nodes are considered as an array of points, the sites of the bcc lattice are defined. Remember that the nodal positions of the tetragonal disphenoid net also define a bcc lattice. When only the 6-connected nodes are considered, a structure is formed in which the nodal position coincides with the vertices of the 4-connected net of [5.18a] defining ¾ of the sites of the primitive cubic lattice. The minimum repeatable unit of the universal network is shown in [6.29]. By a cyclic rotation in 90° increments on each of the [100] branches of this repeat unit, the universal net is formed. Repetition clearly reveals the unit to be the source of the ratio of three 6-connected nodes to one 26-connected node, since there are six 6-connected and two 26-connected nodes. 6/2 = 3/1.

The concepts of the Universal Node and universal network provide the basis for an integrative morphological system. This system allows us to organize known three-dimensional structures in concrete physical terms, by way of models. As we shall see, it is also a powerful means for the discovery and classification of new systems of modular order in three-dimensional physicogeometric space.

6.29 The minimum repeatable unit of the universal network.

7

Principles of Order and the Universal Node System

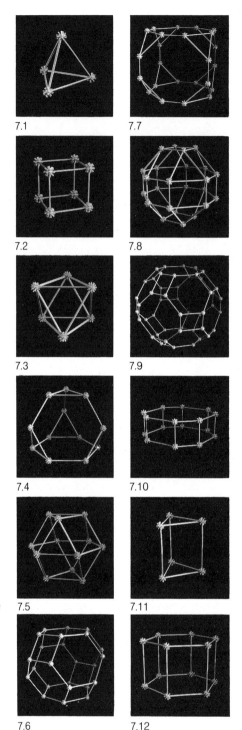

7.1–7.12 Regular and semiregular polyhedra assembled with the Universal Node System. Tetrahedron (7.1); cube (7.2); octahedron (7.3); truncated tetrahedron (7.4); cuboctahedron (7.5); truncated octahedron (7.6); truncated cube (7.7); rhombicuboctahedron (7.8); truncated cuboctahedron (7.9); octagonal prism (7.10); triangular prism (7.11); hexagonal prism (7.12).

Because the physical design of the Universal Node and its associated branches embodies the principles of symmetry which govern the combinatorial possibilities within a large class of periodic structures, a deep-rooted empirical understanding of complex relationships evolves with its use. Because the cross-sectional shapes of the branches correspond to the shapes of their respective spokes on the Universal Node connector, and because these both reflect axes of symmetry, it is impossible to assemble any periodic array in which the Node is incorrectly oriented. By simply taking note of typical vertices, it is possible to "blindly" assemble from nodes and branches the whole of a finite, or a representative sample of an infinite, space filling system. This capability reflects the holistic character of the Universal Node and the universal network. The Universal Node and the universal network are completely interdependent. One cannot exist without the other and they define each other.

Although the principles of symmetry embodied in the Universal Node connector can be expressed in terms of a cube or octahedron, the coordinated branch ratios and their multiples are defined by the periodic association of nodes. An individual cube, for example, is only a subset of the universal net and is a periodic (modular) association of nodes.

Classifying Finite Polyhedra with the Integrative Morphological System

Both the finite polyhedra and the space filling networks can be generated and classified by means of our integrative morphological system. As has already been said, the regular and semiregular polyhedra which were generated by the cubic closest packing of spheres (Table 6.1) are finite subsets of the universal net.

Table 7.1 lists these ten polyhedra and provides recipes for their assembly from the kit of parts which is the Universal Node system. Such "recipes" are perfectly consistent with our interest in dealing with modular structures in terms of physical relationships among components.

We can give a structural recipe for each of these polyhedra by giving the morphological features characteristic of each node. The characteristic Universal Node subset can be given in terms of the direction indices of the occupied nodal spokes. This is identified in Table 7.1 as the "Branch Directions at Node." In this column is indicated how many spokes are occupied in a given direction and the total number of occupied spokes ("Overall Coordination").

The next column gives the total number of nodes for each complete polyhedron. In the next column the numbers and kinds of branches are given and the relative distances between nodes along each branch, i.e., the edge lengths between node centers are given. The total number of branches for a given polyhedron is equal to the total number of nodes multiplied by the overall coordination divided by two.

Next, the inventory and description of the polygonal faces of each polyhedron are given. This includes the total number of faces, the number of each type of face, the kind of face, its symmetry, and the included angles of the face. Also, the face plane directions (Miller indices) are given. They are important in the construction of the dual space filling nets, as they predict the directions of the component branches of the constituent polyhedra.

It can be seen from Table 7.1 that all but two of the cubic polyhedra have faces in the [111] direction, yet there are no cubic polyhedra in this table with [111] branches.

In the last column is shown relative volumes of the polyhedra when the volume of the tetrahedron is taken as unity. Note that all of the polyhedra have volumes which are whole-integer multiples of the tetrahedron. This occurs because the universal network provides a modular dimensional correlation among these diverse polyhedra.

Two polyhedra in the hexagonal system—the triangular prism and hexagonal prism—are also identified in Table 7.1. Photographs of assembled models of these polyhedra are shown in [7.1]–[7.12].

We have now classified the finite polyhedra by means of our integrative morphological system. We now turn to a consideration of infinite periodic systems by returning to the various space filling systems we have identified in Table 5.1.

Classifying Space Filling Systems with the Integrative Morphological System

Recall that in our morphological system each vertex of any given space filling system is a subset of the Universal Node. The network of every space filling system will have its dual space filling system or network. There will be a different kind of polyhedron in the dual system for each different kind of vertex in the original system. A space filling system with vertices all of one kind gives rise to a dual space filling arrangement composed of only one kind of polyhedron. A system composed of two kinds of vertices will give rise to a dual space filling composed of two kinds of polyhedra, etc. All of the space filling systems composed of regular and semiregular polyhedra (Table 5.1) have vertices of one kind, so they will each have dual networks composed of a single type—but in general, a different type for each—of space filling polyhedron.

Only those dual space filling systems that are dual to unary systems will themselves have vertices of a single type. For example, the cubic array is a self dual, and the truncated octahedral array has as its dual the array of tetragonal disphenoids. These are the only dual space filling systems that have all vertices of a single type among the plane faced polyhedra.

The binary, etc., space filling systems of Table 5.1 have vertices of one type; but, because they are composed of more than one kind of polyhedron, they give rise to dual nets composed of as many kinds of vertices as there are different polyhedra within the systems. For example, the tetrahedral/octahedral array has one kind of vertex but is binary. It therefore has a single polyhedron as its space filling dual; but the latter—the rhombic dodecahedron—has two kinds of vertices. The space filling of rhombicuboctahedron/octagonal prism/truncated cube/cube has one kind of polyhedron in its dual net but four different kinds of vertices, one for each polyhedron of the parent system.

Nodal Polyhedra

Space filling systems that are dual to one another form the polyhedral *domains* of each other's vertices. A given polyhedron in a unary or multiple space filling system will always define a vertex of its dual space filling network. The polyhedral domain will have the same number of faces as there are edges emanating from the vertex it surrounds. The edges will usually be perpendicular to the faces and will pass through face centers. As it encloses a vertex such a polyhedral domain will define a subset of the Universal Node, and may, therefore, be called a *nodal polyhedron*. These nodal polyhedra are figures which characterize the coordination of the Universal Node or any of its subsets. Here again, coordination refers to the number of branches or struts that meet at a node.

For example, the nodal polyhedron of the simple cubic net is a cube—one square face for each of its six [100] branches. The nodal polyhedron for the truncated octahedron net is the tetragonal disphenoid with one isosceles triangular face for each of the four [110] branches. Or, to look at the same structure the other way round, the truncated octahedron is the nodal polyhedron for the 14-connected tetragonal disphenoid net. In this case, the Universal Node has six [100] branches and eight [111] branches; these correspond to the six square and eight hexagonal faces of the truncated octahedron, respectively. The nodal polyhedron of the 12-connected tetrahedral/octahedral (fcc) net is the rhombic dodecahedron. The rhombic dodecahedral net, however, requires two nodal polyhedra, one for each of its two kinds of nodal subsets. The tetrahedron is the nodal polyhedron for the 4-connected node and the octahedron is the nodal polyhedron for the 8-connected node.

Table 7.1
Regular and
Semiregular
Polyhedra

				Branch Directions at Node				Total Number of Nodes
				[100]	[110]	[111]	Overall Coord.	
Cubic System	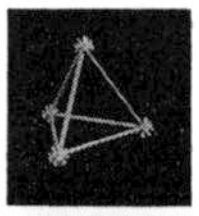	1	Tetrahedron [7.1]		3		3	4
	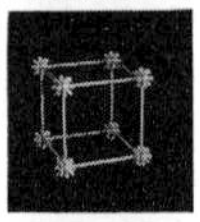	2	Cube [7.2]	3			3	8
	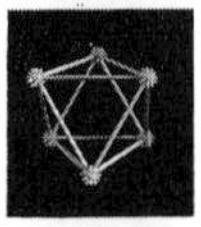	3	Octahedron [7.3]		4		4	6
	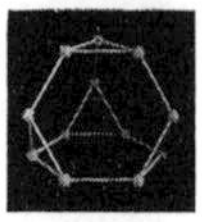	4	Truncated tetrahedron [7.4]		3		3	12
	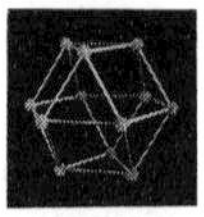	5	Cubocta-hedron [7.5]		4		4	12
	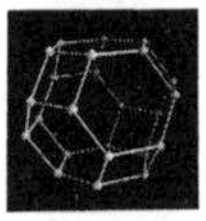	6	Truncated octahedron [7.6]		3		3	24
	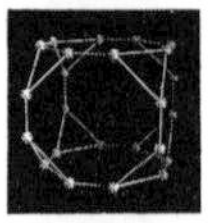	7	Truncated cube [7.7]	1	2		3	24
	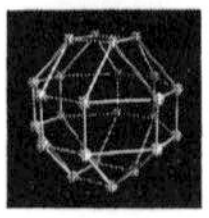	8	Rhombicub-octahedron [7.8]	2	2		4	24
	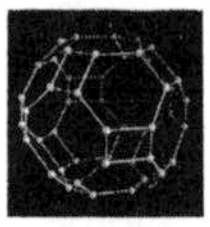	9	Truncated cubocta-hedron [7.9]	1	2		3	48
	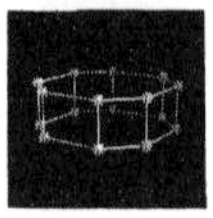	10	Octagonal prism [7.10]	2	1		3	16
		11	Tetragonal prism	1	2		3	8
Hexagonal System	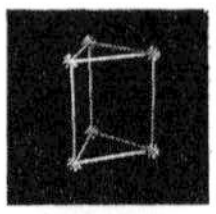	1	Triangular prism [7.11]		2	1	3	6
	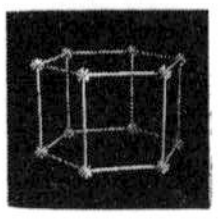	2	Hexagonal prism [7.12]		2	1	3	12

Numbers of Branches [100] A	Numbers of Branches [110] $A\sqrt{2}$	Numbers of Branches [111] $\frac{1}{2}A\sqrt{3}$	Total Number of Branches	Faces Number Tot.	Faces Number Ea.	Faces Type	Faces Symmetry	Faces Included Angles	Face Plane Directions [100]	Face Plane Directions [110]	Face Plane Directions [111]	Relative Volume
	6		6	4	4	Triangle	3-fold	60°			4	1
12			12	6	6	Square	4-fold	90°	6			3
	12		12	8	8	Triangle	3-fold	60°			8	4
	18		18	8	4	Triangle	3-fold	60°			4	23
					4	Hexagon	6-fold	120°			4	
	24		24	14	8	Triangle	3-fold	60°			8	20
					6	Square	4-fold	90°	6			
	36		36	14	8	Hexagon	6-fold	120°			8	96
					6	Square	4-fold	90°	6			
12	24		36	14	8	Triangle	3-fold	60°			8	188
					6	Octagon	4-fold	135°	6			
24	24		48	26	6	Square	4-fold	90°	6			136
					8	Triangle	3-fold	60°			8	
					12	Rectangle	2-fold	90°		12		
24	48		72	26	6	Octagon	4-fold	135°	6			448
					8	Hexagon	6-fold	120°			8	
					12	Rectangle	2-fold	90°		12		
16	8		24	10	2	Octagon	4-fold	135°	2			88
					4	Square	4-fold	90°	4			
					4	Rectangle	2-fold	90°		4		
8	4		12	6	2	Square	4-fold	90°				
					4	Rectangle	2-fold	90°				
	3	6	9	5	2	Triangle	3-fold	60°			2	
					3	Rectangle	2-fold	90°		3		
	12	6	18	8	2	Hexagon	6-fold	120°			2	
					6	Rectangle	2-fold	90°		6		

Branch Angles of the Universal Node Connector

Before we proceed to Table 7.2 and the listing of the cubic space filling systems, it will be useful to look at the Universal Node in more detail.

The Universal Node provides six combinations of two branches which define altogether fourteen possible branch angles of less than 180°. Not all the combinations are needed in the cubic space filling systems but they will all eventually come into play as we explore the many modular options provided by the Universal Node.

In [7.13] are shown five sections through the Universal Node connector taken normal to the various symmetry axes. Note that the section in the center is normal to a [112] axis. This axis does not appear in the Universal Node; it is *not* an axis of rotational symmetry, even though such symmetry is suggested by the sectional view. At the bottom of [7.13] is a list showing the fourteen possible branch angles of the six possible combinations of spokes. It is only coincidental that there are fourteen angles and fourteen space filling structures, or for that matter, the fourteen faces of the truncated octahedron. As we shall see, this *particular* set of fourteen angles gives to the Universal Node its extraordinary modular-configuration capability.

Cubic Space Filling Systems as Subsets of the Universal Network

We now can take a closer look at the space filling systems. Table 7.2 lists the fourteen cubic space filling systems and the nodal polyhedra that define their vertices. This table, like Table 7.1, provides the recipes for the physical assembly of various modular structures. The face plane directions for each nodal polyhedron are identical to the branch directions of the node of the corresponding space filling system.

The faces of each nodal polyhedron are characterized by giving the number of each kind of face, the polygonal type, the symmetry, and the face angles. Both the directions and lengths are given for the branches that circumscribe each face, and, finally, the total number of branches for the entire polyhedron.

Note that although only [100], [110], and [111] branches appear, each branch needs to be provided in full and half lengths. Also, while [111] branches do not occur among the regular and semiregular polyhedra, they do appear quite frequently as edges of the nodal polyhedra. As a matter of fact, only the cube and octagonal prism do not have faces in the [111] directions.

Photographs of models of the space filling systems described in Table 7.2 and their nodal polyhedra are given in [7.14]–[7.27]. From the figures it can be seen that many of the dual space filling systems described by the nodal polyhedra have identical nets. The same net is associated, with different nodal polyhedra by virtue of the various ways in which polygonal circuits may be spanned. An example of this is given by nodal polyhedra of Nos. 5 and 6 of Table 7.2. The former is a square pyramid and the latter is the tetragonal octahedron which is exactly two of the square pyramids put together. They are both associated with the same net, but must be considered distinct space fillers.

7.13 The fourteen possible branch angles of less than 180° of the Universal Node connector:

[100]–[100]	[110]–[110]	[111]–[111]	[100]–[110]	[110]–[111]	[100]–[111]
90°	60°	70°32′	45°	35°16′	54°44′
	90°	109°28′	90°	90°	125°16′
	120°		135°	144°44′	

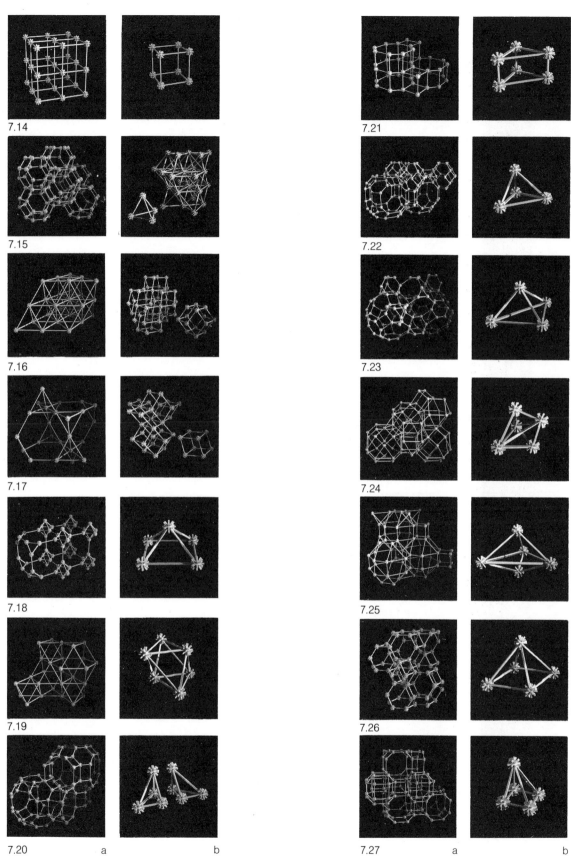

7.14

7.15

7.16

7.17

7.18

7.19

7.20

7.21

7.22

7.23

7.24

7.25

7.26

7.27

a   b

7.14–7.27 Cubic space filling systems built according to the recipes of Table 7.2.

Table 7.2
Space Filling with
Regular and
Semiregular Polyhedra
in the Cubic System

	Space Filling System	Space Filling Ratio	Z	Branch Directions [100]	Branch Directions [110]	Branch Directions [111]
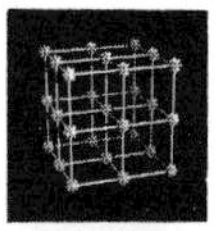 1	Cube [7.14a]		6	6		
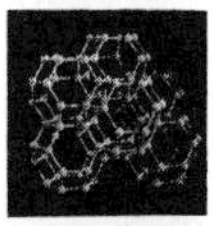 2	Truncated octahedron [7.15a]		4		4	
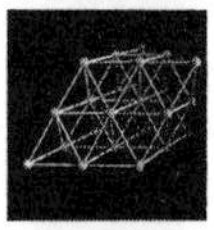 3	Tetrahedron	2	12		12	
	Octahedron [7.16a]	1				
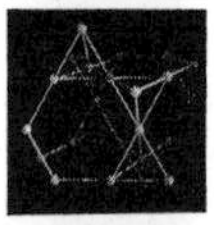 4	Tetrahedron	1	6		6	
	Truncated tetrahedron [7.17a]	1				
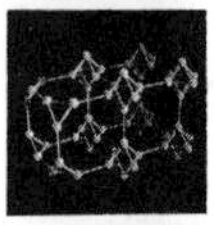 5	Octahedron	1	5	1	4	
	Truncated cube [7.18a]	1				
 6	Octahedron	1	8		8	
	Cuboctahedron [7.19a]	1				
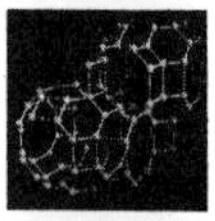 7	Truncated cuboctahedron	1	4	2	2	
	Octagonal prism [7.20a]	3				
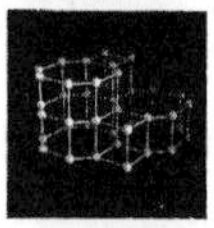 8	Octagonal prism	1	5	4	1	
	Cube [7.21a]	1				
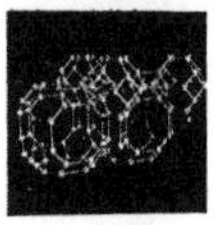 9	Truncated cuboctahedron	1	4	1	3	
	Truncated octahedron	1				
	Square prism [7.22a]	3				
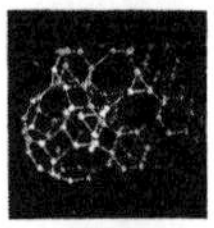 10	Truncated cuboctahedron	1	4	1	3	
	Truncated cube	1				
	Truncated tetrahedron [7.23a]	2				
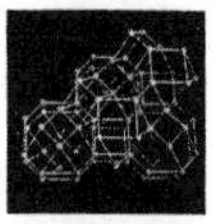 11	Rhombicuboctahedron	1	6	2	4	
	Cuboctahedron	1				
	Square prism [7.24a]	3				
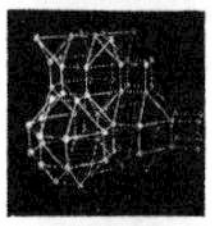 12	Rhombicuboctahedron	1	6	3	3	
	Cube	1				
	Tetrahedron [7.25a]	2				
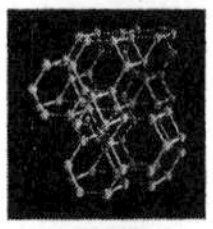 13	Truncated octahedron	1	5		5	
	Cuboctahedron	1				
	Truncated tetrahedron [7.26a]	2				
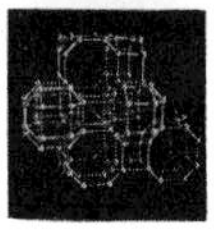 14	Rhombicuboctahedron	1	5	3	2	
	Truncated cube	1				
	Octagonal prism	3				
	Cube [7.27a]	3				

Branch Angles at Node					
[100]–[100]	[110]–[110]	[111]–[111]	[100]–[110]	[110]–[111]	[100]–[111]
90°					
	90°, 120°				
	60°				
	60°, 120°				
	60°		135°		
	60°, 90°				
90°	120°		90°, 135°		
90°			90°, 135°		
	120°, 90°		90°, 135°		
	120°, 60°		90°, 135°		
90°	60°, 90°		90°		
90°	60°		90°		
	60°, 90°, 120°				
90°	60°		90°		

Table 7.2
Continued

	Nodal Polyhedron	Face Plane Directions				Faces		
		Total	[100]	[110]	[111]	Number	Type	Symmetry
	1 Cube [7.14b]	6	6			6	square	4-fold
	2 Tetragonal disphenoid [7.15b]	4		4		4	triangle	mirror
	3 Rhombic dodecahedron [7.16b]	12		12		12	rhombus	2-fold
	4 Rhombic hexahedron [7.17b]	6		6		6	rhombus	2-fold
	5 Square pyramid [7.18b]	5	1	4		1	square	4-fold
						4	triangle	mirror
	6 Tetragonal octahedron [7.19b]	8		8		8	triangle	mirror
	7 Quadrirec-tangular tetrahedron (enantiomorphic) [7.20b]	4	2	2		2	triangle	mirror
						2	triangle	none
	8 Right isosceles triangular prism [7.21b]	5	2			2	triangle	mirror
			1			1	rectangle	2-fold
				2		2	rectangle	2-fold
	9 Trirectangular tetrahedron [7.22b]	4	1			1	triangle	mirror
				1		1	triangle	mirror
				2		2	triangle	none
	10 Right triangular pyramid [7.23b]	4	1			1	triangle	mirror
				1		1	triangle	mirror
					2	2	triangle	mirror
	11 Trirectangular dipyramid [7.24b]	6	2			2	triangle	mirror
				4		4	triangle	none
	12 Monopole trigonal dipyramid [7.25b]	6	3			3	triangle	mirror
				3		3	triangle	mirror
	13 Rhombic pyramid [7.26b]	5		1		1	rhombus	2-fold
				4		4	triangle	mirror
	14 Right square pyramid [7.27b]	5	2			2	triangle	mirror
			1			1	square	4-fold
				2		2	triangle	none

Face Angles	Face Branches [100]		[110]		[111]		Total Branches [100]		[110]		[111]		Total
	A	½A	√2	½√2	√3	½A√3	A	½A	√2	½√2	√3	½A√3	
90°	4						12						12
70°32′, 54°44′	1					2	2					4	6
109°28′, 70°32′						4						24	24
109°28′, 70°32′						4						12	12
90°	4						4					4	8
70°32′, 54°44′	1					2							
70°32′, 54°44′	1					2	4					8	12
90°, 45°	2		1				3		2		1		6
90°, 54°44′, 35°16′	1		1		1								
90°, 45°	1			2			2	3	4				9
90°	2	2											
90°		2		2									
90°, 45°	1			2			1	1		2	2		6
70°32′, 54°44′	1					2							
90°, 54°44′, 35°16′		1		1	1								
90°, 45°	2		1				2		1		3		6
35°16′, 109°28′			1			2							
70°32′, 54°44′	1					2							
90°, 45°	1			2			1	2		4	2		9
90°, 54°44′, 35°16′		1		1	1								
90°, 45°	2		1				3		3		3		9
109°28′, 35°16′			1			2							
109°28′, 70°32′						4	2				6		8
70°32′, 54°44′	1					2							
90°, 45°	2		1				5		2		1		8
90°	4												
90°, 54°44′, 35°16′	1		1		1								

Hexagonal Space Filling Systems as Subsets of the Universal Network

A most remarkable and unexpected discovery is that four of the *hexagonal* space filling configurations are subsets of the universal *cubic* net! These are the triangular prism, hexagonal prism, and the two different multiple systems of triangular and hexagonal prisms (Table 5.1, Nos. 3, 4, 11, 12). The triangular and hexagonal prisms are dual to each other. The dual nets of the two forms of the triangular prism/hexagonal prism binary space filling systems can also be accounted for by the Universal Node system. This means that altogether only five of the twenty-three space filling systems we have inventoried in Table 5.1 cannot be accounted for as simple subsets of the universal net. However, the *topological equivalents** of these five remaining space filling systems may be formed as subsets of the universal net. These are the packings of triangular prisms and cubes (2 cases); triangular and dodecagonal prisms; triangular prisms, cubes, and hexagonal prisms; and hexagonal prisms, cubes, and dodecagonal prisms (Table 5.1, Nos. 13–15, 21, 22).

Figure [7.28] shows in plan how this is possible. The cubes become rhombic prisms and the dodecagons become large hexagons with six additional *nodes* at the midpoints of their edges. All of these but one (hex prism/rhombic prism/dodecagon prism) form uniform nets. However, it is not possible to form any of the dual nets of these five systems with the Universal Node kit of parts.

*Networks (or polyhedra) may be considered topologically equivalent so long as their nodes have the same characteristic coordination and the spatial distribution and inventory of their branches (and polygons) are the same, regardless of whether linear dimensions and angular relationships are the same. For example a simple cube is topologically equivalent to any parallelipiped, and likewise a simple cubic network is topologically equivalent to any network describing a space filling array of parallelepipeds.

Because these five dual nets of the hexagonal system's prism space fillers involve planar combinations of 30°, 60°, 120°, and 90° in single polygons, they cannot be fit into the Universal Node system [4.8]. This reflects the most interesting fact that it is not possible to define a two-dimensional universal network. The reason for this is that there is no unique necessary planar relationship between the equilateral triangle and the square. We have seen that in three-dimensional space this relationship is trivial, as the Universal Node ably demonstrates. There is a fundamental integrative simplicity to periodic structures in three-dimensional space which is not equaled in two dimensions. Can the assumption that is frequently made about the relative simplicity of two-dimensional space be faulty? To the extent that a universal network in two dimensions is not really possible, the correlative aspects of two-dimensional space are far less elegant than the relationships demonstrated in three-dimensional space by the universal network.

7.28 Topological equivalents of 5 space filling prism combinations of the hexagonal system as subsets of the universal network, shown in plan.

Table 7.3 shows the nine hexagonal space filling prism systems; it is in a form identical to that of Table 7.2, except that nodal polyhedra are not given. Figures [7.29]–[7.37] show models of these systems.

Another discovery is that although the hexagonal packing of tetrahedra and octahedra cannot be formed with the Universal Node connector, its dual net of trapezorhombic dodecahedra can by introducing a non-twisted [111] branch as an additional component. Because of this it cannot be formed as a subset of the universal net, but by use of nontwisted [111] branches in combinations with twisted [111] branches it is possible to assemble this configuration [7.38]. We have seen that it is possible to assemble with the Universal Node kit of parts topologically equivalent versions of certain prism systems in the hexagonal family.

7.29–7.37 Hexagonal space filling systems built according to the recipes of Table 7.3.

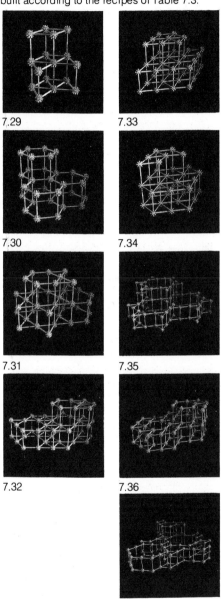

7.29

7.30

7.31

7.32

7.33

7.34

7.35

7.36

7.37

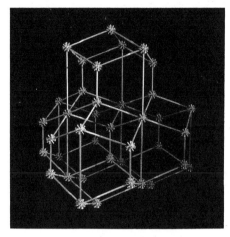

7.38 The network of space filling trapezorhombic dodecahedra.

Table 7.3
Hexagonal Space
Filling Systems

Space Filling Systems		Space Filling Ratio	Branch Directions			Branch Angles at Node					
		Z	[100]	[110]	[111]	[100]–[100]	[110]–[110]	[111]–[111]	[100]–[110]	[110]–[111]	[100]–[111]
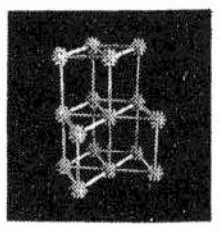 1	Triangular prism [7.29]	8	6	2		60°			90°		
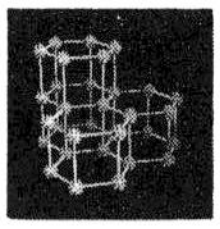 2	Hexagonal prism [7.30]	5	3	2		120°			90°		
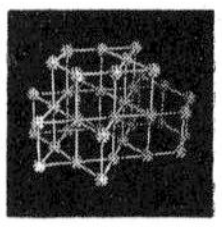 3	Triangular prism	2	6	4	2	60°, 120°			90°		
	Hexagonal prism [7.31]	1									
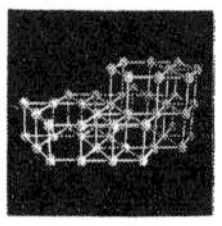 4	Triangular prism	8	7	5	2	60°, 120°			90°		
	Hexagonal prism [7.32]	1									
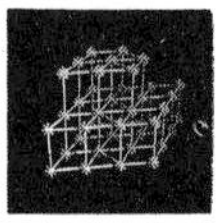 5	Triangular prism	2	7	5	2	60°, 120°			90°		
	Rhombic prism (cube) [7.33]	1									
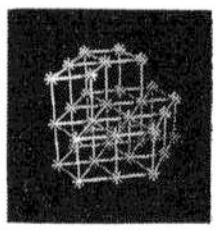 6	Triangular prism	2	7	5	2	60°, 120°			90°		
	Rhombic prism (cube) [7.34]	1									
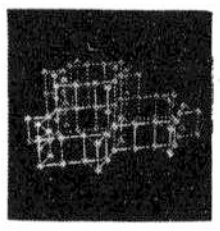 7	Triangular prism	2	5	3	2	60°, 120°, 180°			90°		
	12-prism [7.35]	1									
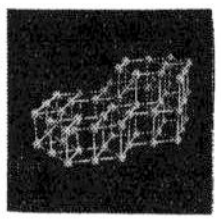 8	Hexagonal prism	1	6	4	2	60°, 120°			90°		
	Triangular prism	2									
	Rhombic prism [7.36]	3									
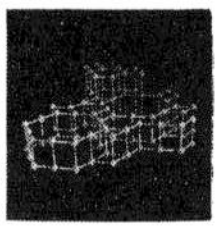 9	Hexagonal prism	2	5	3	2	60°, 120°, 180°, 120°			90°, 90°		
	12-prism	1									
	Rhombic prism [7.37]	3									

Table 7.4
Dodecahedral Space Filling Systems

Space Filling System	Space Filling Ratio	Branch Directions				Branch Angles at Node					
		Z	[100]	[110]	[111]	[100]–[100]	[110]–[110]	[111]–[111]	[100]–[110]	[110]–[111]	[100]–[111]
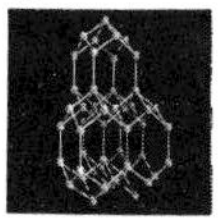 1 Elongated dodecahedron [7.40]		4			4			109°28′			
		5	1		4			70°32′			125°16′
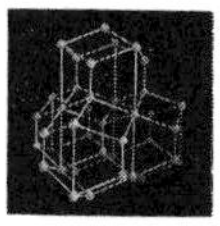 2 Trapezo-rhombic dodecahedron [7.38]		4			4			109°28′			
		8			8			70°32′			
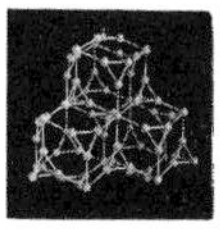 3 Octahedrally truncated rhombic dodecahedron	1	4		3	1		60°			144°44′	
		8			8			70°32′			
Tetrahedron [7.41]	2										
 4 Cubically truncated rhombic dodecahedron	1	4	3		1	90°					125°16′
		4			4			109°28′			
Cube [7.42]	1										
5 Cuboctahedrally truncated rhombic dodecahedron	1	4	3		1	90°					125°16′
		4		3	1		60°			144°44′	
Cube	1										
Tetrahedron	2										
6 Truncated rhombi-cuboctahedron	1	6		4	2		60°	109°28′		90°	
		6		4	2		90°	70°32′		90°	
Cuboctahedron	1										
Octahedron	2										
Triangular prism	8										
7 Truncated rhombi-cuboctahedron	1	4		3	1		60°, 120°			90°, 144°44′	
		4	1	2	1		60°		135°	90°	125°16′
Truncated cube	1										
Truncated tetrahedron	2										
Triangular prism	8										

It is also possible to assemble a topological equivalent in the hexagonal system of the tetrahedral/octahedral net. This is shown in [7.39]. It is achieved by the use of [110] and [100] branches. At each node, nine [110] branches and three [100] branches meet to form a uniform structure. In this configuration every other layer is collapsed by 50%, with regular octahedra stacked vertically on collapsed octahedra having the symmetry of the hexagonal prism.

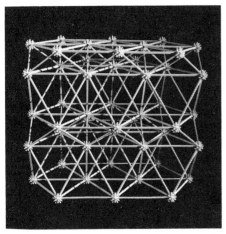

7.39 Topological equivalent in the hexagonal system of the tetrahedral/octahedral network.

Dodecahedral Space Filling Systems

There are four more space filling systems that are, along with their duals, subsets of the universal net. These are the elongated dodecahedron and the three truncated versions of the rhombic dodecahedron which combine with cubes and/or tetrahedra to fill all space (see Chapter 5 [5.15]). The recipes for these systems along with the trapezorhombic dodecahedral system are given in the usual form in Table 7.4. Nodal polyhedra are not given in the table; they may be easily constructed. The elongated dodecahedral and two of the three truncated rhombic dodecahedral systems are shown in [7.40]–[7.42]. The two truncated rhombicuboctahedral systems described in Chapter 5 (p. 49) are also included in Table 7.4 (Nos. 6, 7), but are not illustrated here.

We have discovered that Universal Node imposes an inherent order. Every new structure assembled with this integrative morphological system is instantly understood and may be classified in terms of its relation to the whole. The Universal Node itself allows us to anticipate and then to build a diverse array of alternative modular configurations, in which the notion of *subsets of the whole* emerges as an ordering principle.

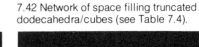

7.42 Network of space filling truncated dodecahedra/cubes (see Table 7.4).

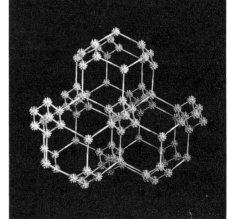

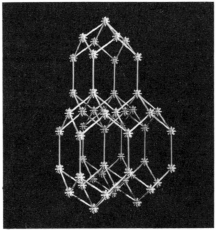

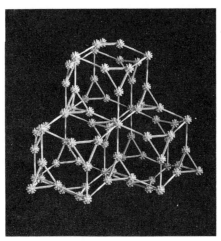

7.40 Network of space filling elongated dodecahedron (see Table 7.4).

7.41 Network of space filling truncated rhombic dodecahedra/tetrahedra (see Table 7.4).

Triangulated Structures Derived from the Universal Network

In our inventory of periodic structures based on the universal network, we have seen very few triangulated systems, particularly those in which a minimum deviation in branch lengths is exhibited.* We are familiar with the tetrahedron/octahedron system [7.16a] (which is composed of equilateral triangles) and the space filling of tetragonal disphenoids that forms the 14-connected bcc network [7.15b]. The bcc network is composed of two branch lengths ([100] and [111]) which vary in length by only 15%. The space filling tetragonal octahedron [7.19b] is composed of the same two branches and forms a triangular network with 8- and 14-connected nodes.

There are some other triangulated systems among the dual nets (nodal polyhedra) of Table 7.2, but their edge-length ratios deviate considerably (by approximately 39%) from the equilateral ideal. In spite of this, any of these networks might serve as useful structures in certain applications.

*Triangulated structures tend to be more energy efficient when differences in branch lengths are minimized. See the Law of Closest Packing and Triangulation in Chapter 1.

There are two other efficient periodic triangulated systems which can be considered subsets of the universal net and which relate to the tetragonal disphenoid and tetragonal octahedron. They are based upon two dual nets from the space filling of regular and semiregular polyhedra (Table 7.2)—namely, the space filling of rhombic dodecahedra [7.16b] and rhombic hexahedra [7.17b]. Both of these systems are composed of the same rhombic face, which is formed by four [111] branches. This rhombic face may be easily subdivided into two isosceles triangles by placing a [100] branch across its short diagonal. The triangles, like those of the tetragonal disphenoid and tetragonal octahedron, are formed with branches that differ in length by only 15%, and therefore constitute an efficient basis for triangulated systems. Both the triangulated rhombic dodecahedron and hexahedron networks have 10-connected and 8-connected nodes ([7.43a], dodecahedra; and [7.43b], hexahedra). It is important to point out that neither of these systems suffers from any local instabilities because no new vertices are formed and, therefore, no unsupported planar sets of triangles are to be found.

We have listed all but one of those periodic systems composed of equilateral triangles or *approximately* equilateral triangles that are subsets of the universal network. This is not to say that there are no other systems which relate to the universal net. We will find again and again that the universal node-net concept is constantly reappearing in different forms. We will find that the same principles of symmetry upon which the Universal Node is based govern an array of periodic structures which, although they are not subsets of the universal net, do relate to it in sophisticated and subtle ways.

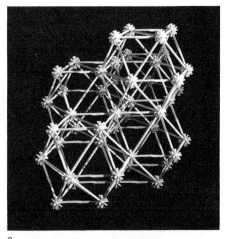

a

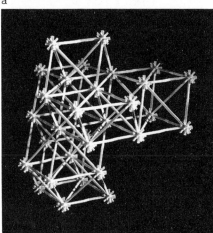

b

7.43 Network of space filling triangulated rhombic dodecahedra (a); network of space filling triangulated rhombic hexahedra (b).

8 Saddle Polyhedra and the Universal Network. The Cube Revisited

In our inventory of space filling systems we have seen two major subsets of the Universal Node: the 6-connected node of the simple cubic network which incorporates all of the [100] directions available on the node [8.1a]; and the 12-connected node of the tetrahedral/octahedral fcc network which incorporates all of the [110] directions of the node [8.1b]. We have not as yet observed the result of connecting the eight [111] directions of the node [8.1c]. This results in an 8-connected [8.1d] network that does not define any plane-faced polyhedron. Its nodes are the site of the bcc lattice, and it is closely related to the network formed by space filling tetragonal disphenoids [8.1e]. If the [100] branches are removed from this latter tetrahedral network, the 8-connected bcc net results.

We now have three uniform networks; these constitute the most symmetrical possibilities for the periodic subdivision of space. They are equivalent to the simple cubic, body centered cubic, and face centered cubic lattices and, therefore, all have full cubic symmetry. We note that symmetry can be preserved even with "incomplete" nodes, i.e., a node with spokes for only the six [100] directions, will still retain full cubic symmetry, as will a node with only the eight [111] directions, or one with only the twelve [110] directions [8.2]. There are no other periodic networks in which the nodes have this much symmetry.* The universal network is a combination of the three most symmetrical coordinate systems into one comprehensive system.

*The 14-connected node of the unary tetrahedron (tetragonal disphenoidal) system has full cubic symmetry but because it has two kinds of branches, ([100] and [111] branches), it does not form a completely homogeneous structure. As I have already pointed out, this 14-connected net is a combination of the simple cubic and bcc nets.

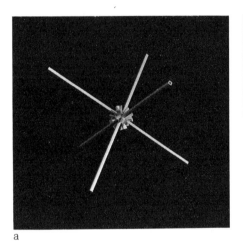

a

b

c

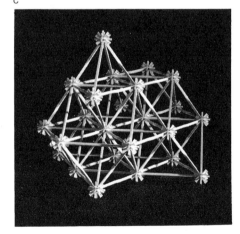

d

e

8.1 The Universal Node connector with all six possible [100] branches attached (a); with all twelve possible [110] branches attached (b); with all eight possible [111] branches attached (c). Note the repeating network with all eight possible [111] branches at each node. Nodes fall at sites of bcc lattice (d); repeating network with all eight possible [111] branches, and with addition of all six possible [100] branches at each node. Nodes of this 14-connected network also fall at sites of bcc lattice (e).

Minimal Surfaces, Mean Curvature

The simple cubic and the fcc networks both have their dual nets, but what of the bcc network just described? Its edges do not define any polyhedron—*at least not any plane-faced polyhedron.* The generation of dual space fillers is a reciprocation process: the centers of contiguous polyhedral cells are joined through their common faces forming a dual space filling network. If we do not have a polyhedral cell then how can we have a dual space filling network?

In our earlier discussion (Chapter 5, p. 50; [5.18]–[5.19]) of three-dimensional connected networks which do not form plane-faced polyhedra, it was pointed out that various kinds of skew polygonal circuits are formed. It is possible to span such a nonplanar skew polygon with a so-called minimal surface, forming a doubly curved saddle shaped module.

A minimal surface is a surface of zero mean curvature; such a surface can be associated with any closed polygon. If the polygon is flat, the minimal surface will be flat. If the polygon is skew, then the minimal surface will be warped, with its positive curvature exactly equal to its negative curvature; hence the surface will be of a saddle shape.

It was shown by Euler that all minimal surfaces must have zero mean curvature at every point of the surface* and that all such surfaces that are nonplanar must be saddle shaped. A minimal surface can be easily formed by immersing a wire frame in a soap solution. Upon removing it, we find that a very thin film of soap spans the frame, arranging itself so as to have the smallest possible area. The film is stressed in pure tension and is in a state of minimal potential energy. If such a surface is duplicated in a rigid material, it can form an extremely strong structure of very small thickness with resistance to both compression and tension forces. Although they can be easily formed and studied empirically, such minimal surfaces are extremely difficult to treat mathematically.**

*Courant and Robbins have defined the minimal surface as follows. "Consider the perpendicular to the surface at [a point] P, and all planes containing it. These planes will intersect the surface in curves which, in general, have different curvatures at P. Now consider the curves of minimum and maximum curvature, respectively. (In general, the planes containing these curves will be perpendicular to each other.) One-half the sum of these two curvatures is the mean curvature of the surface at P."

**In the 1870s, the Belgian physicist Plateau experimented with minimal-surface soap films. The general problem of minimal surfaces is usually referred to as Plateau's problem. Mathematically Plateau's problem is exceedingly difficult as it is connected with the solution of a partial differential equation, or a system of such equations.

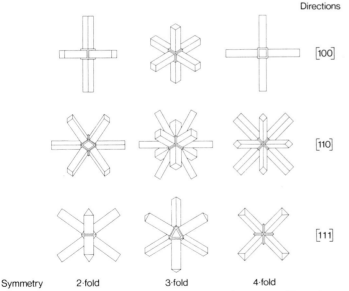

Directions

[100]

[110]

[111]

Symmetry   2·fold   3·fold   4·fold

8.2 Full cubic symmetry is preserved in nodes with only [100] spokes, or [110] spokes, or [111] spokes.

Saddle Surfaces and Interstitial Domains

Some areas on a saddle surface are flatter than others and, therefore, all points on the surface do not respond equally well to concentrated loads. When such saddle surfaces are associated in a periodic array, the physical interaction of one surface on another produces a compensatory effect which greatly increases their efficiency as structures. An isolated saddle polygon is not a fully stable structure. It requires the cooperative effect of associated saddle polygons if its advantages as a doubly curved surface are to be fully realized. This is true whether the surface is a tension system, as in the case of the soap film, or a surface of rigid material capable of resisting tension and compression forces.

The significance of saddle figures for the theory of modular structure is that three-dimensional periodic connected networks that do not describe plane faced polyhedra nonetheless form saddle figures of various kinds. In previous chapters we always started with a polyhedron or a set of polyhedra and then found ways in which these could be generated and combined. For the saddle figures, we are, at least initially, faced with a different problem: the saddle figure must be generated from an existing network. It is a problem of partitioning off some fundamental volumetric region or set of regions with saddle (or plane) faces to form a space filling figure or a set of space filling figures. We shall refer to this fundamental spatial region (or a set of regions) as the *interstitial domain(s)*[*] of the network. The interstitial domain is formed by spanning with a minimal surface the group of polygonal circuits that as a nonintersecting set will combine to form a closed polyhedron or set of closed polyhedra. The appropriate group of polygonal circuits is determined by spanning the smallest, next smallest, . . . polygons until a closed cell or set of cells is found. Both unary and multiple space filling domains can be found by means of this method.

*This term has been proposed by Schoen, who also refers to the domain of the vertex (which is simply the polyhedron of the dual net) as the symmetry domain. Our nodal polyhedron of Chapter 7 is equivalent to Schoen's symmetry domain. The term nodal polyhedron was originally proposed by Schoen as well.

It is important to emphasize the use of *minimal* surfaces to generate the faces of interstitial domains. The plane-faced polyhedra which compose the space filling systems of Table 5.1 are interstitial domains of the uniform networks which they define. If these structures are formed as networks without faces, the faces may be found in the same manner in which the faces of the saddle faced interstitial domains are found, i.e., by spanning with a minimal surface the set of smallest, next smallest, etc. nonintersecting circuits formed by the constituent polygons which compose the network which combine to form closed polyhedral cells.* When the proper interstitial domain (or domains) of a net are found, fundamental repeating space filling units are formed which greatly increase our ability to perceive structure in an array otherwise very difficult to understand. Because of the structural advantages of the saddle surfaces, the saddle polyhedra have significant implications for the design of physical structures.

*In the cases of the dual nets this spanning principle breaks down because of the multiple ways in which identical networks are spanned to form the nodal polyhedra. In such cases, the requirements of duality remove the ambiguities.

Saddle Polyhedra and Connected Networks

The confluence of the notion of three-dimensional connected networks and that of minimal surfaces has led me and others independently to the invention of a new class of polyhedra that are called *saddle polyhedra*. A saddle polyhedron is a closed figure formed by a finite number of saddle polygons bounded by straight edges.* Although, as with plane faced polyhedra, there can be an infinite number of saddle polyhedra, only those figures which can be used to build infinite periodic structures are of concern in the present work. Michael Burt has studied the limiting case of a finite set of non-space-filling saddle polyhedra composed of regular faces which he derives from the Platonic and Archimedean solids.**

*A few infinite regular saddle polyhedra have been discovered by Schoen following upon my earlier invention of (finite) saddle polyhedra. Schoen, with whom I have collaborated, has done major mathematical work on the subject of saddle polyhedra and infinite periodic minimal surfaces, and has discovered many other finite saddle polyhedra which do not fill space but which satisfy rigorous mathematical criteria for regularity. See bibliography for citations of Schoen's work.

**Burt has independently discovered the saddle polyhedron concept, although his emphasis is somewhat different than mine. He has studied some of the space filling saddle polyhedra and the class of infinite periodic minimal surfaces, which is treated later in this book, as well as the non-space-filling finite class mentioned above.

8.3 Space filling bcc saddle tetrahedra.

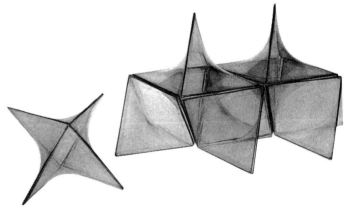

Our first saddle polyhedron is the interstitial domain of the 8-connected bcc network. It is a saddle tetrahedron bounded by four regular saddle tetragons. We, therefore, see the emergence of a space filling bcc saddle tetrahedron. [8.3]. Because the *bond angles* of the bcc network are 70°32′, the saddle tetragon faces of the bcc tetrahedron have included angles of 70°32′. Such included angles or face angles are the crucial data necessary to describe particular saddle faces and, therefore, particular saddle polyhedra. As we shall see, the fourteen possible branch angles provided by the Universal Node account for all of the combinations of face angles that appear in our saddle polyhedra.

Once we have transformed a connected network into an array of space filling saddle polyhedra, it is a simple matter to find the dual space filling network. The interstitial domain will be the nodal polyhedron of the dual net. From this, we know that the network which is dual to the bcc net must have 4-connected vertices because the nodal polyhedron of the dual net will be the bcc saddle tetrahedron with four faces. The dual net of the bcc net is the coplanar 90° 4-connected network of [5.18a]. The interstitial domain of this dual net is a saddle octahedron bounded by regular saddle hexagons with included angles of 90° corresponding to bond angles of the net. This space filling bcc saddle octahedron is then the nodal polyhedron of the bcc network [8.4].

8.4 Space filling bcc saddle octahedra.

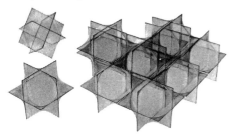

Polyhedra with Less than Four Faces

We find that the network of this saddle bcc octahedron [8.5], like the bcc network itself, is also a subset of the universal net in which four [100] directions meet at each node. In fact, all of the networks described in Chapter 5 are subsets of the universal network. Some also generate extremely significant saddle polyhedra. The 3-connected Laves network of the decagon circuits [5.17a], has as its interstitial domain a saddle trihedron [8.6] bounded by three saddle decagons with included angles of 120°. The node of this net is a coplanar subset of the [110] directions in which three [110] branches meet at 120° in a common plane. This network is shown in [8.7] (which the reader will recognize as being the same as [5.17a].)

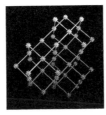

8.5 Network of space filling bcc saddle octahedra.

8.6 Space filling saddle decatrihedra.

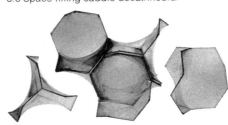

A closed plane-faced polyhedron must have at least four faces. This is no longer true if nonplanar faces are allowed. We see that the saddle trihedron is not only a three-faced polyhedron, but that it is even a unary space filler. This trihedron, like many of the saddle polyhedra we will soon examine, has certain vertices at which only two edges meet. Such 2-connected vertices do not occur amongst any of the plane-faced polyhedra. It might be said that such vertices make possible the existence of saddle polyhedra. Surprisingly, even the saddle polyhedra with such 2-connected vertices still satisfy Euler's theorem for polyhedra (p. 32): faces + vertices = edges + 2. This is so, because for every 2-connected vertex there must also be an extra edge.

This saddle decatrihedron of the Laves network has the symmetry of a triangular prism: one axis of 3-fold symmetry and three axes of 2-fold symmetry. The dual of the decatrihedronal space filling system is the mirror image of the original network, i.e., the system is an enantiomorphic self-dual. A model of these dual networks juxtaposed is shown in [8.8].

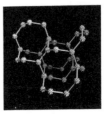

8.7 Network of space filling saddle decatrihedra.

8.8 By juxtaposing networks of right- and left-handed space filling decatrihedra we see them to be duals to each other.

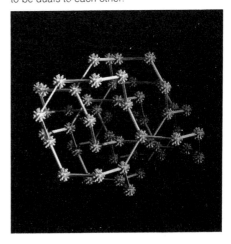

The Diamond Network

The 4-connected diamond net was also introduced in Chapter 5 [5.18b]. In its simplicity and symmetry, it is one of the most fundamental of all periodic structures. It is rivaled only by the three cubic nets in the hierarchy of fundamental three-dimensional structures. The node of the diamond net is a subset of the bcc node; it has four [111] directions disposed at 109°28′ angles. It is assembled by attaching [111] branches to every other [111] directed spoke on the Universal Node [8.9].

The interstitial domain of the diamond net is a saddle tetrahedron bounded by four regular hexagonal saddle faces with included angles of 109°28′ [8.10]. This diamond tetrahedron has the symmetry of the regular tetrahedron. The nodal polyhedron of the diamond net is another diamond tetrahedron. It is a self-dual. The diamond network and the simple cubic network are the only self-dual uniform networks. If enantiomorphism is permitted, the 3-connected Laves network also qualifies as a self-dual. There are apparently no others, although this has not been proven mathematically.*

*There is also one semiuniform net with two kinds of nodes which is a self-dual. This is discussed later in this chapter. It is interesting to note that the regular tetrahedron is the only plane-faced finite polyhedron which is a self-dual and the diamond saddle tetrahedron with full tetrahedral symmetry gives rise to a self-dual space filling system.

8.9 The 4-connected diamond network.

8.10 The diamond saddle tetrahedra.

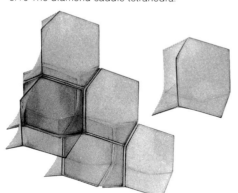

Wurtzite and Carborundum

Wurtzite, a form of zinc sulfide, and Carborundum III, a form of silicon carbide, are two crystals whose atomic positions are the same as in diamond. (Wells 1962a). Therefore, their networks appear to be identical to the diamond network. The use of saddle polyhedra as interstitial domains, however, enables us to clearly distinguish the subtle differences between these seemingly identical structures.

Both wurtzite and Carborundum III may be assembled from the Universal Node system but neither are subsets of the universal network. The wurtzite structure is a subset of the trapezorhombic dodecahedron net and its overall symmetry is hexagonal rather than cubic.

Like the diamond net, all of its nodes are alike surrounded by four branches meeting at 109°28′. It is necessary to use both twisted and nontwisted [111] branches to assemble this structure with the Universal Node System [8.11]. The wurtzite is less symmetrical than the diamond structure, and so is composed of two interstitial domains: a trihedron bounded by three saddle hexagons of 2-fold symmetry, and a pentahedron bounded by two regular saddle hexagons and three 2-fold saddle hexagons [8.12]. All included angles for these various saddle faces are of necessity 109°28′.

8.11 Four-connected network of wurtzite.

8.12 Wurtzite structure formed by space filling of saddle trihedra and saddle pentahedra.

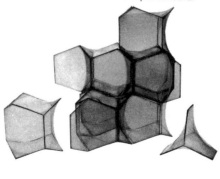

The Carborundum III structure is like both the diamond and wurtzite networks in that all of its nodes are 4-connected with [111] branches (twisted and nontwisted) disposed coequally at 109°28′ [8.13]. However, the interstitial regions of this network give rise to three polyhedral domains: the wurtzite pentahedron and trihedron and the diamond tetrahedron. The admixture of these three polyhedra in a ternary space filling system defines the Carborundum III net [8.14].

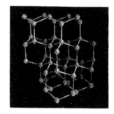

8.13 Four-connected network of Carborundum III.

8.14 Carborundum III structure formed by space filling of saddle trihedra, saddle pentahedra, and diamond saddle tetrahedra.

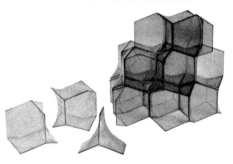

Unlike the diamond net, neither the wurtzite nor Carborundum nets are self-duals, although the nodal polyhedra of the wurtzite and Carborundum nets are very similar to the diamond tetrahedron. Wurtzite has a tetrahedron bounded by one plane regular hexagon and three saddle hexagons with 2-fold symmetry, while Carborundum requires two nodal polyhedra. Both are, of course, tetrahedra: one is bounded by one regular plane hexagon and three saddle hexagons with only mirror symmetry; and the other is bounded by the same three saddle hexagons, but with a single regular saddle hexagon with included face angles of 109°28′. Although the net of the wurtzite nodal tetrahedra can be assembled with the Universal Node system, the pair of Carborundum nodal tetrahedra cannot. The Carborundum network is, in fact, a mixture of cubic and hexagonal structures. Because of this, the Carborundum nodal polyhedra require a special set of branch angle relationships which cannot be accommodated by the Universal Node connector. It is possible, however, to assemble the wurtzite nodal polyhedron in a configuration which is topologically equivalent to the network formed by the packing of Carborundum nodal tetrahedra.

Describing the Universal Network with Saddle Polyhedra

I have not as yet described the interstitial domains or nodal polyhedra for the universal net. We already know that there will be two kinds of nodal polyhedra due to the two kinds of nodal subsets. I have noted in Chapter 6 that the universal network has three 6-connected nodes for every 26-connected node. We know from this that we are looking for a multiple space filling system which consists of a 26-faced nodal polyhedron with full cubic symmetry and a 6-faced nodal polyhedron with tetragonal symmetry which together fill space in the ratio of one to three. There is no example of such an array in our space filling inventory (Table 5.1) so we can be fairly sure that we will need saddle polyhedra. We find that the interstitial domains of the universal net consist of two kinds of polyhedra: an orthorhombic* saddle tetrahedron bounded by four 2-fold saddle quadrilaterals (face angles of 90°, 45°, 90°, 45°); and an enantiomorphic pair of trihedra, each bounded by the same two right triangular faces (included angles of 90°, 54°44′, 35°16′,) and one 2-fold saddle quadrilateral [8.15]. This trihedron has one axis of 2-fold symmetry. This set fills space in the ratio of one tetrahedron for every four trihedra. We shall call its members the universal tetrahedron and universal trihedron.

These interstitial domains tell us that the dual network which defines the nodal polyhedra will have two kinds of vertices. Careful examination of these interstitial polyhedra shows that there will be 3-connected nodes with branches meeting at 120° on a common plane and 4-connected nodes with branches meeting at 90° on a common plane. The nodal polyhedra that are generated are of considerable interest.

*Figures of the orthorhombic class have three 2-fold axes of symmetry.

8.15 Interstitial domains of the universal network: universal tetrahedron and an enantiomorphic pair of universal trihedra.

The 26-faced nodal polyhedron of the Universal Node is bounded by eight plane regular hexagonal faces in the [111] directions, twelve 2-fold saddle hexagons in the [110] directions (face angles of 90° and 120°), and six 4-fold saddle dodecagons in the [100] directions (face angles 90° and 120°). The six-faced nodal polyhedron is bounded by two of the 4-fold saddle dodecagons in the [100] directions, and four of the 2-fold saddle hexagons in the [110] directions. These we will call the universal cuboctadodecahedron and the universal hexahedron; they are shown in [8.16]. These two polyhedra fill space in the ratio of 1:3, just as the nodal ratio of the universal network leads us to expect. A space filling array is shown in [8.17]. The universal cuboctadodecahedron has full cubic symmetry and the universal hexahedron has tetragonal symmetry, so the symmetry requirements of the nodes are satisfied.

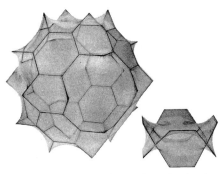

8.16 Nodal polyhedra of the universal network: universal cuboctadodecahedron and universal hexahedron.

8.17 Space filling of universal cuboctadodecahedra and universal hexahedra.

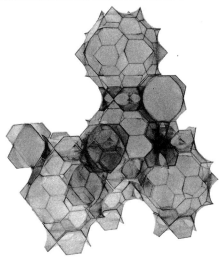

Visualizing the Universal Network

The universal network may be visualized with the aid of an assembly of three enantiomorphic pairs of universal trihedra. These six trihedra share a common [111] branch when grouped and their collective vertices fall exactly at the eight corners of the cube [8.18]. The corresponding relative branch lengths are: for the [100] direction, 1; for [110], $\sqrt{2}$; and for [111], $\sqrt{3}$. Note that in this cubical assembly two opposite vertices are 7-connected and that the additional six vertices are only 2-connected. If such a cubical assembly is packed with others of the same species, such that the 7-connected corners are always matched and that 2-connected corners are always matched, each collection of 7-connected vertices becomes a 26-connected vertex; i.e., a Universal Node vertex, and each collection of 2-connected vertices becomes a 6-connected vertex. A space filling collection of these cubically assembled trihedra gives rise to a second interstitial space which takes the form of the universal tetrahedron. The ratio of three 6-connected nodes for every 26-connected node is clearly explained by the cubical assembly of trihedra. Note that there are two 7-connected nodes for every six 2-connected nodes: i.e., a ratio of one to three. A space filling array of universal trihedra and universal tetrahedra can be seen in [8.19].

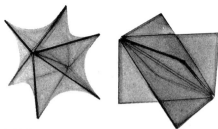

8.18 Cubical assembly of three enantiomorphic pairs of universal trihedra can repeat to describe the universal network.

8.19 Space filling of universal trihedra and universal tetrahedra.

The unit cell of the universal network is an array of eight cubical sets of six universal trihedra. This complex will repeat by simple translation along the [100] directions to define the entire universal network. Its network is shown in [8.20a] along with the network of the cubical set of six universal trihedra [8.20b]. The cubical set of six trihedra will repeat to define the entire structure but not by simple translation since a reflection through [100]-directed mirror planes or a rotation about all [100] branches is required. We see in the unit cell of the universal net that the 26-connected Universal Nodes fall on the sites of the body centered cubic lattice, and the 6-connected Universal Node subsets fall on three-fourths of the sites of the simple cubic lattice.

8.20 The unit cell of the universal network (a), and the network of the cubical set of six universal trihedra showing the sites of the 26-connected and 6-connected Universal Nodes (b).

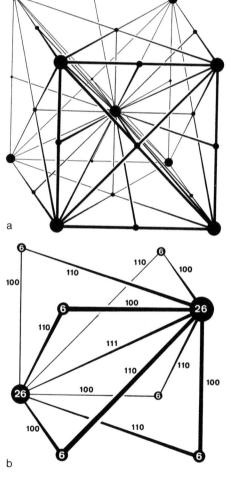

Regular and Semiregular Saddle Polyhedra

I now return to a discussion of the general characteristics of the saddle polyhedra. We have already seen that there can be an infinite number of saddle polyhedra, and I have already restricted our inquiry to those polyhedra that can be used to assemble infinite periodic structures.

Because saddle polyhedra usually have sets of vertices in which two edges meet, it is difficult, if not impossible, to find saddle polyhedra which have all their vertices alike. Because of this, there are no simple cases of regular or semiregular saddle polyhedra. Schoen has identified a set of nine finite regular saddle polyhedra in which all vertices are uniform, but these are comparable to the Kepler-Poinsot stellated polyhedra in which faces are permitted to intersect.*

Three of these regular saddle polyhedra are related to the regular tetrahedron, octahedron, and cube, respectively. The six others are related to the icosahedron and cannot form periodic structures. The former three are shown in [8.21]. They are the tetrahedral hemihexahedron with three saddle tetragons (60° angles) at each vertex and 3 intersecting faces; the octahedral hemioctahedron with four saddle hexagons (60° and 90° angles) at each vertex and 4 intersecting faces; and the cubic hemioctahedron with three saddle hexagons (60°, 90°, 90°, 90° angles) at each vertex and four intersecting faces** As far as I know, the only regular and semiregular saddle polyhedra which do not have intersecting faces are infinite systems. Some of these will be described in Chapter 9. These are derived from space fillings of finite saddle polyhedra with certain of their faces omitted; they have also been identified by Schoen (1970).

*Schoen (1968a). These are the metric realizations of a class of regular maps enumerated by Coxeter and Moser (1964, p. 112).

**The names of these polyhedra are due to Norman Johnson.

8.21 Regular saddle polyhedra: octahedral hemioctahedron, tetrahedral hemihexahedron, and cubic hemioctahedron.

Of all of the saddle polyhedra that we will examine (which total altogether over fifty examples), there are four which have special significance, three of which have already been described (the bcc tetrahedron, the bcc octahedron, and the diamond tetrahedron). They are characterized by the fact that they are bounded exclusively by one kind of regular skew polygon. If it were not for the fact that they each have a secondary set of 2-connected vertices, and, therefore, have two kinds of vertices, these polyhedra would qualify as regular polyhedra. When they are packed to fill space, the 2-connected vertices disappear and only one kind of vertex remains. These figures and the nets to which they belong are uniform and constitute a unique class of polyhedra, perhaps as unique as the Platonic figures.

A fourth saddle polyhedron ranks with the foregoing three in importance. It is a ten-sided polyhedron bounded by six regular skew saddle quadrilaterals (60° angles) and four regular skew hexagons (60° angles) [8.22]. It has tetrahedral symmetry and we shall call it the tetrahedral decahedron. It is a unary space filling polyhedron and is derived from a 6-connected (rather than fully 12-connected) version of the fcc network [8.23]. Because it has more than one kind of regular face it is analogous to the semiregular polyhedra, except, again, for the fact of the 2-connected vertices. The 6-connected fcc network is yet another branch system that may be used to connect the points of a given lattice. These four polyhedra—the bcc tetrahedron, the bcc octahedron, the diamond tetrahedron, and the tetrahedral decahedron—are the only known saddle polyhedra, which fill space alone or in combination with other polyhedra, that are bounded exclusively by regular saddle polygons.

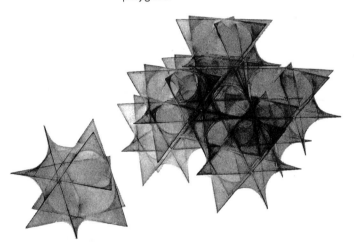

8.22 Space filling of tetrahedral decahedra.

8.23 Network of space filling tetrahedral decahedra is 6-connected subset of 12-connected fcc network.

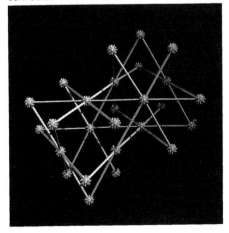

Characteristics of Skew Polygons

The many additional saddle polyhedra that have been discovered are bounded by a variety of skew polygonal faces of varying degrees of symmetry. In review, the regular polygon is defined as any circuit, plane or skew, of straight line segments that is equilateral and equiangular and in which all vertices are equidistant from a common central point. In projection, all regular skew polygons can be made to yield regular plane polygons. As we are about to see, the requirement of equal edges and equal angles is not enough to uniquely define a regular skew polygon. Note that while the rotational symmetry of a regular plane polygon corresponds exactly to the number of sides, the rotational symmetry of a regular skew polygon is exactly half the number of sides. For example, a plane square has 4-fold symmetry, while a regular skew tetragon has only 2-fold symmetry. A regular plane hexagon has 6-fold symmetry, while a regular skew hexagon will have only 3-fold symmetry.

A curious class of polygons emerges which, although it consists of equal edges and equal included angles, is still not regular because of the particular manner in which the included angles are directed. An example of this is the skew decagon of the decatrihedron we have already discussed. This saddle polygon is equilateral and equiangular but has only 2-fold symmetry. All of its angles are 120°, but these are oriented in such a manner that an irregular 2-fold ten-sided polygon is formed [8.24]. Two other examples of this class of face are found in the faces of a truncated tetrahedral decahedron which is bounded by four regular plane hexagons, six saddle octagons and four saddle dodecagons [8.25]. Both of the saddle faces are equiangular (120° included angles) and equilateral. However, they are not regular—the octagon has only 2-fold symmetry and the dodecagon has only 3-fold symmetry. As suggested by an examination of the polyhedron to which these faces belong, the octagon is simply a truncated regular saddle quadrilateral of 60° angles and the dodecagon is a truncated regular saddle hexagon of 60° angles. The truncated polygons have the same symmetry as their parent figures.

Another frequently occurring class of skew polygons consists of equal sides but face angles of two different kinds. Such polygons frequently appear to be regular when viewed in projection and tend to be relatively symmetrical. They have two classes of vertices, one set of which falls at the intersection of two edges which when viewed in projection have included angles of 180°. This has the effect of transforming an n-gon into a (n / 2)-gon when it is viewed in plan. An example of this class of skew polygon is an eight-sided saddle polygon with equal edges but included angles of 60° and 90°. Another example is an octagon with included angles of 70°32′ and 109°28′ [8.26]. These octagons have 4-fold symmetry. In the inventory of saddle polyhedra there are also various saddle polygons which consist of two kinds of edges and two kinds of included angles. There are also saddle polygons which have two edge types and one kind of included angle.

8.26 Skew octagon (4-fold symmetry).

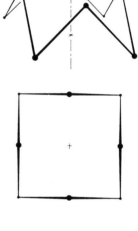

8.24 Skew decagon of decatrihedron (2-fold symmetry).

8.25 Skew octagon (2-fold symmetry, a), and skew dodecagon (3-fold symmetry, b) are the faces of a truncated tetrahedral decahedron.

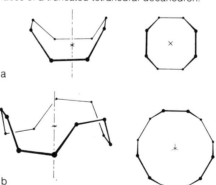

a

b

Saddle Polyhedra: An Inventory of Possibilities

Because of our success with the universal net as a means of accounting for all of the space filling systems composed of plane-faced polyhedra, and because it is also possible to consider the nets of all of the saddle polyhedra so far described to be subsets of the universal net, we will consider *only* those additional saddle polyhedra and related nets which can be defined by this system.

Many different modes of exploration were used to discover numerous saddle polyhedra. In some cases, they have been derived directly from networks. This is how the concept first saw realization—the bcc tetrahedron and diamond tetrahedron being the first discovered in that order. Many others were derived by a process of truncation of vertices or augmentation of vertices. New uniform and semiuniform* networks have been derived by an exploration of the various combinatorial possibilities of previously established saddle polyhedra or saddle polygons. The Universal Node concept is a powerful tool for the systematic empirical exploration and analysis of the concept of periodic nets as they relate to saddle polyhedra.

*We know that a periodic network is uniform when all of its vertices are equivalent (congruent). A semiuniform network is a system in which more than one kind of vertex appears, but which is still periodic. Typically, semiuniform nets have two or three kinds of vertices and there are a few which have up to four different vertex types.

Many saddle polyhedra and saddle polyhedral space filling systems have been discovered. I have not attempted to exhaust all of the possible combinations and permutations of the universal net system which will give rise to uniform or semiuniform saddle polyhedral networks. There is no question that there are additional structures to be discovered, particularly in the realm of the larger class of semiuniform networks. How many more is difficult to suggest. Table 8.1 lists 53 saddle polyhedra, all of which relate to periodic networks which are identified in Table 8.2. Only those saddle polyhedra are described that are components of space filling systems and that are, therefore, related to the global behavior of the periodic structures to which they belong—again, a synthesis of the parts and the whole.*

* No attempt has been made to consider the set of dual polyhedra for the finite saddle polyhedron cells. Because of the typical 2-connected vertices of the finite saddle polyhedron cells, their duals are not obvious and are subject to some interpretation.

Complete specifications of the 53 saddle polyhedra are given in Table 8.1. They are identified according to their symmetry and grouped according to the numbers of faces. Names have been derived which reflect either their symmetry properties or their origins and/or the number of faces, or all of these factors. In effect, recipes are given in Table 8.1 for the construction of these saddle polyhedra using the Universal Node system. Models are shown for 38 of these 53 saddle polyhedra. Figures [8.27]–[8.64] show two views of each of these polyhedra assembled from plastic surfaces and a third view of the network of the polyhedron assembled from Universal Node connectors and branches.

Forty-two space filling combinations are possible with the saddle polyhedra listed in Table 8.1. These saddle polyhedral space filling systems are enumerated in Table 8.2, and recipes for the construction of their networks using the Universal Node system are given. Models of 38 of these 42 systems are shown [8.65]–[8.96] as packings of closed polyhedra assembled from plastic surfaces, and as networks assembled from Universal Node connectors and branches.

From these many examples of saddle polyhedral systems we again see the extraordinary range of options provided by the Universal Node system within the constraints of a very simple set of geometric relationships. Quite clearly, the minimum inventory/maximum diversity concept posited earlier has been powerfully fulfilled with the Universal Node system.

Table 8.1
Saddle Polyhedra
Classified According
to the Universal
Node® System

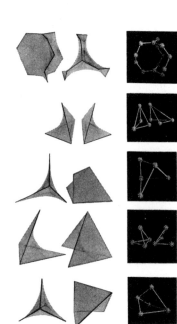

Complete recipes are given for 53 saddle polyhedra. Although the list is not exhaustive it does include the most important known saddle polyhedra.

The second column identifies the number of symmetry axes each of 2-, 3-, 4-, and 6-fold rotation. The third column lists the symmetry class within which each polyhedron falls. In addition to the seven crystal classes already described, the terms *triangular*, *digonal*, and *tetrahedral* have also been used to indicate symmetry. *Triangular* refers to figures which have the symmetry of an equilateral triangular prism. *Digonal* refers to figures which have only a single 2-fold rotation axis. *Tetrahedral* refers to figures with the symmetry of the regular tetrahedron. The nodal characteristics are given in the fourth column. Note that all of the saddle polyhedra have two kinds of nodes—a primary and a secondary. The secondary nodes in all but two cases are 2-connected vertices. Complete specifications are given regarding the numbers and types of branches and faces.

Following the table, [8.27]–[8.64] show models of 38 of the listed saddle polyhedra.

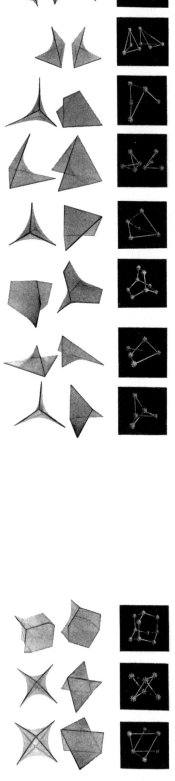

| Saddle Polyhedron | Symmetry Axes | | | | Symmetry |
	2-f	3-f	4-f	6-f	
1 Decatrihedron [8.27]	3	1			Triangular
2 Universal trihedron (enantiomorphic) [8.28]	1				Digonal
3 Trirectangular trihedron [8.29]	1				Digonal
4 Digonal trihedron (enantiomorphic) [8.30]	1				Digonal
5 Trigonal trihedron [8.31]		1			Trigonal
6 Wurtzite trihedron [8.32]	3	1			Triangular
7 Delta trihedron [8.33]					mirror
8 bcc trihedron [8.34]		1			Trigonal
9 Rectangular trihedron (enantiomorphic)					no symmetry
10 Double rectangular trihedron					mirror
11 Diamond tetrahedron [8.35]	3	4			Tetrahedral
12 bcc tetrahedron [8.36]	4		1		Tetragonal
13 fcc tetragonal tetrahedron [8.37]	4		1		Tetragonal

Nodes					Branches				Faces					Face Plane Directions		
Primary		Secondary							Number				Included			
Z	No.	Z	No.	Tot.	[100]	[110]	[111]	Tot.	Tot.	Ea.	Type	Symmetry	Angles	[100]	[110]	[111]
3	2	2	12	14		15		15	3	3	10-gon	2-fold	120°		3	
3	2	2	2	4	2	2	1	5	3	1	4-gon (enantio)	2-fold	90°, 45°, 90°, 45°		1	
										2	3-gon	no symmetry	90°, 54°44′, 35°16′		2	
3	2	2	3	5	2	4		6	3	1	4-gon	2-fold	60°, 90°		1	
										2	4-gon	mirror	60°, 90°, 90°, 90°			2
3	2	2	2	4	2		3	5	3	1	4-gon (enantio)	2-fold	54°44′		1	
										2	3-gon	mirror	54°44′, 70°32′, 54°44′		2	
3	2	2	3	5	3	3		6	3	3	4-gon	mirror	60°, 90°, 90°, 90°			3
3	2	2	6	8			9	9	3	3	6-gon	2-fold	109°28′		3	
3	2	2	3	5	4		2	6	3	1	3-gon	mirror	54°44′, 70°32′, 54°44′		1	
										2	4-gon (enantio)	no symmetry	90°, 54°44′, 54°44′, 90°			2
3	2	2	3	5	3		3	6	3	3	4-gon	mirror	109°28′, 54°44′, 90° 54°44′		3	
3	2	2	2	4	2	1	2	5	3	1	3-gon	no symmetry	35°16′, 90°, 54°44′		1	
										1	3-gon	mirror	54°44′, 70°32′ 54°44′		1	
										1	4-gon (enantio)	no symmetry	90°, 45°, 54°44′, 54°44′		1	
3	2	2	3	5	3	2	1	6	3	1	3-gon	mirror	45°, 90°, 45°		1	
										1	4-gon (right)	no symmetry	90°, 45°, 54°44′, 54°44′		1	
										1	4-gon (left)	no symmetry	90°, 45°, 54°44′, 54°44′		1	
3	4	2	6	10		12		12	4	4	6-gon (regular)	3-fold	109°28′			4
4	2	2	4	6			8	8	4	4	4-gon (regular)	2-fold	70°32′	4		
4	2	2	4	6		8		8	4	4	4-gon	2-fold	60°, 90°, 60°, 90°		4	

Table 8.1
Continued

	Saddle Polyhedron	Symmetry Axes				Symmetry
		2-f	3-f	4-f	6-f	
14	fcc orthorhombic tetrahedron [8.38]	3				Orthorhombic
15	Universal tetrahedron [8.39]	3				Orthorhombic
16	Digonal tetrahedron [8.40]	1				Digonal
17	Truncated orthorhombic tetrahedron [8.41]	3				Orthorhombic
18	Digonal hemisaddle tetrahedron	1				Digonal
19	Wurtzite nodal tetrahedron		1			Trigonal
20	bcc orthorhombic tetrahedron [8.42]	3				Orthorhombic
21	Rectangular orthorhombic tetrahedron	3				Orthorhombic
22	Hemisaddle digonal disphenoid	1				Digonal
23	Double delta tetrahedron	1				Digonal
24	Trigonal pentahedron [8.43]		1			Trigonal
25	Wurtzite pentahedron [8.44]	3	1			Triangular
26	Digonal pentahedron [8.45]	1				Digonal

| Nodes | | | | | Branches | | | | Faces | | | | | Face Plane Directions | | |
| Primary | | Secondary | | | | | | | Number | | | | | | | |
Z	No.	Z	No.	Tot.	[100]	[110]	[111]	Tot.	Tot.	Ea.	Type	Symmetry	Included Angles	[100]	[110]	[111]
4	2	2	4	6	8			8	4	2	4-gon (regular)	2-fold	60°	2		
										2	4-gon	2-fold	60°, 90°, 60°, 90°		2	
4	2	2	4	6	4	4		8	4	2	4-gon (right)	2-fold	90°, 45°, 90°, 45°		2	
										2	4-gon (left)	2-fold	90°, 45°, 90°, 45°		2	
4	2	2	4	6	6		2	8	4	2	4-gon (right)	no symmetry	90°, 54°44', 54°44', 90°			2
										2	4-gon (left)	no symmetry	90°, 54°44', 54°44', 90°			2
3	4	2	8	12		14		14	4	2	6-gon	2-fold	90°,120°,120°, 90°,120°,120°		2	
										2	8-gon	2-fold	120°	2		
3	4	2	5	9	5	6		11	4	2	5-gon (plane)	mirror	90°, 90°, 180°,90°,90°		2	
										2	6-gon	mirror	90°		2	
3	4	2	6	10	9		3	12	4	1	6-gon (regular)	6-fold	120°			1
										3	6-gon	mirror	90°, 90°, 120°, 90°, 90°, 120°			3
4	2	2	4	6	4		4	8	4	4	4-gon	mirror	109°28',54°44', 90°, 54°44'		4	
4	2	2	6	8	6	4		10	4	4	5-gon	mirror	90°		4	
3	4	2	4	8	6	4		10	4	2	5-gon	mirror	90°		2	
										2	5-gon	mirror	90°, 90°, 180°, 90°,90°		2	
4	2	2	4	6	4	2	2	8	4	2	4-gon (right)	no symmetry	54°44', 54°44', 90°, 45°		2	
										2	4-gon (left)	no symmetry	54°44', 54°44', 90°, 45°		2	
4	3	2	6	9	6	6		12	5	1	6-gon (regular)	3-fold	60°			1
										1	6-gon (regular)	3-fold	90°			1
										3	4-gon	mirror	60°, 90°, 90°, 90°			3
3	6	2	6	12			15	15	5	2	6-gon (regular)	3-fold	109°28'			2
						3				3	6-gon	2-fold	109°28'		3	
4	1	3	4	5	2	4	2	8	5	1	4-gon	2-fold	69°, 90°, 60°, 90°		1	
										2	3-gon (right)	no symmetry	90°, 54°44', 35°16'		2	
										2	3-gon (left)	no symmetry	90°, 54°44', 35°16'		2	

Table 8.1
Continued

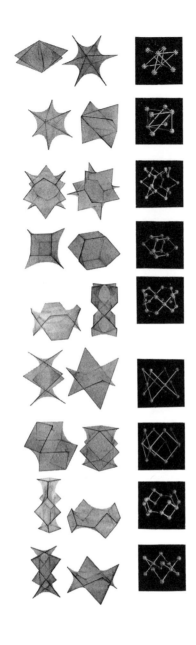

	Saddle Polyhedron	Symmetry Axes				Symmetry
		2-f	3-f	4-f	6-f	
27	Triangular hexahedron [8.46]	3	1			Triangular
28	Cubical saddle hexahedron [8.47]	3	1			Triangular
29	Saddle cube [8.48]	6	4	3		Cubic
30	Truncated tetragonal tetrahedron [8.49]	4		1		Tetragonal
31	Universal hexahedron [8.50]	4		1		Tetragonal
32	Augmented universal hexahedron [8.51]	4		1		Tetragonal
33	Bioctagonal hexahedron [8.52]	4		1		Tetragonal
34	Bidodecagonal hexahedron [8.53]	4		1		Tetragonal
35	Tetragonal saddle hexahedron [8.54]	4		1		Tetragonal
36	Fissioned tetragonal saddle hexahedron	4		1		Tetragonal
37	Tetragonal octagonal hexahedron	4		1		Tetragonal
38	Trigonal hexahedron		1			Trigonal
39	Trapezoidal trigonal hexahedron		1			Trigonal

| Nodes | | | | | | | | | Faces | | | | | | | |
| Primary | | Secondary | | | Branches | | | | Number | | | | | Face Plane Directions | | |
Z	No.	Z	No.	Tot.	[100]	[110]	[111]	Tot.	Tot.	Ea.	Type	Symmetry	Included Angles	[100]	[110]	[111]
6	2	2	6	8	6		6	12	6	3	4-gon (right)	2-fold	54°44′		3	
										3	4-gon (left)	2-fold	54°44′		3	
6	2	2	6	8	6	6		12	6	3	4-gon (right)	2-fold	90°, 45°, 90°, 45°		3	
										3	4-gon (left)	2-fold	90°, 45°, 90°, 45°		3	
3	8	2	12	20			24	24	6	6	8-gon	4-fold	70°32′,109°28′, 70°32′,109°28′, 70°32′,109°28′, 70°32′,109°28′	6		
3	8	2	4	12		16		16	6	2	square	4-fold	90°	2		
										4	6-gon	2-fold	90°, 120°, 120°, 90°, 120°, 120°		4	
4	4	2	16	20		24		24	6	2	12-gon	4-fold	90°, 120°, 120°, 90°, 120°, 120°, 90°, etc.	2		
										4	6-gon	2-fold	90°, 120°, 120°, 90°, 120°, 120°		4	
4	4	2	8	12		16		16	6	2	8-gon	4-fold	90°, 90°, 60°, 90°, etc.	2		
										4	4-gon	2-fold	60°, 90°, 60°, 90°		4	
4	4	2	8	12		16		16	6	2	8-gon	4-fold	60°, 90°, 60°, 90°	2		
										4	square	4-fold	90°	4		
3	8	2	8	16		20		20	6	2	12-gon	4-fold	90°, 120°, 120°, 90°, 120°, 120°, 90° etc.	2		
										4	square	4-fold	90°	4		
4	4	2	8	12			16	16	6	2	8-gon	4-fold	109°28′,70°32′, 109°28′,70°32′	2		
										4	4-gon (regular)	2-fold	70°32′	4		
3	8	2	8	16		4	16	20	6	2	12-gon	4-fold	70°32′,144°44′, 144°44′,70°32′, 144°44′, etc.	2		
										4	4-gon (regular)	2-fold	70°32′	4		
3	8	2	12	20		8	16	24	6	2	8-gon	4-fold	70°32′, 109°28′, etc.	2		
										4	8-gon	2-fold	90°, 144°44′, 109°28′, 144°44′, 90°, etc.		4	
3	2	2	9	14			18	18	6	3	6-gon	mirror	70°32′,109°28′		3	
4	3									3	6-gon (regular)	3-fold	109°28′	3		
6	2	2	6	8	6	3	3	12	6	3	4-gon (right)	no symmetry	54°44′,54°44′, 90°, 45°		3	
										3	4-gon (left)	no symmetry	54°44′,54°44′, 90°, 45°		3	

Table 8.1
Continued

| Saddle Polyhedron | Symmetry Axes | | | | Symmetry |
	2-f	3-f	4-f	6-f	
40 bcc octahedron [8.55]	6	4	3		Cubic
41 fcc saddle octahedron	4		1		Tetragonal
42 Tetragonal pentagonal octahedron	4		1		Tetragonal
43 Tetrahedral decahedron [8.56]	3	4			Tetrahedral
44 Saddle dodecahedron [8.57]	6	4	3		Cubic
45 Blunted saddle dodecahedron	6	4	3		Cubic
46 Truncated tetrahedral decahedron [8.58]	3	4			Tetrahedral
47 bcc saddle cuboctahedron [8.59]	6	4	3		Cubic
48 Fissioned bcc saddle cuboctahedron	6	4	3		Cubic
49 fcc saddle cuboctahedron [8.60]	6	4	3		Cubic
50 Truncated fcc saddle cuboctahedron [8.61]	6	4	3		Cubic
51 Saddle cube dodecahedron [8.62]	6	4	3		Cubic
52 Truncated saddle dodecahedron [8.63]	6	4	3		Cubic
53 Universal cuboctadodecahedron [8.64]	6	4	3		Cubic

| Nodes | | | | | Branches | | | | Faces | | | | | Face Plane Directions | | |
| Primary | | Secondary | | | | | | | Number | | | | | | | |
Z	No.	Z	No.	Tot.	[100]	[110]	[111]	Tot.	Tot.	Ea.	Type	Symmetry	Included Angles	[100]	[110]	[111]
4	6	2	12	18	24			24	8	8	6-gon (regular)	3-fold	90°			8
4	6	2	12	18	8	16		24	8	8	6-gon	mirror	90°		8	
4	6	2	8	14	12	8		20	8	8	5-gon	mirror	90°		8	
6	4	2	12	16		24		24	10	4	6-gon (regular)	3-fold	60°			4
										6	4-gon (regular)	2-fold	60°	6		
4	6	3	8	14		24		24	12	12	4-gon	2-fold	60°, 90°, 60°, 90°		12	
4 3	6 8	2	24	38		24	24	48	12	12	8-gon	2-fold	90°,144°44', 109°28', 144°44', 90°, etc.		12	
3	24	2	24	48		60		60	14	4	6-gon (regular)	6-fold	120°			4
										4	12-gon	3-fold	120°			4
										6	8-gon	2-fold	120°	6		
4	12	2	24	36			48	48	14	6	8-gon	4-fold	109°28', 70°32'	6		
										8	6-gon (regular)	3-fold	109°28'			8
3	24	2	48	72		36	48	84	14	6	12-gon	4-fold	144°44',70°32', 144°44',144°44', 70°32',144°44', 144°44', etc.	6		
										8	12-gon	3-fold	144°44'			8
4	12	2	24	36		48		48	14	6	8-gon	4-fold	60°, 90°, etc.	6		
										8	6-gon (regular)	3-fold	60°			8
3	24	2	48	72		84		84	14	6	12-gon	4-fold	90°,120°,120°, 90°,120°,120°, etc.	6		
										8	12-gon	3-fold	120°			8
6	8	2	24	32		48		48	18	6	8-gon	4-fold	60°,90°,60°, 90°, etc.	6		
										12	4-gon	2-fold	60°,90°,60°, 90°		12	
4	6	3	24	30		48		48	20	8	triangle	3-fold	60°			8
										12	6-gon	2-fold	90°,120°,120°, 90°		12	
3	48	2	24	72		96		96	26	6	12-gon	4-fold	120°,90°,120°, 120°,90° etc.	6		
										8	hexagon (regular)	6-fold	120°			8
										12	6-gon	2-fold	90°,120°,120°, 90°,120°,120°		12	

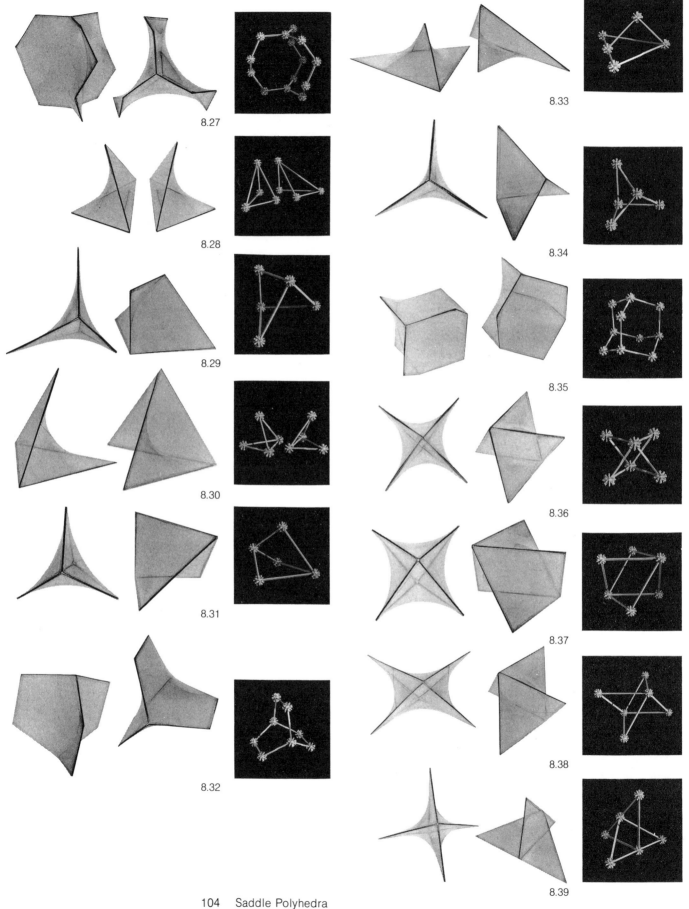

8.27–8.64 Saddle polyhedra from Table 8.1.

8.27

8.28

8.29

8.30

8.31

8.32

8.33

8.34

8.35

8.36

8.37

8.38

8.39

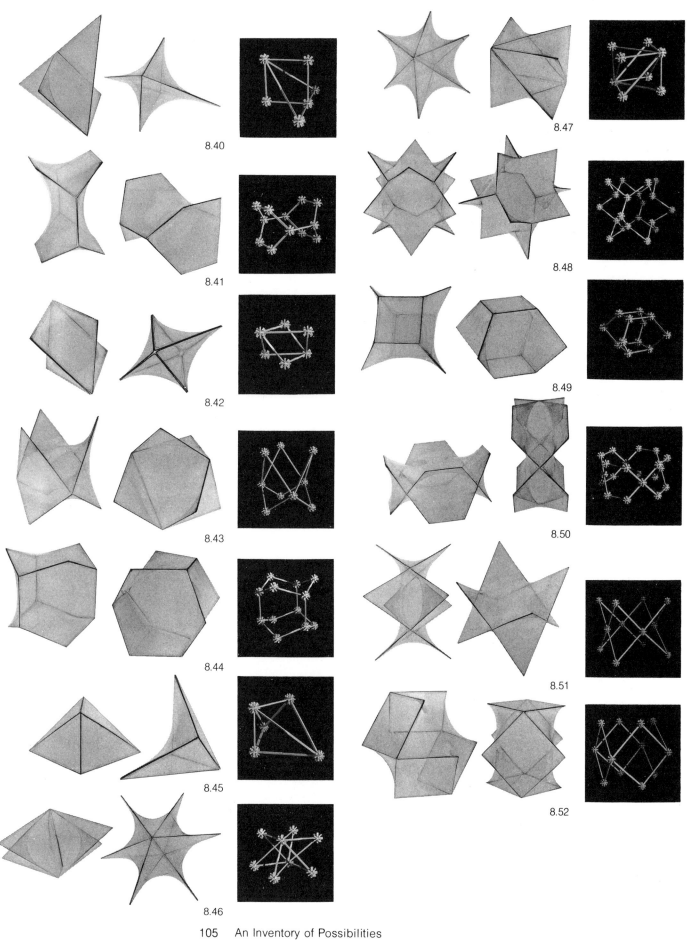

8.40

8.41

8.42

8.43

8.44

8.45

8.46

8.47

8.48

8.49

8.50

8.51

8.52

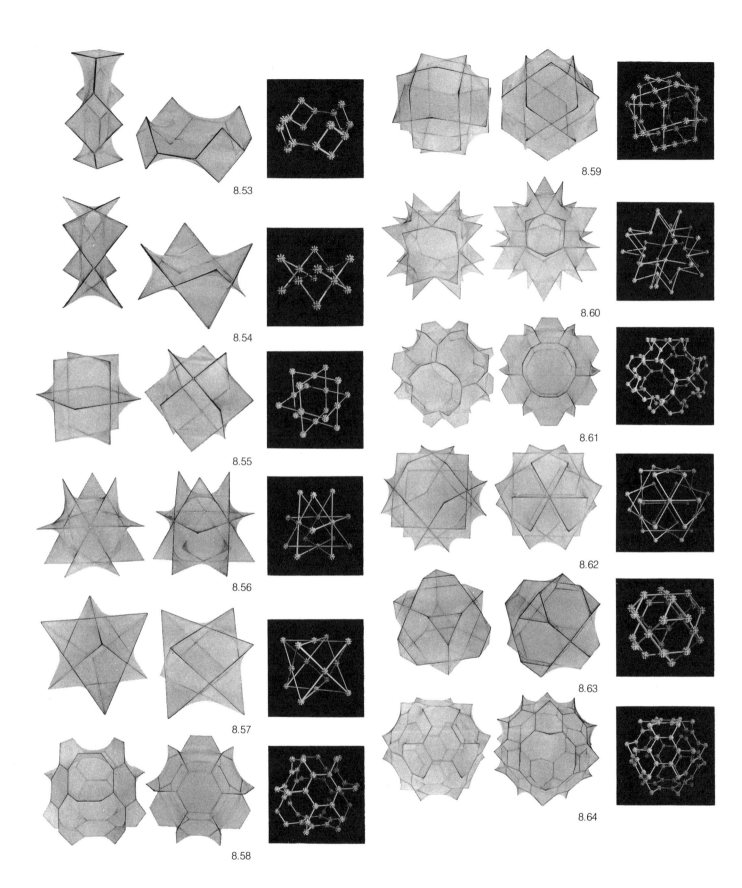

8.53

8.54

8.55

8.56

8.57

8.58

8.59

8.60

8.61

8.62

8.63

8.64

Unary Space Fillers and Uniform Networks

Of the 42 space filling systems that are listed in Table 8.2, we note that 14 are unary space filling saddle polyhedra—which brings the total of all unary space filling polyhedra we have as yet inventoried (including plane faced polyhedra) up to 35. We have seen that there are an infinite number of space filling polyhedra; the significance, therefore, of newly discovered systems is a function of the ordering principles from which they are derived. The 14 unary space filling saddle polyhedra are not all of equal stature. As I have already suggested, the bcc tetrahedron, bcc nodal octahedron, the diamond tetrahedron, and the tetrahedral decahedron are the most important of these unary systems. Including these four, there are 8 unary systems which define uniform networks among the 14 unary saddle polyhedral space filling systems. The six remaining space filling saddle polyhedra define semiuniform networks. The total number of unary space filling saddle and flat polyhedra which define uniform nets is 13: the eight saddle polyhedra plus the cube, truncated octahedron, triangular prism, hexagonal prism and tetragonal disphenoid.

Perhaps far more significant a concept than that of unary space filling is that of the uniform net. Our inventory shows a total of 17 uniform nets formed by the saddle polyhedra. In addition to the eight formed by unary systems, eight are formed as binary systems and one as a ternary system. If we add to that the fourteen cubic space filling systems, all of which are uniform nets, plus the nine uniform nets from the hexagonal class, we have a grand total of 40 uniform nets. If we add the total of 42 saddle polyhedral space filling systems (uniform and semiuniform) to all those systems previously inventoried, we find a total of 92 different space filling systems. Eighty-five of these systems may be accounted for by the Universal Node system (with topological license permitted in the hexagonal system). See Chapter 7, pp. 74–84.

Diverse Networks Share Common Point Lattices

Now that we have inventoried a vast collection of orderly spatial networks it should be useful to summarize which networks share common point lattices. As the reader should by now expect, each of the three most symmetrical point lattices—simple cubic (p), bcc, and fcc—can be alternatively interlinked with branches to form vastly different networks.

As mentioned in Chapter 6 and as shown in [8.20], all the nodes of the universal network fall at the sites of a simple cubic lattice. This fact reveals the importance and usefulness of considering spatial organization in terms of networks rather than solely in terms of lattice points. The position of points in space in no way predicts the interlinkages between points. It is clear that a given point lattice (or point lattice subset) may be the basis of many different uniform and semiuniform networks. It is startling to realize that the simple cubic lattice usually identified with the 6-connected cubical network gives rise to a structure of such apparent complexity as the universal network. Another example in our inventory with its nodes positioned at the sites of the simple cubic lattice is the 18 / 6-connected net found with space filling of cubical saddle hexahedra and universal tetrahedra. ([8.86], No. 27, Table 8.2.)

The bcc lattice gives rise to a host of uniform and semiuniform networks. There are four uniform networks: the 14-connected tetragonal disphenoid net; the 8-connected bcc tetrahedron net ([8.67], No. 3, Table 8.2); the 10-connected triangular hexahedron net ([8.70], No. 6, Table 8.2); and the 14-connected digonal trihedron net ([8.72], Table 8.2). Among the space filling systems dual to the regular and semiregular polyhedra space filling systems (Table 5.1), there are three semiuniform networks with their nodes positioned on the bcc lattice, including space filling of rhombic hexahedra [5.11b] (4 / 8-connected); square pyramid [5.11c], tetragonal octahedron [5.11d] and rhombic pyramid [5.11p] (all on the same 8/14-connected net); and, finally the right triangular pyramid [5.11m] (24/14/8-connected).

The fcc lattice can be formed by the 12-connected tetrahedra/octahedra space filling system, the 6-connected tetrahedral decahedron system ([8.69], No. 5, Table 8.2), and the 8-connected fcc tetragonal tetrahedron/fcc orthorhombic tetrahedron system ([8.76], No. 16, Table 8.2), all of which are uniform networks.

The aforementioned is not an exhaustive list of networks; in particular, many more semiuniform cases may be given. It is interesting to note that of the alternative uniform systems, each lattice (p, bcc, fcc) accounts for a single plane-faced polyhedral system, i.e., packings of cubes (p), tetragonal disphenoids (bcc), or tetrahedra and octahedra (fcc). The remaining uniform networks are systems composed of saddle polyhedra of various kinds, again emphasizing the morphological significance of the saddle polyhedra. We will come to appreciate the saddle polyhedra even more in the next chapter as we go on to describe a special class of systems derived from the special properties of polyhedra bounded by minimal surfaces.

Table 8.2
Space Filling
with Saddle
Polyhedra

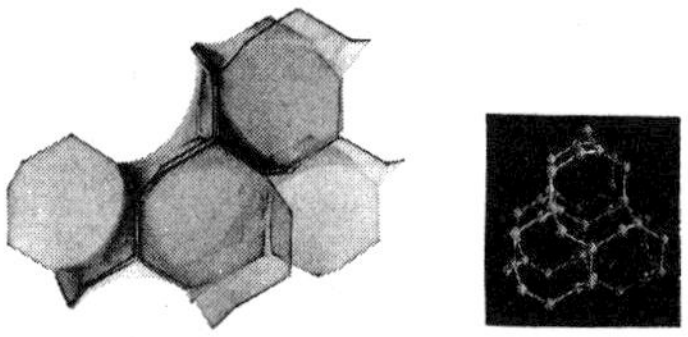

8.65

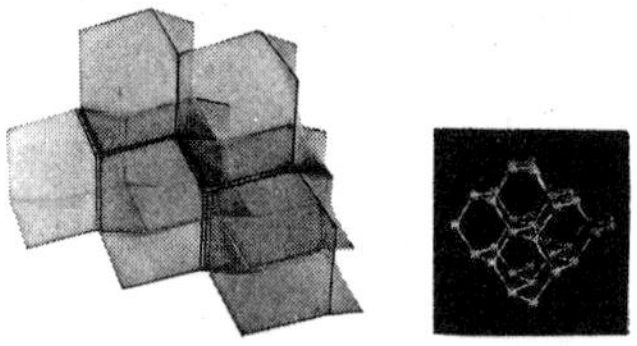

8.66

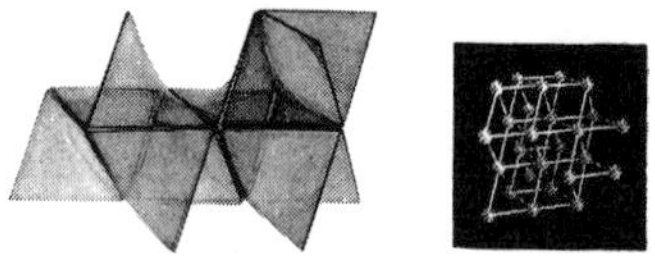

8.67

8.68

8.69

8.70

8.71

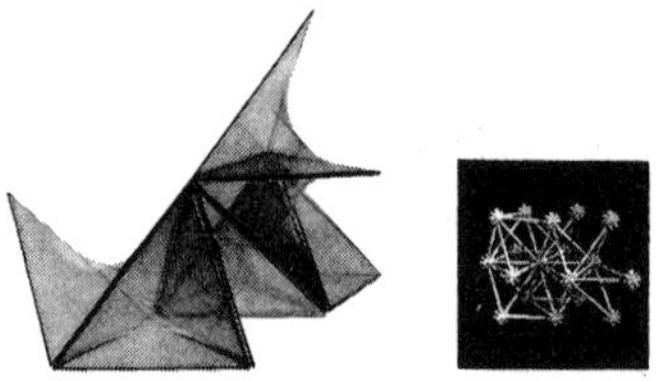

8.72

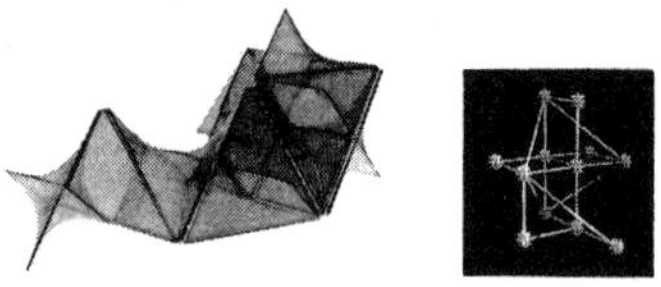

8.73

In this table are listed 42 space filling combinations that are possible with the polyhedra given in Table 8.1. For each system in Table 8.2, there is given the space filling ratio, the space filling type, the net type, the nodal coordination, branch directions, and the angles at which the branches meet the nodes. In the case of semiuniform nets, entries differ for each different node. Note that the nodal polyhedra listed in the last column for each system are all in the first column as well. It is difficult, if not impossible, to separate the saddle polyhedra and their nets into the categories that are available for the plane-faced regular and semiregular polyhedra. This is true at least in the sense that the nodal polyhedra of the space filling systems which are composed of regular and semiregular polyhedra are clearly of a separate category if for no other reason than that they are not bounded by regular faces. No such clear distinction exists for the saddle polyhedra.

Models of 32 of the 48 systems listed in Table 8.2 are shown in [8.65]–[8.96] following the table.

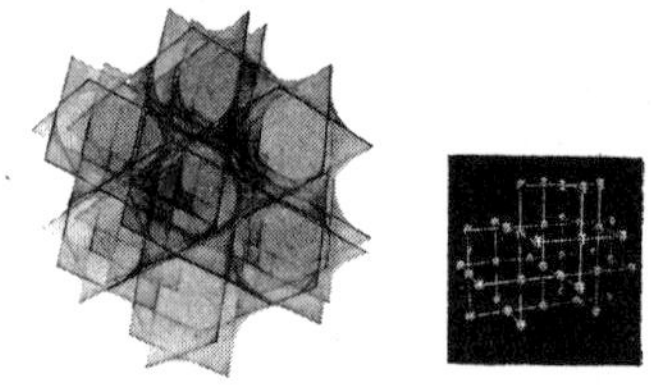

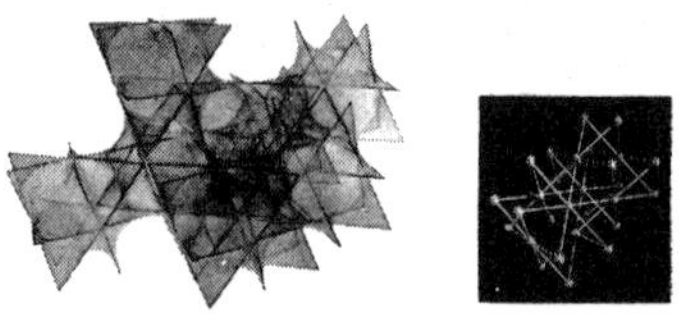

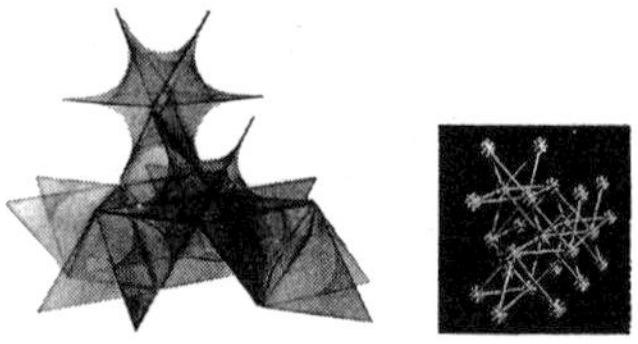

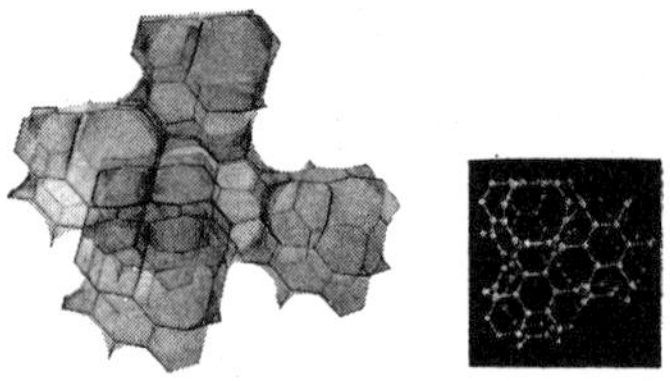

	Space Filling System	Entry in Table 8.1	Space Filling Ratio	Net Type	Z
1	Decatrihedron (right) [8.65]	1		uniform	3
2	Diamond tetrahedron [8.66]	11		uniform	4
3	bcc tetrahedron [8.67]	12		uniform	8
4	bcc octahedron [8.68]	40		uniform	4
5	Tetrahedral decahedron [8.69]	43		uniform	6
6	Triangular hexahedron [8.70]	27		uniform	10
7	Truncated tetrahedral decahedron [8.71]	46		uniform	3
8	Digonal trihedron (enantiomorphic) [8.72]	4		uniform	14
9	Digonal tetrahedron [8.73]	16		semiuniform	6
					14
10	Trigonal hexahedron	38		semiuniform	3
					5
11	fcc saddle octahedron	41		semiuniform	4
					4
12	Digonal hemisaddle tetrahedron	18		semiuniform	6
					4

Branch Directions			Branch Angles at Node						Nodal Polyhedra
[100]	[110]	[111]	[100]–[100]	[110]–[110]	[111]–[111]	[100]–[110]	[110]–[111]	[100]–[111]	
	3			120°					1 Decatrihedron (left) (self-dual with change in handedness)
	4				109°28′				2 Diamond tetrahedron (self-dual)
	8				70°32′				4 bcc octahedron
4			90°						3 bcc tetrahedron
	6			60°					6 Triangular hexahedron
6	4						54°44′		5 Tetrahedral decahedron
	3			120°					8 Digonal trihedron (enantiomorphic)
6	8		90°		70°32′		54°44′		7 Truncated tetrahedral decahedron
6			90°						15 Tetrahedral saddle hexahedron and bcc saddle cuboctahedron
6	8		90°		70°32′		54°44′		20 bioctagonal hexahedron and fcc saddle cuboctahedron
		3			109°28′				18 Trigonal trihedron
		5			109°28′, 70°32′				Trigonal pentahedron
	4			90°					16 fcc tetragonal tetrahedron
2	2					90°			fcc orthorhombic tetrahedron
2	4			90°		90°			17 Truncated tetragonal tetrahedron
2	2					90°			Truncated orthorhombic tetrahedron

Table 8.2
Continued

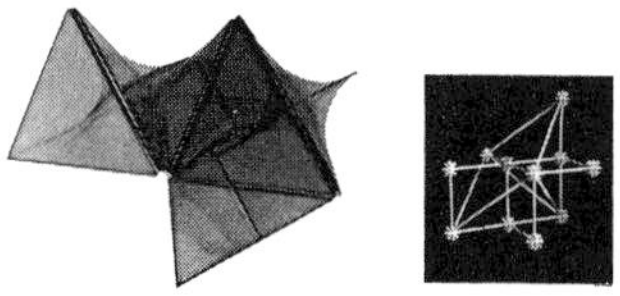

8.74

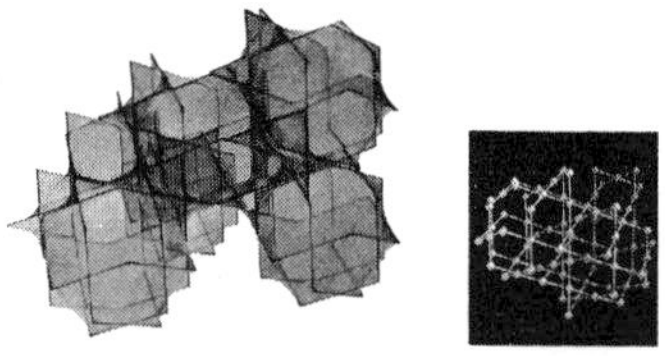

8.75

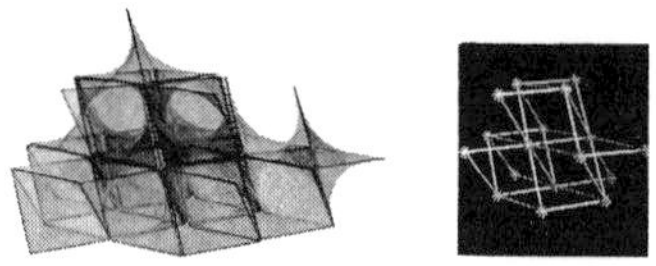

8.76

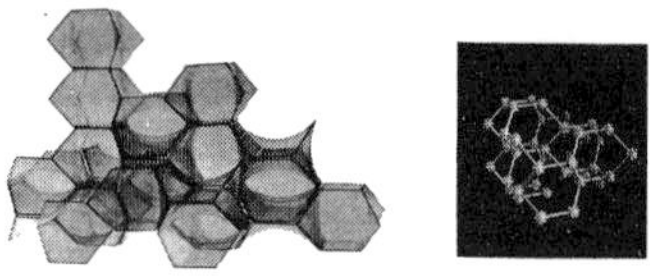

8.77

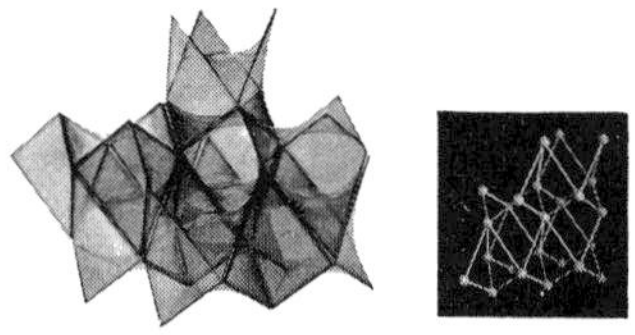

8.78

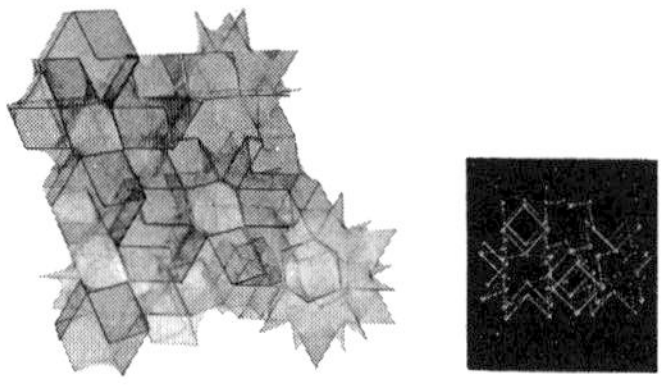

8.79

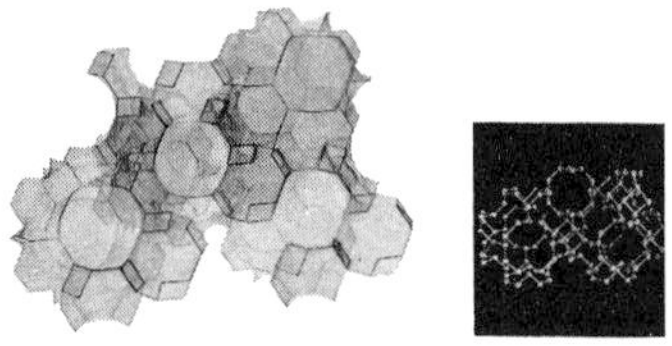

8.80

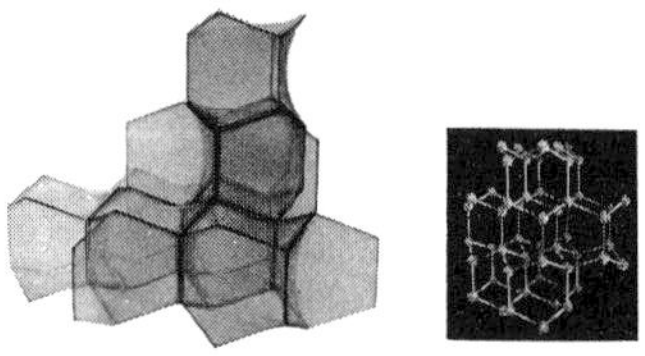

8.81

Space Filling System	Entry in Table 8.1	Space Filling Ratio	Net Type	Z
13 Delta trihedron [8.74]	7		semiuniform	14
				6
14 Wurtzite nodal tetrahedron	19		semiuniform	3
				5
15 bcc saddle cuboctahedron	47	1	uniform	4
Tetragonal saddle hexahedron [8.75]	35	3		
16 fcc tetragonal tetrahedron	13	1	uniform	8
fcc orthorhombic tetrahedron [8.76]	14	1		
17 Truncated tetragonal tetrahedron	30	1	uniform	4
Truncated orthorhombic tetrahedron [8.77]	17	1		
18 Trigonal trihedron	5	1	uniform	6
Trigonal pentahedron [8.78]	24	1		
19 Fissioned bcc saddle cuboctahedron	48	1	uniform	3
Fissioned tetragonal saddle hexahedron	36	3		
20 fcc saddle cuboctahedron	49	1	uniform	4
Bioctagonal hexahedron [8.79]	33	3		
21 Truncated fcc saddle cuboctahedron	50	1	uniform	3
Bidodecagonal hexahedron [8.80]	34	3		
22 Wurtzite trihedron	6	1	uniform	4
Wurtzite pentahedron [8.81]	25	1		

Branch Directions			Branch Angles at Node						Nodal Polyhedra
[100]	[110]	[111]	[100]–[100]	[110]–[110]	[111]–[111]	[100]–[110]	[110]–[111]	[100]–[111]	
6		8	90°		70°32′			54°44′	19 Fissioned bcc saddle cuboctahedron, and fissioned tetragonal saddle hexahedron
6			90°						21 Truncated fcc saddle cuboctahedron, and bidodecagonal hexahedron
	3			120°					22 Wurtzite trihedron
	3	2		120°			90°		Wurtzite pentahedron
		4			70°32′				9 Digonal tetrahedron
	8			60°,90°					11 fcc saddle octahedron
	4			90°, 120°					12 Digonal hemisaddle tetrahedron
3	3		90°	60°		90°			10 Trigonal hexahedron
	1	2			70°32′		144°44′		13 Delta trihedron
	4			60°, 90°					9 Digonal tetrahedron
	3			120°, 90°, 120°					13 Delta trihedron
		4			109°28′				14 Wurtzite nodal tetrahedron

Table 8.2
Continued

8.82

8.83

8.84

8.85

8.86

8.87

8.88

Space Filling System	Entry in Table 8.1	Space Filling Ratio	Net Type	Z
23 fcc tetragonal tetrahedron	13	3	semiuniform	4
Saddle dodecahedron [8.82]	44	1		12
24 Universal tetrahedron	15	1	semiuniform	6
Universal trihedron (enantiomorphic) [8.83]	2	4		26
25 Universal cuboctadodecahedron	53	1	semiuniform	3
Universal hexahedron [8.84]	31	3		4
26 Saddle cube dodecahedron	51	1	semiuniform	6
Augmented universal hexahedron [8.85]	32	3		4
27 Cubical saddle hexahedron	28	2	semiuniform	18
Universal tetrahedron [8.86]	15	3		6
28 bcc trihedron	8	4	semiuniform	14
bcc orthorhombic tetrahedron [8.87]	20	3		6
				4
29 fcc tetragonal tetrahedron	13	1	semiuniform	14
Digonal pentahedron [8.88]	26	4		20
				6
30 Rectangular orthorhombic tetrahedron	21	2	semiuniform	6
Tetragonal pentagonal octahedron	42	1		6
				4
31 Rectangular orthorhombic tetrahedron	21	1	semiuniform	6
Hemisaddle digonal disphenoid	22	2		6
				6
32 Rectangular trihedron	9	2	semiuniform	26
Double rectangular trihedron	10	1		14
				14
				4
33 Double delta tetrahedron	23	3	semiuniform	14
Trapezoidal trigonal hexahedron	39	2		18
				10
				4

[100]	[110]	[111]	[100]–[100]	[110]–[110]	[111]–[111]	[100]–[110]	[110]–[111]	[100]–[111]	Nodal Polyhedra
	4			90°					23 Saddle dodecahedron
	12			60°					fcc tetragonal tetrahedron (self-dual)
2	4			90°		90°			25 Universal hexahedron
6	12	8				45°	35°16′	54°44′	Universal cuboctadodecahedron
	3			120°					24 Universal trihedron
	4			90°					Universal tetrahedron
	6			60°					27 Cubical saddle hexahedron
	4			90°					Universal tetrahedron
6	12			60°		45°			26 Saddle cube dodecahedron
2	4			90°		90°			Augmented universal hexahedron
6		8	90°		70°32′			54°44′	35 bcc saddle cuboctahedron
6			90°						Saddle cube
		4			109°28′				Diamond tetrahedron
6		8	90°		70°32′			54°44′	36 Cuboctahedron
	12	8		60°			35°16′		Truncated saddle dodecahedron
2	4			90°		90°			Truncated tetragonal tetrahedron
6			90°						37 Bioctagonal hexahedron
2	4			90°		90°			Augmented universal hexahedron
	4			90°					fcc tetragonal tetrahedron
6			90°						38 Bidodecagonal hexahedron
2	4			90°		90°			Universal hexahedron
2	4			90°		90°			Truncated tetragonal tetrahedron
6	12	8				45°	35°16′	54°44′	41 Universal cuboctadodecahedron
6		8	90°		70°32′			54°44′	Truncated fcc saddle cuboctahedron
6		8	90°		70°32′			54°44′	Truncated tetrahedral decahedron
2	2					90°			Truncated orthorhombic tetrahedron
6		8	90°		70°32′			54°44′	42 fcc saddle cuboctahedron
6	12			60°		45°			Saddle cube dodecahedron
6		4						54°44′	Tetrahedral decahedron
2	2					90°			fcc orthorhombic tetrahedron

Table 8.2
Continued

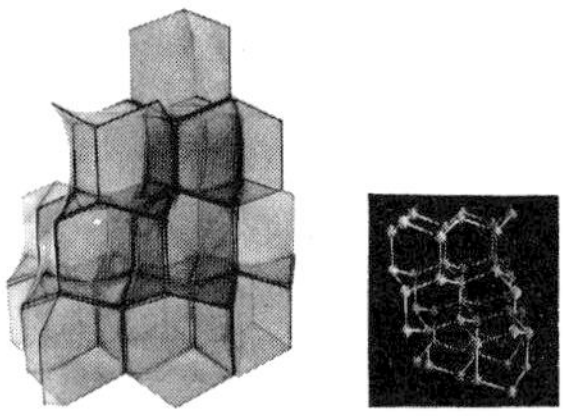

8.89

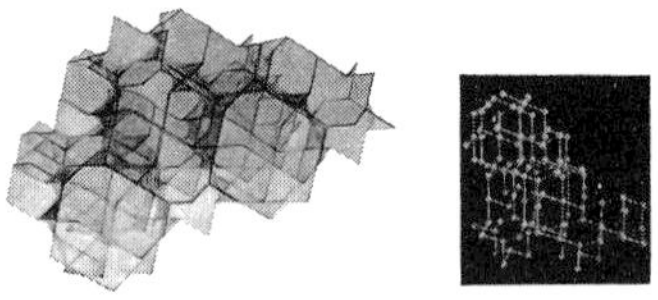

8.90

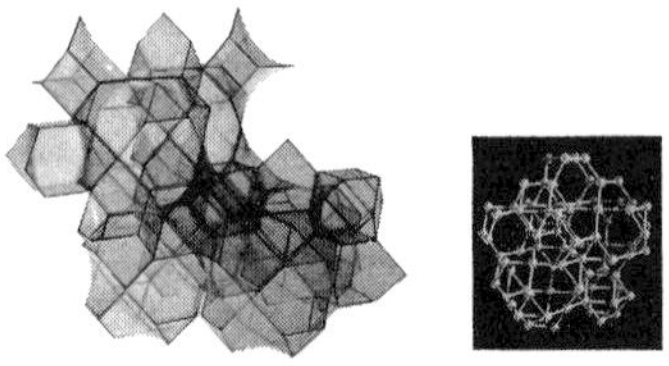

8.91

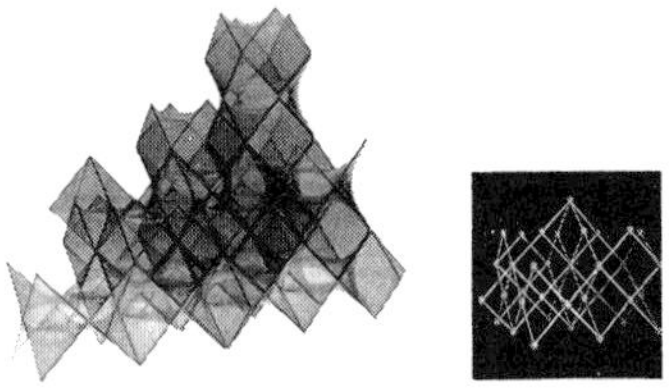

8.92

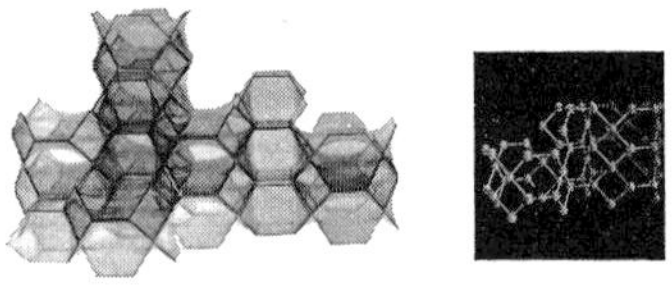

8.93

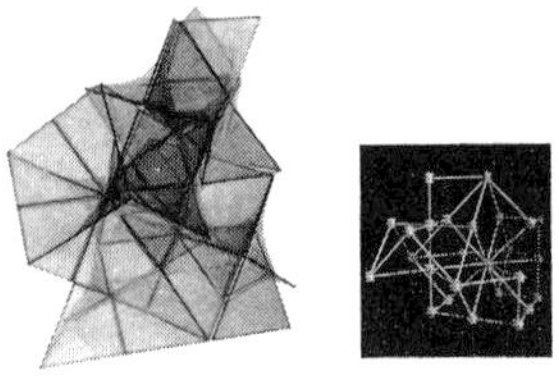

8.94

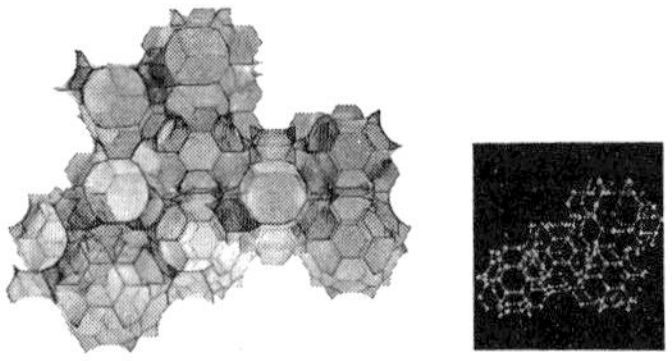

8.95

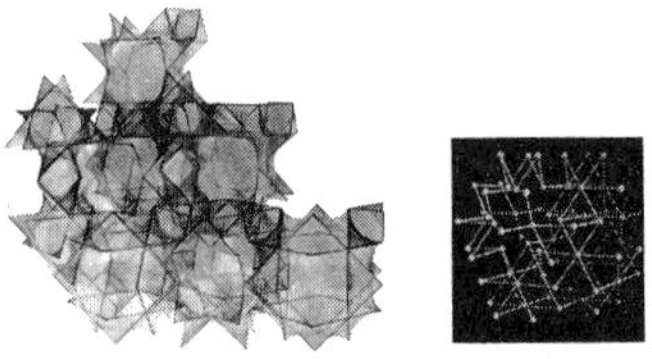

8.96

	Space Filling System	Entry in Table 8.1	Space Filling Ratio	Net Type	Z
34	Wurtzite trihedron	6	1	uniform	
	Wurtzite pentahedron	25	1		4
	Diamond tetrahedron [8.89]	11	2		
35	bcc saddle cuboctahedron	47	1	semiuniform	3
	Saddle cube	29	1		4
	Diamond tetrahedron	11	2		
36	Truncated saddle dodecahedron	52	1	semiuniform	4
	Truncated tetragonal tetrahedron	30	3		5
	Cuboctahedron [8.91]		1		
37	Bioctagonal hexahedron	33	1	semiuniform	4
	Augmented universal hexahedron	32	1		8
	fcc tetragonal tetrahedron [8.92]	13	1		
38	Universal hexahedron	31	1	semiuniform	4
	Bidodecagonal hexahedron	34	1		4
	Truncated tetragonal tetrahedron [8.93]	30	1		
39	fcc tetragonal tetrahedron	13	3	semiuniform	6
	Trigonal trihedron	5	8		6
	Trirectangular trihedron [8.94]	3	12		12
40	Saddle cube	29	1	semiuniform	3
	Tetragonal octagonal hexahedron	37	3		3
	Blunted saddle dodecahedron	45	1		4
41	Universal cuboctadodecahedron	53	1	semiuniform	3
	Truncated tetrahedral decahedron	46	2		3
	Truncated fcc saddle cuboctahedron	50	1		
	Truncated orthorhombic tetrahedron [8.95]	17	6		
42	fcc saddle cuboctahedron	49	1	semiuniform	4
	Saddle cube dodecahedron	51	1		6
	Tetrahedral decahedron	43	2		
	fcc orthorhombic tetrahedron [8.96]	14	6		

Branch Directions			Branch Angles at Node						
[100]	[110]	[111]	[100]–[100]	[110]–[110]	[111]–[111]	[100]–[110]	[110]–[111]	[100]–[111]	Nodal Polyhedra
									Carborundum tetrahedron
		4			109°28′				Diamond tetrahedron
		3			109°28′				28 bcc trihedron
		4			70°32′, 109°28′				bcc orthorhombic tetrahedron
	4				90°				29 fcc tetragonal tetrahedron
	5				60°, 90°, 120°				Digonal pentahedron
	4				90°				30 Rectangular orthorhombic tetrahedron
	8				60°, 90°				Tetragonal pentagonal octahedron
	4			90°, 120°					31 Hemisaddle digonal disphenoid
	4			90°					Rectangular orthorhombic tetrahedron
	6		90°						40 Saddle cube
2	4			90°		90°			Tetragonal octagonal hexahedron
	12			60°					Blunted saddle dodecahedron
		3			109°28′				39 Trigonal trihedron
	1	2			70°32′		144°44′		Trirectangular trihedron
	4			90°					fcc tetragonal tetrahedron
	3				120°				32 Rectangular trihedron
	3				90°, 120°				Double rectangular trihedron
	4				60°, 90°				33 Double delta tetrahedron
	6				60°				Trapezoidal trigonal hexahedron

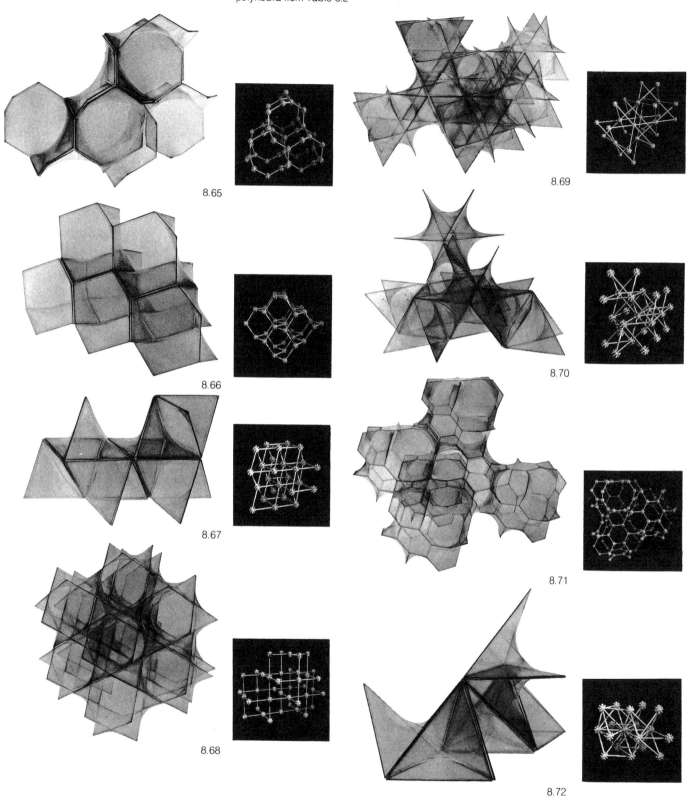

8.65–8.96 Space filling combinations of saddle
polyhedra from Table 8.2

8.65

8.66

8.67

8.68

8.69

8.70

8.71

8.72

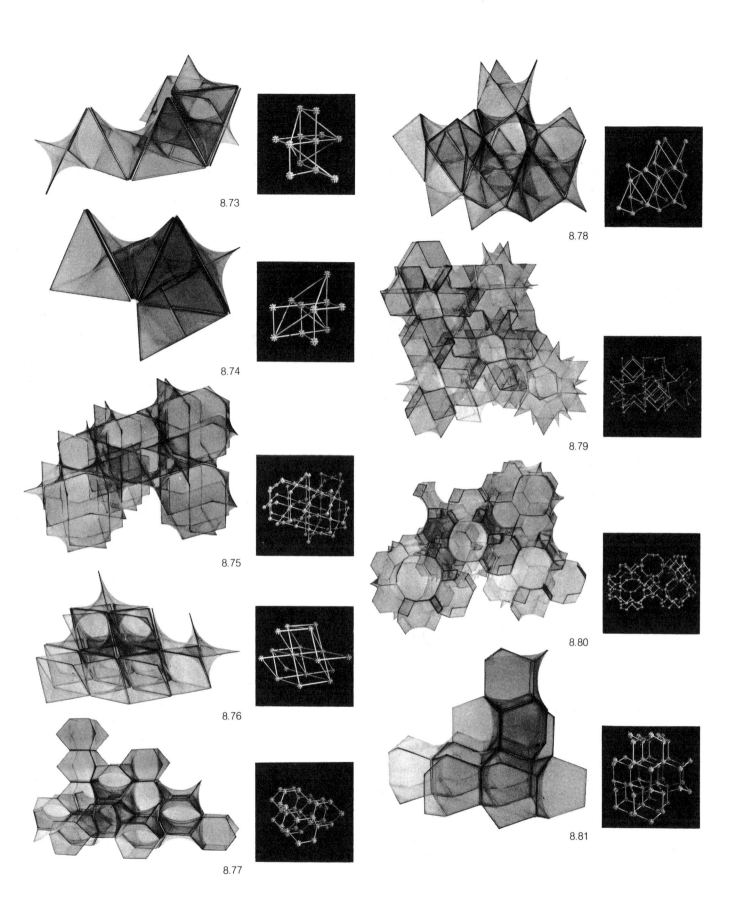

8.73

8.74

8.75

8.76

8.77

8.78

8.79

8.80

8.81

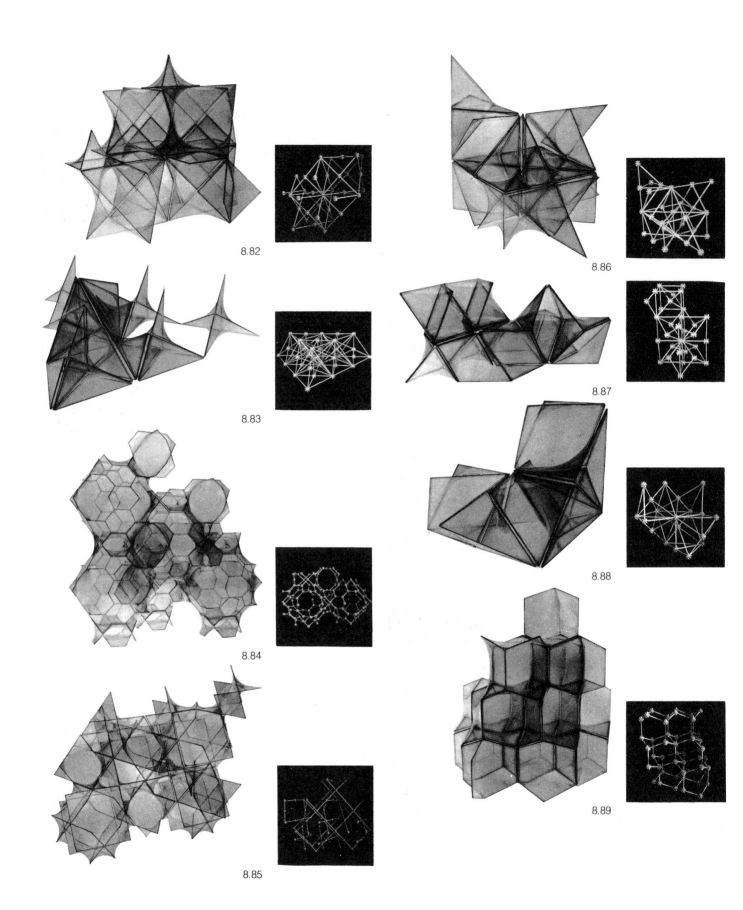

8.82

8.86

8.83

8.87

8.84

8.88

8.85

8.89

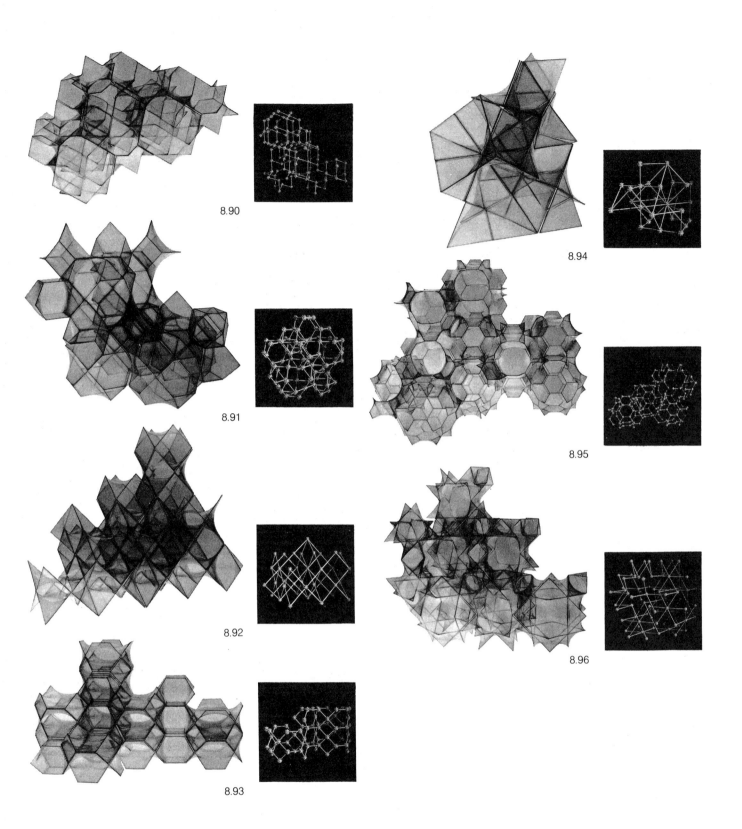

8.90

8.94

8.91

8.95

8.92

8.96

8.93

The Universal Network as Interactive Process

We have now reached the point in our study of morphology where we may consider any specific structure to be the expression of a moment in the transition from one state of a system to another. To go even further—all *structures* are *processes*. The morphological function of the partitioning of three-dimensional networks into volumetric regions by means of plane or saddle faces is the explication of process. Partitioning not only contributes to identification and differentiation, but also echoes and reflects the symmetries that govern the structural options of three-dimensional space.

Self-Replication of the Universal Network

We saw that the universal network consisted of interstitial domains—saddle polyhedra—which clarified its morphology. Its pattern of repetition in space included two kinds of nodes— 6-connected and 26-connected. We earlier observed that the 6-connected node is merely a subset of the 26 spokes of the Universal Node connector. When the unfilled spokes of the 6-connected subset of the universal node are filled with branches so that all of the original nodes are 26-connected, branches cross, forming new subset nodes. It is never possible to form a network in which all nodes are 26-connected. New subsets continue to appear, ad infinitum, as branches inevitably cross. Suddenly it becomes clear that the universal network is *inherently self-replicating*.

The universal network replicates itself in two steps. Each time it reappears, its branches are half as long as in the parent stage. They always bisect each other as they cross. In the first step when the 6-connected subset nodes are filled with 26 branches, two new nodal subsets are formed: 8-connected and 4-connected. In the second phase, 18 more branches are added to the 8-connected subset node making it 26-connected. This does not alter the nodes that are already 26-connected but transforms the 26-8-4 network into the universal network as the 6-connected nodes are once again formed.

This two-step process can be continued indefinitely. The fact that there must always be some nodes which have fewer than 26 branches implies that it is impossible to conceive a structure that is final; it is always in a state of transition. The universal network is a dynamic system that perpetuates inherent growth—it is never "finished." The character of its growth implies a process which is simultaneously additive and subtractive. By *adding* more branches to the *growth implying* unfilled nodes, the overall structure is subdivided into progressively smaller submodules—a synthesis wholly consistent with the holism underpinning this work.

Process and Hierarchy

If the universal network is considered as a three-dimensional graph, its remarkable properties of integration, self-replication, and spatial growth make it a tantalizing model of hierarchical process. It opens up new possibilities for the visualization of hierarchical processes in which *levels* do not imply *caste*. Rather, process is seen as an *integration* of levels by means of a three-dimensionally coordinated array of concrete elements which are determined by and which determine or control each other. Such a synthesis can be expressed as a collection of interrelated priorities which are constantly subject to reciprocation. Functional priorities in terms of sequences, not caste, are thus established.

The conceptual hierarchy which is represented by the two-dimensionality and 3-connected nodes of the usual *tree graph* is misleading in its influence on our visualizations of relationships. Its very form implies caste. It is based upon a two-dimensional logic of limited options, in which the subdivisions are always the slaves of the apices. When we move into the development of new three-dimensional *integrative graphs,* unanticipated conceptual relationships can be visualized that are the basis of an entirely new emergent perception of the interrelationship of the parts to the whole—a new mind set in which reciprocal and complementary processes are accepted as the norm. Cause becomes effect and effect becomes cause.

The Cube Reconsidered

At the beginning of this book, I questioned the structural and morphological significance of the cube and the dominance of its use. The Universal Node system, and particularly the universal network with its simple cube lattice, reveals that when the cube is described in terms of an integrative morphological system it can be viewed in a new perspective unanticipated by those laboring under a cubical spatial bias. The cube itself is only one of many possible structures, and as the basis of a spatial sensibility is extremely limiting. However, in terms of the holism of the universal network, it emerges as both the basis of and the result of an integrative process. It can be both cause and effect. With such a strategy, expanded possibilities result from an interaction of the whole and the parts—a synthesis of holism and atomism.

9

Continuous Surfaces and Labyrinths

Continuous Surfaces Derived from Space Filling Saddle Polyhedra

At this point in our exploration we see clearly the morphological significance of the saddle polyhedra, particularly in their relation to periodic structures. The structural significance has only been touched upon and is treated in more detail in Chapter 10. There is another class of geometric systems that may be derived from space filling saddle polyhedra that is important in its own right. This class takes the form of periodic continuous surfaces. These surfaces are derived from space filling saddle polyhedra by removing certain symmetrically disposed faces such that the remaining faces of the space filling array form continuous surfaces; these surfaces usually divide the whole of space into two infinite regions. Such continuous surfaces are smooth throughout. Even at the intersection of one face to another, there exists no abrupt change in direction of the surface. The dihedral angles are generally 180° or something very close to that.*

*In a strict sense, for figures made up of periodic associations of saddle polygons, all dihedral angles would have to be precisely 180° in order for the overall surface to be smooth and continuous. For many such systems we will discuss, this is true. However, there are others in which the dihedral angle is only approximately 180°. I shall here use the term "continuous surface" in a descriptive rather than in a rigorous sense, and will consider spatial labyrinths of polygons to be composed of continuous surfaces even when dihedral angles are only approximately 180°.

Dividing Space into Two Congruent Regions

An important class of continuous surfaces is made up of the so-called infinite periodic minimal surfaces.* These are formed by the periodic repetition of saddle polygons by rotating each polygon 180° about its edges. There are two major forms in this class in which the faces do not intersect. They both form *tunnel* systems in which space is divided into a three-dimensional labyrinth of two congruent infinite regions. Such infinite periodic minimal surfaces are like the sphere insofar as (1) their surfaces are smooth everywhere and (2) they divide space into two exclusive regions. However, whereas for the sphere we have a finite inner and an infinite outer region each bounded by a wall (the surface of the sphere) that is for the one region convex and for the other concave, here the two regions are both infinite and bounded by a wall of the same overall curvature, regardless of from which of the two regions it is viewed.

*Schoen notes that, although the saddle polyhedron concept was not known, such infinite periodic minimal surfaces were known to Schwarz and to Schwarz's student Neovius in the nineteenth century (Schoen 1968, 1970; Neovius 1883; Schwarz, 1890).

These two major forms of the periodic minimal surface can be derived from the space filling of the tetrahedral decahedron. In an infinite space filling array, if the saddle hexagons are omitted, the saddle quadrilaterals remain and form a smooth continuous two-sided surface. This surface defines two *four-tunnel* congruent regions of space corresponding to the diamond network. That is, the tunnels are directed along the branches of the diamond net; and the two regions illustrate the self-duality of the diamond net. Two views of a model of this structure are shown in [9.1].

If in the same space filling array of tetrahedral decahedra, the quadrilateral faces are omitted instead of the hexagons, the hexagons form a continuous perfectly smooth surface of two *six-tunnel* congruent regions corresponding to the simple cubic net [9.2]. These tunnels are directed along the [100] branches of the simple cubic network and illustrate its self-duality. Since the diamond and simple cubic are the only self-dual uniform networks, it follows that any continuous surface system which divides space into two congruent regions must correspond to one of these two networks. The 3-connected Laves net is only a self-dual if enantiomorphism is permitted. Schoen (1970) has discovered a periodic minimal surface corresponding to this 3-connected net, but if it is to be perfectly smooth, i.e., if all dihedral angles equal 180°, it cannot be composed of polygons with straight edges. It cannot be defined as a subset of any of the space filling systems we have inventoried, so is not considered in this study.

9.2 Six-tunnel continuous surface derived from space filling of tetrahedral decahedra corresponding to the simple cubic network.

9.1 Four-tunnel continuous surface derived from space filling of tetrahedral decahedra corresponding to the diamond network.

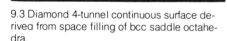

The diamond four-tunnel continuous surface can also be generated from the space filling of bcc saddle octahedra by omitting every other face [9.3].* It is, therefore, possible to form the same surface with two different saddle or skew polygons. Both of these systems may be considered regular infinite polyhedra, as Schoen (1968) has proposed. When this four-tunnel system is composed of the regular saddle quadrilaterals, each vertex is equally surrounded by six faces and when it is composed of the bcc octahedron's regular saddle hexagons, the faces meet four at each vertex. These two tessellations on the same surface form reciprocal networks to each other with respect to that surface. This reciprocity defines a saddle quadrilateral that is common to both the 60° regular quadrilateral and the 90° regular hexagon [9.4]. This common quadrilateral has one 60° included angle and three 90° included angles and has mirror symmetry.

*Note that the opaque model in [9.3] is assembled such that the terminal openings include cut segments of saddle hexagons revealing arc edges.

9.4 The quadrilateral (tetragon) common to both the 90° regular saddle hexagon and the 60° regular saddle quadrilateral.

The six-tunnel continuous surface may also be considered an infinite regular polyhedron in which six regular saddle hexagons of 60° included angles meet at each vertex. The reciprocal of this tessellation of the six-tunnel continuous surface is another tessellation of 60° regular saddle hexagons. It is a self-dual with respect to the surface it defines. This self-duality defines a common quadrilateral of 2-fold symmetry which has included angles of 60° and 90° in equal numbers [9.5]. We find then that both the diamond four-tunnel and cubic six-tunnel infinite periodic minimal surfaces may be generated by simple quadrilaterals.

9.5 The saddle quadrilateral generated by overlapping 60° regular saddle hexagons.

9.3 Diamond 4-tunnel continuous surface derived from space filling of bcc saddle octahedra.

9.6 Diamond 4-tunnel continuous surface derived from space filling truncated tetrahedral decahedra.

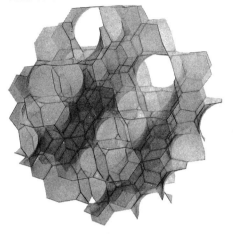

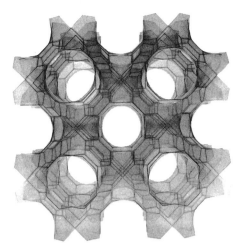

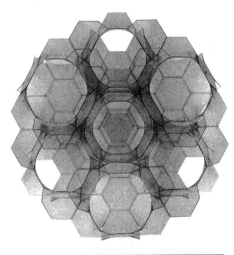

If each vertex is truncated, in the diamond four-tunnel system composed of 60° regular saddle quadrilaterals, regular plane hexagons are formed throughout this four-tunnel surface. This same labyrinth configuration can be derived from the space filling of truncated tetrahedral decahedra in which the saddle dodecagons are omitted, leaving only 120° 2-fold octagons and regular plane hexagons [9.6].* Similarly, when the six-tunnel cubic system is composed of 60°, 90° 2-fold quadrilaterals in which only the 6-connected vertices are truncated, the six-tunnel system formed also includes regular plane hexagons [9.7]. This system can be simply derived from the space filling of universal cuboctadodecahedra and universal hexahedra with the dodecagons omitted, leaving the 90°, 120° hexagons and plane regular hexagons. Both of these systems with the plane hexagons have interesting spatial and structural properties that have applications in building; such applications are discussed later.** Neither of these labyrinths can be considered to be true periodic minimal surfaces, although they are very close approximations.

*Note that the opaque models in [9.6] are assembled such that the terminal openings include cut segments of saddle octagons revealing arc edges.

**Adaptations of these particular labyrinth structures and a family of related labyrinths and saddle polyhedral structures are the subject of U.S. Patents 3925941 and 3931697.

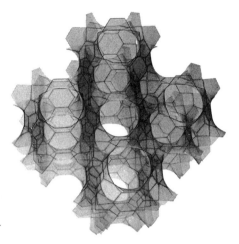

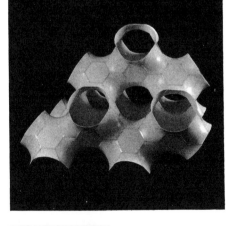

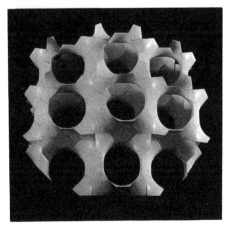

9.7 Cubic 6-tunnel continuous surface derived from space filling of universal cuboctadodecahedra and universal hexahedra.

The six-tunnel continuous surface system composed of the 60°, 90° saddle quadrilateral can be derived from the space filling of the saddle cube dodecahedron and augmented universal hexahedron by omitting the octagonal faces. On the other hand, if in such a space filling system the octagonal faces remain and the quadrilaterals are omitted, a very curious surface results. We have seen so far that the diamond tunnel system and simple cubic tunnel system correspond to uniform networks that are self-dual. A tunnel system is formed by this new surface which corresponds to a semiuniform net based on space filling of the saddle dodecahedron and the fcc tetragonal tetrahedron (No. 23, Table 8.2). This net, which is 12-connected and 4-connected, is the only semiuniform net known to me which is a self-dual. The resulting surface, therefore, divides all of space into two congruent tunnel systems which each have intersections including sets of both twelve and four tunnels [9.8]. This system completes the inventory of tunnel arrangements for continuous surfaces in which all of space is divided into two congruent regions. We know this because of their correspondence to the three networks which are self-duals. This is not to say that we have completed the inventory of all cases of continuous surfaces which correspond to these three different tunnel systems, i.e., the 4-tunnel, 6-tunnel, and 12-tunnel/4-tunnel (12/4-tunnel) systems.

It should be pointed out that the 12/4-tunnel system can also be considered a rigorous infinite periodic minimal surface because it can be generated by 180° rotation about the edges of the 60°, 90° saddle octagons from which it is composed. Therefore, the dihedral angles are all 180° so that the continuous surface is exactly smooth everywhere.

Only a few of the labyrinth systems we will discuss satisfy the strict mathematical criteria which define a true periodic minimal surface. However, as I have pointed out above, all of the continuous surface systems are close approximations to infinite periodic minimal surfaces. Since dihedral angles are always approximately 180°, the transition from one polygon in the surface to another is generally smooth. The physical differences between the strictly defined infinite periodic minimal surface and our spatial labyrinths are insignificant.

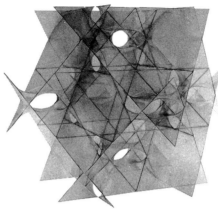

9.8 A continuous surface tunnel system corresponding to a 12/4-connected network generated by the space filling of saddle cubedodecahedra and augmented universal hexahedra.

The space filling of universal cuboctadodecahedra and universal hexahedra (No. 25, Table 8.2) generates a 12/4-tunnel system by omitting the 90°, 120° saddle hexagons [9.9]. Another simple cubic tunnel system can be generated with the space filling of bcc saddle cuboctahedra and tetragonal saddle hexahedra (No. 15, Table 8.2). This surface, like the others just mentioned, cannot be considered a periodic minimal surface for the reasons already outlined, but it is smooth and continuous.

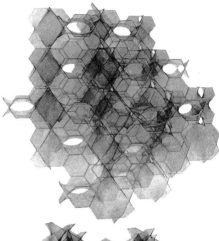

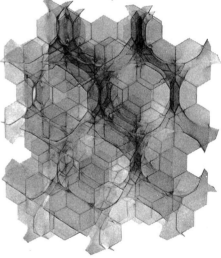

9.9 A 12/4-tunnel system generated by the space filling of universal cuboctadodecahedra and universal hexahedra.

Dividing Space into Two Complementary Regions

In addition to the diamond, simple cubic, and 12/4-tunnel continuous surface systems, which form congruent self-dual regions, there are two other tunnel systems that give rise to two infinite regions which, although dual to each other, are not congruent. That is, they are not self-dual. One of these tunnel systems corresponds to the 8-connected bcc network and its 4-connected dual network. It can be generated by the space filling of fcc saddle cuboctahedra and bioctagonal hexahedra (No. 20, Table 8.2) by omitting all of the faces of this system but the 60°, 90° octagons [9.10], and by the space filling of truncated fcc saddle cuboctahedra and bidodecagonal hexahedra (No. 21, Table 8.2) by omitting all the faces but the 90°, 120° dodecagons [9.11].

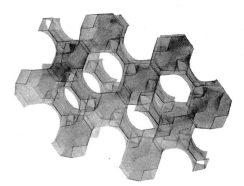

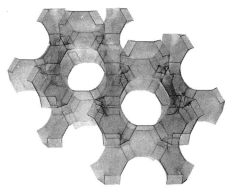

9.11 Space filling of truncated fcc saddle cuboctahedra and bidodecagonal hexahedra generates a tunnel system corresponding to the 8-connected bcc network and its 4-connected dual network.

Note that in these two manifestations of the same tunnel system, the relative volumes of the complementary labyrinths differ markedly. This is caused by the differences in proportion between the 60°, 90° octagon and the 90°, 120° dodecagon, and because the complementary 8-tunnel and 4-tunnel regions are not congruent.

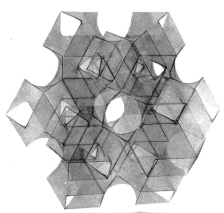

9.10 Space filling of fcc saddle cuboctahedra and bioctagonal hexahedra generates a tunnel system corresponding to the 8-connected bcc network and its 4-connected dual network.

We have now seen the simple cubic and bcc nets represented by continuous surface systems. It is not surprising, then, to learn that the fcc 12-connected network may also be represented by continuous surface systems. Again, from our earlier studies, we know that the reciprocal network of the 12-connected fcc network is the network defined by the space filling rhombic dodecahedra which has both 4- and 8-connected nodes. From this, we know that the 12-tunnel fcc system will have as its dual region a semiuniform system in which both four and eight tunnels meet. There are two continuous surface systems which define the 12-tunnel (and its complement, the 4/8-tunnel) configuration. One is derived from space filling of fcc saddle cuboctahedra/saddle cubedodecahedra/tetrahedral decahedra/fcc orthorhombic tetrahedra (No. 42, Table 8.2) by using only the 60°, 90° octagon and the 60° quadrilateral [9.12]. The other is derived from space filling of universal cuboctadodecahedron/truncated tetrahedral decahedron/truncated fcc saddle cuboctahedron/truncated orthorhombic fcc saddle tetrahedron (No. 41, Table 8.2) by using the 90°, 120° dodecagon, the 120° octagon and the plane regular hexagon [9.13]. Again, we see differing relative volumes of these two versions of the same labyrinth system because of the different proportions of the respective component polygons of each version.

These various continuous surface systems well illustrate the usefulness of our integrative morphological system for the understanding of spatial systems. Because all of these continuous surfaces can be generated from the space filling saddle polyhedra, their networks are common to such space filling systems. This not only means that the networks that define such continuous surfaces are subsets of the universal network, but all of the tunnels formed by the continuous surfaces are directed along combinations of the three branches of the universal network, i.e., the [100], [110], and/or the [111] branches.

9.12 Space filling of fcc saddle cuboctahedra/saddle cubedodecahedra/tetrahedral decahedra/fcc orthorhombic tetrahedra generates a tunnel system corresponding to 12-connected fcc network and its dual rhombic dodecahedron network.

9.13 Space filling of universal cuboctadodecahedra/truncated tetrahedral decahedra/truncated fcc saddle cuboctahedra/truncated orthorhombic fcc saddle tetrahedra generates a tunnel system corresponding to 12-connected fcc network and its dual rhombic dodecahedron network.

The characteristics of this series of continuous surfaces are presented in Table 9.1. From this table we will be able to see the interelatedness of the continuous surfaces to a series of three-dimensional networks. The columns labeled "Labyrinth Configuration" give the basic tunnel arrangements. The labels "A" and "B" identify the two complementary tunnel configurations.

Note that Nos. 1–4 in Table 9.1 have the same tunnel systems and that tunnel system A is congruent with tunnel system B. this tunnel configuration corresponds to the diamond net. A simple way to think of this labyrinth is to imagine inflating the branches of the diamond net until the two congruent regions are formed. As a matter of fact, any of these continuous surfaces may be thought of as inflated networks or networks assembled with very fat branches. Entries 1–4 in Table 9.1 show that there are four alternative systems which form the diamond labyrinth. All of the component polygons required for assembly constitute subsystems borrowed from "Parent Space Filling Systems" which are identified in Table 8.2. As described earlier, the continuous surfaces have been derived by omitting certain faces from these various space filling systems. The polygons listed are those which remain from a given space filling system.

Configuration numbers 5–8 identify simple cubic six-tunnel labyrinths. The self-duality of the simple cubic net is again reflected in the congruence of tunnel system A and tunnel system B. Numbers 9 and 10 also have congruence of the complementary tunnel labyrinths and are based on the only self-dual semiuniform net. Because this system derives from a semiuniform net with both 12- and 4-connected nodes, two angles for each tunnel system must be given. (This network is defined by the branches of the space filling system No. 23, Table 8.2.) Numbers 11 and 12 form tunnel labyrinths around the bcc 8-connected network and its 4-connected complement (Nos. 3, 4 Table 8.2), and numbers 13 and 14 in Table 9.1 form tunnel labyrinths around the 12-connected fcc network and its complement, the 4/8-connected rhombic dodecahedron network.

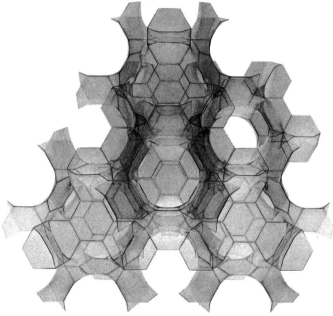

Table 9.1
Continuous
Surfaces

		Labyrinth Configuration						
		Tunnel A			Tunnel B			
		No. of Intersecting Tunnels	Tunnel Directions	Angles at Which Tunnels Meet	No. of Intersecting Tunnels	Tunnel Directions	Angles at Which Tunnels Meet	Component Polygons Required for Assembly
Diamond net	1	4	[111]	109°28′	4	[111]	109°28′	60° tetragon
	2	4	[111]	109°28′	4	[111]	109°28′	90° hexagon
	3	4	[111]	109°28′	4	[111]	109°28′	60°-90°-90°-90° tetragon
	4	4	[111]	109°28′	4	[111]	109°28′	120° octagon; 120° hexagon
Simple cubic net	5	6	[100]	90°	6	[100]	90°	60° hexagon
	6	6	[100]	90°	6	[100]	90°	60°-90°-60°-90° tetragon
	7	6	[100]	90°	6	[100]	90°	90°-120° hexagon; 120° hexagon
	8	6	[100]	90°	6	[100]	90°	70°32′ tetragon 109°28′ hexagon
12/4 net	9	12/4	[110]	60°,90°	12/4	[110]	60°,90°	60°-90° octagon
	10	12/4	[110]	60°,90°	12/4	[110]	60°,90°	90°-120° dodecagon; 120° hexagon
bcc 8-connected net	11	8	[111]	70°32′	4	[100]	90°	60°-90° octagon
	12	8	[111]	70°32′	4	[100]	90°	90°-120° dodecagon
fcc 12-connected net	13	12	[110]	60°	4/8	[111]	109°28′, 70°32′	60°90° octagon; 60° tetragon
	14	12	[110]	60°	4/8	[111]	109°28′, 70°32′	90°-120° dodecagon; 120° octagon; 120° hexagon

Parent Space Filling System From Table 8.2	Figure Number
#5 — Tetrahedral decahedron	9.1
#4 — bcc octahedron	9.3
Overlapping of #4 and #5	—
#7 — Truncated tetrahedral decahedron	9.6
#5 — Tetrahedral decahedron	9.2
#26 — Saddle cubedodecahedron; Augmented universal hexahedron	—
#25 — Universal cuboctadodecahedron; Universal hexahedron	9.7
#15 — bcc saddle cuboctahedron; Tetragonal saddle hexahedron	—
#26 — Saddle cubedodecahedron; Augmented universal hexahedron	9.8
#25 — Universal cuboctadodecahedron; Universal hexahedron	9.9
#20 — fcc saddle cuboctahedron; Bioctagonal hexahedron	9.10
#21 — Truncated fcc saddle cuboctahedron; Bidodecagonal hexahedron	9.11
#42 — fcc saddle cuboctahedron; Saddle cubedodecahedron; Tetrahedral decahedron; fcc orthorhombic tetrahedron	9.12
#41 — Universal cuboctadodecahedron; Truncated tetrahedral decahedron; Truncated fcc saddle cuboctahedron; Truncated orthorhombic tetrahedron	9.13

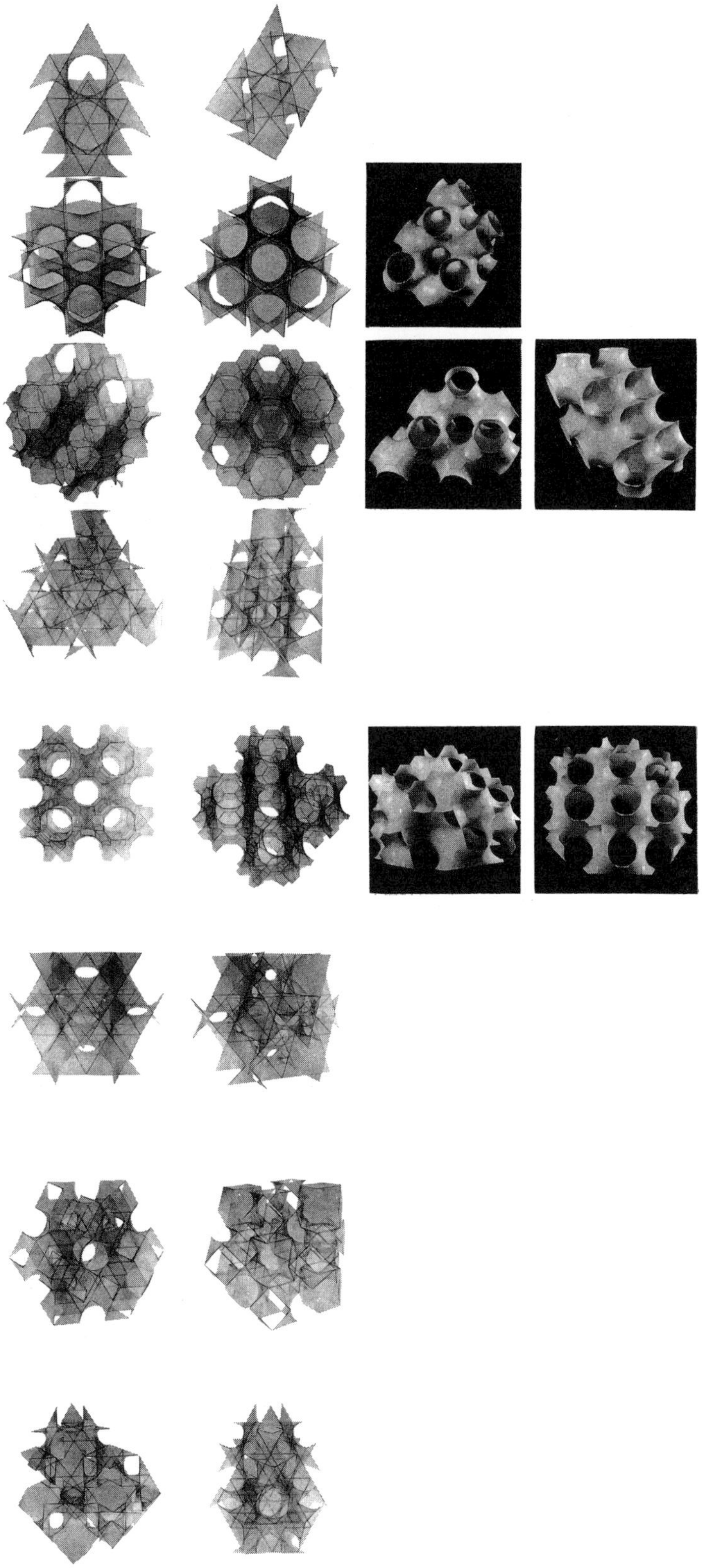

Labyrinths Derived from Plane Faced Polyhedra

Periodic continuous surfaces have counterparts derived from the space filling of plane-faced polyhedra.

Infinite Skew Polyhedra

Coxeter has identified a set of three infinite labyrinths which he calls "regular skew polyhedra" (Coxeter 1968. p. 75). Like the periodic minimal surfaces, they divide all of space into two congruent regions and they can be derived from simple space filling systems. They do not form continuous smooth surfaces because their dihedral angles are not 180° and consequently form spatial labyrinths in which adjacent polygons form discontinuities at their common edges. These three systems can be derived from space fillings of (1) cubes, (2) truncated octahedra, and (3) truncated tetrahedra/tetrahedra by omitting one half of the square faces, all of the square faces, and all of the triangular faces, respectively. These systems can be classed as infinite regular polyhedra because they are composed of congruent regular polygons and congruent vertices. They are called skew because the faces meeting at each vertex are arranged in a convexoconcave (skew) configuration. It should be emphasized that the networks from which these three systems are derived remain unchanged from the parent space filling configurations.

Labyrinths Formed by Omitting Faces from Polyhedral Space Filling Systems

It becomes apparent from these examples and the examples of the continuous surfaces that many systems of infinite labyrinths can be derived by the process of systematic omission of certain faces of space filling polyhedral arrangements. In a similar way, it is also possible to form "open packings" of polyhedra in which one single infinite labyrinth is complemented by a periodic chain of closed polyhedra joined face to face. In such systems, certain of the faces are shared with adjacent polyhedra and the other faces form the walls of the infinite labyrinths. A simple example of this system is an open packing in which cubes are attached to each square face of truncated octahedra [9.14]. The hexagonal faces of the truncated octahedra and four of the six square faces of the cubes form the walls of the infinite labyrinth. The cube/truncated octahedron complex forms an infinite multidirectional chain. This particular packing is equivalent to the space filling of truncated cuboctahedra/truncated octahedra/cubes [5.10], in which the octagon faces of the truncated cuboctahedron have been omitted. Both systems are defined by the same network. I have not made a systematic study of all of the possible symmetrical ways that faces can be omitted from the space filling polyhedra to form infinite labyrinths and/or open packings of polyhedra. *No new networks* would in any case be found, so such an investigation is less important than other aspects of our studies.

9.14 Labyrinth generated from space filling of truncated cuboctahedra/truncated octahedra/cubes.

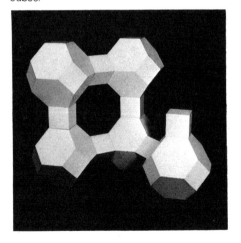

Labyrinths Formed by Open Packings of Polyhedra

There are a few open packings which are not derived from space filling systems, but which form uniform nets and which can be considered subsets of the universal net. Four examples follow; these do not exhaust the possibilities, although I suspect that they are the principal cases.

Two of these consist of open packings of truncated octahedra and hexagonal prisms. In one case, four of the eight hexagonal faces of the truncated octahedra have hexagonal prisms attached. When this system is repeated, the truncated octahedra are found to lie at the nodes of the diamond net. In the other case, all eight of the hexagonal faces of the truncated octahedra have hex prisms attached and this forms an open packing in which the truncated octahedra are positioned at the sites of the bcc lattice. In both cases, the hex prisms serve as "branch linkages" between the truncated octahedra which serve as nodal regions in the open packing. The networks formed by these "open packings" assembled from the Universal Node kit are shown in [9.15a] (diamond) and [9.15b] (bcc lattice).

The third example is an open packing of truncated tetrahedra and hexagonal prisms in which the prisms are attached to all four of the hexagonal faces of the truncated tetrahedra [9.16]. This system also corresponds to the diamond net with the truncated tetrahedra occupying the nodal positions.

The fourth example is an open packing of truncated cuboctahedra and hexagonal prisms in which the prisms are attached to the eight hexagonal faces of the larger polyhedra [9.17]. This system forms an arrangement in which the truncated cuboctahedra are found at the sites of the bcc lattice and the prisms serve as "bond linkages."

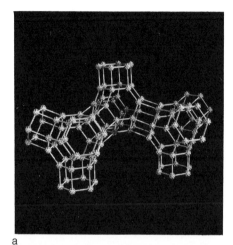

a

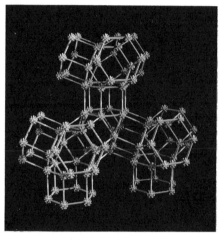

9.16 A network of open packing of truncated tetrahedra and hexagonal prisms forms a diamond labyrinth.

9.17 A network of open packing of truncated cuboctahedra and hexagonal prisms forms a bcc labyrinth.

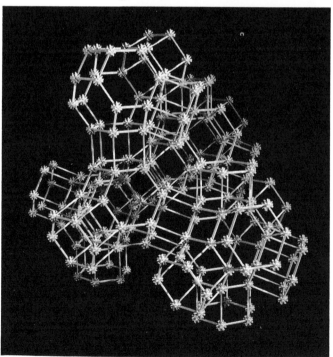

b

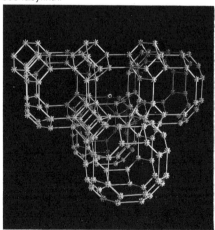

9.15 Networks of open packings of truncated octahedra and hexagonal prisms form a labyrinth corresponding to the diamond network (a), and to the bcc network (b).

The four foregoing systems are listed in Table 9.2. The last column of this table indicates the network which corresponds to the overall configuration of the open packing. The complementary regions of these open packings form infinite labyrinths. These infinite labyrinths may be decomposed into polyhedra that are bounded by both plane and saddle faces. I will not here identify these polyhedra or describe the dual nets of these systems. Open packings of polyhedra will appear again in Chapter 11 of this book when we look more closely at infinite periodic triangulated structures.

In the introduction of this book I stated that a major concern was the discovery and understanding of intrinsic force systems as they relate to design strategies for modular environments. I suggested that the discovery of the comprehensive intrinsic force systems that govern options in three-dimensional space will make evident the practicality of an unprecedented host of structures. I have also suggested that an understanding of these intrinsic force systems would provide the basis for the development of minimum inventory/maximum diversity modular systems.

Although I have yet to show specific architectural applications, it is clear that the range of spatial options and possibilities for adaptive systems has been substantially extended by the development of the comprehensive morphological geometry of the Universal Node system. The meaning and usefulness of "intrinsic force" becomes quite clear to one working with the Universal Node connector. Because the Universal Node system is a direct phenomenological embodiment of the physicogeometric "rules" of nature, it can never become obsolete as a basic kit of parts. In fact, the many examples of networks, labyrinths, and open-packed structures described in these last few chapters make it clear that the Universal Node system is a canonical form of a minimum inventory/maximum diversity system of spatial possibilities. This is not to suggest that all possible systems can be formed with the Universal Node kit, but as we shall continue to discover, it is ubiquitous. For the moment, I shall move on to a discussion of the structural implications of saddle polyhedra in infinite continuous surfaces and their relationships to triangulated structures.

Table 9.2
Uniform Nets Formed
by Open Packings
of Polyhedra

Open Polyhedral Packing	Z	Branch Directions at Typical Node			Branch Angles at Node						Network of Labyrinth
		[100]	[110]	[111]	[100]–[100]	[110]–[110]	[111]–[111]	[100]–[110]	[110]–[111]	[100]–[111]	
Truncated octahedron	4		3	1		90°, 120°			90°, 144°44′		Diamond
Hexagonal prism											
Truncated tetrahedron	5		3	2		60°, 120°	109°28′		90°		Diamond
Hexagonal prism											
Truncated octahedron	5		3	2		90°, 120°	70°32′		90°, 144°44′		8-connected bcc
Hexagonal prism											
Truncated cuboctahedron	4	1	2	1		120°		90°, 135°	90°	124°76′	8-connected bcc
Hexagonal prism											

A
Theory of
Structure

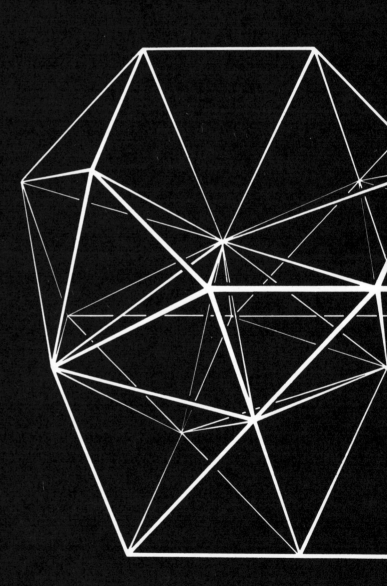

10 Continuous Surfaces as Triangulated Networks

Structural Characteristics of Continuous Triangulated Networks

I have already suggested that the space filling saddle polyhedra are high efficiency structures due to the modular interaction of the already efficient doubly curved surfaces. In the first place, these interactions are such that the structure is self-stabilizing. Furthermore, the periodic continuous surfaces are optimal forms in that they form nonredundant structures. Finally, they are characterized by a large contained volume for the given surface area, and although there is no actual formation of an array of finite volumetric units or cells, such cells are implicit in the tunneling system. Perhaps even more than the space filling polyhedra, these periodic continuous surfaces open up wholly unprecedented possibilities of architectural structure.

Although it is implicit in all of the configurations discussed in this book, it is with the continuous-surface systems that we clearly abandon any reference to the conventional spatial-orientation constraints usually associated with architecture. The spatial labyrinths of continuous surfaces have no inherent inside or outside, up or down, or horizontal or vertical. All of these orientations can be assigned to a structure, but they are not dictated by the geometry of the structure itself. I have already pointed out that these labyrinths divide space into two regions; that is, they create two-sided surfaces. "Inside" can be either of the two sides. This will usually depend on the means by which these infinite systems are *terminated* or closed off into finite structures. "Up and down" and "horizontal and vertical" may be determined by specific environmental contexts, but not by the structure itself.

In order to differentiate an inside from an outside, it is necessary to subdivide space into two regions. Any simple finite cell such as a single sphere or cube does this very well. If one wishes to subdivide space infinitely or even in a finite but repeatable way, then the continuous surfaces are extremely useful.

It can be shown, for example, that the simple cubic and diamond spatial labyrinths will infinitely subdivide space into two regions with a smaller surface/volume ratio than any other possible system.* This, in connection with their efficiency as physical structures, promises systems of *minimum redundancy*, i.e., structures which enclose a great amount of repeatable volume while requiring a minimum of invested resources.

Geometric Stability with Saddle Surfaces and Linear Frameworks

A surprising similarity of physical behavior between linear frameworks and saddle surfaces becomes evident when they are both viewed in terms of periodic modular associations. A very simple observation has been the underpinning of our study. It is that those spatial arrangements of physical modules, (be they *linear branches* or *surfaces*) which form fully stable geometrical arrangements will be more efficient as structures than those which do not form stable geometric arrangements. Such inherently stable geometric arrangements insure conditions of axial or membrane stress, respectively. Efficiency is taken here to mean the ratio of resource investment required to resist a given amount of stress (or stresses), to the amount of volume enclosed. To state it another way: It will take less material to resist a given amount of stress while enclosing a given amount of volume with a modular system that is inherently stable than with a system that is not inherently stable.

The basic principles of geometric stability govern the behavior of both branch and surface systems. In the case of finite branch systems, the principle of geometric stability is simple enough, as we have already seen: only fully triangulated systems are inherently stable. If a finite system is entirely enclosed by surfaces it will also be stable. If these surfaces are flat, as in the plane faced polyhedra, local instability results when concentrated loads are applied to the faces. If the surfaces are curved the local instability is diminished or eliminated. This is equivalent in effect to the faceting, etc., discussed in Chapter 3. Only fully triangulated polyhedra or fully surfaced polyhedra may be considered closed and, therefore, stable, and the saddle polyhedra because of their compound curvature overcome, to a large extent, the local instabilities that are evident in the plane faced polyhedra.

---

*Of these two systems, the diamond labyrinth can be shown to have approximately 19% less surface area per unit volume that the cubic labyrinth, although they both represent highly efficient systems when compared to other infinite subdivisions of three-dimensional space.

A finite saddle polyhedron clearly illustrates the structural enhancement of doubly curved saddle surfaces when they are aggregated. The isolated saddle surface, used so well by Candela (Faber), undergoes stress that is completely cancelled out by the interaction of saddle surfaces in an aggregate. The isolated saddle surface is invariably expected to function as a cantilever, which introduces bending stresses that simply do not appear in periodic arrays of such surfaces. This can be appreciated by working with scale models. For example, the bcc tetrahedron is composed of four identical regular saddle quadrilaterals. These individual surfaces, when formed from thin plastic, are quite flexible and easily bent. When four are assembled to form the bcc tetrahedron, they become extraordinarily rigid by virtue of the manner in which they *must* interact with each other. An inherently stable configuration is formed which is like the fully triangulated network structure in its ability to distribute stress.

Stability in Infinite Periodic Structures

With infinite periodic structures, the question of stability is far more subtle and interesting than it is for finite triangulated frameworks. There are two basic classes of infinite periodic structures, which have counterparts in both triangulated systems and surface systems. First, there are those systems that are aggregates of stable finite polyhedra, and second, there are those systems that are continuous infinite labyrinths. Such infinite labyrinths are frequently derived from periodic arrays of finite polyhedra but they are not of themselves composed of finite *stable* cells. So far, we have only seen continuous labyrinths that are composed of saddle surfaces. Later in this chapter and in subsequent chapters we will see a number of interesting examples of triangulated-framework systems that can be considered to be continuous labyrinths. Infinite labyrinths are always composed of simple repeat units or modules. We have seen examples of this in the cases of the periodic continuous surfaces. With triangulated labyrinth structures, the module is frequently a polyhedron which is only partially triangulated. Such a polyhedron becomes stable only by association with others like it.

Infinite labyrinths, be they surface or framework systems, are theoretically only stable when they are infinitely large. When such infinite systems are arbitrarily terminated, they become unstable at the terminations; however, this does not always affect stability at the center of such structures. Of course, it is not possible to realize an infinite structure; all built labyrinths must eventually be terminated. If total stability is to be maintained it is necessary for such structures to be *closed* by *surfaces* or *triangulated* frameworks.

The class of periodic structures which are composed of finite stable cells do not, of course, suffer from this problem. They can be stopped at any arbitrary multiple of complete stable cells and will remain stable. The continuous surfaces as infinite systems are highly stable when properly terminated; and the smoothness of transition of one surface module into another leads one to anticipate a successful distribution of stress, whether due to concentrated or distributed loads. From an experimental point of view, the stability of any system can be determined by means of assemblies in which the joining of all elements, be they branches or surfaces, is by way of hinged connectors. For the branch systems, a multidirectional hinge is desirable; but for saddle surfaces, which join along common edges, a simple hinge is appropriate. A very slight load (usually just the weight of the model) will reveal an unstable condition.

Periodic Triangulated Networks Derived from Continuous Surfaces

The relation of continuous surfaces to periodic triangulated labyrinths can be explored by considering the tessellations of triangles that approximate the curvatures of the minimal surfaces from which the continuous surfaces are composed. Such tessellations may have their *edges* in the surface and would, therefore, be curved; or they may be chordal subdivisions in which only the *vertices* are in the surface. If we are to consider such systems as simple physical framework structures, then they would more properly consist of chords. Such a chordal interpretation or approximation of a continuous minimal surface can be considered an infinite periodic analog to a finite geodesic sphere system.

In the remainder of this chapter, we will begin to see something of the relationships between continuous surfaces and continuous triangulated labyrinths. For example, the modular surfaces of the six-tunnel periodic minimal surface of 60°, 90° quadrilaterals (Table 9.1) may be subdivided into more clearly equilateral triangles than most of the other surfaces. This means that the differences in edge lengths are minimized, regardless of the frequency of subdivision. It is clear that the saddle quadrilateral can be subdivided into any arbitrarily large number of triangular facets.

The minimum triangulated approximation of the saddle surface has at least one point falling on the surface of the saddle polygon. If this is placed on the center of the saddle surface, the surface naturally divides into eight triangles [10.1]. Tessellations of progressively higher and higher degrees of modular subdivision can be envisioned. However, just as for the triangulated domes, as the frequency of modular subdivision increases, the shrinking "neighborhood" of each vertex becomes more and more planar, gradually losing its resistance to local concentrated loads (Chapter 3, esp. [3.9]). Such high frequency structures can be built, but they require the incorporation of double-layer space-frames for stability. Progressively higher subdivisions of the basic 60°, 90° saddle quadrilateral are shown in [10.2].

If we consider the 6-tunnel infinite periodic minimal surface assembled from 60°, 90° saddle quadrilaterals as a structural model, there exist certain regions of relative flatness (where the 60° corners come together) and are thus locally unstable. Now all of the flat spots (which in this case are regular hexagons) could be cut out of the infinite periodic minimal surface without greatly affecting its global stability. A 6-tunnel continuous surface system has already been described which is precisely that—namely, the surface derived from the space filling of the universal cuboctadodecahedra and universal hexahedra (No. 7, Table 9.1). When the flat regular hexagons are left out, the module which remains is simply the 60°, 90° saddle quadrilateral with its 60° corners truncated, giving 90°, 120° saddle hexagons.

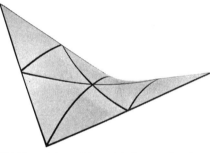

10.1 The minimum triangulated approximation of the 60°, 90° saddle quadrilateral.

10.2 Progressively higher triangulated subdivisions of the 60°, 90° saddle quadrilateral.

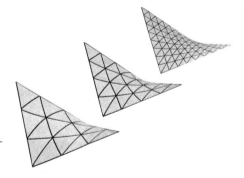

The elimination of all these flat regions enables more total volume to be differentiated with even less surface. However, it must be pointed out that if space is to be totally enclosed, i.e., separated into two regions of space by a continuous partition, the flat regular hexagons must be included in the assembly, even though they are not required for structural stability. I have already suggested the highly nonredundant character of the general class of continuous surfaces described earlier in this study. We can anticipate economic advantages from this surface composed of 90°, 120° saddle hexagons. Due to the relative small size of the basic modules for the volume that is enclosed, this particular system should have considerable practical significance.

Because we are concerned at this point with the simple cases of triangulated infinite labyrinths and their relations to continuous surfaces, we shall consider only the minimum triangulated approximation of the saddle surface. The basic 60°, 90° quadrilateral is minimally subdivided into eight triangles. When this module is combined to approximate the 6-tunnel infinite periodic minimal surface, the 60° corners meet in sixes and account for the relatively flat regions which were observed in the continuous surface. Regular plane hexagons composed of six equilateral triangles are formed in these flat regions and like the flat regions in the continuous surfaces, they are locally unstable. If these hexagonal groups of equilateral triangles are everywhere omitted from the structure, global stability is nonetheless preserved. The basic repeating unit becomes the triangulated approximation of the 90°, 120° saddle hexagon which again is simply a truncated version of the 60°, 90° saddle quadrilateral. The triangulated approximation of this 90°, 120° saddle hexagon is composed of six triangles, two isosceles and four scalene, which constitute combinations of three different edge lengths. The shortest of these lengths differs from the longest by approximately 20%.

If the continuous surface cubic labyrinth composed of 90°, 120° saddle hexagons is a minimally redundant structural system, as has been suggested, then it can be assumed that the triangulated labyrinth which approximates this continuous surface is an inherently stable linear network of minimum redundancy for the periodic structuring of space. Figure [10.3] shows a comparison of the continuous surface and the triangulated approximation based on the 90°, 120° hexagon. The configuration shown consists of 36 modular units assembled in a symmetrical arrangement. Note that the three cubic axes of symmetry, 2-fold, 3-fold, and 4-fold are shown. Figure [10.4] shows an arbitrarily terminated sample of the triangulated labyrinth.

We must remind ourselves that in the case of both the continuous surface and its triangulated approximation, an arbitrarily terminated array is unstable unless special peripheral conditions are satisfied. An arbitrarily terminated structure assembled from the 90°,120° saddle hexagons and plane regular hexagon modules exhibits a remarkable structural behavior. With the modules linked to each other with hingeable joints (Mylar tape along the edges of shared polygons), the structure is unstable only in a limited sense. When local loads are applied to the structure the deflection is observed to be of equal magnitude *throughout the entire structure.* Even this unstabilized structure will not totally collapse. When the direction of the load is reversed the entire structure deflects in the opposite direction. This behavior suggests an extraordinary tendency to distribute stress, so that even concentrated local loads are resisted by a very large part of the structure.

10.3 Three symmetrical views of a cubic labyrinth section assembled from 90°,120° saddle hexagons, comparing continuous surface modules to triangulated modules.

a

b

c

d

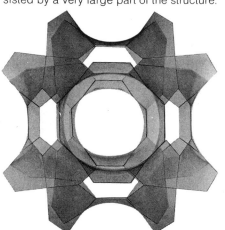

e

f

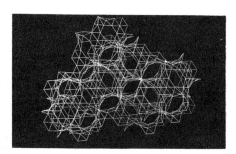

10.4 Arbitrarily terminated sample of the triangulated cubic labyrinth assembled from 90°,120° hexagons.

I have discovered that the same 90°, 120° hexagon modules from which the continuous labyrinths are assembled can be used to stabilize the structure. This is achieved by a simple redirection or inversion of the modules such that the labyrinth is closed off at its terminal regions. No matter how large the structure becomes, once the peripheral regions are stabilized by closing off, the entire structure becomes perfectly rigid.

The hingeable joint is an effective way to verify the inherent stability of this system. In the case of triangulated framework structures, all loads remain axially in the members and no bending loads are induced. The same principle is operative in the case of the fully stable continuous labyrinth.That is, all loads remain *in* the surface and bending is minimized if not altogether eliminated. Thus a condition of "membrane stress" is maintained.

Figure [10.5a,c,e] shows different views of the same structural assembly composed of 90°,120° hexagons and plane regular hexagons. It forms eight volumetric regions joined to each other by tunnels such that a central ninth volumetric region is defined. This configuration requires 24 terminal assemblies each composed of four inverted 90°,120° hexagons. Note the occurrence of triangular holes. This structure is completely stable. Once such a structure is enclosed by the terminal modules, an inside and outside are defined. In this particular configuration, the eight volumetric regions are inside, and the central ninth volumetric region is actually "outside."

Figure [10.5b,d,f] shows the triangulated approximation of the structure. The behavior of this skeletal configuration is similar to its counterpart composed of 90°, 120° hexagonal surface modules. However, the model shown in the photographs has no terminal modules installed, and is, therefore, not totally stable. The reader will note that in the skeletal structure the plane regular hexagons are omitted. Also note that both the skeletal and surface configurations have cubic symmetry. A view along a 4-fold axis can be seen in [10.5 a, b]; a view along a 3-fold axis can be seen in [10.5 c, d]; and, a view along a 2-fold axis can be seen in [10.5 e, f]. Details of the skeletal configuration can be seen in [10.6].

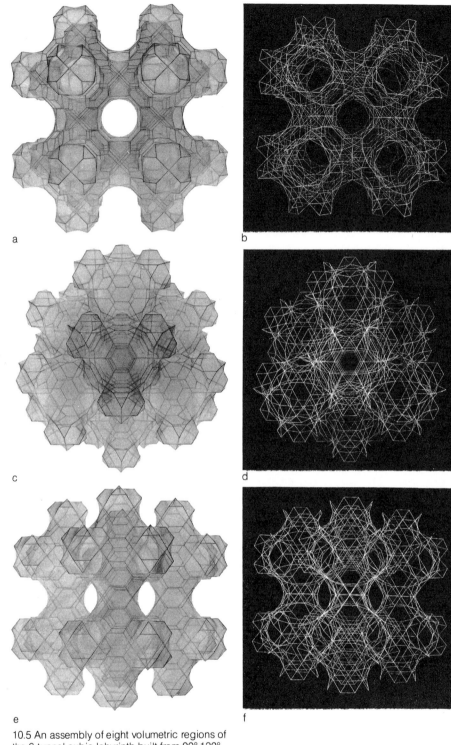

a

b

c

d

e

f

10.5 An assembly of eight volumetric regions of the 6-tunnel cubic labyrinth built from 90°,120° saddle hexagons, comparing a continuous surface to its triangulated approximation, and viewed along the three cubic symmetry axes: [100] (a, b); [111] (c, d); and [110] (e, f).

Although all of the continuous surfaces may be used to derive efficient triangulated labyrinths, some are more effective than others from the point of view of minimizing differences in edge lengths. The 4-tunnel diamond minimal surface based upon the 60° regular saddle quadrilateral (No. 1, Table 9.1) and its truncated form, the 120° saddle octagon (No. 4, Table 9.1) give rise to systems probably exceeding the efficiency of the 6-tunnel cubic system described in detail above.

In [10.7] can be seen two views of an assembly of 120° octagons, plane regular hexagons and, surprisingly, 90°,120° hexagons, which are used as termination modules in sets of three. Note the occurrence of triangular and square openings. The behavior and efficiency of this 4-tunnel structure are similar to those of the 6-tunnel one assembled from 90°,120° hexagons. A triangulated skeletal approximation of this structure can also be formed. The 120° octagon is decomposed into eight identical isosceles triangles with two edge lengths which differ by approximately 20%.

The 4-tunnel diamond and 6-tunnel simple cubic systems represent two sophisticated examples of periodic triangulated networks. In the search for periodic triangulated networks, high emphasis is placed on the criterion that all edges be as nearly equal as possible. Such a requirement leads not only to structural advantages for such complex multidirectional systems, but also to practical production advantages.

At this moment, we will not further explore the architectural implications of these saddle polyhedra–derived structures. Nor are we ready to investigate the architectural possibilities generally indicated by an integrative morphological system. I have shown an array of possibilities and to some extent have discussed their structural implications. I have shown the extraordinary interrelationships among a collection of diverse structures. It is remarkable to realize that systems of such complex three-dimensional curvature as that exhibited by the continuous surfaces may also be easily described as networks composed of straight branches and simple nodes indeed, as subsets of the universal network. The simplicity and integrative capability of our morphological system is a decisive step toward a comprehensive theory of modular structure, but it is not by any means the end of the story.

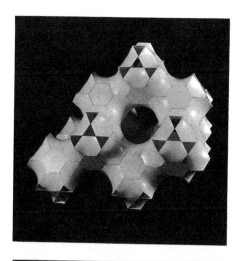

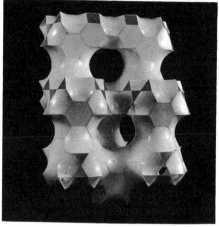

10.7 Two views of a terminated diamond labyrinth assembled from 120° saddle octagons and plane regular hexagons, with 90°,120° saddle hexagons used to close off the tunnels for stability. Note the occurrence of triangles and squares which are not closed on this model.

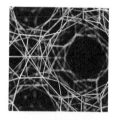

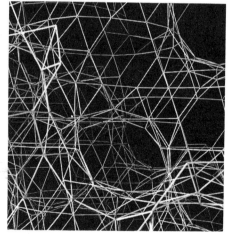

10.6 Details of the triangulated framework structure which approximate the cubic 6-tunnel continuous surface.

11

Infinite Spatial Networks from Equilateral Triangles

Though we have, so far, covered the general principles governing three-dimensional modular space, we do not have a comprehensive overview of the periodic triangulation of three-dimensional space. In our discussion of the triangulated approximations of the continuous surface labyrinths (Chapter 10), and in our discussions of triangulated networks derived from closest packing (Chapter 1), we have come to appreciate some of the properties of triangulated spatial systems. The importance of triangulated structures has been stressed because of their characteristically high strength-to-weight ratio (Chapter 3).

As a corollary to the law of closest packing and triangulation of Chapter 1, it can be stated that complex three-dimensional triangulated structures tend to be more energy efficient when the differences in their branch lengths are minimized or eliminated. Such equilateral triangulated structures tend to evenly distribute stresses acting on them, and this distribution improves as the structure becomes more uniform. Therefore, it may be taken for granted that the more uniform a triangulated structure, the less resource investment it will require. Due to the stress-distribution property of such structures, the specific directions of the forces acting on them are far less significant than for nontriangulated systems.

Periodic Systems of Equilateral Triangles

In Chapter 4 I listed the possible finite convex figures that could be formed with equilateral triangles. In addition to the regular tetrahedron, octahedron, and icosahedron, there were five other figures, bounded by 6, 8, 10, 12, 14, and 16 faces, respectively (see [4.20]). Of all these, only the regular tetrahedron and octahedron can be accounted for by the universal net system. However, because of our special interest in both triangulated structures and infinite periodic structures, we need not be content with only the few triangulated structures already described.

This aforementioned inventory of finite convex deltahedra suggests an investigation of the possibilities of infinite periodic spatial structures composed *exclusively* of equilateral triangles. So far we have identified only one such system, the 12-connected fcc network (tetrahedral/octahedral space filling). However, we must find systematic, albeit empirical, methods to explore other possibilities. One cannot expect to get very far very quickly by random attempts to combine equilateral triangles in space.

We have seen the limits of space filling systems per se, as far as periodic arrangements of equilateral triangles are concerned. The highly symmetrical icosahedron has been notably absent from our discussion of space filling and this is a disturbing point which deserves further investigation. We have touched briefly on the possibilities for open packings of polyhedra. Perhaps this would be a fruitful course to study in a search for an inventory of periodic equilateral triangular structures.

Open Packings of Tetrahedra, Octahedra, and Icosahedra

It will be useful at this point to put forth some morphological principles which can guide the search for open packings of polyhedra. The universal node-net system can again serve to clarify the nature of such structures. Open packings of polyhedra can be compared to networks in which certain polyhedra function as nodes and certain other polyhedra function as branches. We have already seen examples of this correspondence in the open packings of truncated octahedra and hexagonal prisms described in Chapter 10, in which the truncated octahedra were positioned at the sites of nodes in the diamond net or the bcc 8-connected net, and hexagonal prisms were aligned with the branches of such nets. That is, the truncated octahedra functioned as very large nodes and the hexagonal prisms as very stubby branches. When given polyhedra have some symmetrical correspondence to the Universal Node or any of its three branches, it is likely that they can combine in various arrangements to form open packings. It is characteristic of many open packings of polyhedra, when joined on certain face planes, that certain polyhedra must serve as nodes and others as branches. There are also open packings of polyhedra which combine on face planes in such a way that all polyhedra serve as nodes of a network. We will also find a few cases of open packings in which polyhedra are linked by their edges.

Let us first consider the three regular triangulated figures: the tetrahedron, octahedron, and icosahedron, from the point of view of open packings. The tetrahedron has four axes of 3-fold symmetry in the [111] directions, and three axes of 2-fold symmetry in the [100] directions. Its four faces are parallel to (111) planes and its six edges are parallel to (100) planes. If tetrahedra are joined edge to edge, they combine to form the 12-connected fcc network, so we have not discovered anything new. It is quickly found that tetrahedra alone will not fill space. If they are joined face to face they will not repeat in space. If they represent nodes of a network, they must be separated from each other by branches having a very special property. The reader will recall that the [111] branches of the Universal Node connector had to have a longitudinal twist of 60° in order to maintain the proper orientation of the nodes.

If equilateral triangles are formed at each end of the branch, one must be rotated by 60° from the other about a common axis [11.1]. Any polyhedron which has two parallel equilateral triangular faces that share a common axis about which they are twisted by 60° with respect to each other can serve as a [111] branch. If the parallel planes are regular hexagons, such a polyhedron can also serve as a branch separating the polyhedra which have corresponding hexagonal faces in [111] directions. The need for the twisted branch is obscured by the hexagonal faces, because they can accommodate the twist by virtue of the fact that they have twice as many sides as the triangular face. Limiting ourselves to triangular polyhedra, we find that both the regular octahedron and the icosahedron have sets of parallel faces which are disposed about a common axis at 60°. Therefore, they qualify as [111] branches. If octahedra are placed on each face of the regular tetrahedron, a subset of the 12-connected fcc network is created in which only nine edges and nine triangles meet at each vertex (Wells 1969).

11.1 Any polyhedron which has two parallel equilateral triangular faces axially displaced 60° with respect to each other can serve as a [111] branch.

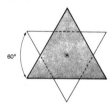

Since the fcc network is a subset of the universal network and since this open packing of regular tetrahedra and regular octahedra is a subset of the 12-connected fcc net, it is also a subset of the universal network. In this structure, the tetrahedra are found at the nodes of the diamond net and the octahedra function as [111] branches. Although the net of this structure can be assembled from Universal Node components, I show it here as an open packing of polyhedra [11.2].

If icosahedra are placed on each face of a tetrahedron another interesting periodic structure results. Like the open packing of tetrahedra and octahedra mentioned above, the diamond structure is again formed with the tetrahedra found at the nodal sites of the diamond net and the icosahedra functioning as [111] branches [11.3]. The network formed by the edges of the tetrahedra and icosahedra is semiuniform with 12-connected and 5-connected vertices.

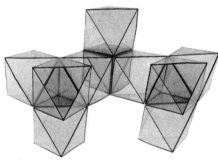

11.2 An open packing with tetrahedra as nodes and octahedra as branches forms the diamond structure.

11.3 The diamond structure as an open packing of tetrahedra (nodes) and icosahedra (branches).

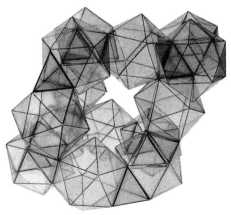

The octahedron is more interesting. It has four axes of 3-fold symmetry, three axes of 4-fold symmetry and twelve axes of 2-fold symmetry. If octahedra are joined edge to edge, like tetrahedra, the 12-connected fcc network is again formed. However, to join octahedra on their faces is another story. The eight faces of the octahedron are parallel to the (111) planes. It is, therefore, possible to use the octahedron as the node for the 8-connected bcc network or its subset, the 4-connected diamond net, and we have already observed that octahedra can serve as [111] branches. Two extremely interesting structures are thus formed. Both have uniform vertices.

In the first system, the octahedra are found at the sites of the bcc lattice with additional octahedra functioning as branches. The node octahedra have branch octahedra attached to all eight of their faces, while the branch octahedra share only two parallel, oppositely disposed faces with node octahedra. This fully triangulated net has 12-connected vertices and, although the triangles are equilateral, as is the case with the 12-connected fcc net, it should not be confused with the latter. It can be seen in [11.4].

11.4 An open packing of octahedra as both nodes and branches, forming the bcc structure.

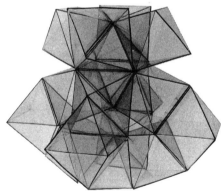

The other system is simply a subset of this bcc arrangement in which octahedra are found at the nodal sites of the diamond network with additional octahedra serving as branches. In this case, branch octahedra are attached to only four of the eight faces of the node octahedra. The fully triangulated network of this arrangement has uniformly connected vertices in which 8 branches meet [11.5]. Both of these open packings of octahedra give rise to infinite spatial labyrinths which complements the connected chain formed by the periodic associations of polyhedra.

11.5 Diamond structure formed by an open packing of octahedra as both nodes and branches.

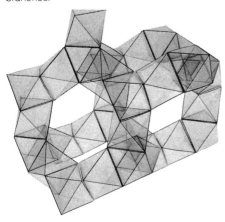

Open Packings of Icosahedra (Continued)

Let us now review the symmetry characteristics of the icosahedron. Due to its relative complexity one might expect some fruitful possibilities in spite of its 5-fold symmetry. We have already seen that 5-fold symmetries are not permissible in infinite periodic structures, except in the limited case of concentric arrangements about a unique center of symmetry (see [4.7]). The icosahedron has been frequently dismissed as having no capability for forming periodic structures. Its special place in the theory of polyhedra stems from the fact that it is the only regular polyhedron with a set of 5-fold symmetry axes. It has altogether six 5-fold axes of rotational symmetry. Thus it is easy to overlook the fact that this figure also has ten axes of 3-fold symmetry and fifteen axes of 2-fold symmetry. Even this is not so significant for periodic systems until it is realized that the regular icosahedron has eight of its twenty triangular faces parallel to the eight faces of the octahedron (the (111) planes) [11.6] and six of its 30 edges parallel to the faces of the cube (the (100) planes) [11.7].

11.6 Eight faces of the icosahedron are parallel to the faces of the regular octahedron.

11.7 Six edges of the icosahedron are parallel to the faces of the cube.

We have already noted that the icosahedron can qualify as a [111] branch in open packing systems because it has parallel sets of faces rotated 60° with respect to each other on common axes. With eight of its faces parallel to the [111] planes, it becomes clear that the icosahedron may also serve as a node. As might be expected, both the 8-connected bcc network and the 4-connected diamond net can be formed. In the former, eight branch icosahedra are attached to each node icosahedron on its eight (111) faces [11.8]. In the latter, only four branch icosahedra are attached to half of the (111) faces of each node icosahedron [11.9]. Neither of these structures forms uniform nets because in both cases the branch icosahedra have sets of equatorial vertices which remain 5-fold as they do not come into contact with the node icosahedra. However, these nets could be considered semiuniform in that, in both cases, only two different kinds of vertices appear. In the bcc case, the node icosahedron has eleven triangles meeting at each vertex, and in the diamond case the node icosahedron has eight triangles meeting at each vertex. Therefore these structures have, respectively, 11- and 5-connected vertices and 8- and 5-connected vertices.

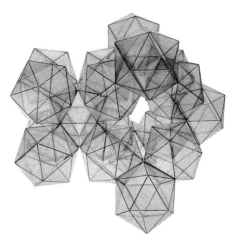

11.8 An open packing of icosahedra as both nodes and branches forms the bcc structure.

Another series of three related structures can be formed by the admixture of icosahedra and octahedra in which these two polyhedra are alternately used as nodes or branches. With node icosahedra positioned at bcc sites, eight branch octahedra may be attached to each (111) face forming a completely uniform 9-connected fully triangulated network [11.10]. Due to an incompatibility of dihedral angles, this system cannot be reversed with the icosahedra serving as branches and the octahedra as nodes.

Four branch icosahedra may be attached to four of the eight faces of the node octahedron [11.11]. This configuration forms a semiuniform net in which the vertices shared by nodal and branch polyhedra are each surrounded by ten triangles, and the vertices found exclusively with the branch icosahedra are surrounded by five triangles each. If this sytem is reversed, branch octahedra are attached to four of the eight (111) faces of a node icosahedron, resulting in a completely uniform net in which seven equilateral triangles surround each vertex [11.12].

Packing Icosahedra Edge to Edge

In addition to these face coordinated open packing systems which utilize the icosahedron, there are three significant systems in which icosahedra are joined edge to edge (edge-coordinated) and which do not require branch polyhedra. The simplest of these is organized according to a simple cubic lattice with an icosahedron at each site. Icosahedra are joined on their six edges which are parallel to the cube planes [11.7] and [11.13] This forms a stable triangulated 9-connected uniform network.

11.13 Icosahedra positioned at the sites of the simple cubic lattice joined by edges parallel to the (100) planes.

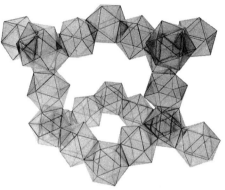

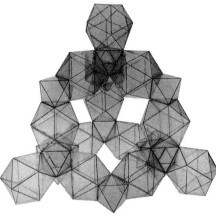

11.9 Diamond structure formed by an open packing of icosahedra as both nodes and branches.

11.10 An open packing of icosahedra (nodes) and octahedra (branches) forms the bcc structure.

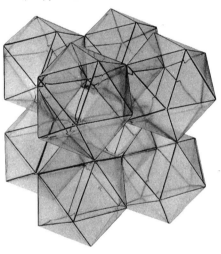

11.11 The diamond structure as an open packing of octahedra (nodes) and icosahedra (branches).

11.12 The diamond structure as an open packing of icosahedra (nodes) and octahedra (branches).

There is a second system which also joins icosahedra on six of the thirty edges. It is somewhat more difficult to describe as the six edges in question do not correspond to the cube planes (the (100) planes). They are approximately parallel to the (111) planes. The icosahedra are organized in an arrangement which approximately corresponds to a 6-connected bcc network* defined by the space filling of rhombic hexahedra. The specific edges of the icosahedron which are shared with neighboring icosahedra in the array are approximately parallel to six "equatorial" faces of the regular octahedron [11.14]. This periodic structure, like the other icosahedron systems, is fully stable [11.15].

*The icosahedra actually fall at the sites of a tetragonal body centered lattice. (See Chapter 5 and [5.4].)

11.14 An icosahedron within an octahedron. Six icosahedral edges are approximately parallel to corresponding faces ((111) planes) of the octahedron.

11.15 Icosahedra positioned at the approximate sites of the bcc lattice, joined by edges parallel to six octahedral faces.

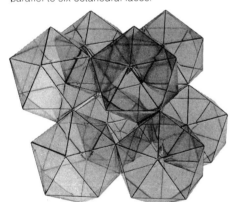

A third edge-coordinated system is a very ingenious construction, called to my attention by Dennis Johnson. It is a hierarchical concentric packing with a unique center of symmetry. The concentric packing will expand infinitely but at any level or layer the total packing has full icosahedral symmetry about its center. This is one factor which contributes to its complexity. The first phase of its formation consists of joining twelve icosahedra together by their edges around a common center. This results in a complex which itself defines a larger single icosahedron [11.16]. Each face of this larger icosahedron consists of a planar packing of three icosahedra in which the vertices and three coplanar face segments are provided. This larger icosahedral group of twelve smaller icosahedra may then be combined with eleven others just alike, and this collection, which totals 144 smaller icosahedra, forms still another larger icosahedron [11.17]. This icosahedron of 144 smaller units will also combine with eleven other like units to form a still larger icosahedrally arranged array consisting of 12 × 144, or 1,728 icosahedra of the original small size. This process can be repeated indefinitely.

11.16 Twelve icosahedra joined by edges around a common center to form planes of a larger icosahedron.

11.17 A hierarchical packing of 133 icosahedra describes the planes of a larger icosahedron.

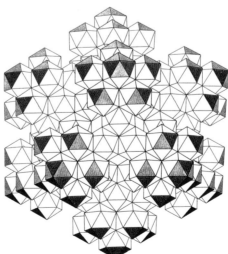

There is still another way in which icosahedra may be aggregated. It is a system in which icosahedra are joined to each other by both edges and faces. If an icosahedron is viewed along one of its 3-fold rotation axes, it will be seen in projection to form a regular hexagon around its periphery. This is a projection of the skew hexagonal equator characteristic of the icosahedron. A planar array of icosahedra may be packed in such a way that these skew hexagonal equators join edge to edge in a regular hexagonal tessellation [11.18]. Layers of such icosahedral tessellations may then be stacked face on face and so form a fully stable triangulated infinite periodic structure [11.19]. This structure is a semi-uniform net with both 8- and 11-connected nodes. The icosahedra in such an arrangement are positioned at the nodal sites of a network of triangular prisms.

11.18 An edge-coordinated planar tessellation of icosahedra.

11.19 Layers of planar tessellations of icosahedra form a three-dimensional periodic structure.

Unidirectional Indefinite Networks of Equilateral Triangles

The foregoing completes the inventory of periodic structures composed of regular tetrahedra, octahedra, and icosahedra and combinations thereof. We now return to our search for packings of triangles and immediately find a series of unidirectional infinite packings composed entirely of equilateral triangles. It is obvious that octahedra and icosahedra can be infinitely stacked on sets of parallel and opposite faces to form columnar structures [11.20]. When it is realized that the octahedron is nothing but a triangular antiprism, it becomes clear that all antiprisms are capable of such stacking arrangements; and, as long as the antiprisms have no more than 16 sides (octagonal antiprism), they form stable structures [11.21]. If antiprisms are used that have greater numbers of sides they tend to suffer from local instability as dihedral angles approach 180°.

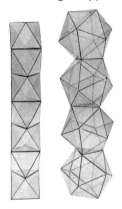

11.20 Octahedra and icosahedra can stack to form infinite columnar structures.

11.21 Antiprisms stack to form fully triangulated infinite columnar structures. Square and octagonal antiprisms are shown here.

Far more subtle is an infinite columnar structure, the tetrahelix, described by Fuller (1963a, p. 161). It consists of tetrahedra attached face upon face in such a fashion that an infinite helical array is formed [11.22].

The octahedron and icosahedron each have sets of four planes that are parallel to the regular tetrahedron (the (111) planes), so both of these structures can also form helical columns. We can call these the octahelix [11.23a] and the icosahelix [11.23b]. We can also imagine admixtures of all three figures in various combinations that would give rise to similar helical forms. The significance of such helical structures for architecture is at present remote, but because of the similarity of their shape to the shape of biomolecules they may be of interest to scientists.

11.22 Infinite helical columnar structure assembled from regular tetrahedra: the tetrahelix (Fuller).

11.23 Infinite helical columnar structures assembled from regular octahedra and regular icosahedra: the octahelix (a) and the icosahelix (b).

a

b

The tetrahelix is an optimum form in the sense that it is a fully triangulated columnar structure, requires only a single edge length, and is constructed with fewer components for a given column length than any other triangulated columnar system. Such a tetrahelical structure may constitute a highly efficient modular structure for resistance to axial compression or tension loads. For example, a microscale tetrahelix could theoretically be substituted for the branches of any of the triangulated structures we have discussed.

Packings of Snub Cuboctahedra

There are two more periodic structures in our inventory which are composed entirely of equilateral triangles. Of the Platonic and Archimedean polyhedra, there is still one figure which we have not mentioned. It is the snub cuboctahedron, and it appears in both right- and left-handed form. The snub cuboctahedron is the only polyhedron of the Platonic/Archimedean collection with cubic symmetry which is not accountable for by the universal net. We have already discussed the icosahedron and its derivative forms, all of which have icosahedral symmetry and, therefore, do not fit simply into the cubic scheme of things. The snub cuboctahedron is in a class by itself.*

It is bounded by 32 equilateral triangles and 6 squares. Eight of its triangles are parallel to the (111) or octahedral planes, but the remaining 24 do not correspond to any of the three cubic planes. The 6 square faces are, of course, parallel to the (100) or cube planes. Right- and left-handed snub cuboctahedra may be combined on their square faces to form a fully stable periodic network with uniform 8-connected nodes [11.24]. The snub cuboctahedra are positioned at the nodal sites of the simple cubic lattice. The finite snub cuboctahedron, due to its square faces, forms an unstable network. However, in this open packing structure, the square faces stabilize each other. In a periodic array, only the terminal cells need have their square faces triangulated if complete stability is to be achieved.

*There is also a snub dodecahedron with icosahedral symmetry.

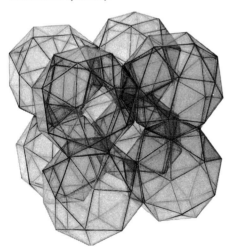

11.24 Enantiomorphic pairs of snub cuboctahedra combine on square faces to form a uniform infinite periodic triangulated structure.

If a model of the snub cuboctahedron is constructed from branches joined together with hingeable nodes, the instability of the square faces is immediately apparent. When the square faces are deflected they also become skew. The squares that are common to adjacent polyhedra in the periodic array tend to deflect in opposite directions and, therefore, stabilize each other. As long as squares (or any polygon with more than three sides) are shared by contiguous cells of an otherwise fully triangulated system, they will aways stabilize each other. If the squares are not shared they will be unstable. This explains that when a structure such as the repeating snub cuboctahedron system is infinite, it is fully stable, but that when such a periodic structure is terminated it becomes unstable in the peripheral regions unless additional triangulation is incorporated into the terminal faces.

Packing of Truncated Tetrahedra and Hexagonal Antiprisms

The final structure in the inventory of systems composed of equilateral triangles is a semiuniform network with both 6- and 7-connected nodes. This is an open-packed binary system, composed of truncated tetrahedra positioned at the nodal sites of the diamond network with double arrangements of hexagonal antiprisms serving as the branch polyhedra. The repeat unit of this system is formed by placing a hexagonal antiprism on each hexagonal face of the truncated tetrahedron [11.25]. When this repeat unit is combined with others like it, the periodic structure is formed [11.26]. There are always two face-to-face antiprisms between each truncated tetrahedron. All of the hexagonal faces are stabilized (except terminal ones) according to the same principles of interaction described in relation to the snub cuboctahedron system. This structure forms an infinite periodic labyrinth similar to the snub cuboctahedron system.

Table 11.1 lists the periodic structures composed of equilateral triangles that have been described in this chapter. In addition to showing which polyhedra function as nodes and which as branches, the networks which these "node" and "branch" polyhedra form are indicated. The coordination of the networks is given. A single number indicates one kind of vertex in a periodic array and hence a uniform network, and a double number indicates two kinds of vertices and hence a semiuniform network.

As I pointed out early in this chapter, in addition to the tetrahedron, octahedron, and icosahedron, there are five other convex deltahedra. The six-faced deltahedron is merely two face-to-face regular tetrahedra, and, as such, occurs in the version of the tetrahedron/octahedron triangulated space filling system, which exhibits overall hexagonal symmetry, described by the hexagonal closest packed spheres (see Chapter 6). The remaining four deltahedra comprised of 10, 12, 14, and 16 faces do not give rise to space filling or open packing systems. Therefore, no additional periodic structures from equilateral triangles may be derived from these polyhedra.

11.25 Hexagonal antiprisms placed on each face of the truncated tetrahedron.

11.26 Periodic triangulated structure formed by the spatial repetition of the assembly of [11.25], in which paired hexagonal antiprisms form branches between truncated tetrahedra positioned at the sites of nodes in the diamond structure.

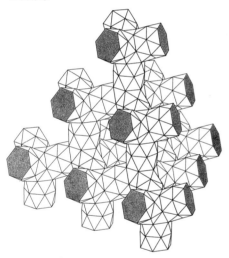

Table 11.1
Periodic Structures
Composed of
Equilateral Triangles
(Derived from Open
Packings of Polyhedra)

Node Polyhedron	Branch Polyhedron	Network	Face Joined	Edge Joined	Z	Uniform	Semi-uniform	Figure Number	
1 Tetrahedron	Octahedron	Diamond	√		9	√		11.2	
2 Tetrahedron	Icosahedron	Diamond	√		12/5		√	11.3	
3 Octahedron	Octahedron	bcc (Z = 8)	√		12	√		11.4	
4 Octahedron	Octahedron	Diamond	√		8	√		11.5	
5 Icosahedron	Icosahedron	bcc (Z = 8)	√		11/5		√	11.8	
6 Icosahedron	Icosahedron	Diamond	√		8/5		√	11.9	
7 Icosahedron	Octahedron	bcc (Z = 8)	√		9	√		11.10	
8 Octahedron	Icosahedron	Diamond	√		10/5		√	11.11	

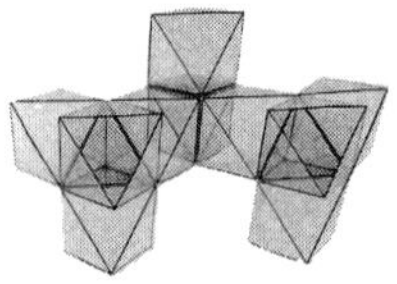

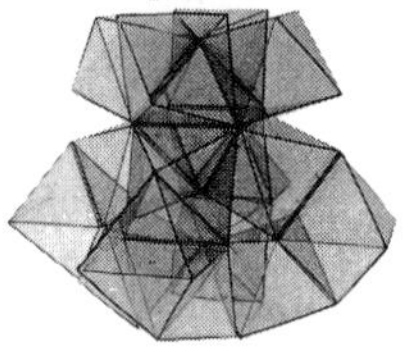

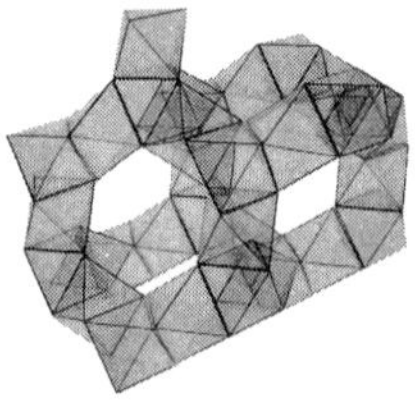

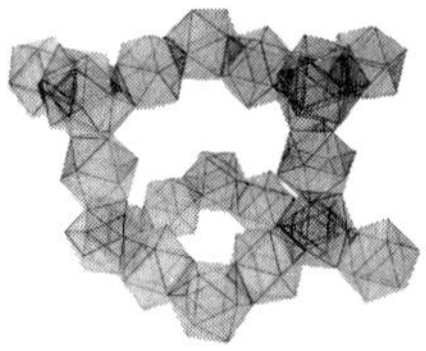

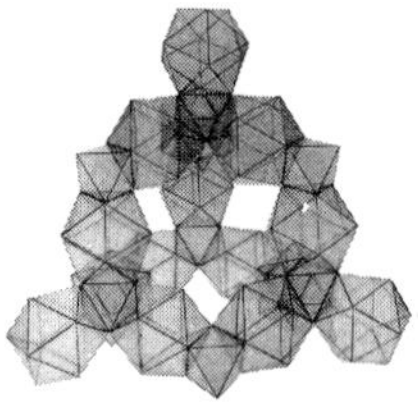

Table 11.1
Continued

Node Polyhedron	Branch Polyhedron	Network	Face Joined	Edge Joined	Z	Uniform	Semi-uniform	Figure Number
9 Icosahedron	Octahedron	Diamond	√		7	√		11.12
10 Icosahedron		Simple cubic		√	9	√		11.13
11 Icosahedron		Approximate bcc (Z = 6)		√	9	√		11.15
12 Icosahedron		Concentric 5-fold net		√				11.16
13 Icosahedron		Triangular prism	√	√	8/9		√	11.19,
14 Snub cubocta-hedron (rt. & left)		Simple cubic	√		8	√		11.24
15 Truncated tetrahedron	Hexagonal antiprism (double)	Diamond	√		6/7		√	11.25,

12 Closest Packed Cells and the Triangulation of Space

Triangulated Structures Derived from Closest Packed Cellular Systems

Our inventory in the preceding chapter uncovered very few possibilities of structures composed exclusively of equilateral triangles. A few examples of periodic triangulated structures consisting of nearly equal edges have also been described in previous chapters, most notably the 14-connected bcc net and the triangulated approximations to continuous surfaces. These systems suggest the possibilities of other approximately equilateral triangulated periodic networks. "Approximately equilateral" can be taken to mean that 25% is a reasonable maximum difference in edge length, remembering that, as I have stressed earlier (especially in Chapter 11), the smaller the differences in edge lengths, the more energy-efficient a structure will tend to be.

As I pointed out in Chapter 1, all closest packed cellular aggregates form dual networks that are fully triangulated (according to the law of closest packing and triangulation). Therefore, any periodic solutions to this problem will yield triangulated structures composed of nearly equal branches, providing, of course, that all cells are of approximately equal volume throughout. Therefore, closest packed space filling systems composed of approximately equivolume polyhedra could be a basis for deriving new periodic triangulated structures. They may also provide a solution to the ideal soap bubble packing that is more consistent with experimental evidence than the Kelvin proposal introduced in Chapter 1.

As Matzke (1946) showed, typical cell aggregates are never composed of identical shapes even when their volumes are the same. Some conjectures about the reasons for this have been presented in Chapter 1, along with a detailed discussion of the general characteristics of closest packed polyhedral cells. I have suggested that the 15% difference in the distances between cell centers that is created by the packing of minimal tetrakaidecahedra may be too great to satisfy the law of closest packing and triangulation when the soap bubbles are of equal volume. Perhaps the solution lies not in a single cell shape, but in some complementary space filling system which may be composed of two, three, or even four different cell shapes, all with equal volume, but not necessarily of the same number of faces. The reader is reminded that Matzke's (1946) study of arrays of equivolume bubbles uncovered an average of 13.70 faces per polyhedron, with faces having included angles of 109°28′, and with the majority of faces being pentagons. Therefore, we can anticipate that if such a periodic complementary system exists, it will be composed of polyhedra ranging from approximately 12 to 16 faces.

The Distorted Pentagonal Dodecahedron

It is tempting to consider the pentagonal dodecahedron, which has been notably absent from our discussion of space filling, as a component of a complementary space filling system. Not only does it have the pentagonal faces which dominate the bubble arrays, but its face angles of 108° are very close to 109°28′, requiring far less distortion of this figure than that which is necessary to distort the truncated octahedron with 90° and 120° face angles into the Kelvin minimal tetrakaidecahedron with its 109°28′ face angles. Beyond this, the pentagonal dodecahedron has slightly less surface area per unit volume than the truncated octahedron and only slightly more than Kelvin's minimal tetrakaidecahedron. This relationship is shown in Table 12.1, which compares surface-to-volume ratios of various polyhedra and the sphere.

Table 12.1

Surface-to-Volume Ratios in Terms of the Geometrical Invariant

Three-dimensional figures may be characterized by the geometrical invariant $I = S / V^{2/3}$, where S is the measured surface area and V the measured volume of the figure. Since I is dimensionless, its value for a given type of figure is independent of the size of the figure. Values of I for the sphere and various polyhedra are given here. For figures of unit volume, I is equal to the surface area. The surface area S of a figure of arbitrary volume V is given by $S = I\,V^{2/3}$, and the surface-to-volume ratio by $S / V = I / V^{1/3}$.

Figure		I
1	Sphere	4.83598
2	Icosahedron	5.14836
3	Minimal tetrakaidecahedron	5.30632
4	Pentagonal dodecahedron	5.31163
5	Truncated octahedron	5.31474
6	Rhombic dodecahedron	5.34539
7	Regular octahedron	5.71911
8	Tetragonal octahedron	5.88337
9	Cube	6.00000
10	Rhombic hexahedron	6.73477
11	Regular tetrahedron	7.20562
12	Tetragonal disphenoid	7.41285

The regular dodecahedron will not combine with itself to fill space due to its icosahedral symmetry, as has been discussed in Chapter 5. If this dodecahedron is formed such that all of its face angles are 109°28', as Kelvin did with the truncated octahedron, it is distorted very slightly. The edges become very slight arcs, and the faces become saddle-like. The equivalent distortion of the truncated octahedron is much more noticeable. Although calculations would be difficult and I have not attempted them, there is no doubt that this distorted dodecahedron would have less surface per unit of volume than its plane-faced counterpart and may even have less surface area per volume than the Kelvin figure. However, even this distorted dodecahedron will still not fill space in a periodic arrangement. If we let all the nodes be surrounded by equal length branches, all meeting at 109°28', and we allow the branches to distort into whatever curves they may require, it is possible to form a radial or concentric packing of pentagonal dodecahedra [12.1].

It should be noted that there is no unique solution to this problem. The nuclear dodecahedron could be precisely regular with flat faces, straight edges, and 108° face angles. In this case, the successively packed dodecahedra could distort in such a way that all the edges remained straight and equal—but many different face angles begin to appear. Topologically, the systems are equivalent. In the present context we are more interested in a minimal solution exhibiting only 109°28' face angles.

In such an arrangement only the nuclear dodecahedron retains its full symmetry; in each successive layer the dodecahedra become progressively more distorted. This structure can theoretically progress to infinity, but the outer layers of dodecahedra will be considerably distorted. The dual network of this structure will be a fully triangulated concentric system, but great differences in branch lengths will result due to the extreme distortion of the dodecahedral cells. This cannot be considered periodic except in the limited sense of a radial progression. It is probably not a solution to the closest packed cells problem, not only because its cells do not have the number of faces shown by experimental arrays (it has only twelve faces), but also because it does not possess any inherent tendency to equalize the distances between neighboring cell centers; rather, its tendency is to increase the differences in these distances.

Pauling (1960) and Wells (1962) have shown that the pentagonal dodecahedron appears in the chemistry of certain hydrate structures and that it fills space in association with other polyhedra consisting of 14, 15, and 16 faces. I discussed these three polyhedra briefly in Chapter 1 (see [1.12]); a paper of K. W. Allen describes their geometry in detail. It is easily seen that there is no unique solution to any of these figures. Allen defines them in terms of plane faces and unequal straight edges. However, it is also possible to form them with all face angles equal to 109°28' and with equal branches. This, of course, requires that the branches be curved, as they are in the case of Kelvin's minimal tetrakaidecahedron.

The Tetrakaidecahedron and Space Filling

The 14-faced figure is bounded by two hexagons and 12 pentagons and has been called the *tetrakaidecahedron*.* When all face angles are 109°28', none of the faces are regular. We can form this tetrakaidecahedron with regular hexagons, but then the pentagons will not be regular. It is also possible to form the figure with as many as four pentagons that are regular, but in this case, if all faces are to remain plane, the hexagons will not be regular. Figure [12.2] shows the tetrakaidecahedron with all face angles equal to 109°28' and all branches of equal length.

*This is a source of some confusion because of Kelvin's earlier use of that term. To minimize this confusion, the Kelvin figure will always be referred to as the *minimal* tetrakaidecahedron and the newer figure will be simply called the *tetrakaidecahedron*.

12.2 The tetrakaidecahedron with all face angles equal to 109°28'.

12.1 Concentric packing of distorted pentagonal dodecahedra.

This 14-faced polyhedron fills space in the ratio of 3 tetrakaidecahedra for every dodecahedron. The dodecahedra in this system never touch each other; therefore, they may be regular. The tetrakaidecahedron will have seven axes of 2-fold symmetry (six equatorial axes and one polar axis). For the case in which all face angles are 109°28' and all edges, although arced, are of equal length, the average number of faces for each cell will be 13.50. There is an average of 5.14 sides associated with each face. These statistics are remarkably close to the experimental evidence cited in Chapter 1, and the 5.14 sides correspond exactly with the packing of minimal tetrakaidecahedra. The network which defines this dodecahedron/tetrakaidecahedron packing arrangement is shown in [12.3].

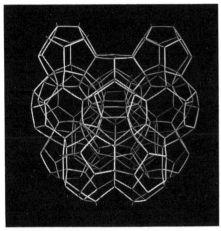

12.3 Network formed by space filling of pentagonal dodecahedra and tetrakaidecahedra with all face angles equal to 109°28'.

We have already noted that the dodecahedron contains more volume with less surface than the truncated octahedron. (Since the minimal tetrakaidecahedron has only 0.103% less surface than the truncated octahedron, we can assume that it also has somewhat more surface per unit volume than the corresponding minimal dodecahedron). Although no calculations have been made, it is likely that the tetrakaidecahedron bounded by 12 pentagons and 2 hexagons will also have less surface per volume than Lord Kelvin's ideal figure. It will at least be its equal in this respect. We have, then, a binary system which seems to go far in satisfying the properties of soap bubble arrays.

One difficulty is that if all edges are of equal length, then the volume of the tetrakaidecahedron will be greater than that of the dodecahedron. Consequently, the distances from the centers of adjacent cells will not be any more equalized than with the packing of minimal tetrakaidecahedra (the 14-connected bcc network). Actually, even with these volumetric differences, there still appears to be only about a 15%–20% variation in the distances between cell centers. It is conceivable that a packing of these two polyhedra could be formed in which they would both be nearly equal in volume by allowing difference of edge lengths while still maintaining the 109°28' face angles. Under such circumstances, variation of distances between cell centers may be minimized. Preliminary inspections suggest that these variations could be reduced to as little as 11%.

Such speculations notwithstanding, the closest packed space filling system composed of the pentagonal dodecahedron and the tetrakaidecahedron gives rise to a very interesting fully triangulated dual network composed of both 12- and 14-connected nodes. This system is composed of six different edge lengths. As there is no metrically unique solution to the space filling system from which this triangulated network is derived, there is also no unique solution to the triangulated system itself. It may be simply described in terms of a packing of a specially modified hexagonal antiprism and is shown in [12.4].

Such an antiprism will be bounded by two congruent parallel hexagons with 2-fold symmetry, oppositely oriented. The hexagons are joined to each other by an equatorial ring of twelve triangles of two different kinds. In this example, four of the twelve triangles will join the hexagonal planes at dihedral angles of 90° and will be equilateral triangles. The remaining eight triangles are isosceles. A planar array of these antiprisms may be formed by matching the "vertical" equilateral triangles. The remaining voids can be filled with tetrahedra of two kinds, neither of which are quite regular. Such planar arrays may be stacked by matching up the 2-fold hexagonal faces. The triangulation of the system is then completed by placing a node at the center of each antiprism, which node is then joined by branches to the vertices of the antiprism and to the centers of the antiprisms directly above and below.

12.4 Fully triangulated dual network of dodecahedral/tetrakaidecahedral packing of [12.3].

The Pentakaidecahedron and Space Filling

The 15-sided pentakaidecahedron as described by K. W. Allen is composed of plane faces; but it may also be formed with face angles all of 109°28' and with equal-length edges [12.5]. Like the tetrakaidecahedron, it is bounded by twelve pentagons; but instead of two hexagons, it has three. It has the symmetry of a triangular prism with one axis of 3-fold symmetry and three axes of 2-fold symmetry. This figure will fill space with the pentagonal dodecahedron and the tetrakaidecahedron in the ratio of three dodecahedra, two tetrakaidecahedra, and two pentakaidecahedra. The network which defines this system is shown in [12.6] with 109°28' face angles and equal-length, but slightly curved, branches. It is important to point out that although the tetrakaidecahedron appearing in this system is topologically identical to the one that appears in the binary dodecahedron/tetrakaidecahedron packing, it is more symmetrical (having one axis of 3-fold symmetry and six axes of 2-fold symmetry). The dodecahedron, which has full icosahedral symmetry in the binary system, has only tetragonal symmetry in this ternary packing.

The average cell in the dodecahedral/ tetrakaidecahedral/pentakaidecahedral system has 13.43 faces, and the average face again will have slightly more than 5 sides. This system also comes very near to satisfying the statistical evidence demonstrated by closest packed bubble systems. However, in this system we are confronted with cells of three sizes and, therefore, may expect even more deviation in the distances which separate cell centers.

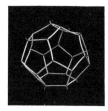

12.5 The pentakaidecahedron with all face angles equal to 109°28'.

12.6 Network formed by space filling of pentagonal dodecahedra, tetrakaidecahedra and pentakaidecahedra with all face angles equal to 109°28'.

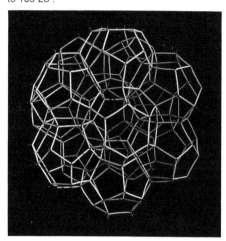

The dual network of this system is another fully triangulated arrangement in which the variations in branch lengths are relatively small and compare favorably to the 14-connected bcc network with its 15% variation. Its superficial organization is similar to the 12/14 connected network, and it can also be described in terms of a packing of modified hexagonal antiprisms [12.7]. In this case, the antiprisms are bounded by two regular hexagons of slightly different size and twelve triangles, of which half may be equilateral. It is necessary that half of the triangles meet the hexagons at dihedral angles of 90°. These may either be the equilateral triangles or isosceles triangles. The antiprisms are then packed into a planar array which contains tetrahedral voids. The planar array may then be stacked on its hexagonal faces. To complete the triangulation, we then place a new node at the center of each antiprism, which node is joined with branches to the antiprism vertices and to centers of the antiprisms above and below. A fully triangulated network is formed with 12-, 14-, and 15-connected nodes in which all space is filled with periodic arrangements of five different kinds of tetrahedra composed of five different but nearly equal edge lengths.

Like the dodecahedral/tetrakaidecahedral closest packed system, this dodecahedral/tetrakaidecahedral/pentakaidecahedral system could probably be adjusted so that all of the cells contained equal volume. Under such conditions, the distances between cell centers may very well be minimized, although it would be impossible to have absolute equality of distances. The variation in distances between centers appears to be reducible to something less than 15% but probably is not as little as the anticipated 11% of the dodecahedral/tetrakaidecahedral system.

12.7 Fully triangulated dual network of dodecahedral/tetrakaidecahedral/pentakaidecahedral packing of [12.6].

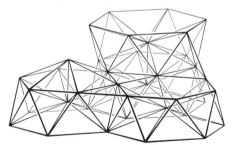

The Hexakaidecahedron and Space Filling

Perhaps of greatest interest is a cellular array with dodecahedra filling space in a binary system in which the complementary polyhedron is a 16-faced figure bounded by 12 pentagons and 4 hexagons (hexakaidecahedron). The space filling ratio is two dodecahedra to one hexakaidecahedron. The average cell has 13.30 faces and the average polygon has again slightly more than 5 sides. The dodecahedra are found in clusters of four with their centers at the vertices of a regular tetrahedron. This requires that each dodecahedron has one axis of 3-fold symmetry and three axes of 2-fold symmetry and that the face angles surrounding the 3-fold axis must be 109°28'.

If the dodecahedron is to have plane faces then there will only be six such angles. However, I have again assumed all vertices to be surrounded with equal branches meeting at 109°28'. This version of the hexakaidecahedron is shown in [12.8]. In terms of minimal surfaces, this system may be the best of all the systems examined. The hexakaidecahedron has more facets and is generally more spherical than the minimal tetrakaidecahedron, tetrakaidecahedron, or pentakaidecahedron. When this hexakaidecahedron combines in a closest packed cellular system with the minimal dodecahedron (which is already a slight improvement over the minimal tetrakaidecahedron), a significant reduction in total surface area per given volume can be expected over that provided for the Kelvin figure. This dodecahedral/hexakaidecahedral system can be seen in [12.9].

12.8 The hexakaidecahedron with all face angles equal to 109°28'.

12.9 Network formed by space filling of pentagonal dodecahedra and hexakaidecahedra with all face angles equal to 109°28'.

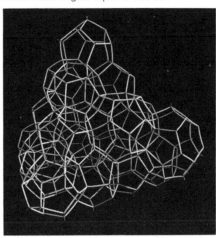

The distances between cell centers exhibit a variation of approximately 15%, which can also be improved upon if the volumes of the different types of polyhedra are equalized. The fully triangulated network derived from this system consists of only three different kinds of tetrahedra (including some regular tetrahedra), comprised altogether of three branch lengths differing by approximately 15%. This system may be easily derived from a space filling of regular tetrahedra and truncated tetrahedra by joining the vertices of each truncated tetrahedron to their centers and by then, in turn, joining the centers of adjacent truncated tetrahedra to each other. The latter system is shown in [12.10].

12.10 Fully triangulated dual network of dodecahedral / hexakaidecahedral packing of [12.9].

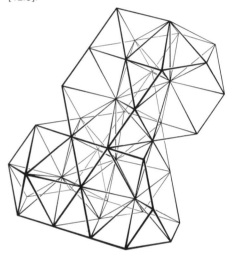

Multiple Solutions to a Single Problem

This completes our survey of closest packed cellular systems modeled on the statistics found in soap bubble packings. I have drawn attention to these systems, not only because they give rise to efficient periodic triangulated networks, but because of their possible use in explaining (or at least describing) the results of experiments with minimal surface cellular aggregations. It is probable that one, if not all, of the three dodecahedral closest packing systems that have just been described provides a better "ideal" solution to the problem of closest packed cells than Lord Kelvin's minimal tetrakaidecahedron. These examples indicate another direction to the solution of a problem which to date has been thought of in terms of a single archetypal cellular form. We see in this a strong pluralism at work; an illustration of the fact that, in nature, there is almost always more than one solution to a problem.

It should be pointed out in passing that the 12/14-, 12/14/15-, and 12/16-connected periodic triangulated networks I have just described are the same structures that Frank and Kasper describe as sphere packings in their papers on the alloy structures that we discussed in Chapter 1. Frank and Kasper have compared packings of spheres of slightly different sizes to various complex alloy structures. They have found packing systems which are somewhat more dense than the twelve-around-one packing coordination of equal spheres. Such structures are periodic but not homogeneous, as they exhibit various combinations of 12, 14, 15, and 16 spheres packed around another sphere. The dodecahedra, tetrakaidecahedra, pentakaidecahedra, and hexakaidecahedra precisely account for these various coordinations. The same triangulated networks may be derived from the Frank and Kasper sphere packings as from our packings of polyhedra.

It is worthy of note that the inherently stable triangulated frameworks we have just discussed are found in metal structures, while their dual nets—which as physical frameworks have no inherent stability—have been found in the composition of water molecules. The rigidity of the metal structure as compared to the fluidity of the water structure seems to be the consequence of geometric relationships.

Triangulated Labyrinths Derived from Dodecahedra and Hexakaidecahedra

The Pentakis Dodecahedron

The dual triangulated networks derived from the closest packed cellular systems described above, comprised of packing combinations of dodecahedra, tetrakaidecahedra, pentakaidecahedra, and hexakaidecahedra, have been structures with high densities of branches (high nodal coordination numbers) and very small interstitial volumes (polyhedra). It is also possible to derive open triangulated labyrinths with large interstitial volumes having low branch densities from these same dodecahedral packings.

A fully triangulated convex polyhedron may be built up from an individual pentagonal dodecahedron by placing a shallow pyramid on each pentagonal face. If we set the altitudes of the pyramids equal to each other, the resulting figure will be composed of 60 identical isosceles triangles. This polyhedron is known as the pentakis dodecahedron; it is the polyhedral dual of the truncated icosahedron [12.11]. The dihedral angle of this figure is 156°43′ and the face angles are 55°41.5′ and 68°37′ (Cundy and Rollett, Table II), so that the isosceles triangles are very nearly equilateral. The entire figure is composed of only two different branches which differ in length by approximately 10%.

12.11 The pentakis dodecahedron is formed by placing pentagonal pyramids on each face of the dodecahedron.

The pentakis dodecahedron with its full icosahedral symmetry illustrates the fact that it is impossible to form a convex polyhedron with more than sixty identical non-right triangles. If right triangles are permitted then each isosceles triangle of the pentakis dodecahedron can be subdivided into two coplanar right triangles, giving 120 as the greatest number of like units which can be used to form a convex polyhedron. It is this 120th lowest-common-denominator "icosahedral triangle" from which Fuller has derived his geodesic domes. The pentakis dodecahedron is topologically equivalent to the simplest of Fuller's geodesic domes.

Of the three dodecahedral closest packed systems that have been described, the dodecahedron / hexakaidecahedron (see [12.9]) is perhaps the most interesting. This is because it can be considered as an open packing of dodecahedra or an open packing of hexakaidecahedra. It is the only system of the three in which any single type of constituent polyhedron is repeated in a continuous arrangement. In the other two systems, the polyhedra are either completely isolated from others of the same type or they combine in purely linear stackings or planar arrangements. Though they still may give rise to interesting possibilities, it suggests that they are more complex, since any triangulated structure that is derived must require a combination of two or three different types of polyhedra. Since the pentakis dodecahedron is the simplest and most symmetrical of the four types of polyhedra, it is likely to be of greatest interest when it can combine with itself.

The Triangulated Hexakaidecahedron

We are also reminded that the tetrahedral hexakaidecahedron, which is composed of 12 pentagons and 4 hexagons, is more symmetrical and spherelike than the tetrakaidecahedron or the pentakaidecahedron. In fact, it should be observed that although it is less symmetrical than the icosahedron, its composition of nearly regular hexagons and only slightly distorted pentagons suggests that it could very well approach the icosahedron as a basis for the symmetrical subdivision of the sphere into triangulated polyhedra. The regular hexagon and the regular pentagon subdivide into more nearly equal-edged triangles than can any other polygon. The plane hexagon, of course, divides into six equilateral triangles and the plane pentagon subdivides into five isosceles triangles with face angles of 72°, 54°, and 54°.*

As the triangulated pentagon becomes a pyramid, the edges of the five triangles approach equality. As the triangulated hexagon becomes a pyramid, the edges radiating from the apex (center) increase in length forming isosceles triangles. Nevertheless, the altitude of the hexagonal pyramid can increase substantially over the plane hexagonal group of triangles before a great difference in the length of the circumferential and radial branches is exhibited. The hexakaidecahedron may be triangulated into a polyhedron composed of 84 triangles of nearly equal-length branches [12.12].

*The septagon divides into seven isosceles triangles with face angles of 51.42°, 64.29°, and 64.29°. However, since it does not occur in any of the polyhedra in question, we need not be concerned with it here.

Open Packing of Dodecahedra

Let us now consider the possibility of an open packing of dodecahedra and the consequences of their triangulation. In my first description of dodecahedral/hexakaidecahedral packing, I pointed out that tetrahedral clusters of dodecahedra were grouped around hexakaidecahedra [12.14]. In the open packing of these dodecahedra in which the hexakaidecahedra are omitted, it is found that six of the twelve faces of the dodecahedron are shared with neighboring dodecahedra while the remaining six define the continuous region originally occupied by the complementary polyhedra. When the dodecahedra are triangulated to form an open packing of pentakis dodecahedra (or simple geodesic spheres) it is found that the faces that are common to adjacent polyhedra need not be triangulated. Instead of forming a packing of pentakis dodecahedra, an open labyrinth structure is formed. The inherent stability is insured without the need to triangulate the interfaces of common polyhedra. The result is an open labyrinth similar in character to the continuous-surface system derived from the saddle polyhedra.

The details of this system may best be disclosed by a description of the development of the underlying packing system of dodecahedra, which, as we have earlier noted, must be slightly distorted if they are to pack. In the present instance, the requirement that all face angles be 109°28′ is abandoned. As with all labyrinth systems, this one must either be infinitely large or triangulated where it is terminated if it is to be completely stable. In this instance, the spherical approximation of the triangulated pentakis dodecahedron is an ideal terminal system. Consequently, the required distortions were made in such a manner as to minimally alter the regular dodecahedron.

12.12 Hexakaidecahedron and triangulated hexakaidecahedron.

a

b

c

d

e

f

g

h

i

j

k

l

12.13 Transforming the pentagonal dodecahedron for space filling by changing its face angles and symmetry. Deriving polar and equatorial cores (a, b, c); connecting equatorial cores (d, e, f); equatorial cores plus polar caps and alternate polar caps (g, h, i, j, k, l) combined to fill space.

Distorting the Dodecahedron

The regular dodecahedron has face angles of 108°. Because this packing arrangement consists of clusters of four tetrahedrally disposed dodecahedra surrounding a common point, it is necessary that the face angles around that point, and only those, be 109°28'. In a periodic arrangement the dodecahedron must have two oppositely disposed vertices which are surrounded by the 109°28' angle. The overall symmetry of the dodecahedron is transformed from full icosahedral to triangular, with a single 3-fold axis of symmetry and three 2-fold axes. I have developed a simple method of achieving this distortion of the regular figure.

The first step is to designate one of the 3-fold axes of the regular dodecahedron as a polar axis. Two slices are made perpendicularly to this polar axis, such that two "caps" are removed from the dodecahedron. Each cap includes three regular pentagonal faces meeting at the polar apex, plus three isosceles triangles removed from the ends of the equatorial pentagons. This process is shown in [12.13a, b]. Once the two polar caps are removed an equatorial core remains [12.13c]. This core has a major axis of 3-fold symmetry that corresponds to the original polar axis that was assigned to the dodecahedron and is bounded by six trapezoids which are partial truncations of regular pentagons, and two irregular hexagons of 3-fold symmetry in the planes of truncation. Three of the six edges of each hexagon are edges of the original pentagons. It is possible to form a three-dimensional periodic arrangement of the equatorial cores by connecting them together on these pentagon edges [12.13d, e].

Once such a periodic formation is established it becomes apparent that an open packing of dodecahedra may be subsequently formed by simply replacing the polar caps of the regular dodecahedra with alternate polar caps in which the proper angular adjustments have been made. Such an alternate cap must have three pentagons meeting at its apex with face angles of 109°28'. One very important feature of this infinite system is that when a given assembly is terminated, as it must eventually be, the polar cap of the regular dodecahedron may be used rather than the alternate polar cap. In other words, the dodecahedron remains

regular except where it shares an interface with another like unit. As we shall see, this has important consequences for the development of fully triangulated labyrinths.

Figure [12.13g] shows three dodecahedral cores with a single alternate cap added to each, allowing them to come together and share faces. Figure [12.13h] shows the same cluster of three with a regular cap placed where the fourth cell would go to complete a basic tetrahedral arrangement of four dodecahedra.

It can be observed that there is a very slight discrepancy that does not allow for a precise meshing of the regular cap. In Figure [12.13i] the regular cap has been replaced with the alternate cap, and it may now be seen that a precise meshing has occurred. Figure [12.13j] shows a cluster of three dodecahedra with alternate polar caps where they meet each other and regular caps on the opposite terminal regions. Figure [12.13k] shows a tetrahedral cluster of dodecahedral cores with the alternate caps added where they come together. Figure [12.13l] shows a tetrahedral cluster of four complete dodecahedra with the proper adjustments necessary for repetition in space. The space filling dodecahedron has two different pentagonal faces with angles of 109°28', 105°48', 109°28', 105°48', 109°28'; and 108°, 105°33.5', 112°53', 105°33.5', 108°. It is composed of two different edges which differ in length by less than 3%.

Figures [12.14] and [12.15] show periodic arrangements with dodecahedra and hexakaidecahedra. An open packing of sixteen dodecahedra reveals hexakaidecahedral holes. The network for an open packing of five hexakaidecahedra can be seen in [12.15c]. In this arrangement there are four hexakaidecahedra around a fifth; the figures are attached to each other on their hexagonal faces. If such an open packing is indefinitely extended, the centers of the hexakaidecahedra fall at the nodes of the diamond network. The centers of packed dodecahedra fall at the nodes of the network defined by space filling tetrahedra and truncated tetrahedra.

As was noted earlier, the hexakaidecahedron is bounded by 12 pentagons and 4 hexagons. The particular version formed in association with the adjusted space-filling dodecahedron is bounded by a special set of polygons. The 12 pentagons are not regular but correspond to the distorted pentagons that appear in the adjusted space filling dodecahedron with face angles of 108°, 105°33.5', 112°53', 105°33.5', 108°. Only this one kind of pentagon is required. These pentagons appear in groups of three meeting at a common vertex surrounded by the 112°53' face angles. Because this hexakaidecahedron is derived from a system of dodecahedra which has been adjusted to meet the requirement of space filling, it does not need to be considered in terms of a basic core as was the dodecahedron.

Triangulating Open Packed Distorted Dodecahedra

An initial attempt at the development of a packing of triangulated dodecahedra would seem to be simple enough—we merely placed pentagonal pyramids on all pentagonal faces of an array. This, of course, presents no difficulty when the pentagons do not form interfaces between cells. However, when such faces are shared by two cells, into which cells will the pyramids be directed if the pentagonal faces are to become pyramidal? This question has no important structural implications. As long as we employ pyramidal faces a stable structure will result, regardless of which cells the pyramids invade. However, the symmetry of the system must be altered with some cells having concave partitions while others have convex partitions.

However, we must not forget the simpler solution to the problem of interfaces, which is always applicable. As I have mentioned, it is possible simply to omit altogether the interfaces that are shared by adjacent cells. When this is done the infinite structure is still completely stable. It is only when the periodic system is terminated that it becomes necessary to stabilize the regions of the cell which normally form interfaces.

A periodic system of a most satisfying simplicity may be derived from the system of packed pentakis dodecahedra.

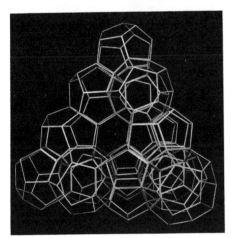

12.14 Open packing of distorted pentagonal dodecahedra.

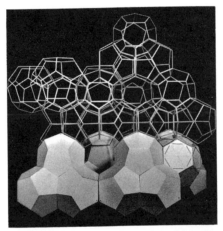

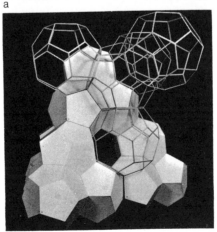

a

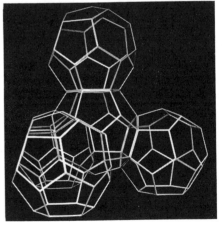

b

c

12.15 Packing arrangements of dodecahedra and hexakaidecahedra.

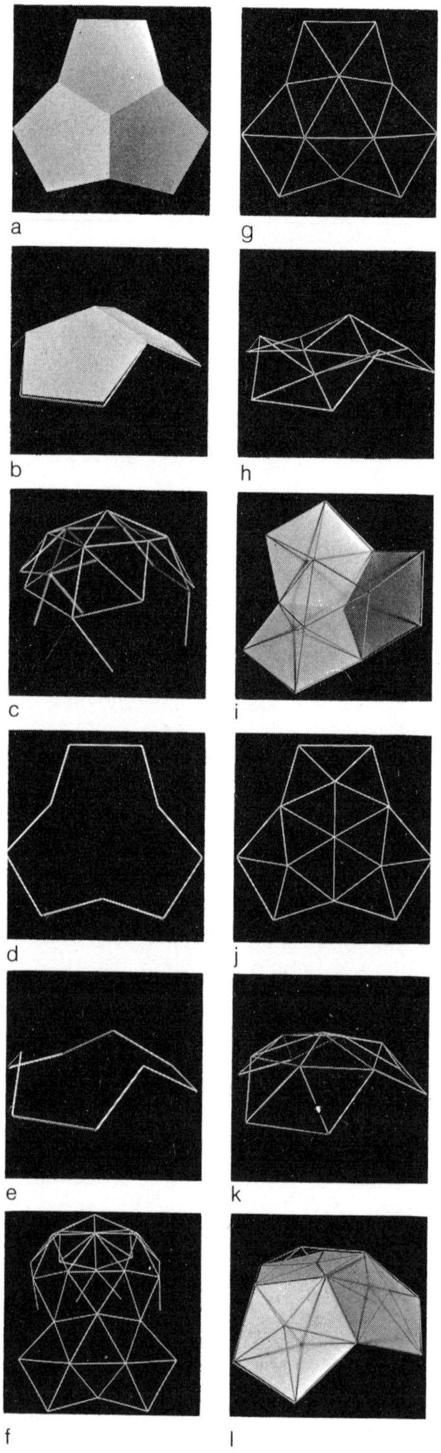

a

g

b

h

c

i

d

j

e

k

f

l

12.16 A nine-sided repeat unit is the basis for
the triangulation of open packings of distorted
pentagonal dodecahedra or hexakaidecahedra.

A Nine-Sided Elementary Repeat Unit

In [12.13l] can be seen a forward facing
set of three pentagons whose apex is directed towards the center of the tetrahedral cluster of four dodecahedra. This set
forms a concave region in the tetrahedral
cluster of dodecahedra and a convex region on the single hexakaidecahedron.
The set of three pentagons forms a nine-sided boundary which defines an elementary unit. It is illustrated in [12.16a, b, d, e].

If three pentagonal pyramids are placed
on the concave side of this repeat unit,
the distances separating their apices is
very nearly the same length as the edge
length of the original pentagon. A simplification can be achieved by joining the
apices of the pentagonal pyramids with
an equilateral triangle and by omitting the
six triangles which meet at the point
where the three original pentagons meet.
This results in a convex-concave collection of thirteen triangles bounded by a
nine-sided polygonal circuit. It is shown
in [12.16g, h, i] and brings to mind the
doubly curved saddle polygons. This
nine-sided unit of thirteen triangles can
be repeated infinitely to form a fully triangulated labyrinth not unlike the triangulated approximations of the periodic continuous surfaces described in Chapter 10.

Triangulated Dodecahedra Form a Diamond Labyrinth

While the packing of dodecahedra found
their centers at the nodes of the tetrahedral/truncated tetrahedral network, the
elimination of the interfaces achieved by
this triangulated system results in a
three-dimensional continuous labyrinth
which conforms to the diamond network.
We have seen that the diamond network is
a self-dual, so we can be sure that this
labyrinth divides space into two diamond
labyrinths. However, unlike the infinite
periodic minimal surface, the two regions
are of different volumes. The larger volume is that originally occupied by the
dodecahedra and the smaller region is
that originally occupied by the hexakaidecahedra.

The termination of the infinite labyrinth
formed by multiples of the basic repeat
unit is achieved with a collection of six
pentagonal pyramids which form exactly
half of the regular pentakis dodecahedron. This spherical terminal unit is shown
in [12.16c], and its relationship to the
nine-sided repeat unit is explained by
[12.16f].

In [12.13f] is shown the relationship of the
triangulated terminal tetrahedral cluster of
pentakis dodecahedra to the packing of
the four dodecahedral cores from which
they are derived.

Starting with the single pentakis dodecahedron, we may progressively add the equivalent of additional dodecahedral cells; although by the time four cells are combined the space is no longer cellular, but rather has become a three-dimensional continuous labyrinth. Nevertheless, the original sites of the dodecahedra can always be accounted for. The periodicity of this system is shown by two views of a model in [12.17] and [12.18]; the complex system shown in these figures consists of the equivalent of 28 dodecahedral cells.

Like all of the other multiple arrangements of this pentakis dodecahedral-derived system, this large structure consists of only three branch lengths which vary in length by no more than 10%.

Figures [12.19a–d] show details of the 28-cell structure. The terminal spherelike region is clearly shown in [12.19a], and in [12.19b] can be seen the nine-sided repeat unit of 13 triangles as it appears in the context of the periodic array. Figures [12.19c, d] give some feeling for the nature of the spatial labyrinth formed by this kind of structure. In relatively large arrays, such as the one shown here, a fourth branch may be added that is still within the 10% range of length variance. This branch joins two adjacent triangles to form a nearly regular tetrahedron. Such tetrahedra may be formed periodically in the structure and serve to increase both local stability as well as the overall stability of the structure.

12.19 Details of the triangulated labyrinth of [12.17] and [12.18].

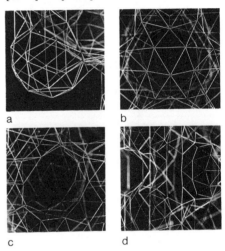

a   b

c   d

12.17 A triangulated labyrinth structure derived from an open packing of 28 pentagonal dodecahedra.

12.18 Another view of the structure shown in [12.17].

Triangulating Open Packings of Hexakaidecahedra

For the dodecahedron-oriented system just discussed, we began our study by placing pentagonal pyramids on the concave side of the set of three pentagons. If we place the same pentagonal pyramids on the convex side of this cluster, a significantly different result is formed. Instead, of the nine-sided convex-concave repeat unit, a nine-sided domical repeat unit consisting of 15 triangles is formed. Figures [12.16j, k, l] show this new configuration.

Four such units combine with four appropriately sized hexagonal pyramids to form a triangulated hexakaidecahedron (see [12.12].) An open packing of this polyhedron forms a system quite different from that derived from the dodecahedral packing. Rather than an infinite continuous-labyrinth structure, an open packing of spherelike polyhedra is formed. Earlier in this chapter I noted that the hexakaidecahedron packs together by sharing hexagonal faces. In a periodic array of triangulated hexakaidecahedra, the same hexagons form the common faces of these cells as they repeat with the symmetry of the diamond network. The triangulation of the hexagonal interfaces is unnecessary, as they are stabilized by the interaction of adjacent cells. The hexagonal pyramids which normally stabilize these hexagons in a single cell only need to be used at the terminal regions of a periodic array. Figures [12.20] and [12.21] show different views of the same periodic array of 14 triangulated hexakaidecahedra.

Such periodic triangulated hexakaidecahedra structures require four different branch lengths in the nine-sided 15-triangle repeat unit; an additional length must be added for the triangulation of the hexagonal terminal faces. The variation of lengths of branches does not exceed 10%. Because the hexakaidecahedral packing is the complement to the dodecahedral packing, and because the triangulated structures derived from these two systems both use the same basic nine-sided repeat unit, it is misleading to think of them as separate systems. It is certainly true that the general character of the triangulated labyrinth derived from the open packing of dodecahedra is quite different from that of the periodic array of triangulated hexakaidecahedra, but nevertheless they are both developments of the same system; both are based on the same nine-sided repeat unit. Which system is formed depends entirely on which mode of triangulation of the nine-sided repeat unit is used.

The common repeat unit makes it possible to arbitrarily and asymmetrically combine and interchange the two systems. This provides for endless permutations, all of which will be stable structural configurations. So here we have another example of diversity within the constraints of a simple minimum-inventory system.

12.20 An open packing of 14 triangular hexakaidecahedra.

12.21 Another view of the structure shown in [12.21].

Triangulated Packings of Rhombic Triacontahedra and Starred Dodecahedra

There are two additional systems that are closely related to the open packing of dodecahedra from which the pentakis dodecahedron–based triangulated structure was derived. They both have their origins in the basic dodecahedron.

Forming the Rhombic Triacontahedron

The metric properties of the pentagonal pyramids [12.13] can be adjusted so that when they are placed on the faces of the dodecahedron, 180° dihedral angles are formed between the two triangles which share a common dodecahedron edge. Because of the 180° dihedral angle, the two adjacent triangles become a single plane rhombus. The polyhedron that is formed is called the rhombic triacontahedron; it is bounded by 30 rhombic faces [12.22]. It is the polyhedral dual of the icosidodecahedron.

Because we are interested here in the framework of such polyhedra rather than their surface characteristics, we may still consider the rhombic triacontahedron to be composed of 60 identical triangles by retaining the original edges of the dodecahedra. These edges divide the rhombic faces into two equal isosceles triangles with angles of 58°17′ and 63°26′ and which are thus closer to the equilateral ideal than those of the pentakis dodecahedron. However, this figure, because it is less spherical, contains less volume per unit of surface and is likely to have less stress-distribution capability. Nonetheless, it is still a very stable and efficient form.

12.22 Forming the rhombic triacontahedron.

Forming the Starred Dodecahedra

The third dodecahedron-based system may be formed by again placing pentagonal pyramids upon each face of the dodecahedron. However, we will now let the pyramids be composed of equilateral triangles. The resulting polyhedron is bounded by 60 equilateral triangles; it is not as well mannered as the other two. It is not a simple convex polyhedron but is rather convex-concave. That is, some of its dihedral angles are less than 180° but others are greater than 180° [12.23]. We shall call it the starred dodecahedron. Unlike its two counterparts, it is not the dual of any semiregular polyhedron.

12.23 Forming the starred dodecahedron.

Two More Versions of the Nine-Sided Repeat Unit

Because of their common morphological origins, both the rhombic triacontahedron and the starred dodecahedron relate to the packing of dodecahedra in the same manner as does the pentakis dodecahedron. Therefore, two new versions of the nine-sided repeat unit can be envisioned. These new repeat units are topologically identical to the 13-triangle pentakis system and are derived by means of the same method we used for that system. The only difference is in the relative lengths of edges. Figure [12.24a–c] shows comparative tetrahedral clusters of all three systems. Their similarities and differences become apparent with careful study of this photograph.

12.24 Tetrahedral clusters of pentakis dodecahedra (a), rhombic triacontahedra (b), and starred dodecahedra (c).

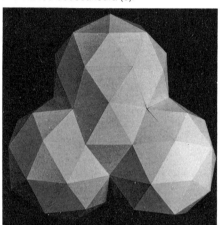

a

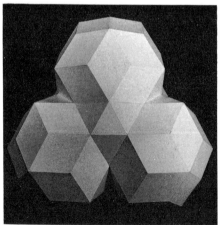

b

The rhombic triacontahedron–derived system [12.24b] is composed of three branch lengths which vary by 20%. The starred dodecahedron–derived system [12.24c] is composed of only two branches, which, however, vary in length by 35%. Both systems give rise to infinite periodic labyrinths very similar to that of the pentakis dodecahedron–derived structure. In each of these, the highly symmetrical form tends to counteract the loss of efficiency occasioned by the greater difference in component-branch lengths.

We saw that the pentakis-derived system could be adapted to either the concave or convex side of the nine-sided repeat unit of three pentagons. These two new systems may also be adapted in the same way. One can envision, therefore, an open packing of rhombic hexakaidecahedra as well as an open packing of starred hexakaidecahedra. With this set of systems we have developed an inventory of six fundamental geometrically significant alternative modes for the triangulation of the basic nine-sided polygonal repeat unit which is common to them all.

c

Alternative Modes of a Comprehensive System

Due to the relationship of each of these three systems to the common edges of the original dodecahedron, it is possible to conceive of a comprehensive structural system which would incorporate all of these alternative modes. It would be possible in a given construct to move, at will, from one mode to the other without any breakdown of the modularity of the system. Such a comprehensive structural system would, in this case, consist of an inventory of 12 branches, 10 of which would vary in length by no more than 10%. The combinations and permutations possible with such a system would give rise to a staggering number of spatial possibilities, all possessing complete structural stability. Although immediate architectural applications of the spaces created by such a super-system may not be apparent, this should not deter a closer look. This particular system emerges as an extremely important exemplary form, which, while adhering to and governed by a strict periodicity, can accommodate the most extraordinary demands for subtle spatial variations.

Dodecahedral/Hexakaidecahedral Packings and the Universal Node System

The fundamental closest packed space filling system composed of slightly modified regular pentagonal dodecahedra and hexakaidecahedra has yielded an extremely interesting array of infinite periodic triangulated structures. As will soon be apparent, we have still not exhausted the possible structures that may be derived from this packing arrangement. Before moving on to the further possibilities based upon the dodecahedron, it will be useful to relate the space filling of dodecahedra and hexakaidecahedra to our universal net-node system. The network common to all of the triangulated structures derived from this packing system is not a subset of the universal net. We have seen that the centers of the dodecahedra in these arrays fall at the nodes of the network defined by space-filling regular tetrahedra and truncated tetrahedra. From this, it is easily seen that while the undistorted regular dodecahedron has no face planes parallel to any of the three cubic planes, i.e., the (100), (110), or (111) planes, the adjusted dodecahedra will have six of its twelve faces facing the [110] directions. These are the interfaces shared by adjacent dodecahedra. The other six faces have no such direct relationship to the universal network.

The open packing of hexakaidecahedra has the symmetry of the diamond network. The four hexagonal faces of the hexakaidecahedron are parallel to the four faces of a regular tetrahedron and are consequently (111) planes. In the periodic array, these [111]-directed hexagonal planes are the shared interfaces between adjacent polyhedra. The centers of the polyhedra in the array are of necessity coincident with the nodes of the diamond network. The twelve pentagonal faces of the hexakaidecahedron do not correspond to any of the three directions of the Universal Node.

Thus, although there is only a partial correspondence between the dodecahedra / hexakaidecahedra closest-packed space filling system and the Universal Node system, it is a clear correspondence of the greatest significance. The appearance of these most fundamental principles of symmetry do not only govern the relationships upon which the system is based, but also explain the richness of the system. The other two closest packed dodecahedral systems* do not demonstrate the fundamental relationships exhibited by the dodecahedral/hexakaidecahedral system. They show no direct relationship to the Universal Node system and are far less interesting as generators of infinite periodic triangulated structures.

*Dodecahedra/tetrakaidecahedra, and dodecahedra/tetrakaidecahedra/pentakaidecahedra.

Triangulated Structures Derived from Truncations of the Dodecahedral/Hexakaidecahedral Packing

We noted in Chapter 4 that a number of semiregular polyhedra can be derived directly from the regular dodecahedron or its dual, the regular icosahedron. There are six such cases: the icosidodecahedron, the truncated dodecahedron, the truncated icosahedron, the rhombicosidodecahedron, the truncated icosidodecahedron, and the snub icosidodecahedron. These polyhedra are bounded by either 32, 62, or 92 faces. In all six cases exactly twelve of the total number of faces are either pentagons or decagons and they are parallel to the original faces of the regular dodecahedron. Of these six, three are bounded by pentagons and hexagons or equilateral triangles, and hence can be easily transformed into fully triangulated spherelike polyhedra, bounded by *nearly* equilateral triangles.

Triangulating the Icosidodecahedron, Snub Icosidodecahedron, and Truncated Icosahedron

Two of these three semiregular figures, the icosidodecahedron and truncated icosahedron, each have a set of twelve faces parallel to the faces of the dodecahedron. When they are derived from the modified space filling dodecahedron, they too will be capable of repetition in space to form structures which correspond exactly to the dodecahedron/hexakaidecahedron closest packed system. However, the enantiomorphic configuration of the snub icosidodecahedron creates a misalignment of pentagonal faces when packing is attempted. This difficulty precludes an infinite structure; however, we have still derived a fully triangulated finite snub-hexakaidecahedral structure.

If pentagonal pyramids are placed upon the twelve pentagonal faces of the icosidodecahedron which is bounded by twelve pentagons and 20 triangles, such that its apices fall on a sphere common to the vertices of the original figure, a spherelike polyhedron results bounded by 80 triangles [12.25]. If pentagonal pyramids are similarly placed upon the 12 pentagonal faces of the snub icosidodecahedron, which is bounded by 12 pentagons and 80 equilateral triangles, a spherelike polyhedron results which is bounded by 140 triangles [12.26].

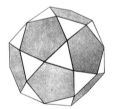

12.25 Icosidodecahedron and triangulated icosidodecahedron.

12.26 Snub icosidodecahedron and its triangulation.

The truncated icosahedron can also be so treated. However, it is bounded by 12 pentagons and 20 hexagons, so requires the use of both pentagonal and hexagonal pyramids. A spherelike polyhedron can be formed which is bounded by 180 triangles, none of which are exactly equilateral [12.27]. This triangulated truncated icosahedron requires three different edge lengths, giving in this case isosceles triangles of two different kinds. On the other hand, the snub icosidodecahedron and the icosidodecahedron require only two edge lengths, and are each bounded by both equilateral triangles and isosceles triangles of a single type. All three triangulated polyhedra form efficient fully stable frameworks in which branch lengths vary by approximately 10%.

12.27 Truncated icosahedron and its triangulation.

The triangulated icosidodecahedron is equivalent to what Fuller calls an "alternate two-frequency geodesic sphere," and the triangulated truncated icosahedron is called by Fuller the "alternate three-frequency geodesic sphere" (Popko). The triangulated snub icosidodecahedron does not appear in Fuller's system. This figure exists in right- and left-hand forms; these enantiomorphs are not disclosed by the particular morphological system from which Fuller derives his geodesic structures. Due to this enantiomorphism, it is somewhat more difficult to use the snub icosidodecahedron as a partial sphere (dome), because it has no clearly defined equatorial region. However, as a structural configuration, this figure is of great interest because it is composed of more equilateral triangles than any other convex polyhedron. As previously noted, it is comprised of 80 equilateral triangles, and, when fully triangulated, 60 additional isosceles triangles.

Truncating the Hexakaidecahedron

Just as the three semiregular polyhedra being discussed in this chapter serve as counterparts to the dodecahedron in the space-filling array, so must there also be corresponding counterparts to the hexakaidecahedron. What emerges in the case of the icosidecahedron and the truncated icosahedron are corresponding truncated hexakaidecahedra of two different kinds, which complement each polyhedron, respectively. Both of these truncated hexakaidecahedra are bounded by 44 faces. The complement to the icosidodecahedron is composed of 4 hexagonal faces, 12 pentagonal faces, and 28 triangular faces [12.28].

When properly distorted, the icosidodecahedron and this truncated hexakaidecahedron will fit together to form a periodic spatial structure. Strictly speaking, all space is not filled unless additional tetrahedra are also included in the array. These tetrahedra have their centers positioned at the nodes of the original dodecahedron/hexakaidecahedron network and form a continuous periodic chain in which tetrahedra are connected to each other at their vertices. Some of the tetrahedra are regular but most are slightly distorted when the system is strictly derived from the distorted dodecahedron [12.13] described in detail earlier in this section.*

*All of the tetrahedra in the continuous chain can be regular; but this gives rise to badly warped faces on the icosidodecahedra and truncated hexakaidecahedra.

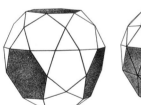

12.28 The truncated hexakaidecahedron and the triangulated truncated hexakaidecahedron.

Packing the Icosidodecahedron

Figure [12.29a, b] shows a tetrahedral collection of four properly adjusted icosidodecahedra. When it is realized that in space filling array tetrahedra are positioned on every triangular face of the icosidodecahedra (and truncated hexakaidecahedra), continuous chains of tetrahedra can be visualized. Regular tetrahedra appear at the nucleus of the basic tetrahedral cluster of icosidodecahedra. These are the only tetrahedra which do not share some of their faces with the truncated hexakaidecahedra. Because most of the triangular faces must be slightly distorted from equilateral, slightly irregular tetrahedra appear.

a   b

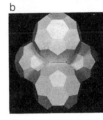
c   d

12.29 Tetrahedral clusters of four adjusted icosidodecahedra (a, b), and four adjusted truncated icosahedra (c, d).

Truncating the Icosioctahedron

The truncated hexakaidecahedron which is complementary to the truncated icosahedron is similar to its counterpart which relates to the icosidodecahedron. Just as the truncated icosahedron is more easily derived from the icosahedron rather than its dual, the dodecahedron (hence its name), this truncated hexakaidecahedron is more easily derived from the polyhedron which is dual to the hexakaidecahedron. We have not as yet identified such a dual polyhedron. It is bounded by 28 triangular faces, 4 of which are equilateral triangles and 24 are equal isosceles triangles [12.30]. It may be easily formed by placing hexagonal pyramids on the four hexagonal faces of the truncated tetrahedron. Since this polyhedron has 28 faces and the symmetry of the regular tetrahedron, I shall call it the tetrahedral icosioctahedron.

To avoid possible confusion of the truncated hexakaidecahedron of the icosidodecahedron with the truncated hexakaidecahedron of the truncated icosahedron, I will refer to the latter as the truncated tetrahedral icosioctahedron, or more simply the truncated icosioctahedron. Like the truncated hexakaidecahedron, the truncated icosioctahedron also has 44 faces [12.31]. It is bounded by 12 pentagons and 32 hexagons. Twenty-eight of these 32 hexagons correspond to the 32 triangles of the truncated hexakaidecahedron, and the other four hexagons correspond to the four hexagons of the truncated hexakaidecahedron.

12.30 The 28-faced icosioctahedron: dual polyhedron of the hexakaidecahedron.

12.31 The truncated icosioctahedron and the triangulated icosioctahedron.

Packing the Truncated Icosahedron

The truncated icosahedron with its 12 pentagonal faces parallel to the distorted dodecahedron can pack together to form an open periodic structure. Two views of a tetrahedral cluster of four such figures can be seen in [12.29]. In order to fill all space, not only must we add the complementary truncated icosioctahedron, but truncated tetrahedra are also required. At the nucleus of the tetrahedral cluster of truncated icosahedra is found a true semiregular truncated tetrahedron. This is the only position where truncated tetrahedra do not share any faces with the complementary truncated icosioctahedron.

The truncated tetrahedra share their triangular faces with each other and form a continuous chain in which their centers are positioned at the nodes of the network formed by the space filling of dodecahedra and hexakaidecahedra. All of the hexagonal faces on the truncated icosahedra in the space filling array are common to truncated tetrahedra. The continuous chain of these figures can be visualized from [12.29c, d] if the reader imagines a truncated tetrahedron placed upon each hexagonal face of the tetrahedral cluster of truncated icosahedra. Four of the 32 hexagonal faces of the truncated icosioctahedron are parallel to the hexagonal faces of the hexakaidecahedron (and to a regular tetrahedron), and are the interfaces between neighboring polyhedra of the same kind. The remaining 28 hexagons are shared with truncated tetrahedra in the space filling array. The chain of truncated tetrahedra in this system corresponds to the chain of tetrahedra formed in the packing of icosidodecahedra and truncated hexakaidecahedra.

Triangulated Structures from Repeating Icosidodecahedra and Truncated Icosahedra

Fully triangulated infinite labyrinth structures can be easily derived from both the icosidodecahedral/truncated hexakaidecahedral/tetrahedral and the truncated icosahedral/truncated icosioctahedral/truncated tetrahedral space-filling systems. They are both very similar in fundamental properties to the triangulated systems derived from the dodecahedral/hexakaidecahedral system, but more nearly approximate what might be thought of as a packing of geodesic spheres than the latter. Neither of these two systems are as simple as the dodecahedral/hexakaidecahedral-derived systems and cannot be as conveniently reduced to a basic polygonal repeat unit. They are less like the continuous labyrinth structure and more like an open packing of closed polyedra.

Figures [12.32] and [12.33] show an open packing of 16 triangulated icosidodecahedra. The shared pentagonal faces are not triangulated, as they are stabilized by the interaction of adjacent polyhedra in the array. This omission of the triangulation of these interfaces provides a continuity of space. Although not a structural necessity, inclusion of the continuous chain of tetrahedra within the overall system seems to enhance the efficiency of this structure. Each pentagonal interface is surrounded by tetrahedra. This can be seen in [12.34]. This structure requires five different branch lengths, but all are within 10% of each other. A similar structure can be formed with the array of truncated icosahedra. Such a structure can be formed which is composed of 6 different branch lengths, all within 15% of each other. It differs from the triangulated icosidodecahedron packing system only in that its pentagonal interfaces are smaller in relationship to the circumference of each polyhedral cell. The pentagonal edges of the icosidodecahedron are 1/10 its circumference while the pentagonal edges of the truncated icosahedron are only 1/15 its circumference. This can be seen by comparing [12.29a] with [12.29c]. The tetrahedral cluster of truncated icosahedra suggests the closest packing of spheres much more clearly than the tetrahedral cluster of icosidodecahedra.

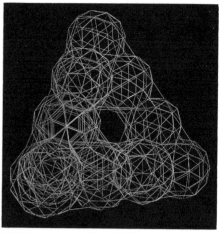

12.32 An open packing of 16 triangulated icosidodecahedra.

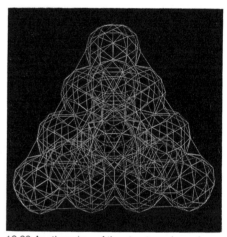

12.33 Another view of the structure shown in [12.32].

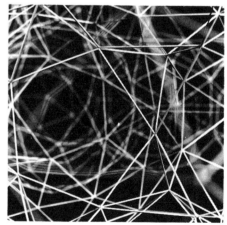

12.34 Details of an open packing of triangulated icosidodecahedra; linked tetrahedra surround pentagons within the interior of the structure.

Triangulating the Truncated Hexakaidecahedron and the Truncated Icosioctahedron

Just as we saw that the hexakaidecahedron can be triangulated into an efficient spherelike polyhedron, so can the truncated hexakaidecahedron and the truncated icosioctahedron. When the pentagons and hexagons of the former are triangulated, a polyhedron results which is bounded by 112 triangular faces [12.28b], and when the pentagons and hexagons of the latter are likewise triangulated, a polyhedron is formed which is composed of 252 triangular faces [12.31b]. In both cases, the variation in branch lengths does not exceed 15%. Both of these figures can form open structures similar to those formed by the open packing of triangulated hexakaidecahedra with their centers found at the nodal sites of the diamond network.

These truncated polyhedra exhibit a distinct applelike shape, which becomes even more apparent when their faces are triangulated. Such an ovoid configuration has interesting implications for dome structures. A spherical dome is a spherical dome regardless of how it is terminated. With the hexakaidecahedron-derived ovoid structures, a variety of dome shapes are possible depending on where the equatorial base plane is taken. The floor plan can be round or oval and the elevation can be semicircular or approximately parabolic.

The ovoid form of these polyhedra is largely the result of their tetrahedral symmetry. Since tetrahedral symmetry is a relatively high order symmetry for an oblate ovoid, the "apple" shape quality is misleading since perfect apples have a single polar axis of rotational symmetry. Our ovoid structures can be thought of as applelike configurations which have four polar axes, tetrahedrally disposed towards each other.

Triangulating the Snub Hexakaidecahedron

The snub icosidodecahedron, with a complementary snub hexakaidecahedron, would also seem to give rise to a fully triangulated infinite periodic structure. However, as we mentioned above, the enantiomorphism of these snub figures makes the alignment of pentagonal and hexagonal faces impossible. Therefore, it is not possible to pack these two figures to form a periodic structure. In spite of this, I have derived a snub hexakaidecahedron [12.35a]. It is bounded by 12 pentagons, 4 hexagons, and 70 triangles. When the pentagons and hexagons of this figure are triangulated, a polyhedron is formed which is bounded by 154 triangles [12.35b]. Like the truncated hexakaidecahedron and the truncated icosioctahedron, a distinct ovoid configuration is apparent in this polyhedron which forms an interesting fully triangulated finite structure with only a small variation in edge lengths.

12.35 The snub hexakaidecahedron and the triangulated snub hexakaidecahedron.

 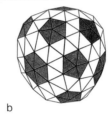

a   b

The Space Filling of Icosahedra, Icosioctahedra, and Octahedra

In Chapter 11, a number of open packings of structures composed of icosahedra and octahedra were described. One of these systems is of particular interest because of the way it relates to the packing of dodecahedra and hexakaidecahedra, and because it is the basis of a complete space filling system composed of regular icosahedra, a 28-face triangulated polyhedron and regular and irregular octahedra. The 28-face polyhedron was described earlier in this chapter and identified as the tetrahedral icosioctahedron. It is dual to the hexakaidecahedron.

The original open packing (see [11.22])
consists of tetrahedral clusters of icosahedra surrounding regular octahedra in
such a way that the octahedra form node
polyhedra and the icosahedra form
branch polyhedra organized according to
the diamond net. As this open packing
grows it forms a structure in which large
voids appear. Such voids can be occupied by tetrahedral icosioctahedra. Two
views of a tetrahedral cluster of 16
icosahedra with the icosioctahedron occupying the center of the cluster are
shown in [12.36]. This system can prolif-
erate in a manner identical to the packing
of dodecahedra and hexakaidecahedra in
which icosahedra are found to occupy the
dodecahedral sites and the icosioctahedra are found to occupy the hexakaidecahedral sites. All space can be filled by
this system with additional irregular octahedra occupying the balance of the interstitial regions. The network defined by this
space filling of icosahedra/icosioc-
tahedra/octahedra is shown in [12.37]
and [12.38].

12.36 Two views of a tetrahedral cluster of the
space filling system of icosahedra, icosioctahedra, and octahedra, showing sixteen
icosahedra surrounding a single icosioctahedron. The icosahedra and all octahedra shown
are regular. The unfilled spaces would be occupied by nonregular octahedra.

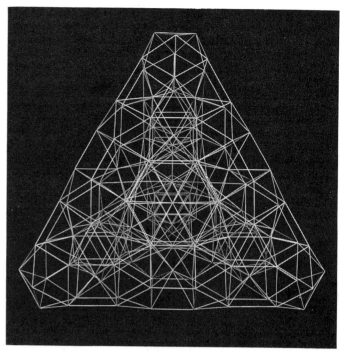

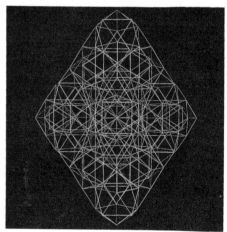

12.37 The triangulated network of the space
filling of icosahedra/icosioctahedra/octahedra.

12.38 Another view of the structure shown in
[12.37].

Dodecahedral/Hexakaidecahedral Systems and Derivatives Modeled as Sphere Packings

The icosahedra packing system just described and all of the other dodecahedron/hexakaidecahedron derived systems I have presented can be thought of as open sphere packings in which equal spheres are positioned at the sites of the dodecahedron derivatives (or icosahedra, since they are at equivalent positions). In order to give some feeling of larger aggregates of these structures, I exhibit here a number of sphere packing models [12.39]. The open spaces are where the hexakaidecahedra derivatives (or icosioctahedra) would be found when the spheres are considered dodecahedron derivatives (or icosahedra). These sphere packing models begin to suggest large scale architectural possibilities.

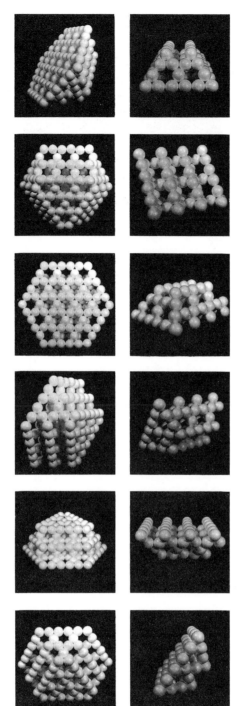

12.39 Open sphere packings represent larger arrays of open packings of pentagonal dodecahedra and its derivative structures.

Periodic Structures Composed of Distorted Icosahedra

I have pointed out that the space filling system composed of icosahedra and icosioctahedra required the use of somewhat distorted octahedra if all space was to be occupied. It is clear from that fact that all branches in the system will not be equal in length. The four branch lengths required for this system vary by less than 15%. The distorted octahedra suggest another avenue of exploration—namely, periodic structures composed of distorted icosahedra.

There are in fact, three interesting systems composed of systematically distorted icosahedra in which efficient triangulated structures are formed. Earlier, it was pointed out that the icosahedron does not lend itself to space filling because of both its high symmetry and the fact that its dihedral angles were incompatible with space filling requirements. I have found a simple method of distortion which alters both the symmetry and the dihedral angles of the icosahedron such that an interesting periodic structure can be formed.

The Oblate Icosahedron

This distortion is accomplished by increasing the edge length of the icosahedron's skew hexagonal equator which is normal to a polar axis defined by two opposite "polar" triangles. The dihedral angle of a regular icosahedron is 138°11'. As the skew hexagonal equator is varied by changing its edge length, alternative dihedral angles can be provided. If this distortion is carried out such that the dihedral angles formed are 144°44' (between the triangles immediately adjacent to the polar triangles and the polar triangles themselves), a remarkable packing arrangement becomes possible. These icosahedra, which may be called *oblate*, will combine periodically in tetrahedral clusters with four icosahedra surrounding a nuclear regular tetrahedron and sharing faces with each other. Such a packing of oblate icosahedra is shown in [12.40]. The oblate icosahedron is composed of two nearly equal edge lengths which define 8 equilateral and 12 identical isosceles triangles. It no longer has full icosahedral symmetry but the symmetry of a triangular prism—one axis of 3-fold symmetry (the polar axis) and three axes of 2-fold symmetry. The oblateness of this figure is apparent in [12.41c].

With just the oblate icosahedra and the regular tetrahedra, an open packing is formed. Figure [12.41a, b] shows a network of this system in which additional irregular tetrahedra and regular octahedra are required if all space is to be occupied.

12.40 Tetrahedral cluster of sixteen oblate icosahedra.

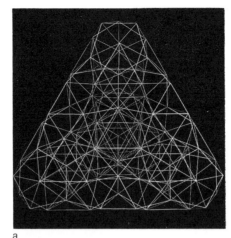

a

b

c

12.41 Two views of the triangulated network of the space filling of oblate icosahedra, tetrahedra (regular and nonregular), and regular octahedra (a, b). An oblate icosahedron (c).

The Prolate Icosahedron

Just as it is possible to increase certain dihedral angles of the icosahedron by enlarging the edge length of a designated skew hexagonal equator, it is also possible to decrease the same dihedral angle by shortening the edge of a designated skew hexagonal equator. If the dihedral angle is decreased to 125°16', it is possible to symmetrically dispose eight *prolate* icosahedra on the eight faces of the regular octahedron. This gives rise to a periodic system which is organized according to an 8-connected bcc network with the regular octahedra functioning as node polyhedra and the prolate icosahedra functioning as branch polyhedra. The icosahedron becomes prolate, as can be seen in [12.42a] and, like its oblate counterpart, consists of two edge lengths, giving 8 equilateral and 12 identical isosceles triangles.

Figure [12.42b, c] shows a basic cluster of 8 prolate icosahedra surrounding a single octahedron. This periodic structure is still an open packing, but all space can be filled with the addition of slightly irregular tetrahedra and regular octahedra.

12.42 The prolate icosahedron (a), and a cluster of eight prolate icosahedra surrounding a single regular octahedron (b, c).

a

c

b

The Contracted Icosahedron

Quite a number of years ago, Fuller discovered that the cuboctahedron, when constructed as a framework with flexible joints, can go through a series of transformations which take it first to the icosahedron and then the octahedron. The required rotations and translations of the triangular faces whereby the cuboctahedron contracts symmetrically about its center, are illustrated in [12.43]. Stuart, inspired by this work of Fuller, has done some brilliant work in extending this transformation principle to all of the Platonic and Archimedean polyhedra (Stuart 1961).

This cuboctahedral transformation gives rise to a most interesting distorted icosahedral space filling system. It is possible to consider a cuboctahedral transformation within a space filling array. In Chapter 5 I have identified a space filling system composed of cuboctahedra and octahedra (see [5.10d] and [12.44a]). In this configuration, the cuboctahedra are at the sites of a simple cubic lattice. As the cuboctahedra begin to contract in such an arrangement, the octahedra begin to expand [12.44b]. In the cuboctahedral/octahedral space filling system, there is exactly the same number of each polyhedron. Because of this, the transformation will ultimately lead to an exchange of positions of the two polyhedra.

The moment the octahedra begin opening up, they immediately become irregular icosahedra with eight equilateral triangular faces and twelve identical isosceles triangular faces. The octahedra are expanding toward regular icosahedra and ultimately cuboctahedra. In like manner, the moment the cuboctahedra begin to contract, they immediately become irregular icosahedra with eight equilateral triangular faces and twelve identical isosceles triangular faces, and are contracting toward icosahedra and ultimately octahedra.

12.44 The transformation of the space filling of cuboctahedra and octahedra. A space filling of contracted icosahedra and isosceles tetrahedra is formed at the midpoint of the transformation.

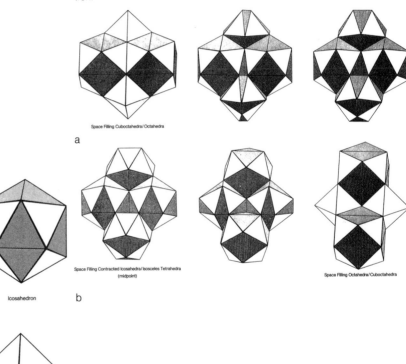

Space Filling Cuboctahedra/Octahedra

a

Space Filling Contracted Icosahedra/Isosceles Tetrahedra
(midpoint)

b

Space Filling Octahedra/Cuboctahedra

12.43 The transformation by symmetrical contraction of the cuboctahedron to the octahedron (after Fuller). A contracted icosahedron is formed at the midpoint of the transformation.

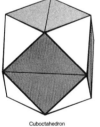

Cuboctahedron

Icosahedron

Contracted Icosahedron
(midpoint)

Octahedron

Because the cuboctahedron's square faces are transformed into two adjacent triangles with a dihedral angle of less than 180°, additional identical irregular tetrahedral voids suddenly appear when the transformation begins. At that moment, the result is space filling with groups of two different irregular icosahedra and a group of identical irregular tetrahedra [12.44b]. This arrangement requires three edge lengths. As the transformation continues, it comes to a position in which one group of icosahedra have become precisely regular [12.44c]. This gives rise to space filling with regular icosahedra, irregular contracted icosahedra, and irregular tetrahedra. This system requires altogether two edge lengths. If only the regular icosahedra are left in this system, an open packing is formed in which the icosahedra are joined edge to edge, and fall at the sites of a simple cubic lattice. This open packing was described earlier in Chapter 11 [11.14].

As the transformation continues past the position in which half of the icosahedra are regular, it comes to an exact midpoint where both sets of icosahedra are identical [12.44d]. As the transformation continues past this midpoint, we again reach the position where half the icosahedra are regular [12.44e]. When the transformation is complete, it returns to the cuboctahedral/octahedral arrangement, but with the positions of the two sets of polyhedra exchanged [12.44f].

12.45 The contracted icosahedron superimposed within the truncated octahedron.

The midpoint of this transformation is extremely interesting, not only because there is only one icosahedron involved, but also because this icosahedron is related in an unambiguous way to the truncated octahedron. The eight regular faces of this icosahedron are not only parallel to the eight hex faces of the truncated octahedron, but the vertices of the regular faces coincide exactly with 12 of the truncated octahedron's 24 vertices. Figures [12.45] and [12.46] illustrate this unique icosahedral system. This icosahedron has two edge lengths, the longer of which belongs to the equilateral triangles and occurs 24 times.

12.46 Two views of the triangulated network of space filling contracted icosahedra and isosceles tetrahedra (a, b), and its association with the network of space filling truncated octahedra (c).

Figure [12.45] shows a model with the truncated octahedron and contracted icosahedron superimposed, revealing their relationship to each other; [12.46a, b] shows two different views of an aggregate of 14 icosahedra around a nuclear icosahedron typifying the characteristic 14-around-one coordination of the truncated octahedral packing. An aggregate of truncated octahedra is shown in association with the icosahedron system in [12.46c]. This icosahedral system is a very efficient manner with which to stabilize (triangulate) the truncated octahedral space filling system.

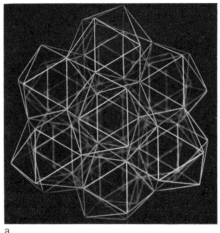

a

b

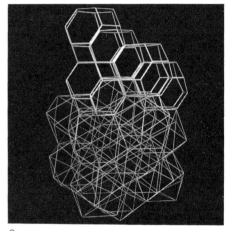

c

Other Icosahedron-Related Structures

The Packing of Polyhedral Duals: Dodecahedron/Tetrakaidecahedron

The foregoing completes the discussion of systems based upon distorted icosahedral forms. However, there are still a few more systems for the periodic triangulation of space based on icosahedral-derived forms which must not be overlooked. I have described a system composed of regular icosahedra, icosioctahedra, and octahedra (see [12.36], [12.37], and [12.38]). This triangulated system was derived from the packing of hexakaidecahedra and dodecahedra, since the icosioctahedron is the polyhedral dual of the former and the icosahedron is the polyhedral dual of the latter. In the same way, the packing of dodecahedra/tetrakaidecahedra and the packing of dodecahedra/tetrakaidecahedra/pentakaidecahedra may also be the basis of similar systems. The dodecahedral/tetrakaidecahedral packing is shown in [12.47a].

By replacing the dodecahedron with its dual icosahedron and by replacing the tetrakaidecahedron with its dual, a 24-face figure composed of 12 equilateral and 12 isosceles triangles—a periodic triangulated network—can be formed. It is shown in [12.47b]. Note that the icosahedra and 24-hedra are joined to each other on the vertices, which gives rise to octahedra. Although I do not illustrate it here, one can easily imagine a system derived from the dodecahedral/tetrakaidecahedral/pentakaidecahedral system. It would be composed of icosahedra, 24-hedra, and 26-hedra.

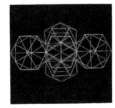

a   b

12.47 If, in a space filling of pentagonal dodecahedra and tetrakaidecahedra (a), dual polyhedra are substituted (b), a triangulated structure results composed of icosahedra, 24-hedra, and octahedra.

Face to Face With Truncated Icosahedra and Rhombic Triacontahedra

There are yet two more systems related to the icosahedron that must be mentioned. One is an open packing of truncated icosahedra and the other is an open packing of the rhombic triacontahedron. In the former, truncated icosahedra combine by sharing eight hexagonal (111) faces which are parallel to the faces of a regular octahedron, and are positioned at the sites of the bcc lattice. This system is shown in [12.48]. It is obvious that this open packing can be fully stabilized by the triangulation of unshared hexagonal faces and the pentagons.

12.48 Truncated icosahedra pack on the bcc lattice by joining on faces parallel to planes normal to the [111] directions (i. e., parallel to (111) planes).

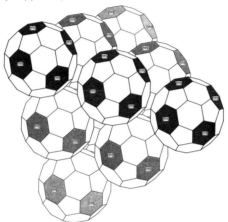

The rhombic triacontahedron will combine by sharing faces which are normal to the [100] or cubic axes, in such a way that the center of each polyhedron is at the corner of a cube in a simple space-filling array [12.49]. The triacontahedron system may be easily triangulated by dividing each rhombus into two triangles. Nearly equilateral triangles are formed with face angles of 63°26′ and 58°17′.

12.49 Rhombic triacontahedra pack on the simple cubic lattice by joining on faces parallel to (100) planes.

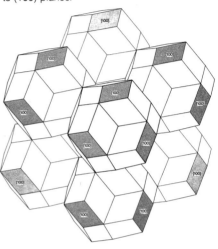

Triangulation of the Kelvin Minimal Tetrakaidecahedron

There is a final system which must be mentioned. In thinking about the triangulation of the truncated octahedra in space filling arrays, it became apparent to me that an interesting structure might be derived from a faceted approximation of the Kelvin minimal tetrakaidecahedron. Such a faceted approximation may be simply derived by substituting the curved edges with their tangents taken at the 109°28′ vertices of the Kelvin figure. When this is done new vertices are fortuitously created where the tangent lines meet at a point just below the midedge of the original curved edges of the minimal truncated octahedron. This is shown in [12.50] for the square face. Once these tangent lines are established, the saddle hexagon faces may be divided into six congruent trapezium faces (with mirror symmetry). This is accomplished by connecting, with straight lines, the vertices (created by the intersection of the tangent lines) that are opposite each other.

12.50 Approximating the arc-edged face of the Kelvin minimal tetrakaidecahedron with tangent edges.

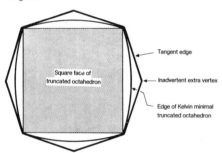

Tangent edge

Square face of truncated octahedron

Inadvertent extra vertex

Edge of Kelvin minimal truncated octahedron

Figure [12.51a] shows a truncated octahedron identically oriented to the faceted minimal truncated octahedron of [12.51b]. A comparison of these two photographs makes clear the figures' relationship to one another. The faceted approximation of the minimal truncated octahedron is composed of 48 identical trapezium faces and 6 identical octagon faces. I have already mentioned that the trapezium faces have mirror symmetry; it is important to note that the octagons have only 4-fold symmetry. It is important to emphasize that although this new faceted polyhedron is not wholly convex, it will still fill all space.

The faceted minimal truncated octahedron is still not a triangulated system, but becomes the basis for such a system. By truncating the twenty-four 109°28′ vertices of the faceted polyhedron, 24 equilateral triangles are formed. This has the additional effect that the trapezium faces are transformed into triangles as well, and although they are not equilateral, they are nearly so. The result is a polyhedron composed of 72 triangular faces and 6 square faces, the squares resulting from the truncation of the 4-fold octagons [12.51c]. This polyhedron has the full cubic symmetry of the truncated octahedron, since the symmetry has not been altered by these manipulations.

12.51 The truncated octahedron (a) gives rise to the arc-edged minimal tetrakaidecahedron, which in turn gives rise to a 48-faced approximation of the minimal tetrakaidecahedron (b). Truncating this polyhedron produces a figure composed of 48 isosceles triangles, 24 equilateral triangles, and 6 squares (c).

a

b

c

The truncated polyhedron is not fully triangulated since it still has six square faces. Also, it will not fill space by itself. When it is packed together the triangular faces of the truncated corners form regular tetrahedra. It, therefore, forms a binary space filling system. In a periodic array the interaction of the tetrahedra with the larger polyhedra has the effect of stabilizing the square faces. Like other structures we have discussed, the terminal square faces remain locally unstable.

Figure [12.52] shows two packing arrangements of the polyhedra derived from the Kelvin minimal truncated octahedron. A fully triangulated structure is shown in [12.53] and [12.54], in which 14 truncated versions of the faceted minimal truncated octahedron surround a central cell in the typical fourteen-around-one configuration of the truncated octahedron. Figure [12.53] is a view along the [111] axis; and [12.54] is a view along the [100] axis. None of the branches of this triangulated network are Universal Node branches. Details of this structure are shown in [12.55] where we again see the principles of symmetry embodied in the Universal Node.

12.52 Packing arrangements of polyhedra derived from the Kelvin minimal tetrakaidecahedron.

12.53 A fully triangulated structure consisting of the faceted approximations of 15 truncated minimal tetrakaidecahedra.

12.54 Another view of the figure shown in [12.53].

12.55 Details of the structure shown in [12.53] and [12.54].

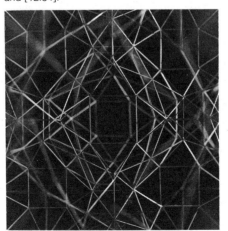

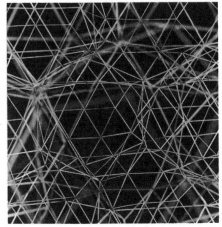

Diversity and Order Prevailing in the Triangulation of Space

In Chapters 11 and 12, we have studied at great length, although by no means exhaustively, the periodic triangulation of space. In this investigation we have found many morphologiclal interrelationships and have seen that, although the Universal Node system cannot be used as a universal recipe, it certainly helps us to classify and understand many of these systems. However, it is quite clear that many of the triangulated structures described are not easily organized into an integrated scheme, certainly not one of the power of the universal net-node system. All this aside, we can still begin to appreciate the remarkable juxtaposition of diversity and order that prevails in the study of fundamental structure and morphology.

We have covered considerable ground. We have inventoried many alternative ways to modulate physical space. We have seen several approaches to the minimum inventory/maximum diversity principle, and a number of physical realizations of this principle. We have found strategies based on natural structural behavior that would allow us to conserve natural resources while creating adaptive physical environments. We have begun to develop a new integrative language of form and structure, an intrinsic force system, which enables the design of environments to be accomplished with a strategy that can be responsive to the human and ecological realities of change and diversity. In the next two chapters I will move into a more specific discussion of the applications of all this to architecture.

The Reduction to Practice

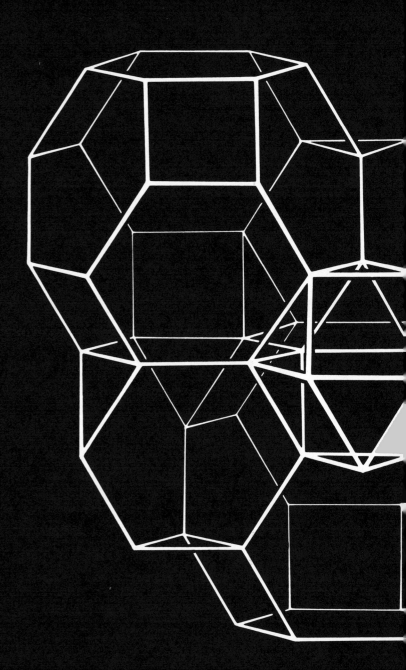

13 Minimum Inventory/ Maximum Diversity Building Systems

In the preceding chapters we have attempted to understand in a fundamental way the characteristics of minimum inventory/maximum diversity systems. We have seen an archetypal model of such systems in the structure of the snowflake. The snowflake exhibits a unifying modular principle which is a function of the molecular constitution of the crystal structure, yet within these rigorous modular constraints, infinite variety is possible. In an attempt to translate my study of integrative morphological systems into useful building systems a number of possibilities have emerged.

None of these systems has seen any full scale construction, but fairly detailed models have been built. The hardware for such systems will not be discussed here, since that hardware is still under development. The same attitudes that have guided the basic investigation of modular systems are being applied to the more immediately practical problems of hardware design and engineering details. Initial work in this area has been fruitful.

We have seen that modular structures can be defined in terms of volumes, surfaces, or linear frameworks, as well as point arrays. Description in terms of linear frames leads to complete structures, as surfaces can be defined by linear frames, and volumes can be defined by surfaces and frames.

As we have seen, a framework must consist of nodes (or vertices) and branches (or edges). In a built system the points or nodes become connectors, and the branches become linear structural components or struts.

In addition to a consideration of the purely *combinatorial* properties of modular systems (be they frames, surfaces, or volumes) it is also necessary to study carefully the physical consequences of alternative spatial arrangements. Insofar as framework structures are concerned, I have emphasized that triangulated configurations give rise to the most efficient systems from the point of view of strength per unit of invested resources. There is a two-fold advantage in inherently stable triangulated structures: first, their tendency to disperse concentrated and distributed loads over a very large part of the structure and, second, the fact that loads are distributed axially through the linear members. Both of these are ideal conditions for the efficient use of materials.

With complex triangulated frameworks, the direction of loads becomes far less important than with the usual rectangular geometry found in most building design.

One of the principle reasons why triangulated systems have not been used very much in architectural structures is that they are largely incompatible with the architectural profession's 90° biased spatial sensibilities. Not by abandoning the obvious usefulness of 90° relationships, but rather by looking at space from a more fundamental and comprehensive point of view, we have been able to develop a modular spatial approach which can yield inherently stable, high efficiency, low redundancy structures based upon fully triangulated configurations. Although such structures are derived primarily from triangular arrays, we shall see that rather than excluding the spatial possibilities inherent in rectangular geometry, we have augmented and redefined them in such a way as to yield a vast array of new options.

One of the disadvantages of triangulated systems is the complexity of the nodes. This disadvantage is overcome by industrial production techniques, which in sophisticated joint systems become economically feasible. And even though the nodes can be complex, they can be easily understood; for the design of the joints derives directly from the underlying principles of modular structures upon which the building systems themselves are based.

The Min-a-Max Building System

The building system I shall now describe has great advantages as a reduction to practice of the minimum inventory/maximum diversity principle. This Min-a-Max Building System is an adaptable system with potential application in almost any environmental context. It consists of a minimum inventory of prefabricated component types designed according to our integrative modular principles. Because of this, the set of components can be assembled to form a vast array of structures. In addition, the geometric coordination of these components was developed with structural principles in mind, such that the great variety of building forms that are possible may all satisfy requirements of structural integrity. It is a system not only able to take maximum advantage of industrial production techniques while facing head-on the requirements of adaptation and diversity, but a system which uses materials economically.

The Structural Framing and Interstitial Panels

The Min-a-Max Building System* consists of structural framing to which various interstitial panels are attached forming a space-enclosing system—a weather envelope. There are three primary and three secondary linear components which, in turn, combine to fit around various interstitial panels.

The interrelationships of the six linear components are shown in [13.1]. The edge length ratios are given as functions of a unit edge A. These ratios are center-to-center distances and not actual component lengths since the bulk of the joints would have to be allowed for. Actual lengths of structural members need not be given, since it is the coordinated length ratios that comprise the system. Appropriate specific member sizes emerge from adaptations of the system to the requirements of particular building applications. The A, B, and C components are primary by virtue of the frequency of their use, and the D, E, and F components are secondary.

*The Min-a-Max Building System described in this chapter is the subject of a comprehensive pending patent (U.S. Patent 3974600).

For the most part, the Min-a-Max kit derives from the Universal Node system in a fairly obvious way, but there are some subtleties involved. Three of the six linear components shown in [13.1] are equivalent to the three branches of the Universal Node system. The A component is equivalent to the [110] branch; the B component is equivalent to the [111] branch; and, the D component is equivalent to the [100] branch. The C component has no equivalent branch, and although the E and F components are directed along [111] axes, they have no equivalence as far as length ratios are concerned. The symmetry of the branches and the corresponding symmetry properties of the nodal intersections are not explicitly considered in the design of the Min-a-Max system.

The triangular interstitial panels derived from the linear components are shown in [13.2]. As for the linear components, these nine surfaces are ranked according to the frequency of their use. Later we will have to introduce a set of *terminal* components which cannot be assembled from the basic kit of parts.

13.1 The six basic linear components of the Min-a-Max Building System.

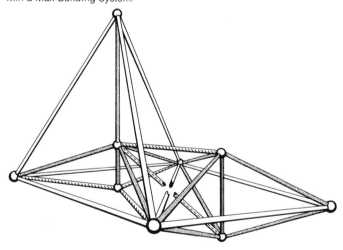

The Six Basic Linear Components of the Min-a-Max Building System

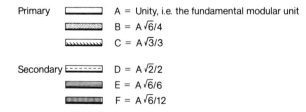

Primary		A = Unity, i.e. the fundamental modular unit
		B = A $\sqrt{6}/4$
		C = A $\sqrt{3}/3$
Secondary		D = A $\sqrt{2}/2$
		E = A $\sqrt{6}/6$
		F = A $\sqrt{6}/12$

Interstitial Panels

Primary

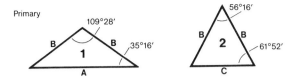

Secondary

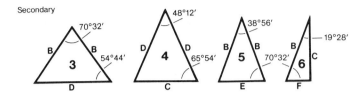

Tertiary

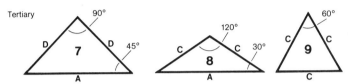

13.2 The triangular interstitial panels of the Min-a-Max Building System.

Each panel can be produced as an opaque surface, as a translucent surface, or as a transparent window. Other panel functions may also be assigned, such as solar collectors, or ventilation louvers. It might also be possible to have panels of differing coefficients of reflectance of radiant energy. The linear framework is envisioned as a demountable system that facilitates both erection and change, and the panels are intended to be replaceable and changeable as well. Removal of the panels would be easy, since the structural integrity is entirely in the frame—the panels being only required to resist local loads.

The interstitial panels defined by the linear kit of parts are not all of equal importance. Panels 1 and 2 constitute a primary set; panels 3 to 6 constitute a secondary set; and panels 7 to 9 comprise a tertiary set. The primary set in this case is all that is required to define the basic options, with the secondary panels being useful ancillary components. The tertiary panels can be used to extend the options available to the system.

Various kinds of stressed-skin systems can be derived from this same geometry, and can yield extremely efficient structural arrangements. However, where maximum adaptability is the goal, such stressed-skin systems are less effective because the panels cannot be removed without dismantling the superstructure.

This simple collection of components can be assembled in great varieties of architectural configurations including single story domelike dwellings, multilevel low and high rise structures, large planar and domical clear spans, and even bridgelike structures. The system provides for the structural framework, the space-enclosing and finish surfaces, a partitioning system for interior space, and a flooring system including integral foundations. Such an adaptable environmental system may be used wherever high strength-to-weight, mass-producible, economical, flexible, and diverse human environments are desired.

The Space Units—A Spatial Vocabulary

The relationships of the six basic components illustrated in [13.1] do not even begin to suggest the kind of spatial arrangements that may be formed with this system. Our research in modular structures suggests a basic set of space filling polyhedral volumes which are closely related to the set of five components. These five polyhedra are the tetrahedron, octahedron, cuboctahedron, truncated tetrahedron, and the truncated octahedron [13.3]. Of these, only the truncated octahedron will fill space alone. The other volumes fill space in various admixtures. (See Table 5.1.)

Of this group, the truncated octahedron is the simplest space filling system and, for this reason alone, it is the more useful system. Another important advantage is that among uniform polyhedra, the truncated octahedron is the space filling system which contains the greatest volume with the least surface area. We have discussed the relationship of the truncated octahedron to cell shapes in Chapter 1, and, although perfect truncated octahedra rarely occur in nature, the shape remains a nonetheless useful canonical form.

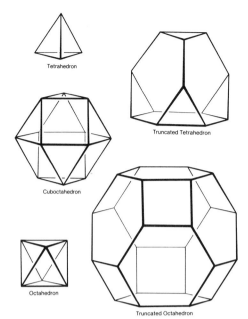

Tetrahedron

Truncated Tetrahedron

Cuboctahedron

Octahedron

Truncated Octahedron

13.3 Five polyhedra are the basis of a spatial vocabulary for the Min-a-Max system.

13.4 The possible space filling systems composed of the five polyhedra of [13.3].

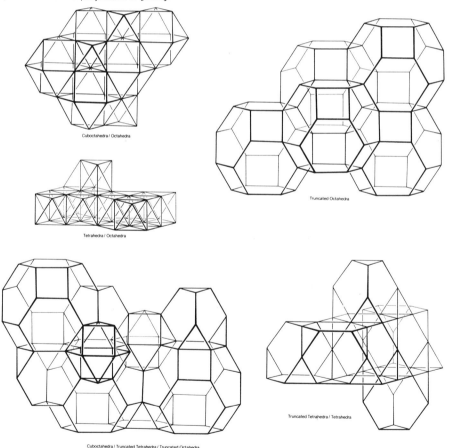

Cuboctahedra / Octahedra

Tetrahedra / Octahedra

Truncated Octahedra

Cuboctahedra / Truncated Tetrahedra / Truncated Octahedra

Truncated Tetrahedra / Tetrahedra

With two exceptions, the space-filling arrangements of these polyhedra [13.4] do not provide for continuous layers of parallel surfaces, an essential requirement if we are to create floors for multilevel buildings. For this reason, it is useful to subdivide three of the five polyhedra into "ceiling-floor" space units. The truncated octahedron can be conveniently divided into three space units [13.5]. Note that there are actually only two different space units: the central equatorial core which is bounded by two hexagons, each with sides of *one* (x) and *two* (2x) units of length, and by six trapezoids; and two identical polar caps that are each bounded by one equilateral hexagon, by one hexagon of sides x and 2x, by three trapezoids, and by three square faces.

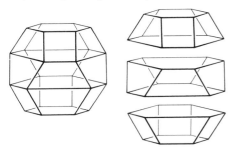

13.5 The truncated octahedron is subdivided into three volumetric regions, forming two kinds of space units: polar and equatorial.

The two space units that are derived by subdividing the truncated octahedron will combine to fill all space. However, unlike the complete truncated octahedron, they can also fill the plane. They become the basis of a system which relates space filling of truncated octahedra to a common plane of reference; i.e., which allows infinite growth along a common plane. Figure [13.6] shows a space filling arrangement of truncated octahedra that incorporates into the array its two space units in order that the entire assembly may sit on a common plane. The parallel layers of "floors" are clearly shown in this illustration. Note that the floors are formed by the tiling of regular hexagons and hexagons with sides of x and 2x.

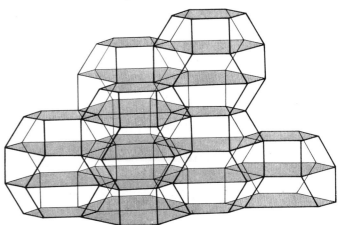

13.6 Parallel floor layers are provided in space filling array of truncated octahedra by means of polar and equatorial space units.

It is also possible to subdivide polyhedra into greater numbers of subunits. The truncated octahedron may be divided into six space units of three different kinds. Figure [13.7] shows a sequence in which the truncated octahedron is thus incrementally lowered to a single layer. It is obvious that such a subdivision could be increased to higher frequencies (thinner slices) ad infinitum. We will here be primarily concerned with the simplest case—the three-unit subdivision of [13.5].

The truncated octahedron is a unary space filling system. Tetrahedra and octahedra will combine in a complementary fashion to form a binary space filling system. Because this particular system does define parallel layers and because the altitudes of the tetrahedra and octahedra are equal to that of the basic space units of the truncated octahedron, there is no need to subdivide these polyhedra [13.4].

Truncated tetrahedra and tetrahedra will also combine in a binary space filling system. Although this system will define parallel layers, it is also possible to subdivide the truncated tetrahedron into two space units [13.8] thereby doubling the number of parallel continuous layers that can be formed.

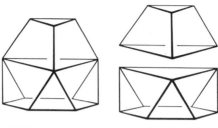

13.8 The truncated tetrahedron divides into two kinds of space units.

The cuboctahedron will combine with the octahedron forming still another binary space filling system. The cuboctahedron divides into two like space units [13.9]. Figures [13.10a–e] show the progressive subdivision of space filling with cuboctahedra and octahedra into the basic space units, finally ending up at one unit of altitude in [13.10e]. A larger aggregate of this system can be seen in [13.10f].

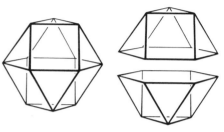

13.9 Dividing the cuboctahedron produces one kind of space unit.

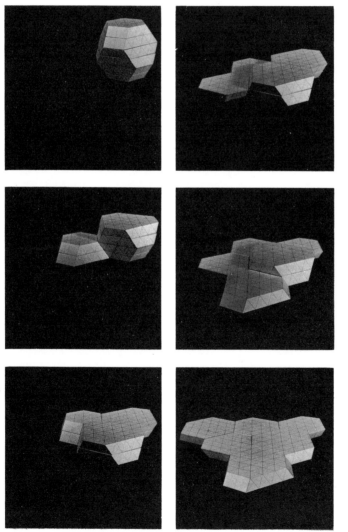

13.7 The truncated octahedron may be subdivided into six volumetric regions, forming three kinds of space units; then these may be incrementally lowered to a common plane.

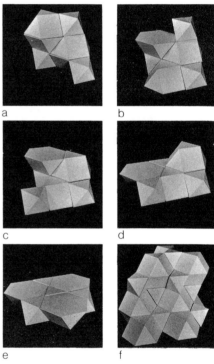

13.10 A space filling of cuboctahedral space units and octahedra (a), subdivided and progressively lowered to a common plane (b–e). A larger array of space filling of cuboctahedral space units and octahedra (f) suggests a multistory building.

In addition to the one unary and three binary systems, there is a single ternary space filling system. It is composed of truncated tetrahedra, cuboctahedra, and truncated octahedra. Since we have already subdivided the three polyhedra comprising this system, no new space units are generated [13.11]. This ternary system completes the collection of space filling arrangements that incorporate combinations of the five polyhedra that are the volumetric modules from which the basic spatial vocabulary of the Min-a-Max system is derived. Three of these polyhedra subdivide to form a total of five basic space units all equal in altitude to the simple tetrahedron and octahedron. The truncated octahedron gives rise to two space units; the truncated tetrahedron gives rise to two space units; and the cuboctahedron gives rise to a single space unit. This brings the total number of volumetric units to ten including the five polyhedra and the five space units. The combinations and permutations possible with this collection of space cells is vast, and although they comprise the basic spatial vocabulary of the Min-a-Max system, they do not constitute the spatial limits of the system. These are the most symmetrical cases and form an intelligible spatial vocabulary from which many other alternatives may be derived. These polyhedral space units are particularly useful for planning small structures or multilevel structures where the accumulation of such volumes has importance.

Triangulation of the Min-a-Max System

None of the polyhedra or space units described above are triangulated systems with the exception of the tetrahedron and octahedron, and, therefore, form unstable frameworks. For this reason, we must discover reasonable ways in which these spatial units may be triangulated. This is not such a difficult problem, since the majority of the faces of the space units can be subdivided into equilateral triangles.

However, as we know from Chapter 3, in performing this triangulation, we must take local instability into account. Recall that this instability occurs within triangulated, but still planar, faces. If a load is placed on any joint that is within and co-planar to a given polygonal face, it will be found *not* to be completely rigid; the loaded joint will tend to move slightly away from the face plane of the polygon with which it is associated.

As we saw, there are two ways to improve this condition. Only one method will allow the polygon to remain planar. This can be accomplished by creating a double-layer space frame structure that corresponds to the plane polygonal faces. The second, and simpler, alternative is to position the joints of the triangulated subdivisions such that a convex or concave arrangement is created on each face. This latter system requires less material, but cannot provide planar faces.

Among our five polyhedra and five space units there are altogether only four faces that may be subdivided into *equilateral* triangles. These are: a regular hexagon of unit (x) edge length; a hexagon with three one-unit (x) edges and three two-unit (2x) edges; a trapezoid with three one-unit (x) edges and one two-unit (2x) edge; and a triangle of two-unit (2x) edges. When these faces are triangulated, only the hexagons have vertices within their periphery [13.12]. The trapezoid, which is actually a half-hexagon, consists of three triangles and, like the two-unit triangle composed of four one-unit triangles, does not suffer from local instability. Therefore, it is only necessary to find a method of stabilizing the two different kinds of hexagons. Incidentally, these are the hexagons that combine to form the parallel layers which become the floors of the multilevel structures based on the space filling array of truncated octahedra, and the space filling array of cuboctahedra/truncated tetrahedra/truncated octahedra (see [13.7], and [13.11].

Both planar and "domical" stabilizations of hexagons have been developed based upon the basic inventory of components. The A components of [13.1] are shown in the arrangement of a regular tetrahedron. The altitude of all of the basic space units is identical to this regular tetrahedron. When three B components are attached to a triangular base composed of A components a low pyramid is formed. The apex of this pyramid falls at the exact center of the original regular tetrahedron formed by the A components, i.e., the altitude of this pyramid is exactly one-fourth of that of the regular tetrahedron.

13.12 Triangulating the faces of the Min-a-Max space units.

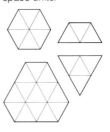

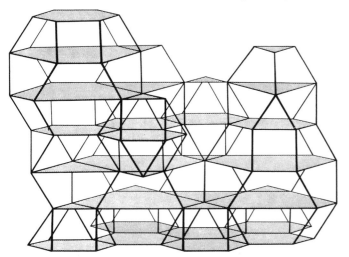

13.11 Parallel floor layers are provided in space filling array of truncated octahedra, truncated tetrahedra, and cuboctahedra by means of five different space units.

The Tetrahex Truss

A space frame system has been developed based upon this triangular pyramid, or "irregular" tetrahedron. The volume of this irregular tetrahedron is, in fact, one-fourth the volume of the full regular tetrahedron. Six of these *quarter tetrahedra* can be arranged on a common plane around a single point. When this is done, the apices of these quarter tetrahedra are joined in a hexagonal ring composed of C components. The six equilateral base triangles, composed of A components, combine to form a regular hexagon. This complex thus serves as a planar stabilization of the regular hexagons of the basic space units [13.13a, b]. This system may be extended infinitely in its plane. When this is done a complex of quarter tetrahedra and hexagonal pyramids is formed. I call this system the tetrahex truss. It is normally used in an inverted position [13.14], with the apices of the quarter tetrahedra pointing downward rather than upward as they are in [13.13a, b].

The hexagon of our space units which is bounded by three edges of one-unit (x) length and three edges of two-unit (2x) length can also be easily accommodated with this tetrahex system. In this case, thirteen quarter tetrahedra are combined and their apices joined with C components [13.15a].

It is easy to convert the planar tetrahex truss to a domical system by redirecting six of the B components. This amounts to the inversion of the central hexagonal pyramid and makes possible the omission of six of the twelve A components of the original planar configuration. This again demonstrates the superior efficiency of domical systems over planar systems. Figure [13.13a] shows the planar stabilized version and [13.13c] shows the domical stabilized version of the regular hexagonal face.

In the case of the second hexagon of x and 2x sides, the same transformation can occur. However, this time there are three hexagonal pyramids which are inverted in the process of redirecting eighteen B components. This arrangement, which eliminates altogether twelve A components, forms a compound triple-hex dome system with three apices. For total stability these three peaks must be joined by an equilateral triangle of A components. Figure [13.15a, b] shows the planar truss and [13.15c] shows the compound dome.

In our discussion so far we have only used three of our six basic components. As has been noted, the A, B, and C components constitute the primary set. Before going on to show the diversity of application of tetrahex planar and domical systems to the polyhedral space unit packings, it will be useful to describe the variety of additional planar and domical systems which can be assembled with the A, B, and C components.

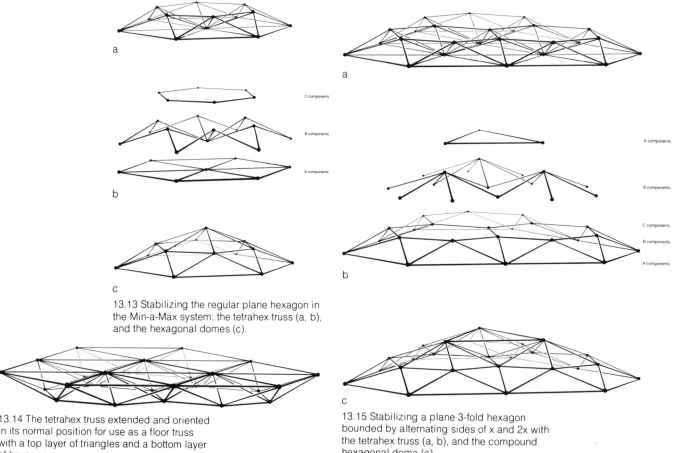

13.13 Stabilizing the regular plane hexagon in the Min-a-Max system: the tetrahex truss (a, b), and the hexagonal domes (c).

13.14 The tetrahex truss extended and oriented in its normal position for use as a floor truss with a top layer of triangles and a bottom layer of hexagons.

13.15 Stabilizing a plane 3-fold hexagon bounded by alternating sides of x and 2x with the tetrahex truss (a, b), and the compound hexagonal dome (c).

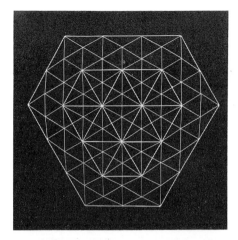

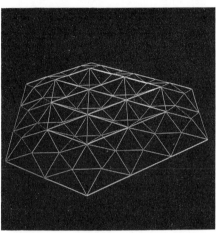

In [13.16], [13.17], and [13.18] can be seen examples of alternative ways that the basic tetrahex truss can be developed into efficient clear span systems. Figure [13.16] shows a semidome arrangement consisting of a central tetrahex truss surrounded by a partial hex dome. Figure [13.17] shows two versions of concentric regular hexagonal domes of two- and three-unit sides. Of these two systems, only the two-unit dome is completely rigid when supported around its periphery. The three-unit dome would require some additional structural members over those shown in the photographs.

As a large clear span system, the planar tetrahex truss could probably function effectively on the basis of a 25 to 1 span-to-depth ratio, although this is misleading because by supporting such systems according to hexagonal plans with supporting members on three sides, this ratio is effectively increased. In order to further increase this span-to-depth ratio, we could use a "double layer" tetrahex truss, in which two tetrahex trusses share the same equilateral triangular planar grid. The two tetrahex trusses face each other, the triangular grid serving as the interface. This double layer system is shown in [13.18]. Because the foregoing systems require only A, B, and C components, it should be a simple matter in any built structure to make the transition from one to another whenever such a change of system is desired.

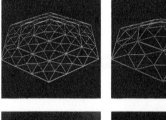

13.17 Three views each of two concentric hexagonal domes: two-unit (right), and a three-unit (left).

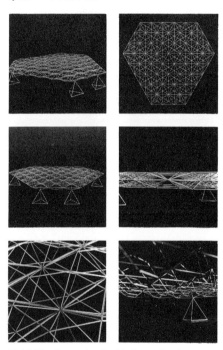

13.18 Six views of a double layer (back to back) tetrahex truss.

13.16 Three views of a semidome structure combining dome and truss.

Triangulating the Space Units

The application of the A, B, and C components to the space units is of both structural and geometric interest. Figure [13.19a] shows a half-cuboctahedron and [13.19b] shows a framework model of this space unit incorporating the tetrahex truss as the regular hexagonal face at the base. Although this structure has three square openings, it is rigid by virtue of the tetrahex truss which provides the necessary stability in combination with the four equilateral triangles comprising the sides and top of the structure. Without the tetrahex truss, which provides a rigid plane on the hexagonal face, this structure is unstable.

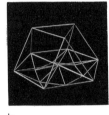

a b

13.19 The space unit of the cuboctahedron (a) is stable when built with a tetrahex truss on a base hexagon (b).

As I have already noted, the truncated octahedron is the simplest and most economical in terms of surface area-to-volume ratio of the space filling systems we have considered in this chapter. Figures [13.20] through [13.23] and [13.26] through [13.29] show applications of the A, B, and C components of the Min-a-Max building system to the truncated octahedron and its space units, and their combinations.

Figure [13.20a] shows a polar space unit sliced from the truncated octahedron. Figure [13.20b] shows a *planar* triangulation of this space unit and [13.20c] shows a *domical* triangulation. In the planar configuration, two tetrahex truss assemblies are separated by twelve A components which form three sets of three triangles each; i.e., nine triangles, which in turn form three half-hexagons. These triangulated half-hexagons, which are parallel to the faces of a tetrahedron, interact with the planar trusses in such a way that it is unnecessary to triangulate the square faces. In [13.20c] can be seen the same polar space unit with the hex dome on the upper surface, half hex domes on the sides, and a lower planar truss. The square faces are again stable. This domical structure still requires only components A, B, and C.

a

b

c

13.20 The polar space unit of the truncated octahedron (a) can be stabilized with planar (b) or domical (c) triangulation.

The equatorial space unit derived from the truncated octahedron is shown in [13.21a]. It is an equatorial unit composed of six half-hexagons around its periphery which separate two equal hexagons with sides equal to x and 2x. Figure [13.21b] shows a planar triangulated version of this space unit. It is only necessary to triangulate three of the half-hexagons for the structure to be stable. The three nontriangulated, open half-hexagons are stable for the same reasons as are the square faces of the previously discussed figure. The three triangulated half-hexagons are parallel to the faces of the regular tetrahedron and interact with the planar trusses stabilizing the open faces. Figure [13.21c] shows the fully stable domed version of this truncated octahedral space unit.

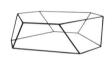

a b

c d

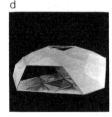

e f

13.21 The equatorial space unit of the truncated octahedron (a) can be stabilized with planar (b) or domical (c–f) triangulation. Stressed-skin domical structure is shown in (d, f) with interior detail in (e).

Efficient stressed-skin versions of this "equatorial" system are possible. Figure [13.21f] shows a model of an identical geometric configuration to that shown in [13.22c] with the exception that the former is a stressed-skin system rather than a triangulated framework with attached panels. Figures [13.21d, e] and [13.22a, b, c] show this surface-structure model from different views. Figure [13.21e] is an interior view. Figure [13.22c, d] compares plan views of the stressed-skin and framework versions of this configuration. The surface version of this system suggests the possibility of stressed-skin plastic structures for which it would be possible to mold very large lightweight component sections.

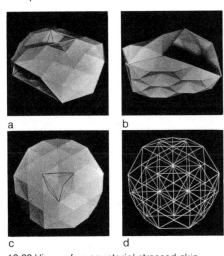

a   b

c   d

13.22 Views of an equatorial stressed-skin dome: oblique top side (a), oblique bottom side (b), with top view (c) compared to top view of skeletal-framework dome (d).

The full truncated octahedron is shown in [13.23a]. The planar triangulated version is shown in [13.23b] and the full domical version in shown in [13.23c]. In order for the planar version to be fully stable it is necessary to include altogether four planar tetrahex trusses separated by A components on the hexagonal faces. As we have seen in the other cases, the square faces need not be triangulated. The full domed truncated octahedron becomes an

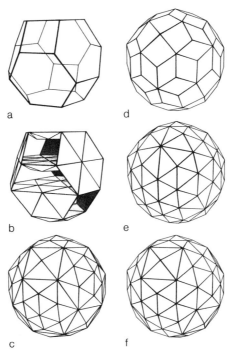

a   d

b   e

c   f

13.23 The full truncated octahedron (a) can be stabilized with planar (b) or domical (c) triangulation. The domical triangulation gives rise to the 84-faced Min-a-Max polyhedron (d) and its triangulated variations (c, e, f).

approximation to a sphere. In this structure it is necessary to triangulate five of the six square faces for complete stability. The triangulation of the square faces introduces a new edge length not previously defined. The square face can be cross-braced with D components. However, this results in a planar triangulation and the by now familiar local instability problem. In order to eliminate local instability, it is necessary to move the joint at the center of the square off the plane of the square face. None of the original components are of such lengths that this can be accomplished. Therefore, it is necessary to invent a new component. Because this component is not critical to the modularity of the Min-a-Max system, it can be of arbitrary length so long as a pyramid is formed on each face of the parent truncated octahedron.

The reader should note that in this "spherical" triangulated truncated octahedron, stability is achieved without the planar tetrahex trusses except for a single truss at the bottom of the structure. Because of this, the "spherical" configuration requires less material than the planar version, revealing again the structural advantage of the nonplanar system.

The Min-a-Max Polyhedron

Even though we can use any arbitrary length of component to form the square pyramid, when we examine the spherelike domical triangulation of the truncated octahedron, there is a length ratio which has a unique consistency with the system as a whole. The triangulated polyhedron in [13.23c] is assembled from two kinds of triangles in addition to the triangles which form the pyramids over the square faces—namely, triangles No. 1 and 2 from [13.2]. There are 48 pairs of No. 2 triangles which meet at 180° on a common C edge, and there are 12 pairs of No. 1 triangles which meet at 180° on a common A edge. Since both these sets of paired triangles meet at 180° dihedral angles, a collection of two kinds of rhombic faces is formed.

Twenty-four additional No. 1 triangles are found positioned around the six square faces of the truncated octahedron. An edge length may be chosen such that the twenty-four faces of the six square pyramids, which are required to fully triangulate the truncated octahedron, meet the corresponding No. 1 triangles on common A edges at 180° dihedral angles. If this is done, the No. 1 triangles and the isosceles triangles from the square pyramids taken as units form a set of 24 plane trapezia. Therefore, a convex polyhedron may be formed which includes these 24 trapezia, the 48 sets of rhombic faces which combine the pairs of No. 2 triangles, and the 12 sets of rhombic faces which combine the pairs of No. 1 triangles. Such a polyhedron, which has a total of 84 faces, is shown in [13.23d].

The advantage of such a polyhedron is that it may be triangulated in a variety of ways without altering its shape. That is, each kind of plane quadrilateral face may be triangulated on a long or short diagonal without altering the 180° common edge relationship between paired triangles. For example, the rhombic face which is assembled from a pair of No. 1 triangles may be triangulated by either the A or D components from [13.1]. We, therefore, have the option of triangulating the rhombic face with either a short or long diagonal. With the basic kit of parts shown in [13.1] we have not provided components for the long-diagonal triangulation of the rhombus formed by the pair of No. 2 triangles, or for the alternate triangulation of the trapezium face.

13.24 The three quadrilateral faces of the Min-a-Max polyhedron.

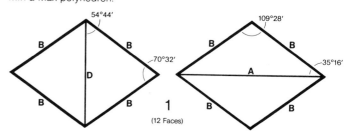

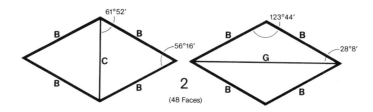

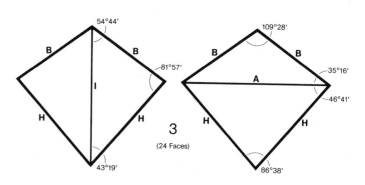

A = Unity, the fundamental modular unit

B = A√6/4 = .6124A	G = A√42/6 = 1.0802A
C = A√3/3 = .5774A	H = A√34/8 = .7289A
D = A√2/2 = .7072A	I = A 5√2/8 = .8839A

In [13.24] can be seen the three faces of our 84-faced polyhedron with all face angles and edge length ratios, including long and short diagonals. From this information, we may add G, H, and I components to the inventory of linear relationships shown in [13.1].

It is important to point out that these new components are important only at the terminal or peripheral regions of structures assembled from the Min-a-Max system. They do not have a role to play in the periodicity of the system. As a practical matter the G component is of little use, but I include it to give a complete description of the system.

In [13.2] were shown nine interstitial panels. All of these panels relate to the periodicity of the system. To this inventory it is useful to add four terminal panels. These are shown in [13.25]. Panels No. 10 and 11 are derived from the trapezia of [13.24]. The rectangular panels No. 12 and 13 are included to complete the inventory of interstitial panels. Their use as termination units will become clear in later examples of structures assembled from the Min-a-Max system.

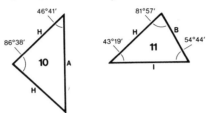

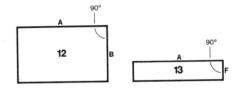

13.25 The terminal interstitial panels of the Min-a-Max system.

One advantage of alternative ways to triangulate the 84 quadrilaterals of our Min-a-Max polyhedron is that it may be "fractured" along a number of different planes, so that domes of different heights and orientations can be obtained. For example, compare c, e, and f of [13.23]. In [13.23c], the Min-a-Max polyhedron is triangulated with long diagonals on the trapezium faces and the No. 1 rhombic face, and short diagonals on the No. 2 rhombic face. In [13.23e] all faces are triangulated with their respective short diagonals. In [13.23f] the trapezium faces have long diagonals and both kinds of rhombic faces have short diagonals. One can imagine from these examples all of the symmetrical and asymmetrical permutations for the triangulation of the Min-a-Max polyhedron.

Other Possibilities Including the Rhombic Dodecahedron

In addition to the spatial systems based upon the "polar" and "equatorial" space units of the truncated octahedron and the full truncated octahedron, it is also useful to consider two alternative spatial systems assembled from a "polar" plus an "equatorial" space unit, i.e., two-thirds of a truncated octahedron. One version has the polar space unit above the equatorial space unit and the other reverses that condition. Figure [13.26a, b] shows these two configurations. The planar and domical triangulated versions are shown in [13.26c–f].

Various other configurations based upon combinations of the truncated octahedron–derived space units are illustrated in [13.27], [13.28], and [13.29].

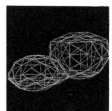

13.27 One equatorial and two polar space units combined and triangulated into a domical structure.

13.28 One equatorial and three polar space units combined and triangulated into planar or domical structures.

13.26 The combination of polar plus equatorial space units of the truncated octahedron (a, b) can be stabilized with planar (c, d) and domical (e, f) triangulation.

13.29 One equatorial and one polar space unit can be combined and triangulated into planar or domical structures.

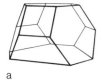
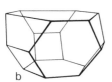

a   b

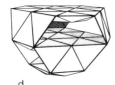

c   d

e   f

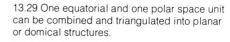

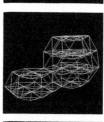
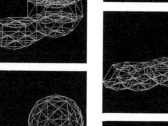

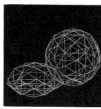
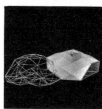

All of the structural configurations we have shown thus far are based upon only components A, B, and C of [13.1] and terminal components H and I of [13.24]. Why then do we even bother with the additional D, E, and F components? A close look at [13.1] shows how closely these three secondary components relate to the three primary components A, B, and C. The D component is an alternative means of stabilizing the rhombus formed by four B components which can also be stabilized by A components. This we saw from the faces of the Min-a-Max polyhedron [13.24]. Where it is appropriate, it is more sensible to stabilize this rhombus with the D component rather than A simply because it is nearly 40% shorter. The E component joins the apices of two "back to back" quarter tetrahedra, and, as we shall see, can serve similar substitutional functions to that of D, as well as permitting many options otherwise not possible. The F component is half the length of the E component and is used to form panel No. 6 in [13.2]. This panel is used primarily for termination purposes in conjunction with panels No. 12 and 13 in [13.25].

When the D component is part of the inventory it is possible to add another space unit to our original set derived from the rhombic dodecahedron. When the edges of a rhombic dodecahedron are comprised of B components, the short diagonals of the rhombic face are exactly the D components. The rhombic dodecahedron can be conveniently divided into two identical space units. This is shown in [13.30a, b]. Higher frequency subdivisions are also possible. For example, [13.30c, d, e, and f] show the rhombic dodecahedron subdivided into four space units of two kinds.

13.30 The rhombic dodecahedron (a) can be divided into two identical space units (b), or four space units of two kinds (c–f).

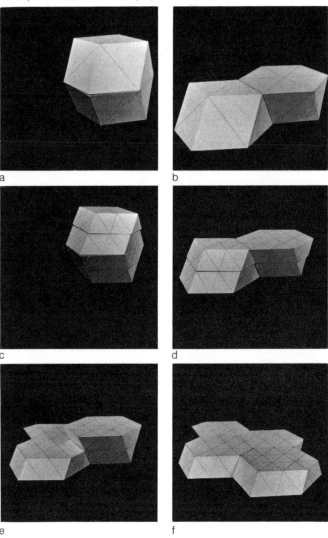

a

b

c

d

e

f

The Octahex Truss and Triprism Hex Truss

For planar space frame systems, the addition of the D and E components to the primary set makes possible the formation of a set of novel structures which have close interrelationships to each other and to our primary tetrahex truss. In [13.18] a double tetrahex truss was shown in which two basic tetrahex trusses are placed back to back such that they share a common horizontal grid of equilateral triangles composed of A components. A variation of this structure can be achieved by removing the horizontal A components and installing E components such that vertically opposite apices of the back to back quarter tetrahedra are connected. This change has the effect of maintaining a fully stable triangulated truss, while at the same time creating a system in which all branches are more nearly equal than is the case of the double tetrahex truss. Components B and C differ in length by a mere 5.7%. The average of the B and C lengths differs from the A component by 40.6%, while it differs from the E component by 31.1%.

The geometry of this new truss is interesting. What is formed is a collection of orthorhombic octahedra clustered in hexagonal sets. I call this the octahex truss. It is shown in [13.31].

A variation of the octahex truss is shown in [13.32]. By substituting B components for E components and D components for certain B components, another octahex truss is formed with monoclinic octahedra. This results in a truss of greater depth per modular increment than the orthorhombic octahex truss. Perhaps what is most significant about this system is that it is possible to change "organically" from the orthorhombic to monoclinic octahex truss without violating the modularity of the system. This makes possible the simple formation of variable-depth trusses [13.33].

In fact, within the constraint of a fixed horizontal modular grid it is possible to effect "organic" transitions from the simple tetrahex truss to the orthorhombic octahex truss, to the monoclinic octahex truss, and beyond. With such a system it is possible within the fixed modular grid to vary truss depth by a factor of 4 or more. The variation in depth between the two types of octahex truss is 33.3%. Such variable depth trusses make possible formation of great variation in clear-span distances while maintaining the rigorous periodicity of a modular system. This is yet another example of diversity within the constraints of simple systems.

With the B, C, and E components that were used to form the orthorhombic octahex truss it is possible to assemble another planar truss. It is shown in [13.34]; I call it the triprism hex truss. It is composed of triangular prisms assembled from C and E components that are arranged in clusters around hexagonal prisms which are triangulated with B components that meet at the center of each hexagonal prism. Again, a fully stable system is formed.

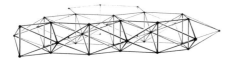

13.31 The octahex truss with vertical E-length components.

13.32 The octahex truss with vertical B-length components used to increase its depth.

13.33 The variable-depth octahex truss with a mixture of vertical B- and E-length components.

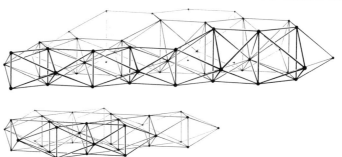

13.34 The triprism hex truss.

Is Minimum Inventory Minimum?

We can begin to see from the examples of these planar trusses the implications of the minimum inventory/maximum diversity concept as a principle. If we limit ourselves to one branch length, say the A component, there is only one possible fully triangulated space frame—that which is composed of regular tetrahedra and regular octahedra. Before we can get any more workable options we have to add two additional components: the B and C branches. This gives us quite a number of new options—both planar trusses (the tetrahex and double tetrahex trusses) and a great variety of domical and partially dome-like structures. If we then add the D and E components to our inventory we add yet even more options, as we have seen. How do we know when we have our minimum inventory?

We are not looking for the *absolute* minimum inventory since that would ultimately be a single component. Although it is quite feasible to envision a system which consists of only one component, it will of necessity have very limited ability to accommodate the requirement for diversity. On the other hand, it does not follow that an infinite number of components will yield any more diversity than a well-chosen minimum set.

The particular Min-a-Max system presented in [13.1], emerges as a minimum set of very high capability. It will take more experience with the system to determine whether the addition of more components will increase the options. As far as structural frameworks are concerned it is not likely that over 7 or 8 primary and secondary branch components will add to the possibilities, for the basic set of 6 components seems nearly optimum. As long as we are aware of possible additions to the inventory, the optimum cut-off point on the inventory will tend to be self-determining.

13.35 The framework of the regular octahedron can be matched to the volume of a vertical-walled hexagonal prism.

Room Partitioning with Min-a-Max

We have so far discussed the basic kit of parts and its application to a spatial vocabulary and its general potential for structural frameworks. We must now move on to discussion of how the Min-a-Max system might be applied to actual building structures, including a system of room partitioning.

It is often typical of environmental structures formed with the Min-a-Max system that no vertical primary structural components occur. This is true even in multistory structures. Because of the three-dimensional triangulation, the members which separate horizontal floors are inclined from the vertical. In spite of this, it is still possible to partition space into rooms with perfectly vertical walls. This is perhaps most easily seen by comparing a hexagonal prism with its vertical walls to an octahedron with its inclined walls. In [13.35a, b] can be seen two views in which the hex prism and the octahedron are superimposed. The linear octahedron forms the triangulated structural frame and the surface hexagonal prism defines the shape and volume of the space enclosed. In such an arrangement the structural system is different from the space-enclosing system. This has implications for the notion of adaptable environments, since changeable partitioning can be envisaged independently of structure.

A modular partitioning system has been developed that is organically coordinated with the Min-a-Max kit of parts shown in [13.1]. The basic geometry of this modular partitioning system is derived from the superposition of a primary equilateral triangular grid defined by component A and a secondary grid defined by component C, forming a compound, multidirectional, rectangular sub-grid over the original triangular grid [13.36]. The combination of rectangular and triangular grids provides a great array of options. The system shares the benefits of triangular and rectangular geometry—conventionally shaped rectangular rooms can be formed along with triangular, trapezoidal, rhombic, hexagonal, and even dodecagonal rooms.

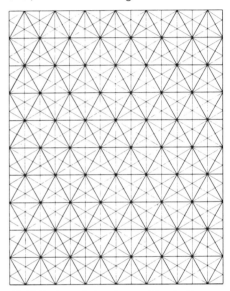

13.36 Equilateral triangles combined with rectangles form the basic floor-plan grid of the Min-a-Max partition system.

The number of room options made possible with Min-a-Max is unlimited both in size and shape. Figure [13.37] shows examples of room plans all of which are formed by various combinations of the set of basic partition modules of [13.38]. The numbers in [13.37] indicate the approximate square footage of each room when the A component is 10 feet long.

13.37 Room sizes and shapes derived from combinations of two partition modules within the Min-a-Max planning grid. Room sizes are given in square feet with a 10-foot A-component.

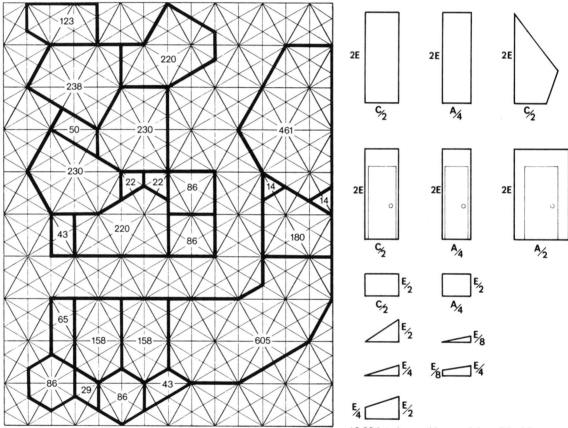

13.38 Interior partition modules of the Min-a-Max system.

Like the exterior surface modules of
[13.2], a set of interior partition modules
is defined in terms of the set of six basic
components of [13.1]. The dimensions of
the partition panels are all multiples or
submultiples of the linear relationships of
these six components. Figure [13.38]
shows a basic set of interior-partition
modules. There are two modular increments in the system corresponding to
submultiples of components A and C.
The small rectangular, triangular, and
trapezoidal modules serve as transition
elements that accommodate the convolu-
tions of the ceiling structure. Figure
[13.39] shows the entrance modules,
which provide the exterior-door options.
Figures [13.40]–[13.42] show a section
from a model, including a floor and ceiling, illustrating the use of the partitions.

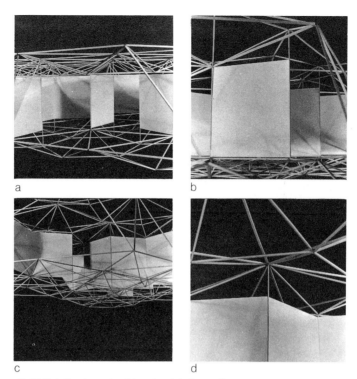

a   b

c   d

13.40 Details of non-load-bearing interior partitions supported by clear span floor and ceiling
tetrahex trusses.

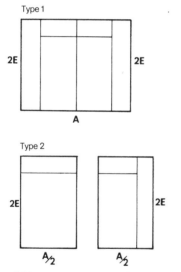

Type 1

2E   2E

A

Type 2

2E   2E

A/2   A/2

13.39 Entrance modules of the Min-a-Max
system.

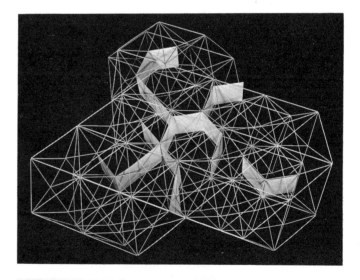

13.41 Oblique top side view of partitions supported by floor and ceiling clear span tetrahex
trusses.

13.42 Elevation view of partitions supported by
floor and ceiling clear span tetrahex trusses.

203   The Min-a-Max Building System

Housing Configurations

In [13.21] and [13.22] we saw a structural enclosing system based upon the equatorial space unit from the truncated octahedron. This configuration constitutes a basic domical unit of great simplicity and usefulness. When the A components have a length of 10 ft., this basic unit has a floor area of 692 sq. ft. When two such domical units are joined, a floor area of 1,328 sq. ft. is provided, and a tricluster of such domical units forms a shelter of 2.119 sq. ft. These structures are shown in [13.43]. The 10 ft. module provides an excellent scale for the Min-a-Max when it is used for single-story structures. The floor plans for the bi- and tri-clusters as housing units are shown in [13.44] and [13.45]. In both cases, exemplary room plans are shown (superimposed on the original partition grid), assembled from the basic partitioning system. It becomes clear from these examples and from [13.37] that a great variety of housing and interior plan arrangements is possible and that varieties of family needs can be readily accommodated.

13.43 Multiple dome housing structures: bicluster and tricluster.

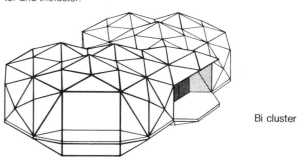

Bi cluster

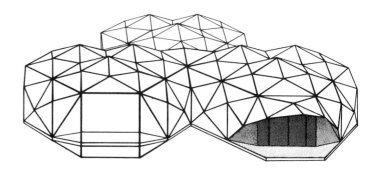

Tri cluster

13.44 Floor plan of the bicluster house superimposed on its planning grid.

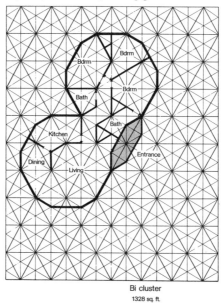

Bi cluster
1328 sq. ft.

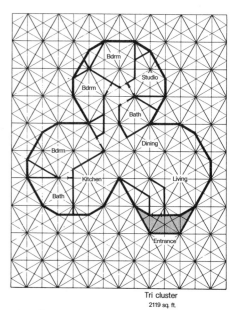

Tri cluster
2119 sq. ft.

13.45 Floor plan of the tricluster house superimposed on its planning grid.

Another possible single-family configuration is shown in [13.46] and [13.47]. With a second level in the large dome, this dwelling has a total floor area of approximately 2,300 sq. ft.

The geometry of this dwelling structure is composed of one full truncated octahedron and three truncated octahedron space units. The model shown in the photograph was originally conceived as a stressed-skin interpretation of the modular geometry of the Min-a-Max system. In either case, stressed-skin or framework, it should be noted that the foundation-floor is an integral part of the structure and requires no reference to a "solid" ground for structural completeness. This, like most of the building configurations shown in this book, can be described as a structurally autonomous system. In [13.47b–d] the view from the underside of the dwelling clearly reveals the tetrahex floor structure. Figure [13.47e, f] shows interior spaces without internal partitions or details.

13.47 The multiple dome of [13.46] is seen in top side (a), bottom side (b), oblique bottom side (c, d), and interior (e, f).

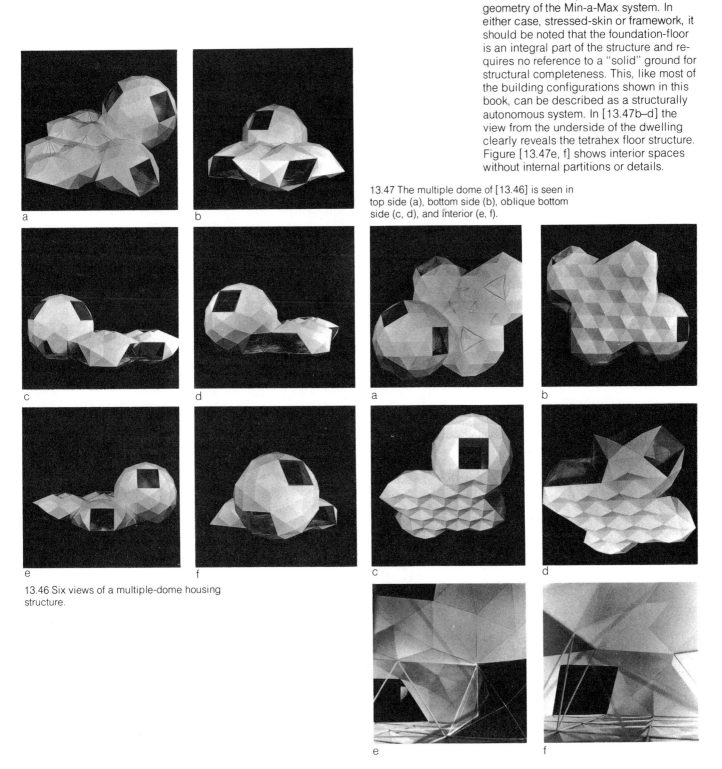

13.46 Six views of a multiple-dome housing structure.

Multilevel Configurations

What is the potential of the Min-a-Max system for multilevel configurations? Figure [13.48a] shows in elevation a fully triangulated skeletal framework for an eight-story building. In [13.48b] the building is shown again with a shell enclosing the framework. The geometry of this eight-story structure is derived from a packing of ten full truncated octahedra and six additional space units derived from the truncated octahedron. This configuration which accounts for the eight horizontal floor layers can be seen in [13.48c].

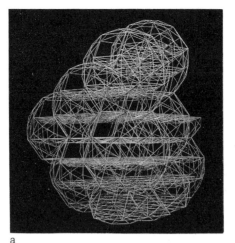

a

The spherical units seen in this configuration provide more floor area per unit of exterior surface than conventional structures, and they have great inherent strength. Another elevation view of this structure is shown in [13.49] and a view of the framework from the underside is seen in [13.50]. Note the vertical coincidence of structural nodes. This view makes it clear that a vertical elevator shaft could be easily installed in spite of the unorthodox geometry. Figure [13.51] shows plan views of all eight levels and [13.52] shows various details. In high rise structures of this kind, it is necessary to increase the length of component A to approximately 13 feet for proper ceiling heights.

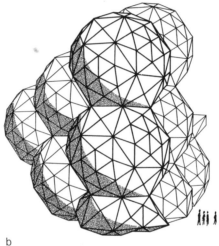

b

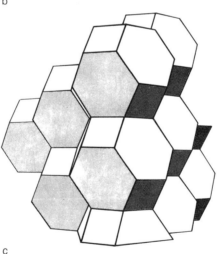

c

13.48 A fully triangulated eight-story building: its framework (a), enclosing shell (b), and the space filling of truncated octahedra from which it was derived (c).

13.49 Another view in elevation of the fully stable triangulated framework of the eight-story building.

13.50 A view of the eight-story building framework from the bottom.

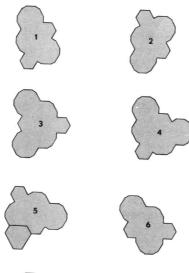

13.51 The eight floors.

It should be emphasized that, with this system, if all structural nodes were multidirectional hinges the structure would still remain completely rigid. The skeletal frame is fully triangulated and is composed entirely of A, B, and C struts. With the exception of local bending loads, stress in this structure is carried axially in the framework members. There are no induced bending moments. The tetrahex planar truss layers which form the floor structures contribute substantially to the overall stability of such a structure; they do not function exclusively as spans or beams. Within the structure, the inclined supporting columns are arranged in hexagonal groups of six equilateral triangles each, all interconnected and co-planar with the faces of the truncated octahedra.

Once again there is a remarkable distribution of forces in such a configuration due to its comprehensive triangulation.*

*This large aggregate of cells has an interesting relationship to soap bubble systems. As in the soap froth, all the surfaces that are not shared with adjacent cells are approximately spherical; all that are shared with adjacent cells are approximately planar. As has already been pointed out, the spherical forms have structural advantages and they also contain the greatest volume with the least surface area. In this particular case, by using spherical hexdomes wherever possible in exterior regions of the structure, a reduction in energy investment results, and at the same time the total volume contained by the structure is significantly increased.

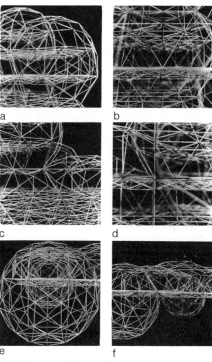

13.52 Details of the eight-story framework.

The Min-a-Max system is capable of forming novel spatial arrangements. In [13.53] the skeletal frame and facade of an arrangement in which three spherical units are connected by a bridgelike structure is seen in elevation. This same structure is shown in oblique view in [13.54] and in plan view in [13.55]. This configuration indicates the potential of Min-a-Max for the innovative use of land. As can be seen in the plan view, the bridge itself is also part of the enclosure. The bridge is developed from a collection of 4 space units which in turn join the three full truncated octahedra from which the spheres are developed.

13.53 Three spheres joined by a bridge.

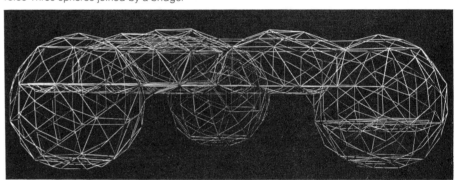

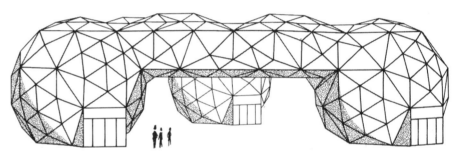

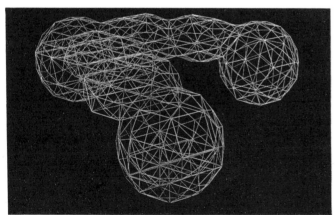

13.54 An oblique top side view of the structure shown in [13.53].

13.55 A top side view of the structure shown in [13.53].

An 11-story structure is shown in [13.56]. Used as an apartment house, this configuration allows almost every apartment to have views in three symmetrically distributed directions, with total privacy. Plans of the eleven levels are shown in [13.57].

The pyramidal form of this configuration constitutes an ideal structural mode for high rise systems. As the altitude of a building increases, the total dead load of the building increases, which places progressively heavier loads on the lower regions of the building. In conventional high rise structures it is necessary to greatly increase the size of the members as they get closer to the ground where the weight is heaviest. In the case of our pyramidal system, there is an accumulation of structural members in direct proportion to the increase in dead load as the structure gets closer to the ground. For this reason, and because the total triangulation of the system disperses stress, uniform or nearly uniform members can be used throughout the structure, thereby keeping the inventory at a minimum. This is a stratagem totally unavailable to conventional architecture.

Pyramidal forms have a low center of gravity. This eliminates the cantilever effect which is characteristic of all high rise structures which grow vertically from a hole in the ground. Such cantilevered arrangements are antithetical to structural efficiency and conservation of materials. With pyramidal forms, structures would be entirely self-supporting. This alone promises considerably more efficient solutions over present approaches to high rise buildings. There is no conclusive evidence that the demands of high density living require that buildings must always be cantilevered vertically from the earth. This again may well prove to be cultural habit with its basis in short range economic considerations or isolated planning.

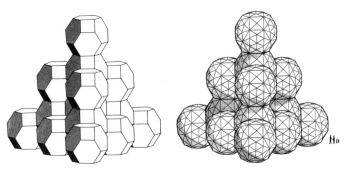

13.56 An 11-story building structure derived from a pyramidal packing of 15 truncated octahedra.

13.57 The 11 floors of the structure [13.56].

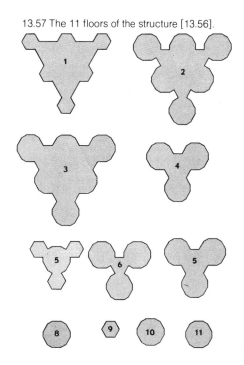

Another high rise system is shown in [13.58]. Here, each spherical unit is a separate house, linked to its neighbors by means of an open framework; so that privacy along with openness of space is achieved while still maintaining higher density than would be possible if the single family dwellings were on the ground. These dwellings would be reached by vertical exterior elevators and elevated walkways. Greenery, including small trees, could be used within the open frameworks connecting the individual houses.

The spherical units are again based on the truncated octahedron; the open triangulated frameworks which separate the truncated octahedra are double hexagonal antiprisms assembled from A components. For this structure, it should definitely not be assumed that the cross section of the A struts used in the living units is the same as the cross section required in the open supporting frameworks. This structural subtlety will require careful analysis. However, such a structure is fully stable and we would expect certain permutations to be quite efficient. It is interesting to note that the geometry of this system is equivalent to that of the diamond structure. Each spherical unit is positioned at the site of a carbon atom with the double antiprisms placed as the chemical bonds.

One can envisage such environmental structures assembled on hillsides in such a way that minimum change in terms of site preparation is required. Such structures might actually hover or bridge over hillsides, touching down only at certain points, thus preserving intact the natural terrain.

13.58 Spherical triangulated truncated octahedra linked in space at the nodal sites of the diamond structure to form a housing complex.

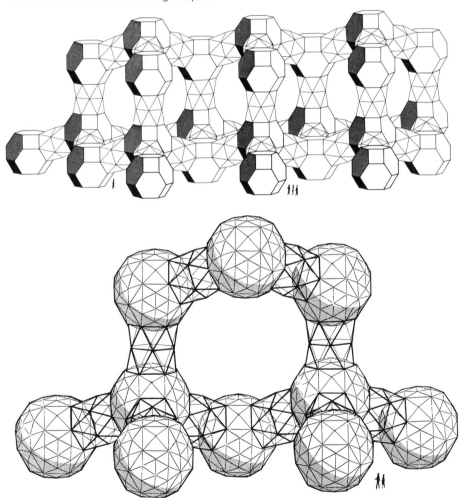

A Min-a-Max School Building

The Min-a-Max system has seen its most detailed development as a study for a child-development center. Figures [13.59] through [13.64] are photographs of a scale model of this building. Although the particular functional constraints of a learning environment are quite different from that of housing, this example goes far in showing the general capabilities of the system.

This model reveals a number of architectural details not described or illustrated in any of the more general structures presented earlier in this chapter. Special notice should be taken of the entrance canopies. They are assembled from the parts shown in [13.2]. In addition, the doorways and window openings are more fully developed than they were in other building examples presented.

The total floor area of the center is 10,954 sq. ft., of which 1,527 sq. ft. is exterior porch. The total surface area of the building is 17,325 sq. ft. It is illuminating to count the numbers of components in this configuration. In the enclosing shell, there are 654 No. 2 panels; 326 No. 1 panels [13.2]; and 8 No. 10 panels [13.25]. There are over twice as many No. 2 panels as there are No. 1 panels, which are the second most frequently occurring panels.

The floor structure of this building is a simple tetrahex truss. All required mechanical systems would be contained in the floor structure, since it does provide considerable room. Like other structures assembled from the Min-a-Max system, the floor truss is an integral structural component of the entire assembly of environmental shells.

13.59–13.64 A Min-a-Max school building.

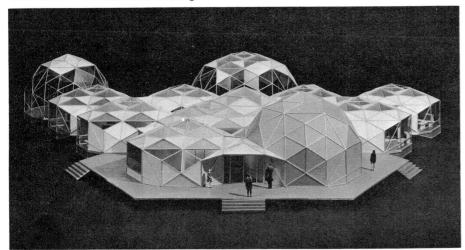

13.59 a

b

Figure [13.60] shows an oblique aerial view of the center in several states of disassembly. The lower-right-hand photograph shows the fully assembled building.

Figure [13.61] is a floor plan of this 10,000 sq. ft. building. The learning/play areas, the learning cluster areas, and the media dome are all clear-span spaces. The administrative dome and the service areas are partitioned into various smaller rooms using the previously outlined Min-a-Max partition system. Figure [13.59a] shows the main entrance of the center, which faces north, and [13.59b] shows the west side of the building. The skylights are oriented to provide an indirect north light inside the facilities.

13.60

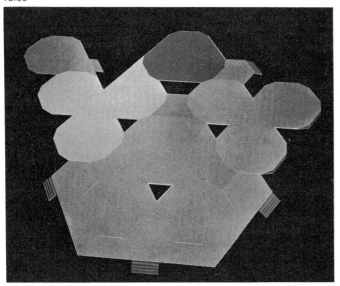

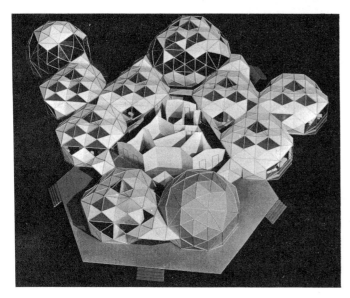

13.61

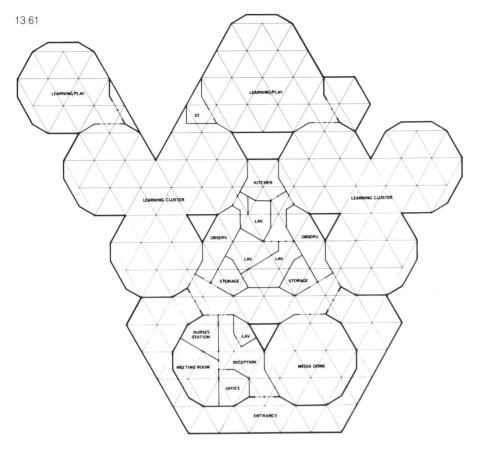

Close-up and interior views are shown in [13.62] and [13.63]. Figure [13.64] shows elevation views—west at the top; west-southwest in the center; and finally a view from due south at the bottom.

13.62

13.63

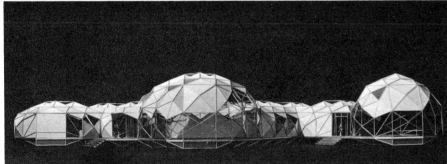

13.64

The Universal Node Building System

I have described the relationship of the Min-a-Max system to the Universal Node system and we know from earlier chapters of the relationships of saddle polyhedra and the continuous surface labyrinths to the Universal Node system. What of the direct application of the Universal Node system to building?

When we impose the requirement that structural frameworks must be fully triangulated, the Universal Node system becomes a system very similar in principle and capability to the Min-a-Max system. In some ways, it is simply another version of the Min-a-Max system and quite clearly it is an embodiment of the minimum inventory/maximum diversity principle.

However, a building system with components based upon the Universal Node system differs from the Min-a-Max system in some important ways. For one thing, because of the constraints imposed by the fixed angles of the universal node, it is impossible to assemble simple convex domes of the type possible with Min-a-Max. (See [13.20]–[13.29].) On the other hand, Universal Node–based architecture requires only one type of joint design, whereas Min-a-Max requires variable-angle or multiple-connector solutions.

One of the fundamental spatial differences in these two related systems is that Min-a-Max relies heavily on the space-unit concept and on domical triangulation and therefore derives many of its structures directly from systems of space-filling polyhedra, while the Universal Node system does not depend as directly on such a spatial vocabulary. The design vocabulary of the Universal Node building system is primarily a function of the properties of symmetry and direction of the node itself, and as such is a system providing finer gauge incrementation than that provided by the relatively large volumetric increments of the Min-a-Max space units. However, the use of such space units and polyhedral cells is clearly not precluded by the Universal Node system. In fact, even though the Min-a-Max system derives from the Universal Node geometry, the latter can be considered a subsystem of the former, at least in the sense that the Universal Node system consists of three out of the six linear components from the Min-a-Max system.

Due to its finer incrementation the Universal Node system is less constrained than Min-a-Max, and is, therefore, theoretically capable of more absolute diversity of form. Also, the connector and framing simplicity of the Universal Node system favors its use for complex multistory structures. By comparison, the Min-a-Max system is more specialized; it is primarily a system based upon multidirectional clusters of variable dome structures. On the other hand, Min-a-Max is potentially more structurally efficient for small structures (particularly single story), and for structures where larger clear spans are required. This is because the C component [13.1] is not included in the Universal Node system, preventing the tetrahex truss and domes, the octahex truss, and the triprism hex truss from being built.

Planar trusses can be built with the Universal Node system with proportions equivalent to the tetrahex truss. They consist of two parallel layers of equilateral triangles of A components separated by pyramids of B components placed on every other triangle, resulting in a distorted (thin) tetrahedral/octahedral truss. In the final analysis, both systems provide efficient fully triangulated embodiments of our minimum inventory/maximum diversity principle, but have somewhat different emphases.

Design Strategy with the Universal Node System

Although our integrative morphological system (Chapters 7, 8) deals with the classification and integration of symmetrical structures, the need for diversity as a function of the adaptation to extrinsic forces suggests that actual building form is likely to be quite unsymmetrical. This seeming contradiction can be accommodated by the Universal Node system's ability to provide orderly asymmetry as a function of symmetrical relationships. Totally random assemblies of components are still governed by the inherent principles of symmetrical order provided by the Universal Node. The inevitable rationality of structures assembled with this system is inescapable. Diversity is, indeed, a function of symmetry.

From the standpoint of function and structure in building design, many structures, symmetrical and otherwise, can be assembled from this system which are not effective. However, the integrative spatial sensibility which the system provides has enabled the development of a novel design vocabulary based upon fully triangulated inherently stable configurations. Low rise, as well as large multistory building structures, have been designed in which comprehensive three-dimensionally triangulated space structures have been totally integrated into the design such that no moment joints are required anywhere in the structures. Like the Min-a-Max system, high strength per weight of material results, while at the same time providing a diverse and functional range of building configurations.

Architectural design flexibility results from the inherent properties, the intrinsic force system, of such a minimum inventory / maximum diversity system. The final "shape" of a given building form emerges as an interaction or synthesis of the extrinsic forces, including building function, structural efficiency, efficient energy use, and environmental adaptation, with the intrinsic forces of the building system. With highly adaptive systems of the types we are describing, building configurations can be anticipated which exhibit a high degree of differentiation from side to side and from upper to lower regions in response to a thorough analysis of relevant extrinsic forces. Because both the Min-a-Max and Universal Node building systems can provide diversity of form with standardized components, the construction of highly differentiated form is not intrinsically difficult or expensive as would likely be the case if such design responses were attempted with conventional building approaches.

The Universal Node as a Building System Connector

Although the present building systems have not been developed into full-scale production, much preliminary design and extensive scale model studies have been completed. In thinking about the Universal Node as a building system connector and its branches as framing members, one may wonder about the value of differentiated cross sections. In addition to the obvious advantages for assembly provided by the self-alignment properties of the Universal Node and its inherent resistance to torsional displacement, the differentiated cross sections are the key to the physical integration of surface panels into the framing system. It is contemplated that in the enlargement of the Universal Node to full-scale building structures, the 26 spokes would be removable from a nodal nucleus. Since, in a building assembly, only a subset of the 26 nodal spokes is normally used, only those spokes that are needed at a given vertex would be included. This minimizes the effective size of the node.

These full-scale "reduction to practice" questions, among many others including choices of appropriate materials, are presently under study, but their further elaboration is beyond the scope of this book. I will here confine myself to a discussion of the basic topology and geometry of Universal Node system and illustrate its potential through exemplary scale models. The building system embodiments represented in the following study models include a Universal Node with removable spokes and the three branches (A, B, D, [13.1]), plus a family of five polygonal interstitial surface modules which include one equilateral triangle (edge length A), three isosceles triangles (Nos. 1, 3, 7, [13.2], and a single rectangle (No. 12, [13.25]). These panels provide the envelope which encloses the building volume. They are attached to and supported by a structural framework assembled from combinations and permutations of the three branch types described above. This enclosed framework provides a polyhedral envelope which can include combinations of convex, concave, and planar regions, and which forms the exterior of the building. This exterior polyhedral envelope can be a self-supporting fully stable clear-span structure enclosing a single floor or can be a configuration requiring additional interior framing struts for roof support, as may be required.

Standardization of Components

Multistory structures are created by hanging floor trusses from the exterior polyhedral envelope. It is typical of such structures that additional interior framing struts are required depending on the size of the spans. The same three linear components from which the polyhedral envelope is assembled are used to assemble the floor trusses and to provide additional interior supports. The fact of three standardized lengths of frame members does not necessarily mean that cross-sectional areas can also be standardized. In fact, the expectation is usually that equal-length frame members are differentiated in section as a function of variation in loads. With the present system the fully stable triangulated geometric options are so extensive that other means of structural differentiation are readily available.

The possibility of truly standardized framing components, including both length, cross-sectional area, and shape can be enhanced by a combination of building form that diminishes in overall size as altitude is increased; by variations in the configurations, positions and density of support framing where loads accumulate and concentrate, such as in the lower levels of a building structure; and by the total absence of moment loads in the joints due to the three-dimensionally integrated (vertical as well as horizontal) triangulation of the structural framing.

The five types of interstitial polygonal surface modules mentioned earlier can be easily standardized, since their structural function is primarily to resist local wind loads. As in Min-a-Max, each panel occurs as an opaque insulated unit or a transparent window unit. Some of the surface modules can also incorporate solar collectors which can be readily integrated into the building form in optimum geometric orientations.

The geometry of the system is adapted to the same system of standardized interior partition modules as that of Min-a-Max, [13.35] through [13.45], which can provide a diverse array of room sizes and shapes. A flooring system is also provided by the system and entryway modules are incorporated into the rectangular surface modules.

Adaptive Form in Architecture

The diversity of structurally valid form available from the standard components enables a given structure to readily and economically adapt its shape to a diverse range of given topographic configurations without the high environmental, social, and economic costs of topographic alterations. Options of form also enable optimal adaptation to earth/sun geometry and prevailing wind conditions in order to facilitate environmental comfort by controlling heat gain and heat loss over daily and seasonal change. This can include even aerodynamic considerations and surface area-to-volume relationships. Many of these factors can have a significant effect on the conservation of external energy supply in the control of temperature and humidity.

The effectiveness of a building from the standpoint of its function and its environmental quality in human terms can be enhanced by the range of form options available to the system. The integration of requirements for privacy and the need for light and view can be readily accomplished by the geometric diversity of the system in either low rise or high rise structures.

The three-dimensionally integrated framework of the building system including the floor trusses and foundation provides for a structural autonomy that is stable independent of any physical support that may be provided by the site. This structural autonomy enables adaptation to marginal geologic conditions, as well as bridge-like spans and even water-borne structures (assuming that adequate buoyancy is also provided). Indeed, structural autonomy of the sort embodied in these systems incorporates properties useful in geographic areas where resistance to seismic loads is a requirement.

Architectural Models Made from the Universal Node System

A series of architectural models have been built which illustrate the Universal Node as a building system. A scale was established in which the longest branch, the rectangle, was assigned the length of 14 feet. The next longest branch, the square, was approximately 10 scale feet long and the shortest, the triangle, was approximately 7 scale feet long. These lengths may be considered optimal with respect to the ratio of truss depth to floor interval and ceiling heights. Also, if the branches are too short the number of nodal connections required is greatly increased. With these lengths, relatively large polygonal surface panels are required, which in some cases may be subdivided into smaller modules.

The models represent an attempt to show a probable range of form options as an expression of responses to the actions of extrinsic forces; that is, form as a diagram of forces. The models were constructed over a brief period of time and do not reflect a rigorous methodology of form development. Rather, some general principles were established, but of necessity these principles were interpreted largely on an intuitive basis. The models clearly show the possibilities for highly differentiated form even within a single structure. Preliminary considerations suggest that the rational expression of extrinsic forces in a building form will most likely result in a structure which is different on all of its sides. This is because extrinsic forces do not act symmetrically upon the structure. The sun does not shine equally on all sides at all times; the wind does not act equally against all sides at all times; gravity does not have the same effect on a tenth floor as it does on a first floor; thus a building's function is not likely to be standardized from side to side and from floor to floor.

In general, the architectural models shown were not designed floor by floor or function by function. In fact, building function was only approximately defined. These structures are an impressionistic view of the possible character of building form that is generated from our minimum inventory/maximum diversity building system in response to the implied action of extrinsic forces.

High Rise Buildings

Figures [13.65] through [13.67] show different views of a hypothetical ten-story building. The building was generally thought of as a commercial center, including a diverse array of shops, restaurants, entertainment facilities and other businesses. Figure [13.65a] is a view from west-southwest showing large areas of opaque surface (light value) and sheltered window areas (dark value). On the left center can be seen an open air mall area covered by an upper region of the building. Figure [13.65b] shows a view of the same ten-story building from south-southwest. In this view can be seen the integral solar collectors covering the oblique roof surfaces, and some of the same sheltered window areas seen in [13.65a]. Also note in [13.65b] the tunnel through the building. A public transit route could be provided including a passenger depot within the tunnel.

Figure [13.65c] shows yet another view of this ten-story building from the northeast and [13.65d] still another view from the north. These two views present a north exposure with considerable surface area committed to windows. The view in [13.65d] shows the tunnel from the opposite end of the view in [13.65b]. Note that the span over the tunnel is a continuation of the roof over the open-air mall seen in [13.65a]. These four views of the same building from different sides illustrate some of the possibilities for assembling a building of highly differentiated form and function from standardized components.

13.65 Ten-story commercial building: west-southwest exposure (a), south-southwest exposure (b), northeast exposure (c).

a

b

c

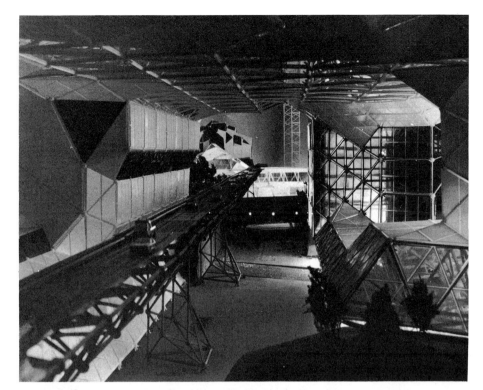

Figure [13.66] shows a detail through the tunnel from the north and [13.67] shows a detail also from the north of three enclosed columnar structures which partially support the region over the open air mall.

A northeast exposure of another building is shown in [13.68]. This eight-story structure was intended to be a general office building offering a diverse array of sizes, shapes, and orientation of office complexes. It would also include open air and interior restaurant facilities. As in the ten-story commercial building of [13.65]–[13.67], a deliberate attempt is made to use the north light to best advantage.

Figure [13.69] shows a southeastern detail of this eight-story office building. The oblique roof surfaces are clad in integral solar collectors directly exposed to the south at an appropriate angle from the horizontal.

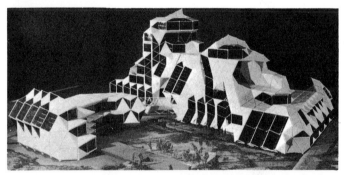

13.66 Ten-story commercial building. Detail of tunnel.

13.67 Ten-story commercial building. Detail of columns.

13.68 Eight-story office building. Northeast exposure.

13.69 Eight-story office building. Detail, southeast exposure.

Housing Units

A three-story, three-family housing structure is shown in [13.70a, b]. The overall form of the building appears remarkably different in the two views—merely a reflection of the spatial requirements of its interior accommodations and its orientation to the environment. The northern exposure of [13.70a] reveals a large surface area for windows, while the southeast exposure of [13.70b] shows the solar collectors in the oblique roof and a large percentage of opaque surface cladding. Although this structure appears to include many rectangular frames, the stability of the framing is preserved by the three-dimensional integration of the triangulated framing.

Although the possibilities for adaptation to nonplanar topographical conditions are clearly implied by examples already given, [13.71] shows a specific adaptation to a hillside site. This multilevel, multistory building was intended to be a two-family housing structure. Three views of another multilevel, multistory housing structure are shown in [13.72a, b, c]. This structure, which is intended for four families, is quite different in character from that shown in [13.71]. Such differentiation is a function of different environmental and site conditions, not to mention different ideas of privacy, and view opportunities, building use, and access. The structure of [13.71] is compact and domelike, while the structure of [13.72], integrated into the land forms of its site, is a more extended linear form.

a

13.71 Multilevel, multistory housing.

b

13.70 Three-family housing unit: north exposure (a), southeast exposure (b).

a

13.72 Four-family, multilevel housing: southeast exposure (a), northeast exposure (b), and detail of southwest exposure (c).

b

c

Internal Structure

In [13.73] is shown a partially enclosed model of a seven-story configuration, revealing some of the internal structure of the building. Some of the interior framing can be seen in [13.74]. Considerable clear space is provided on every floor. Many spatial configurations are possible within the building, while many view options are provided. This structure was designed to fit against a hillside. The overall shape of the building is again intended to demonstrate diversity of form within a single structure as an adaptation to extrinsic forces. The Universal Node connectors are quite visible in this structure, since the unused spokes have not been removed from the model as they were in [13.65] through [13.72].

A skeletal framework without panels is shown in [13.75] and [13.76] of a similar seven-story structure. Space frame floor structures are essentially clear span trusses supported around their peripheries by external building framework, with a few localized internal supports in areas of stress concentration. These trusses, like the tetrahex truss, have a depth of ¼ of the total floor interval. The resulting interior spaces afford great flexibility of use, which can be implemented with the partition system described earlier in this chapter.

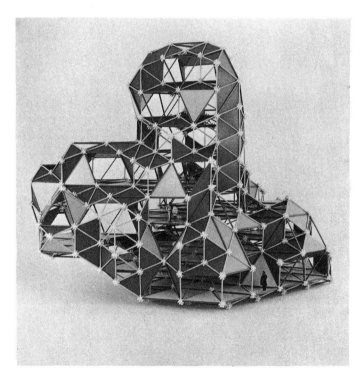

13.73 A partially enclosed seven-story structure built to fit upon a hillside.

13.74 Interior detail of the seven-story structure of [13.73].

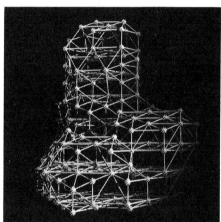

13.75 Skeletal framework of the seven-story building.

13.76 Detail of framework of [13.75].

The structural framework for a 1½-story house is shown in [13.77a, b]. Once again, a stable fully triangulated configuration is provided with clear span interior spaces.

Reasonable Expectations

The models represent an attempt to demonstrate the inherent properties (intrinsic forces) of the minimum inventory/maximum diversity system and its implications for creating adaptive building form from standardized components. The models begin to demonstrate the range of diversity that can be provided by such systems of order and modularity. Since we have already seen responsive systems which provide diversity of form in natural structures governed by minimum-energy phenomena, it is reasonable to expect that such principles of structure in nature can be embodied in man-built architecture. We have only begun to explore the implications of the postulate that successful design solutions are a function of an interaction between intrinsic and extrinsic forces. There is much more work to do at the level of fundamental methodology as well as in the realm of reduction to practice. However, my studies into the applications of minimum inventory/maximum diversity systems to architectural design have convinced me that the design of responsive, adaptive, diverse, and economical environments for human use is within the realm of immediate possibility.

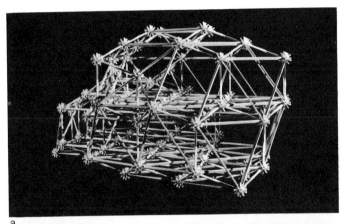

a

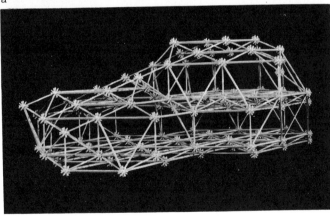

b

13.77 Two views of framework for 1½-story house.

14 Saddle Polyhedra and Continuous Surfaces as Environmental Structures

Saddle Surfaces as Planar Space Structures

I earlier pointed out that certain triangulated space filling polyhedral systems could form the basis of very effective clear-span roof structures. The classic example of such a system is the planar array of regular tetrahedra and octahedra. Additional triangulated space frames were described in Chapter 13. There are a number of possibilities to be found among the space filling saddle polyhedra which can also form clear-span roof structures. In the case of the triangulated space frame structures, all stress is resisted by the linear branch components of the system. If space is to be enclosed with such frameworks it is also necessary to include additional surface panels. A planar space structure can be envisaged which consists entirely of surfaces. There are no branches at all, except, fortuitously, where common edges of the saddle surfaces meet. The interaction of the periodic saddle surfaces suggest that such structures will have very high resistance to both concentrated and distributed loads, comparable or even superior to triangulated planar space frame structures. Such structures could be constructed of thin wall reinforced plastic, or perhaps precast concrete shell modules. Once a flat surface is placed upon a planar triangulated space frame roof system to enclose space, live load bending stresses can be induced in the branches: a phenomenon that does not occur in saddle polyhedra–based structures, since there are no branches.

I have frequently pointed out that the advantage of triangulated structures is that structural members (branches) are loaded along their lengths (axially), in contradistinction to the bending loads (moments) characteristic of nontriangulated structural arrangements. The all-surface space structure derived from the saddle polyhedra displays an inherent rigidity not unlike that of triangulated structures because of the three-dimensional interaction of the curved surfaces of such systems. In addition to their general efficiency, such structures have the advantage that they do not require any additional surface coverings in order to provide shelter, as do open-frame space structures.

From the space filling bcc saddle tetrahedron (Chapter 8) there can be derived a very effective saddle space structure which can function as roof or walls. Examples are shown in [14.1]. The diamond tetrahedron also forms the basis of a saddle space structure as shown in [14.2]. These two are examples of a great many possible systems that can be derived from the inventory of space filling saddle polyhedra.

14.1 A saddle space structure derived from the space filling bcc saddle tetrahedron.

14.2 A saddle space structure derived from the space filling diamond tetrahedron.

Another class of saddle space structures is developed from simple tessellations composed of saddle polygons. Many different saddle polygons are capable of some form of convex-concave planar tessellation and most, if not all, of these tessellations are subsets of space filling systems and, therefore, subsets of the universal network. Some of the most beautiful and efficient examples are derived from tessellations of regular skew hexagons. For instance, [14.3] shows a double layer of tessellations of the 109°28′ regular saddle hexagons. Similar structures can be formed with 90° or 60° regular saddle hexagons and some of the most interesting structures incorporate different hexagons in different layers. For example, a triple-layer structure can be formed in which a central layer of 60° hexagons is covered on both sides by tessellations of 109°28′ hexagons.

With tessellations of saddle polygons, it is not only possible but highly practical to form or mold arbitrary large aggregates of small scale polygons in homogeneous array as a single part. If plane sheets of more saddle tessellations are bonded to both sides of such an array at their apices, a thin panel, say one inch thick, can be created. Such a panel is in actuality a small scale space structure and its strength per unit of invested resources is likely to be unparalleled.

Prior to the discovery of these saddle tessellations and the realization of their small scale possibilities, I had often considered the development of a miniature fully triangulated space structure as a thin, highly efficient structural panel. It is possible to conceive of such a structure built up from, say, one-inch-long struts fastened together at their ends; but fabrication of such small scale, high frequency systems is technically prohibitive. The small scale continuously formed tessellations of saddle polygons make it possible to realize, in virtually equivalent and probably superior form, small scale high efficiency space structures.

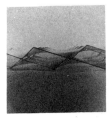

14.3 A saddle space structure derived from a double layer of tessellations of regular saddle hexagons.

Saddle Surfaces Combined with Triangular Networks

Still another possibility of substantial structural interest emerges from the saddle polyhedron concept. Because the saddle polyhedra and tessellations are defined as subsets of our universal network, it is not surprising to learn that structural arrangements are possible which combine in one interactive system both saddle polygons and networks of triangles. Among the simplest examples of such arrangements are structures based, again, on tessellations of regular saddle hexagons. One example is shown in [14.4], in which one planar layer of equilateral triangles has been removed from the tetrahedron/octahedron space frame and replaced by a tessellation of 109°28′ regular saddle hexagons. The saddles function structurally and cooperatively with the linear components of the space frame. If such saddles were produced from reinforced plastic, this could well be the basis of an extremely lightweight structural system in which both rigidity and sheltering were accounted for.

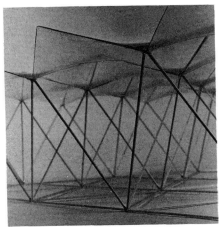

14.4 A structural system formed by combining saddle hexagons with the tetrahedral/octahedral space frame.

Another example of a combined branch and saddle surface structure is seen in [14.5]. This system consists of a tessellation of regular saddle hexagons (109°28′ is shown) in which planar networks of equilateral triangles are attached to the apices formed by the saddles on both sides of the tessellation. An application of such a system to the formation of a space enclosure is shown in [14.6].

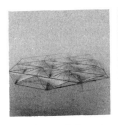

14.5 A tessellation of saddle surfaces combines with a planar network of equilateral triangles.

14.6 A space enclosure formed by the structure shown in [14.5].

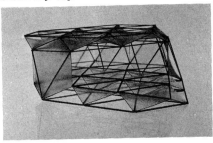

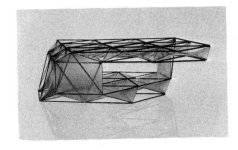

Continuous Surfaces and Their Triangulated Networks as Building Forms

I have already suggested that the space filling saddle polyhedra have some structural advantages due to the modular interaction of their doubly curved surfaces. Such interactions serve a self-stabilizing function. The periodic continuous surfaces have basically the same properties but may be considered optimal forms in the sense that they are minimally redundant structures. They are characterized by an extraordinarily large containment of volume for the surface area, and although there is no actual formation of an array of finite volumetric units or cells, this is implicit in the tunneling system. These periodic continuous surfaces open up novel possibilities for architectural structures.

The Cubic Labyrinth as a Building Form

The simple cubic labyrinth assembled from 60°–90° quadrilaterals was identified in Chapters 9 and 10 as a continuous surface with a desirable surface-to-volume ratio (see Table 9.1). In order to obtain geometrically stable structures, we saw that it was sufficient to truncate the 60°, 90° quadrilateral module to form a 90°,120° hexagon with 2-fold symmetry. We then saw how the continuous surface composed of 90°, 120° hexagons could be approximated by a triangulated network assembled from a module derived by subdividing the hexagon into six triangles (see [10.3]–[10.6]). A building system will now be described in which both the continuous surface and its triangulated approximation can be used.*

*Both the modular continuous surface structures and their triangulated approximation described in this chapter are the subject of pending patents.

When the basic 90°, 120° saddle hexagon module is repeated, the smallest configuration that will enclose space is formed with 36 saddle units. It is shown in [14.7a]. The hexagonal saddle module forms volumetric regions from which can be perimetrically hung five parallel planes, with two additional parallel planes attached on the top and bottom. This arrangement of parallel planes is shown in [14.7b], along with the network of all the edges of the saddle hexagon modules. Each of the parallel planes may be subdivided into equilateral triangles with an edge length common to the edge length of the saddle hexagon module. In addition, it is found that when the planes are subdivided into triangles, certain of the vertices which fall on the perimeters of the planes coincide exactly with certain corners formed by the repeating saddle hexagon modules. Quite clearly, floors for multistory buildings are implied by this arrangement. Because each plane is divided into equilateral triangles, it is a simple matter to build them out of space frame floor structures. For example, the tetrahex truss could be very effectively used. Particularly since, as in the Min-a-Max system, the truss depth is exactly one-fourth the distance between the floors.

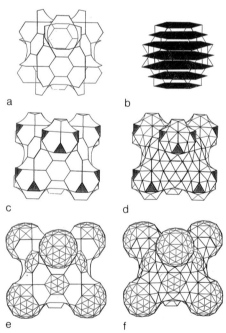

14.7 The smallest configuration of saddle hexagons that will enclose space (a); parallel planes within the structure (b); closing off the open tunnels (c); triangulating the structure (d); closing off the open tunnels with components of the Min-a-Max system (e); and triangulating the entire configuration (f).

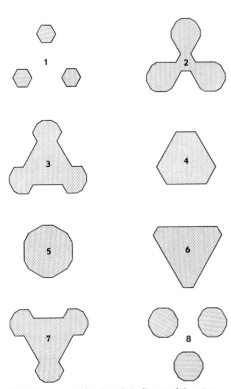

Figure [14.7c] shows the 36-unit configuration with the open tunnels closed off with additional saddles. Figure [14.7d] shows the same structure composed of triangles. Figure [14.7e] shows the 36-unit configuration in which the open tunnels have been closed off with spherical truncated octahedra built with the Min-a-Max system. This configuration can also be composed of triangulated modules as seen in [14.7f]. All four of these structures can form an eight-story structure of very unusual form. The eight plan views are shown in [14.8]. Note that floors one and eight are separated into three coplanar units. A feasible size for a saddle hexagon in such a multistory building would be 14 ft. on edge, which would produce an 11.4 ft. floor interval.

This simple cubic continuous surface structural system has, perhaps, its greatest usefulness in the formation of fairly large multistory buildings. In [14.9] can be seen a 20-story building assembled from over 500 identical saddle hexagon modules. This structure is terminated with Min-a-Max spherical structures. As we discussed in Chapters 9 and 10, this structure divides space into two congruent regions. The structure assembled from our 90°, 120° saddle hexagons also requires plane regular hexagons at intervals if space is to be actually separated into two regions. In the 20-story structure of [14.9], the individual hexagon domes are positioned at the sites of these plane regular hexagons.

The termination of the labyrinth has been done in such a way that one tunnel region is inside and the other is entirely outside. This permits penetration of light and air to a very large part of this essentially pyramidal building as well as permitting numerous view opportunities from inside the building. In the illustration, the dark "holes" represent the tunnels of the exterior part of the labyrinth.

The superstructure formed by the repetition of the single saddle hexagon module is a configuration of enormous structural efficiency. Formed as a thin-shell reinforced-concrete or plastic module, the repeating doubly curved hexagon forms a "stressed skin" system in which no abrupt changes in direction occur while at the same time no flat regions occur. Such a continuous surface system provides a low surface-to-volume ratio; it is difficult to envisage structures of lower redundancy.

14.8 Floor plans for the eight floors of the structure shown in [14.7e, f].

14.9 A 20-story structure assembled from saddle hexagons and spherical triangulated structures from the Min-a-Max system.

It should be pointed out that the same structure can be formed by the repetition of the triangulated module which forms a fully stable network approximation of the continuous-surface structure. Another possibility is the admixture of triangulated modules with curved surface modules. This would permit more options for windows since windows cannot be provided through the saddle surface module without destroying its structural integrity as a stressed skin, while this is easily done with the triangulated framing.

Within the interior labyrinth, twenty levels of tetrahex trusses are perimetrically hung from the superstructure formed by the saddle hexagon modules. A novel floor plan results, in which floors on a common plane are islanded as if they were in separate buildings. All 20 stories are shown in [14.10]. Such a configuration makes possible a great diversity of spatial options within the structure. The floors, as shown, are all clear span spaces which can then be partitioned with the Min-a-Max system into whatever arrangements may be required.

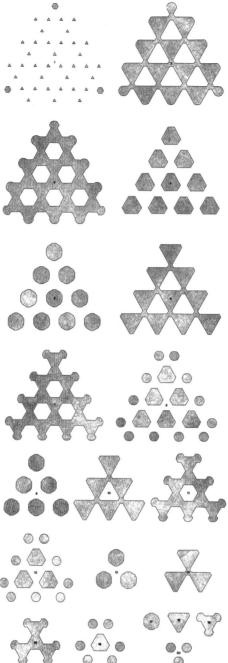

14.10 Floor plans for the structure of [14.9].

The 20-story size of this building is exemplary and not based on any special criteria. Once again the pyramidal form is structurally advantageous, since, as in our other examples of pyramidal structures, the structural components accumulate in direct proportion to the increase in dead load. This has the advantage of permitting the use of structural surface modules which have uniform or nearly uniform thickness. This, in combination with a low center of gravity, promises optimum structural efficiency.

The pyramidal arrangement also has advantages in human terms since more options of view exist and since a series of horizontal plateaus are formed in which trees and gardens can be grown. The entire structure can become a kind of man-made mountain complex. There are many other permutations possible with this structural system than we have suggested. One need only review the discussions and illustrations from the chapters on saddle polyhedra (Chapter 8) and continuous surfaces (Chapters 9, 10) to get a sense of the possibilities.

The Diamond Labyrinth as a Building Form

A related building system is based upon the repetition of a 120° two-fold saddle octagon. It is developed from the 4-tunnel diamond labyrinth derived from the space filling of truncated tetrahedral decahedra. In [14.11a] is shown a basic unit from this system composed of six saddle octagons and four plane hexagons. Figure [14.11b] shows a repetition of this unit. Figure [14.11c] shows how the floor layers relate to the basic framework. Note that it is possible to contain three or six floors in this basic framework. As was the case in the structure assembled from the 90°, 120° hexagon module, the floor planes can be divided into equilateral triangles with certain perimetric vertices coinciding with the nodes of the network. Figure [14.11d] shows a six-story structure with the tunnel openings terminated with domes from the Min-a-Max system.

Figure [14.12] shows a multiple structure assembled from 24 120° octagon saddle surface modules and the Min-a-Max dome system. This structure differs from the one assembled from 90°, 120° hexagons in that the saddle modules are not always connected to one another. This forms a structure less pure insofar as the triangulated frameworks have a substantial role to play in maintaining structural continuity. When this system is sufficiently extended, it becomes clear that only in the terminal regions are the saddle surfaces not fully connected to each other. This system is closely related to the system derived from the simple cubic labyrinth and it is, therefore, possible to coordinate the two systems. It should also be apparent that these two labyrinth systems are organically coordinated with the Min-a-Max and Universal Node systems in such a way as to make it practical to grow one system out of the other. They can be really thought of as a single expanded system in which two saddle modules are added to the original inventory of six linear branch components of the Min-a-Max system or three linear branch components of the Universal Node system. The addition of these two components to either system's inventory increases the options significantly.

Since we know from Chapter 8 that the networks of the continuous surfaces can be assembled with the Universal Node system, we can easily link these two systems. Figure [14.13] shows a model of a 4-story structure. The building is based on the diamond labyrinth, with its saddle surfaces formed by a special saddle pentagon which will be discussed later in this chapter. The planar polyhedral forms are built from the Universal Node parts and the panels of the Universal Node Building System that was introduced in the previous chapter.

14.13 A building structure formed by combining saddle surfaces and the Universal Node system.

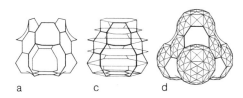

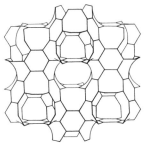

a   c   d

14.11 A basic unit of a building system based on the diamond labyrinth derived from space filling of truncated tetrahedral decahedra (a); repeating the basic unit (b); placing the floor layers in the basic framework (c); and a six-story structure terminated with Min-a-Max domes (d).

b

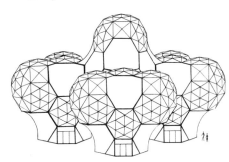

14.12 A structure assembled from octagon saddle surface modules and Min-a-Max domes.

Curved Space Continuous Surfaces as Recreational Environments

The foregoing examples of continuous surfaces as architecture represent some very preliminary investigations into the spatial practicality of such systems. With the help of the staff of my design and manufacturing organization, I have been able to test the validity of such premises with the design, construction and installation of a full-scale "Curved Space"®* continuous surface labyrinth as a recreational/learning environment in the Brooklyn Children's Museum.**

*Curved Space System is the trade name used by Pearce Structures, Inc., manufacturer and developer of this product. It is protected by U.S. Patents 3931697 and 3925941.

**Thanks must go to Edwin Schlossberg and the staff of the Brooklyn Children's Museum for their interest in and support of this project.

Surface Modules

The usefulness of curved space continuous surface systems, whether for large scale architectural or other applications of the type presented here, depends ultimately on the design flexibility of a given system. Such design flexibility is a function of the particular polygonal surface module or set of polygonal surface modules that comprise the system.

We know that the same periodic tunnel system can be derived from different sets of polygonal modules. As a general rule, the larger the size of a polygonal module relative to the volume of the tunnel the less design flexibility is provided. On the other hand, a module that is too small, relative to volume, can become impractical because of an increase in the density of connections.

It has been possible to derive a special coordinated family of polygonal surface modules which provide for optimum design flexibility from the standpoint of both form and structure. This family of surface modules, derived from saddle polyhedra, can be assembled into both major tunnel configurations—the diamond and cubic systems—as well as numerous other labyrinths. Since they can build both systems it is possible to assemble structures in which both systems are integrated. These modules are also provided with efficient and effective terminations, and, in consequence, integrated structural footings.

This optimum family of surface modules consists of three primary polygons: a saddle pentagon, a saddle hexagon, and a plane regular hexagon; and, as a secondary module, a plane square.

The saddle pentagon, when viewed in plan, has mirror symmetry. Its included angles are: 120°, 90°, 90°, 90°, 120°. The boundary of this pentagon is comprised of two edge lengths. The longer edge is $\sqrt{2}$ times as long as the shorter length. The longer edges are adjacent and each falls between 90° included angles. It is a ¼ subdivision of the 120° saddle octagon. We are already familiar with the saddle hexagon. When viewed in plan it has 2-fold rotational as well as mirror symmetry. Its included angles are 120°, 90°, 120°, 120°, 90°, 120°, and it has one edge length equal to the shorter edges of the pentagon. The plane hexagon is regular with all included angles equal to 120°; its single edge length is equal to the short length of the pentagon. The secondary square component is of edge length equal to the short side of the pentagon.

Since the only long edge occurs on the pentagon, it always joins to itself along such edges. In both the case of the saddle pentagon and saddle hexagon, the edges which fall between 90° and 120° included angles are compatible; and the edges which fall between 120° and 120° included angles are compatible. Also, these latter edges are the only ones that are compatible with the plane hexagon and the square.

The Basic Volumetric Cell

The primary modules can be assembled into a 44-faced saddle polyhedron [14.14] consisting of 24 saddle pentagons, 12 saddle hexagons and 8 plane regular hexagons. This saddle polyhedron may be considered the basic volumetric cell of the curved space system. From multiples of this cell either the diamond or cubic labyrinths may be generated. Admixtures of these two fundamental tunnel configurations may be created, as well as a variety of other less symmetrical labyrinthine and closed polyhedral structures.

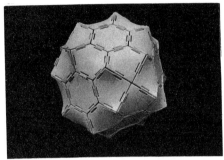

14.14 The 44-faced saddle polyhedron which is the basic volumetric cell of the Curved Space system.

Reduction to Practice

Moving from mathematical abstractions through small scale models to structures of the size used in the installation at the Brooklyn Children's Museum requires considerable attention to details and to the subtleties of three-dimensional space.

The ideal minimal surface is a structure of zero thickness. The surface modules used in the present application have a typical wall thickness of 0.190 inches. The translation of the zero thickness of the ideal minimal surface to a surface module of such a thickness is a technical problem of considerable complexity. The difficulties of such a problem are further compounded by the need to incorporate into the surface modules means by which structures can be assembled. In order to preserve the structural integrity of the branched-shell structures, whatever connector system that is used must provide membrane continuity throughout an assembled labyrinth.

Continuity of form is also a major consideration, since an important recreational intent of the curved space structures is to enable children to slide through the tunnel labyrinths. This requires joining systems without sharp edges and of compact physical dimensions. No matter how compact, any connector system will occupy some space, whether at the vertices of surface modules or between modules along the edges, or both. Since the two major components of the system are nonplanar (skew) polygons, the displacements caused by connector systems must be analyzed three-dimensionally—they defy planar analysis.

Another consideration which adds still further complexity to the development of functioning surface modules relates to the edge conditions of the modules themselves. As was earlier described, the normal relationship in a periodic assembly provides a dihedral angle of 180° between adjacent surface modules. This seems simple enough until it is realized that in 83% of the cases the 180° angle is translated through a helix formed by two saddle surfaces meeting on a common edge. The situation relative to edge conditions becomes even more complex where structures are terminated, because an inversion of the surface modules' normal 180° relationship to each other is required. This changes a 180° helical relationship to a condition in which the dihedral angle progressively changes from 180° to about 90°.

In addition to these considerations, design constraints are imposed by the technique of manufacture. In this case, it was quickly determined that the most economical and effective production method would be injection-molded plastic. Since high impact strength as well as bending stiffness are necessary, and since transparent material is required, polycarbonate material is the logical candidate. In this application all the components including connectors and surface modules were produced in a polycarbonate material produced by General Electric Company and known as Lexan.

Polycarbonates are relatively difficult to mold, and they place more rigorous demands on mold design than other more common plastics. These tendencies of polycarbonates in combination with the relatively complex edge conditions and the three-dimensional contours of the surface modules suggest mold designs of optimum simplicity to insure good molding control. Two-piece molds with simple parting lines around the perimeter of the contoured parts were deemed a requirement. This precluded the use of secondary moving insert slides in the mold; and therefore all undercuts and connector holes were prohibited. All accommodations for connectors and helical edge conditions had to be accomplished on a closed membrane without undercuts. This was easy for the plane hexagon and square modules, since the mold halves opened in a direction normal to their planes. However, for the saddle polygons there are an infinite number of planes tangent to their three-dimensional contours, only one of which is normal to the direction in which the mold halves open.

The accommodation of all of these considerations and the mathematically ideal minimal surface required the use of careful empirical analysis and study. This involved both small scale and full size models as well as observation and analysis of forms created with soap films. Actual size contours were finally developed in clay over machined aluminum supporting plates that defined the exact edge conditions of each of the skew polygons. Each contour that was developed represented the true central membrane of the surface as if it had no thickness. Two resin castings were then made which represented the idealized surface membrane when viewed from opposite sides. Wall thickness was built up on each side and connector and edge details were incorporated. Such models became the patterns from which aluminum molds were directly traced on a 1 to 1 tracing mill.

The scale of the surface modules was decided through the use of full scale cardboard mock-ups of volumetric spaces based upon the polyhedron of [14.14]. An appropriate scale was determined which provided approximately 43 cu. ft. per cell. This resulted in a basic edge length of 10 inches for the polygonal surface modules. The larger edge which occurs only on the pentagon is equal to 10 in. times $\sqrt{2}$, or 14.142 in.

14.15 Vertex clamps of the Curved Space system. Planar (a, b); and two kinds of apex (c–f).

A connection system was developed for joining the polygonal surface modules which fulfilled the considerations outlined above. It consists of a concentric vertex clamp in combination with a linear edge splice. There are three types of vertex clamps: (1) Planar, for assembly of three modules meeting at 120°, 120°, 120°, [14.15a, b] or for assembly of four modules meeting at 90°, 90°, 90°, 90°; (2) Apex, for assembly of three modules meeting at 120°, 120°, 90° [14.15c, d]; and (3) Apex, for assembly of three modules meeting at 90°, 90°, 90° [14.15e, f].

Each vertex clamp is secured by a single nut and bolt assembly. It fits into grooves in the corners of the surface modules such that a rigid and positive joint is effected. The planar vertex clamp is used in the normal 180° dihedral angle condition of repeating surface modules. The apex vertex clamps are used to secure modules in regions of structural termination. All vertex clamps are injection-molded polycarbonate secured by a simple assembly of two washers, a hex cap screw and a self-locking nut. The nut and screw are recessed into the connector assembly and are totally enclosed by molded finishing buttons which are force fitted into place. The finishing buttons create completely smooth vertex clamps and provide security against disassembly. The integration of the surface modules and the vertex clamps provide a continuity of form so as not to interfere with sliding and climbing.

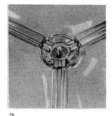

a

b

c

d

e

f

Although these three vertex clamps are a crucial element of the curved space connector system, in and of themselves they do not provide for membrane continuity. In order to achieve membrane continuity, edge splices are required. Like the vertex clamps, the edge splices are also designed to provide smooth transitions between the surface modules. There are two types of edge splice: (1) a 180° dihedral angle splice [14.16a], and (2) a variable dihedral angle splice [14.16b, c].

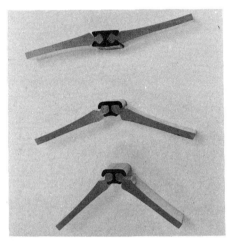

14.16 Two types of edge splice: 180° dihedral angle splice (a); and a variable-angle splice (b, c).

The edge splices run the full length of each edge from vertex clamp to vertex clamp [14.17]. They effectively provide for membrane continuity. The combination of vertex clamps and edge splices provides an effective nonhingeable moment joining system. The edge splices are extruded polycarbonate, and, like all of the other parts, are transparent. They are installed by lightly tapping with a plastic-headed mallet. There is adequate torsional resiliency in these polycarbonate extrusions to allow them to conform to the helical edges while they are tapped into place. The variable angle edge splice contributes less to membrane continuity, since it only occurs at regions of termination. However, it does contribute to the local stability of these regions.

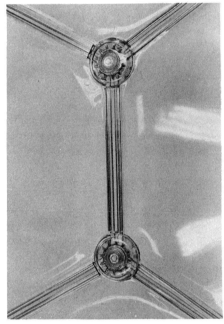

14.17 The edge splice runs the full length of each edge between vertex clamps and provides for membrane continuity.

Earlier I emphasized the need for a labyrinth structure to be closed in order for it to be stable. If we are then to "open it" in order to provide an entryway we lose some local stability. This problem was solved by means of cast aluminum entry frames [14.18]. These frames are substituted for sets of surface modules; they attach with vertex clamps and edge splices. Structural stability is preserved and entry and exit are facilitated. The aluminum frames are either 28 in. x 28 in. or 28 in. × 40 in. and have a ¼-in. average wall thickness. They are coated in a bright epoxy finish so that they can be easily located when climbing in the structure.

The openings made possible by the frames also help ventilate the labyrinth. In addition, all of the secondary square surface modules and half of the flat hexagon surface modules are open triangulated skeletal frameworks. Besides ventilation, these open skeletal modules provide opportunities for varied play activities in addition to sliding and climbing, including hanging and swinging by one's arms and legs.

14.18 The cast-aluminum entry frame.

As was mentioned earlier, three structures were designed for the museum installation. In order to design such structures it was necessary to build a model of the entire museum space within which scale models of curved space labyrinths could be designed and built. These scale models are shown in [14.19]–[14.21]. The modules are 1.5 in. on edge (compared to 10 in. for the full-scale structure), and are injection molded in polystyrene.

The models become, in effect, three-dimensional blueprints for the full-scale structures. Once a configuration is designed through the use of the scale model, it can then be reduced to a drawing, but it would be most misleading to attempt to design such a structure by drawing first. Using the Universal Node system, a three-dimensional skeletal map was devised for each structure. This skeletal map is coded and becomes a simple method for counting components and is a guide for assembly. These same skeletal maps become the basis for the structural analysis described in the following section. Figures [14.22]–[14.24] show the skeletal maps that correspond respectively to [14.19]–[14.21]. The nodes represent cells, the branches represent the tunnels, and the various entryways and terminations are indicated by code. A chart was developed from which parts, including connectors and surface modules, could be counted.

14.19 A scale model of labyrinth No. 1, showing change of level.

14.20 Scale model of labyrinth No. 2, showing bridge span.

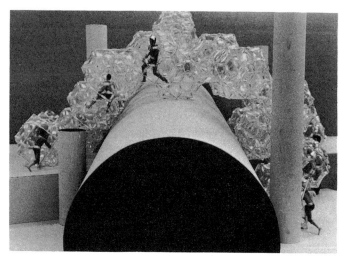

14.21 Scale model of labyrinth No. 3, of sufficient size to demonstrate the congruent tunnels of the diamond labyrinth.

The three structures that were designed had different functions in the museum and were of considerably different size and overall shape. The first and smallest structure [14.19] begins at the main entrance and snakes its way back down to a second level of this multilevel museum. Although this structure is based on the diamond labyrinth, it is more like a protein molecule in its seemingly random organization. It consists of 17 cells with a total volume of 731 cu. ft., reaches a maximum height of 14 ft., is 37 feet long and covers a floor area of 323 sq. ft. It consists of 979 sq. ft. of surface module area, and weighs 1,483 lb. Its components are 438 saddle pentagons, 95 saddle hexagons, 97 plane hexagons, 11 squares, 1,255 vertex clamps, 1,686 edge extrusions and 6 entry/exit frames.

The second structure [14.20] is a combination of diamond and cubic labyrinths. It forms a bridge over a tubular passageway in the museum. It goes from a third level to a second level. The labyrinth starts as a diamond at floor level three and rises to bridge level, at which point it becomes a single horizontal layer of a cubic labyrinth, crosses the passageway in that form, reaches the other side, becomes diamond again, and descends to the floor of the second level.

This second structure consists of 35 cells, with a total volume of 1,505 cu. ft. It reaches a maximum height of 17.5 ft., is 16.5 ft. wide, spans a floor area of 495 sq. ft., consists of 2,057 sq. ft. of surface module area, and weighs 3,121 lb. The components include 556 saddle pentagons, 472 saddle hexagons, 250 plane hexagons, 0 squares, 2,967 vertex clamps, 3,322 edge splices, and 5 entry/exit frames.*

*The final configuration of this second structure as installed in the Brooklyn Children's Museum was modified from this specification and its corresponding skeletal map configuration shown in [14.23]. Although its effect and size is similar, it climbs as cubic, bridges as diamond, and descends as cubic while passing over the tubular passageway [14.27]–[14.30].

The third and final structure [14.21] is the largest and most complex. It is a pure diamond configuration, and is of sufficient size that the congruent tunnels that occur in the curved space labyrinth structures are realized. This structure forms an enclosure for an ecological "habitat" area which is to include a pond stocked with fish, birds, and other animals, and many varieties of vegetation. The children can climb into the labyrinth and observe the habitat from unusual vantage points.

This third structure consists of 66 cells with a total volume of 2,838 cu. ft. It reaches a maximum height of 19.6 ft. and covers a floor area of approximately 715 sq. ft. It consists of 3,534 sq. ft. of surface module area and weighs 5,297 lb. Included are the following components: 1,756 saddle pentagons, 220 saddle hexagons, 326 flat hexagons, 20 squares, 3,945 vertex clamp connectors, 6,110 edge splice extrusions, and 7 entry/exit frames.

The complete Brooklyn Children's Museum installation of three labyrinth structures consists of 118 cells which contain 5,074 cu. ft. of volume and cover 6,570 sq. ft. of surface area, at a total weight of 9,901 lb.

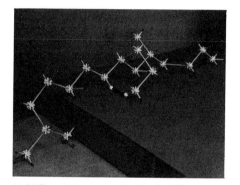

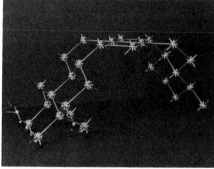

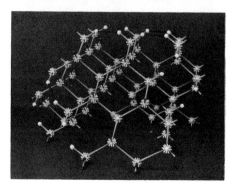

14.22 The skeletal map for labyrinth No. 1.

14.23 The skeletal map for labyrinth No. 2.

14.24 The skeletal map for labyrinth No. 3.

A dramatic and broad range of recreational and learning experiences is provided by these three structures. Figures [14.25]–[14.34] show some typical views in and around these structures.

14.28 Another view of labyrinth No. 2.

14.29 Labyrinth No. 2 as it comes down over the other side of the tubular passageway.

14.30 Detail inside labyrinth No. 1, showing cubic labyrinth.

14.31 Overall view of labyrinth No. 3.

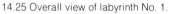

14.25 Overall view of labyrinth No. 1.

14.26 Labyrinth No. 1 changing levels with one cell of labyrinth No. 2 in the foreground.

14.27 Labyrinth No. 2 forming a bridge over a tubular passageway.

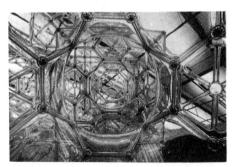

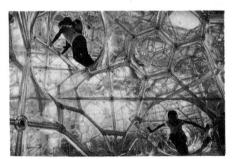

14.32 Another view of labyrinth No. 3.

14.33 Interior region of labyrinth No. 3.

14.34 Climbing inside labyrinth No. 3.

A fourth labyrinth structure was built at the International Design Conference in Aspen, Colorado, in June 1975. It was a 13-cell diamond configuration. Overall views of this structure are shown in [14.35] and [14.36]. Interior views are shown in [14.37] and [14.38] and other details are shown in [14.39] and [14.40].

14.35–14.40 Six views of a 13-cell Curved Space diamond labyrinth.

14.37

14.38

14.39

14.35

14.40

14.36

Structural Analysis*

In the design of most conventional structures, the basic configuration is first developed in sketches and drawings, and then a mathematical analysis is performed. At times, a model is constructed to verify the computationally predicted structural performance. An inverse approach was followed in the Brooklyn Museum project. The design configurations of the branched-shell minimal surface structures were first established at reduced model scales, using modular component elements very similar to the full scale ones. Thus, some measure of the strength and stability performance was established during the design phase. This could only be taken as a preliminary indication, however, since the intermodule connectors differed significantly in the model and the prototype, and many of the loadings could not be properly simulated at reduced scale.

An analytical study of the behavior was therefore necessary. Much other information on the structure was desired as well. The minimal surface structure would sit directly on the museum floor; thus the loads imposed on the museum building had to be known so that additional reinforcements could be provided. The analysis, moreover, would establish the ideal module wall thickness for this application and the magnitudes of load that the intermodule connectors had to resist.

Even at first glance, the rigorous analysis of such branched-shell minimal surface structures appeared to be a task of herculean proportions. It was evident, however, that certain regions of the structure exhibited periodicity and uniformity—with the amplitude and spatial frequency depending on the direction in which the tunnels were developed from the initial cells. A first attempt was made to isolate one of these periodic regions, assume it to be part of an infinite periodic minimal surface, and determine the membrane stress behavior for some simple loads. This might then provide an initial measure of the structural efficiency and help in determining the wall thicknesses. The derivation of the surface equations in a tractable form proved, however, to be such a formidable task in differential geometry that it had to be abandoned in light of the less than complete information it would have provided.

*This analysis was performed by Keto Soosaar of the Charles Stark Draper Laboratory, Cambridge, Mass.

The modular nature of the systems next suggested the possible use of a discrete or finite-element analysis. As mentioned earlier, the modules are joined with vertex clamps at the corners, and with additional edge splices that provide for continuity of slope and deflection. Thus one could derive element stiffness matrices for the saddle pentagon, saddle hexagon, and flat hexagon modules, and then implement these within a general purpose finite-element software package. This approach loses its charm when one reflects that in the largest assembly, there are approximately 2,400 modules and 4,000 corner connectors. With six degrees of freedom per element node, this results in over 25,000 equations for a single assembly. The costs of preparing and executing such an analysis would probably be somewhat greater than a series of full-scale tests on the entire assembly, performed with various module walls to determine the optimum thickness.

It was, therefore, necessary to develop and justify even greater simplifying assumptions to arrive at an analytically and numerically tractable approach. The minimal surface branched shells might be visualized as transformed into a skeletal space frame structure [14.19]–[14.21] of the same overall geometry and topology and with the frame member properties derived from the branched-shell sections. With this approach, the problem is computationally reasonable; the space frame of the largest structure consists of about 66 nodes and 98 branches, and any of a variety of stiffness analysis software packages can be utilized. In this particular case, STRUDL II was used for the computations. The results of such an analysis yield the forces and moments in the members and the reactions applied to the floor. It is assumed thus that the gross distribution of forces, moments and reactions is the same in the skeletal space frame as it is in its equivalent branched shell. This is probably a reasonable assumption, although highly local effects would need special consideration through shell analysis.

At first, considerable pains were taken to apply all of the forces and moments to cylindrical shell branches and then to determine the strength and stability margins based on shell theory. With the relatively large number of branches and their many loading conditions, this soon proved impractical and it was found that almost as good results could be obtained through strength-of-materials approaches, keeping in mind, of course, the general limits of shell stability.

Realistic but conservative loading conditions had to be established for the three-dimensional playground. The structure dead weight and a static lateral equivalent of an earthquake load could be specified quite easily. The expected live loading resulting from the weight of children would, however, be somewhat more difficult to specify. Based on the sizes of the tunnel openings and the dimensions of the cells where branches intersected, it was decided that a "probable heavy" child might weigh 100 lbs. In the case where a large group of children might be arriving together, and then deciding to all occupy one of the structures, the worst possible condition might fit four children into each cell. This would be a highly improbable occurrence, however, since the museum would be limited to about 250 visitors at any one time. Nevertheless, four children was defined as the "unit live load" per cell. This live load was applied in both uniform full as well as various unsymmetrical load combinations to establish the worst cases for each member and to see if net uplift forces could be generated at the supports. Some feel for the worst unsymmetrical load combinations was generated by tactile experiments with the original reduced-scale models.

The module wall thickness of 0.190 inches was based as much on fabricability as on strength and instability criteria. The worst-case material stress, based on highly unsymmetrical loadings, was found to be about 1,000 psi, which is approximately one-ninth of the ultimate strength of Lexan. This occurred only at one location under one load, with the average peak stress being in the order of 400 psi. It was thus decided to use 1,000 psi as a guide for the design of the edge and corner connectors for this application. A much higher strength could be developed without too much trouble but this would have resulted in much bulkier connectors, and would hinder free sliding from one cell to another and increase the hazard to the occupants.

A series of tension load tests were conducted on component subassemblies which verified that the joining system of vertex clamps and edge splices was fully capable of carrying the worst-case stress of 1,000 psi. It was also learned from these tests that as much as a surprising 75% of the tension load is carried by the edge splices alone, insuring membrane continuity, but illustrating the secondary importance of the vertex clamps in the support of tension loads. The connectors were originally designed to operate without benefit of friction. These tests have also shown that friction can act to increase the connector efficiency even further. The vertex clamp and edge splice connection system was also tested for local flexure stress with good results.

In summary, it is felt that a reasonable and conservative approach has been found to the structural analysis of this complex branched-shell structure; and that the safety of the play structure has been established.

It is worthwhile noting that the space frame labyrinths derived from the diamond crystal exhibit primarily space truss action, while the cubic labyrinths behaved mainly in a space frame mode with considerable amount of flexure. While these phenomena are not unexpected when one reflects on the basic structure of matter, they do provide some guidelines for the design strategy.

The Realm of Possibility

The high strength-to-weight and low surface-area-to-volume properties of the Curved Space labyrinth structures are manifestations of a least energy principle. An examination of structure in nature reveals a pervasive tendency for the conditions of minimum potential energy to be fulfilled. The evolution of the Curved Space labyrinth system from the inspiration of the microscopic geometry of the diamond crystal to the small scale plastic models of infinite periodic minimal surfaces, to the development, analysis, and testing of the playground labyrinth provides evidence that such embodiments of natural least effort structural principles are independent of scale. I am confident that the extension of these principles to larger structures such as multistory buildings will follow predictable behavior patterns well established at these smaller scales.

Since the Min-a-Max, Universal Node and continuous surface building systems are so closely related, it is possible (as I have pointed out in the book) to create structural arrays in which one system is interconnected to the other. They become, in effect, a single comprehensive system capable of diverse arrays of alternative structural form.

In the development of our integrative morphological system many unusual and varied geometric possibilities were described. Such an alternative spatial vocabulary was a clear demonstration of the range of possibilities for structural diversity within the constraints of standardized systems.

The examples of structures presented in this chapter and in Chapter 13 do not even begin to exhaust the possibilities for large scale environmental applications of our integrative morphology, since the combinations and permutations are virtually infinite. However, they seem to establish the feasibility of an adaptive architecture conservative of energy and responsive to human needs. They demonstrate the principles and implications of minimum inventory/maximum diversity systems—adaptive molecular structures for architectural design. Indeed, an intrinsic force system has been demonstrated which dramatically increases the options for environmental structure and form, beyond the solutions that emerge from problem analyses limited to enumerations of extrinsic forces or design goals. Structure in nature is a strategy for design.

Bibliography

The references listed here are of varying degrees of importance for the study of structure in nature and its application to environmental systems and modular architecture. This collection of book and article titles is comprehensive as far as structure is concerned, but only suggestive as regards applications. Some of the references cited have played an influential role in the shaping of *Structure in Nature Is a Strategy for Design,* and are important technically and/or philosophically. These documents are marked with an asterisk. The unmarked references are supportive or peripheral, and some are technically esoteric or only obliquely related to the subject at hand. Such references are listed because they will be useful to those who may wish to delve more deeply into special aspects of structural questions, or because they are likely to become important as work on fundamental structure proliferates.

"Materials." *Scientific American,* September, 1967, entire issue.

"Moduledra Building Blocks." *Industrial Design, 10* (July 1962): 44–47.

Allen, J. M., editor, 1967. *Molecular Organization and Biological Function.* New York: Harper & Row.

Allen, K. W., 1964. "Polyhedral Clathrate Hydrates. VIII. The Geometry of the Polyhedra." *Journal of Chemical Physics 41:* 840–844.

Almgren, F. J., Jr., 1966. *Plateau's Problem.* New York: Benjamin.

*Andreini, A., 1907. "Sulle reti di poliedri regolari e semiregolari e sulle corrispondenti reti correlative." *Memorie della Società italiane delle scienze 14:* 75–129.

Apsimon, H., 1950. "Three Facially-Regular Polyhedra." *Canadian Journal of Mathematics 2:* 326–330.

Arnold, B. H., 1962. *Intuitive Concepts in Elementary Topology.* Englewood Cliffs, N.J.: Prentice-Hall.

Azaroff, L. V., 1960. *Introduction to Solids.* New York: McGraw-Hill.

Bagley, B. G., 1965. "Physics: A Dense Packing of Hard Spheres with Five-Fold Symmetry." *Nature 208:* 674–675.

Balamuth, W., 1950. "Volvox," in *Selected Invertebrate Types.* F. A. Brown, Jr., editor. New York: Wiley, pp. 7–10.

*Ball, W. W. R. (Revised by H. S. M. Coxeter), 1962. *Mathematical Recreations and Essays.* New York: Macmillan.

Banigan, S., editor, 1956. *Crystals: Perfect and Imperfect.* New York: Walker.

*Barlow, W., 1883. "Probable Nature of the Internal Symmetry of Crystals." *Nature 29:* 186–188.

*——— 1883a. "Probable Nature of the Internal Symmetry of Crystals." *Nature 29:* 205–207.

*——— 1884. "Probable Nature of the Internal Symmetry of Crystals." *Nature 29:* 404.

*——— 1897. "A Mechanical Cause of Structure and Symmetry Geometrically Investigated with Special Application to Crystals and to Chemical Combination." *Scientific Proceedings, Royal Dublin Society 8:* 526–689.

Barr, S., 1964. *Experiments in Topology.* New York: Crowell.

Barthes, R., and Martin, A., 1964. *La Tour Eiffel.* Lausanne: Delpire.

*Bell, A. G., 1903. "The Tetrahedral Principle in Kite Structure." *National Geographic Magazine 14* (1903): 219–251.

Benfey, O. T., editor, 1963. *Classics in the Theory of Chemical Combination,* New York: Dover.

Benfey, O. T., and Fikes, L., 1966. "The Chemical Prehistory of the Tetrahedron, Octahedron, Icosahedron, and Hexagon," *Advances in Chemistry,* Ser. 61, Kekule Centennial, pp. 111–128.

*Bentley, W. A., and Humphreys, W. J., 1962. *Snow Crystals.* New York: Dover.

Bernal, J. D., 1959. "A Geometrical Approach to the Structure of Liquids." *Nature 183:* 141–147.

——— 1960. "Geometry of the Structure of Monatomic Liquids." *Nature 185:* 68–70.

——— 1960a. "The Structure of Liquids," *Scientific American 201* (August): 124–131.

——— 1967. *The Origin of Life.* Cleveland: World.

Boeke, K., 1967. *Cosmic View: The Universe in Forty Jumps.* New York: Day.

Bonner, J. T., 1963. *Morphogenesis: An Essay on Development.* New York: Atheneum.

——— 1965. *Size and Cycle: An Essay on the Structure of Biology.* Princeton: Princeton University Press.

Borrego, J., 1968. *Space Grid Structures: Skeletal Frameworks and Stressed-Skin Systems.* Cambridge, Mass.: MIT Press.

Bragg, L., 1965. *The Crystalline State: A General Survey.* Ithaca: Cornell University Press.

——— 1968. "X-Ray Crystallography." *Scientific American 219:* 58–70.

——— and Claringbum, G. F., 1968. *Crystal Structures of Minerals.* Ithaca: Cornell University Press.

Bragg, W., 1940. *The Universe of Light.* New York: Dover.

——— 1948. *Concerning the Nature of Things.* New York: Dover.

Brillouin, L., 1953. *Wave Propagation in Periodic Structures.* New York: Dover.

Buchsbaum, R., 1967. *Animals without Backbones.* Chicago: University of Chicago Press.

*Burke, J. G., 1966. *Origins of the Science of Crystals.* Berkeley: University of California Press.

Burt, M., 1966. "Spatial Arrangement and Polyhedra with Curved Surfaces and Their Architectural Applications." Technion — Israel Institute of Technology, Haifa, Master's Thesis.

Buswell, A. M., and Rodebush, W. H., 1965. "Water." *Scientific American 212* (April): 76–89.

Carlson, S. D., Steeves, H. R., VandeBerg, J. S., and Robbins, W. F., 1967. "Vitamin A Deficiency: Effect on Retinal Structure of the Moth *Manduca sexta." Science* 158: 268–270.

Caspar, D. L. D., and Klug, A., 1962. "Physical Principles in the Construction of Regular Viruses." *Symposium on Quantitative Biology* 27: 1–24.

Catalano, E., "Two Warped Surfaces." *Student Publications of the School of Design, North Carolina State College,* 5, pp. 2–17.

Chadwick, G. F., 1961. *The Works of Sir Joseph Paxton.* London: Architectural Press.

Chalmers, B. G., Holland, J. G., Jackson, K. A., and Williams, R. B., 1965. *Crystallography, A Programmed Course in Three Dimensions.* New York: Appleton-Century-Crofts.

Christiansen, G. S., and Garrett, P. H., 1960. *Structure and Change.* San Francisco: Freeman.

Clinton, J. D., 1965. *Structural Design Concepts for Future Space Missions: A Conceptual Investigation of Rotation-Translation Transformation of Platonic Polyhedra.* National Aeronautics and Space Administration Progress Report, NASA Contract NSG-607, November 1.

Committee on Support of Research in the Mathematical Sciences (COSRIMS) with the collaboration of George A. W. Boehm, 1969. *The Mathematical Sciences.* Cambridge, Mass.: MIT Press.

*Courant, R., and Robbins, H., 1963. *What is Mathematics?* London: Oxford University Press.

Coxeter, H. S. M., 1937. "Regular Skew Polyhedra in Three and Four Dimensions and Their Topological Analogues," *Proceedings of the London Mathematical Society,* Ser. 2, *43:* 33–62.

———— 1955. "On Laves' Graph of Girth Ten." *Canadian Journal of Mathematics,* 7: 13–23.

*———— 1961. *Introduction to Geometry.* New York: Wiley.

*———— 1963. *Regular Polytopes.* New York: Macmillan.

———— 1968. *Twelve Geometric Essays.* Carbondale: Southern Illinois University Press.

————, DuVal, P., Flather, H. T., and Petrie, J. F., 1938. *The Fifty-Nine Icosahedra.* Toronto: University of Toronto Press.

———— and Greitzer, S. L., 1967. *Geometry Revisited.* New York: Random House, L. W. Singer Co.

————, Lonquet-Higgins, M. S., and Miller, J.C.P., 1954. "Uniform Polyhedra." *Philosophical Transactions, Royal Society* (London), Ser. A, *246:* 401–450.

———— and Moser, W. O., 1964. *Generations and Relations for Discrete Groups.* New York: Springer-Verlag.

Critchlow, K., 1969. *Order in Space.* New York: The Viking Press.

Cuff, F. B., Jr., and Shetsky, L., 1965. "Dislocation in Metals." *Scientific American* 213 (July): 80–87.

*Cundy, H. M., and Rollett, A. P., 1961. *Mathematical Models.* London: Clarendon.

Dalton, J., 1808. "A New System of Chemical Philosophy" in *Classical Scientific Papers* (Knight).

Davies, R. M., editor, 1968. *Space Structures. Proceedings of the International Conference on Space Structures,* University of Surrey, 1966. New York: John Wiley.

Descartes, R., 1965. *Discourse on Method, Optics, Geometry and Meteorology.* Indianapolis: Bobbs-Merrill. Reprint; original ed., 1637.

Douglas, B. E., 1965. *Concepts and Models of Inorganic Chemistry.* Waltham, Mass.: Blaisdell.

Downs, G. L., and Braun, J. D., 1966. "Pseudo-Fivefold Symmetry in Carbonyl Process Nickel." *Science* 154: 143–144.

Drexler, A., 1964. *Twentieth Century Engineering.* New York: Museum of Modern Art.

Echlin, P., 1968. "Pollen." *Scientific American* 218 (April): 80–90.

Edgar, R. S., and Epstein, R. H., 1965. "The Genetics of Bacterial Virus." *Scientific American* 212 (February): 70–78.

Ehrenfeucht, A., 1964. *The Cube Made Interesting.* New York: Pergamon.

Escher, M. C., 1964. *The Graphic Work of M. C. Escher* (New York: Meredith Press, 1964).

Espinasse, M., 1962. *Robert Hooke.* Berkeley: University of California Press.

*Faber, C., 1963. *Candela: The Shell Builder.* New York: Reinhold.

Feinberg, G., 1967. "Ordinary Matter." *Scientific American* 216 (May): 126–134.

Feininger, A., 1956. *The Anatomy of Nature.* New York: Crown.

Feininger, A., 1966. *Forms of Nature and Life.* New York: Viking.

Finch, J. T., and Klug, A., 1966. "Arrangement of Protein Subunits and the Distribution of Nucleic Acid in Turnip Yellow Mosaic Virus. II. Electron Microscopic Studies." *Journal of Molecular Biology* 15: 344–364.

Fischman, D. A., and Weinbaum, G., 1967. "Hexagonal Pattern in Cell Walls of *Escherichia coli B." Science* 155: 472–474.

Frank, F. C., and Kasper, J. S., 1958. "Complex Alloy Structures Regarded as Sphere Packings. I. Definitions and Basic Principles." *Acta Crystallographica* 11: 184–190.

———— 1959. "Complex Alloy Structures Regarded as Sphere Packings. II. Analysis and Classification of Representative Structures." *Acta Crystallographica* 12: 483–499.

Franke, H. W., 1964. *The Magic of Molecules.* London: Abelard-Schuman.

———— 1966. *Sinnbild der Chemie.* (Microstructures of Chemistry) Basel: Basilius.

Fuller, R. B., 1959. "A Philosophy of Space and Shape." *Consulting Engineer* 13: 90–96.

*———— 1963a. *No more Secondhand God.* Carbondale: Southern Illinois University Press.

*———— 1963b. *Ideas and Integrities: A Spontaneous Autobiographical Disclosure.* Englewood Cliffs, N.J.: Prentice-Hall.

*———— 1965. "Conceptuality of Fundamental Structures," in *Structure in Art and in Science,* Gyorgy Kepes, editor. New York: Braziller.

———— 1969. *Utopia or Oblivion.* Toronto: Bantam.

———— 1975. *Synergetics.* New York: Macmillan.

Gardner, M., 1957. "Mathematical Games." *Scientific American* 196 (June): 166–172.

———— 1964. "Mathematical Games." *Scientific American* 211 (December): 124–130.

———— 1964a. *The Ambidextrous Universe.* New York: Basic Books.

———— 1966. *New Mathematical Diversions from Scientific American.* New York: Simon and Shuster.

———— 1968. "Mathematical Games." *Scientific American* 219 (October): 120–125.

Germer, L. H., 1965. "The Structure of Crystal Surfaces." *Scientific American* 212 (May): 32–41.

Ghyka, M., 1949. *The Geometry of Art and Life.* New York: Sheed and Ward.

Golomb, S. W., 1965. *Polyominoes.* New York: Scribner's.

Gordon, E. K., Samson, S., and Kamb, W. B., 1966. "Crystal Structure of the Zeolite Paulingite." *Science* 154: 1004–1007.

Gott, J. R., III, 1967. "Pseudopolyhedrons." *American Mathematical Monthly* 74: 497–504.

Graziotti, U. A., 1961. *Polyhedra: The Realm of Geometric Beauty.* San Francisco: U. A. Graziotti.

Grebe, J. J., 1968. "A Periodic Table for Fundamental Particles." *Annals of the New York Academy of Sciences* 76: 1–16.

*Haeckel, E., 1887. *Report on the Scientific Results of the Voyage of HMS Challenger, Vol. 18, Part XL – Radiolaria.* Edinburgh 1880–1895. Reprinted, 1966, Johnson Reprint Corp., New York.

Hall, M., Jr., 1967. *Combinatorial Theory.* Waltham, Mass.: Blaisdell.

Hancock, H., 1938. "The Densest Position of Homologous Bodies." *Science* 87: 320–322.

Harrison, W. A., 1961. "The Fermi Surface." *Science 134:* 915–920.

Hellner, E., 1965. "Descriptive Symbols for Crystal-Structure Types and Homeotypes Based on Lattice Complexes." *Acta Crystallographica 19:* 703–712.

Helmcke, J. G., and Otto, F., 1963. "Structures Vivantes et Structures Techniques." *L'Architecture D'Aujourd'hui 108* (June–July): 78–84.

Hertel, H., 1966. *Structure, Form and Movement.* New York: Reinhold.

Heslop-Harrison, J., 1968. "Pollen Wall Development." *Science 161:* 230–237.

Hicks, J. F. G., 1967. "Structure of Silica Glass." *Science 155:* 459–461.

*Hilbert, D., and Cohn-Vossen, S., 1952. *Geometry and the Imagination.* New York: Chelsea.

Hitchborn, J. H. and Hills, G. J., 1967. "Tubular Structures Associated with Turnip Yellow Mosaic Virus *in vivo.*" *Science 157:* 705–706.

Holden, A., 1965. *The Nature of Solids.* New York: Columbia University Press.

——— and Singer, P., 1960. *Crystal and Crystal Growing.* Garden City, N.Y.: Doubleday.

Hooke, R., 1665. *Micrographia or Some Physiological Descriptions of Minute Bodies Made by Magnifying Glasses with Observations and Inquiries Thereupon.* Reprinted, New York: Dover, 1961.

Horne, R. W., 1963. "Electron Microscope Studies on the Structure and Symmetry of Virus Particles," in *Viruses, Nucleic Acids and Cancer (Proceedings of the 17th Annual Symposium on Fundamental Cancer Research, M. D. Anderson Hospital and Tumor Institute, Houston, 1963).* Baltimore: Williams and Wilkins.

*——— 1963a. "The Structure of Viruses." *Scientific American 208* (January): 48–56.

——— and Greville, G. D., 1963. "Observations on Ox-Liver L-Glutamate Dehydrogenase with the Electron Microscope." *Journal of Molecular Biology 6:* 506–509.

——— and Wildy, P., 1961. "Symmetry in Virus Architecture." *Virology 15:* 348–373.

Hubbard, R., and Kropf, A., 1967. "Molecular Isomers in Vision." *Scientific American 216* (June): 64–76.

Hulbary, R. L., 1944. "The Influence of Air Spaces on the Three-dimensional Shapes of Cells in *Elodea* Stems and a Comparison with Pith Cells of *Ailanthus.*" *American Journal of Botany 31:* 561–580.

Hume-Rothery, W., 1963. *Electrons, Atoms, Metals and Alloys.* New York: Dover.

*Hurlbut, C. S., 1966. *Dana's Manual of Mineralogy.* New York: Wiley.

Huxley, H. E., 1958. "The Contraction of Muscle." *Scientific American 199* (November): 66–82.

——— 1965. "The Mechanism of Muscular Contraction." *Scientific American 213* (December): 18–27.

——— and Zubay, G. 1960. "The Structure of the Protein Shell of Turnip Yellow Virus." *Journal of Molecular Biology 2:* 189–196.

Huxtable, A. L., 1960. *Pier Luigi Nervi.* London: Mayflower.

Jaffe, H. W., Robinson P., and Klein, C., Jr., 1968. "Exsolution Lamellae and Optic Orientation of Clinoamphiboles." *Science 160:* 776–778.

Jamnitzer, W., 1964. *Perspectiva Corporum Regularium.* Paris: Alain Brieux.

Jeffrey, G. A., Jordan, T. H., and McMullan, R. K., 1967. "Synthetic Zeolites; Growth of Larger Single Crystals." *Science 155:* 689–691.

*Jírovec, O., Boucek, B., and Fiala, J., 1962. *Life Under the Microscope.* London: Spring Books.

Jöedicke, J., 1963. *Shell Architecture.* New York: Reinhold.

Johnson, N. W., 1966. "Convex Polyhedra with Regular Faces." *Canadian Journal of Mathematics 18:* 169–200.

——— 1966a. *The Theory of Uniform Polytopes and Honeycombs.* University of Toronto Doctoral Thesis.

*Lord Kelvin (William Thompson), 1887. "On the Division of Space with Minimum Partitional Area." *London, Edinburgh, and Dublin Philosophical Magazine and Journal 24:* 503–514.

*——— 1889. "Molecular Constitution of Matter," *Proceedings of the Royal Society of Edinburgh 16:* 693–724.

*——— 1894. "On Homogeneous Division of Space," *Proceedings of the Royal Society 55* (January 18): 1–16.

*Kepes, G., editor, 1963. *The New Landscape in Art and Science.* Chicago: Theobald.

*——— 1965. *Structure in Art and in Science.* New York: Braziller.

*——— 1966. *Module, Proportion, Symmetry.* New York: Braziller.

*Kepler, J., 1966. *The Six Cornered Snowflake.* London: Oxford University Press, reprint; original ed., 1611.

Kikuchi, R., 1956. "Shape Distribution of Two-Dimensional Soap Froths." *Journal of Chemical Physics 24:* 861–867.

Kittel, C., 1967. *Introduction to Solid State Physics.* New York: Wiley.

Klein, F., 1956. *The Icosahedron and the Solution of Equations of the Fifth Degree.* New York: Dover.

Klug, A., and Finch, J. T., 1965. "Structure of Viruses of the Papilloma-Polyoma Type. I. Human Wart Virus." *Journal of Molecular Biology 11:* 403–423.

Klug, A., Longley, W., and Leberman, R., 1966. "Arrangement of Protein Subunits and the Distribution of Nucleic Acid in Turnip Yellow Mosaic Virus. 1. X-Ray Diffraction Studies." *Journal of Molecular Biology 15:* 315–343.

Knight, D. M., editor, 1968. *Classical Scientific Papers: Chemistry.* New York: Elsevier.

Knowles, R. L., 1974. *Energy and Form. An Ecological Approach to Urban Growth.* Cambridge: The MIT Press.

Le Ricolais, R., 1953. "Structural Approach in Hexagonal Planning." *Student Publications of the School of Design, North Carolina State College 3* (Spring): 10–15.

——— 1953a. "Contribution to Space Structures." *Student Publications of the School of Design, North Carolina State College 3* (Spring): 1–5.

——— 1955. "Topology and Architecture." *Student Publications of the School of Design, North Carolina State College 5:* 10–16.

——— 1961. "Tension Structures and Related Research." *New Building Research,* Building Research Institute, National Academy of Science, Washington, D.C., Spring.

——— 1963. "30 Ans de Recherches sur les Structures." *L'Architecture D'Aujourd'hui 108* (June): 86–101.

——— 1968. "The Trihex: New Pattern for Urban Space." *Progressive Architecture,* February, pp. 118–119.

Lesage, J., 1956. "Alexander Graham Bell Museum: Tribute to Genius." *National Geographic Magazine 110* (August): 227–256.

Levinthal, C., 1966. "Molecular Model-building by Computer." *Scientific American 214* (June): 42–52.

Lewis, F. T., 1923. "The Typical Shape of Polyhedral Cells in Vegetable Parenchyma and the Restoration of that Shape Following Cell Division." *Proceedings of the American Academy of Arts and Sciences 58:* 537–552.

——— 1925. "A Further Study of the Polyhedral Shapes of Cells." *Proceedings of the American Academy of Arts and Sciences 61:* 1–34.

——— 1931. "A Comparison Between the Mosaic of Polygons in a Film or Artificial Emulsion and the Pattern of Simple Epithelium in Surface View (Cucumber Epidermis and Human Amnion). *Anatomical Record 50:* 235–265.

——— 1933. "Mathematically Precise Features of Epithelial Mosaics: Observations on the Endothelium of Capillaries." *Anatomical Record 55:* 323–341.

——— 1933a. "The Significance of Cells as Revealed by Their Polyhedral Shapes with Special Reference to Precartilage and A Surmise Concerning Nerve Cells and Neuroglia." *Proceedings of the American Academy of Arts and Sciences 68:* 251–284.

*———— 1943. "A Geometric Accounting for Diverse Shapes of 14-Hedral Cells: The Transition from Dodecahedra to Tetrakaidecahedra." *American Journal of Botany 30:* 74–81.

———— 1944. "The Geometry of Growth and Cell Division in Columnar Parenchyma." *American Journal of Botany 31:* 619–629.

———— 1946. "The Shape of Cells as a Mathematical Problem." *American Scientist 34:* 359–369.

*———— 1949. "The Analogous Shape of Cells and Bubbles." *Proceedings of the American Academy of Arts and Sciences 77:* 147–186.

Li, S., 1962. "Metallic Dome Structure Systems." *Journal of the Structural Division, Proceedings of the American Society of Civil Engineers 88:* 201–226.

Lifshitz, J., 1943. "On the Cellular Division of Space with Minimum Area." *Science, 97:* 268.

Lindgren, H., 1964. *Geometric Dissections.* Princeton: Van Nostrand.

*Lines, L., 1965. *Solid Geometry.* New York: Dover.

Lipscomb, W. N., 1966. "Framework Rearrangements in Boranes and Carboranes." *Science 153:* 373–378.

Lissant, K. J., 1966. "The Geometry of High-Internal Phase-Ratio Emulsions." *Journal of Colloid and Interface Science 22:* 462–468.

Loeb, A., 1958. "A Binary Algebra Describing Crystal Structures with Closely Packed Anions." *Acta Crystallographica 11:* 469–476.

———— 1962. "A Modular Algebra for the Description of Crystal Structures." *Acta Cryst. 15:* 219–226.

———— 1964. "The Subdivision of the Hexagonal Net and the Systematic Generation of Crystal Structures." *Acta Cryst. 17:* 179–182.

———— 1964a. "A Crystal Algebra for Laves Phases." Ledgemont Laboratory, Kennecott Copper Corp., Lexington, Mass., Technical Report 15, March.

———— 1964b. "The Crystograph." Ledgemont Laboratory, Technical Report 40, November.

———— 1965. "Dichromatic Symmetrical Division of the Euclidean Plane." Ledgemont Laboratory, Technical Report 48, February 1.

———— 1965a. "Remarks on Some Elementary Volume Relationships Between Familiar Solids." *The Mathematics Teacher 58:* 417–419.

———— 1966a. "Derivatives of the Body-Centered Cubic Lattice, Ledgemont Laboratory, Technical Report 113, December.

*———— 1966b. "The Architecture of Crystals," in *Module, Proportion, Symmetry and Rhythm,* Gyorgy Kepes, editor. New York: Braziller.

———— 1969. "A Systematic Survey of Cubic Crystal Structures," Ledgemont Laboratory, August.

———— 1971. *Color and Symmetry.* New York: John Wiley.

———— and G. W. Pearsall, 1963. "Moduledra Crystal Modules. A Teaching and Research Aid in Solid-State Physics." *American Journal of Physics 31:* 190–196.

Lyusternik, L. S., 1963. *Convex Figures and Polyhedra.* New York: Dover.

Macgillavry, C., 1965. *Symmetry Aspects of M. C. Escher's Periodic Drawings.* Utrecht: International Union of Crystallography.

Mach, E., 1960. *Space and Geometry.* LaSalle, Illinois: Open Court.

Macior, W. A., and Matzke, E. B., 1951. "An Experimental Analysis of Cell-Wall Curvatures, and Approximations to Minimal Tetrakaidekahedra in the Leaf Parenchyma of Rhoeo Discolor." *American Journal of Botany 38:* 783–793.

Mackay, A. L., 1962. "A Dense Non-Crystallographic Packing of Equal Spheres." *Acta Crystallographica 15:* 916–920.

Mackintosh, A. R., 1963. "The Fermi Surface of Metals." *Scientific American 209* (July): 110–120.

*Makowski, Z. S., 1965. *Steel Space Structures.* London: Michael Joseph.

———— 1966. "Space Structures and the Electronic Computer." *Architectural Design 36* (January): 8–9.

———— 1966a. "A Survey of Recent Three-Dimensional Structures." *Architectural Design 36* (January): 10–41.

*Marks, R. W., 1960. *The Dymaxion World of Buckminster Fuller.* New York: Reinhold.

Marvin, J. W., 1938. "The Shape of Compressed Lead Shot and its Relation to Cell Shape." *American Journal of Botany 25:* 280–287.

———— 1939. "Cell Shape Studies in the Pith of *Eupotorium purpureum.*" *American Journal of Botany 26:* 487–504.

———— 1939a. "The Aggregation of Orthic Tetrakaidecahedra." *Science 83:* 188.

Mason, B. G., 1961. "The Growth of Snow Crystals." *Scientific American 204* (January): 120–131.

Massey, A. G., 1964. "Boron." *Scientific American 200* (January): 88–97.

Matzke, E. B., 1939. "Volume-Shape Relationships in Lead Shot and Their Bearing on Cell Shapes." *American Journal of Botany 26:* 288–295.

*———— 1946. "The Three-Dimensional Shape of Bubbles in Foam—An Analysis of the Role of Surface Forces in Three-Dimensional Cell Shape Determination." *American Journal of Botany 33:* 58–80.

———— 1949. "Three-Dimensional Shape Changes During Cell Division in the Epidermis of the Apical Meristem of *Ancharis densa* (Elodea)" *American Journal of Botany 36:* 584–595.

*———— 1950. "Torreya: in the Twinkling of an Eye." *Bulletin of the Torrey Botanical Club 77:* 222–232.

*———— and Nestler, J., 1946. "Volume-Shape Relationships in Variant Foams—A Further Study of the Role of Surface Forces in Three-Dimensional Cell Shape Determination." *American Journal of Botany 33:* 130–144.

*McHale, J., 1962. *R. Buckminster Fuller.* New York: Braziller.

McHarg, I., 1969. *Design With Nature.* Garden City, N.Y.: Natural History Press.

Mercer, E. H., and Day, M. F., 1952. "The Fine Structure of the Peritrophic Membranes of Certain Insects." *Biological Bulletin 103:* 384–394.

Milman, G., Uzman, G., Mitchell, A., and Langridge, R., 1966. "Pentagonal Aggregation of Virus Particles." *Science 152:* 1381–1383.

Mindel, J., 1962. "Gibbs' Phase Rule and Euler's Formula." *Journal of Chemical Education 39:* 512–514.

Moffatt, W. G., Pearsall, G. W., and Wulff, J., 1964. *The Structure and Properties of Materials, Vol. 1. Structure.* New York: Wiley.

Moore, P. B., and Smith, J. V., 1964. "Archimedean Polyhedra as the Basis of Tetrahedrally Coordinated Frameworks." *Mineralogical Magazine 33:* 1008–1014.

Moore, R. C., 1954. *Treatise of Invertebrate Paleontology.* Laurence, Kan.: University of Kansas Press.

Morris, I. L., and Loeb, A. L., 1960. "A Binary Algebra Describing Crystal Structures with Closely Packed Anions. Part II. A Common System of Reference for Cubic and Hexagonal Structures." *Acta Crystallographica 13:* 434–443.

Mott, N. F., and Jones, H., 1958. *The Theory of the Properties of Metals and Alloys.* New York: Dover.

Muetterties, E. L., and Knoth, W. H., 1966. "Polyhedral Boranes." *Chemical and Engineering News 44:* 88–98.

———— 1968. *Polyhedral Boranes.* New York: Dekker.

Müller, E. W., 1952. "A New Microscope." *Scientific American 186* (May): 591–601.

*———— 1957. "Atoms Visualized." *Scientific American 196* (June): 113–122.

*———— 1960. "Field Ionization and Field Ion Microscopy." *Advances in Electronics and Electron Physics 13:* 83–179.

———— 1965. "Field Ion Microscopy." *Science 149:* 591–601.

———— and Rendulic, K. D., 1967. "Field Ion Microscopical Imaging of Biomolecules." *Science 156:* 961–963.

Munari, B., 1963. *Good Design.* Milan: All'Insegna del Pesce D'Oro.

———— 1965. *Discovery of the Circle.* New York: Wittenborn.

—— 1965a. *Discovery of the Square.* New York: Wittenborn.

Nakaya, U., 1954. *Snow Crystals—Natural and Artificial.* Cambridge, Mass.: Harvard University Press.

Neovius, E. R., 1883. *Bestimmung Zweier Speciellen Periodischen Minimalflachen.* Helsingfors.

Pier Luigi Nervi, P. L., 1956. *Structures.* New York: McGraw-Hill.

—— 1965. *Aesthetics and Technology in Building.* Cambridge, Mass.: Harvard University Press.

Newman, J. R., editor, 1956. *The World of Mathematics. Vols. 1–4.* New York: Simon and Schuster.

Nilsson, L., and Jögersten, G., 1960. *Life in the Sea.* New York: Basic Books.

Odum, E. P., 1963. *Ecology.* New York: Holt, Rinehart and Winston.

Ore, O., 1963. *Graphs and Their Uses.* New York: Random House.

Otto, F., editor, 1967, 1969. *Tensile Structures. Vols. 1, 2.* Cambridge, Mass.: MIT Press.

Pauling, L., 1955. "Modern Structural Chemistry." *Les Prix Nobel en 1954.* Stockholm, pp. 91–99.

—— 1960. *The Nature of the Chemical Bond.* Ithaca, N.Y.: Cornell University Press.

*—— 1964. *The Architecture of Molecules.* San Francisco: Freeman.

—— 1964a. *College Chemistry.* San Francisco: Freeman.

—— 1965. "The Close-Packed Spheron Theory and Nuclear Fission." *Science 150:* 297–305.

Pawley, G. S., 1962. "Plane Groups on Polyhedra." *Acta Crystallographica 15:* 49–53.

Pearce, Peter, and Pearce, Susan, 1978. *Polyhedra Primer.* Palo Alto: Dale Seymour Publications.

Pearce, Peter, and Pearce, Susan, 1980. *Experiments in Form.* New York: Van Nostrand Reinhold.

Perutz, M. F., 1964. "The Hemoglobin Molecule." *Scientific American 211* (November): 64–76.

Philibert, J., 1968. "Diffusion in Solids." *Science and Technology 80:* 47–54.

Phillips, D. C., 1966. "The Three-Dimensional Structure of an Enzyme Molecule." *Scientific American 215* (November): 78–90.

Phillips, F. C., 1963. *An Introduction to Crystallography.* New York: Wiley.

Phillips, H. B., 1967. *Vector Analysis.* New York: Wiley.

Picken, L., 1962. *The Organization of Cells and Other Organisms.* Oxford: Clarendon.

Popko, L., 1968. *Geodesics.* Detroit: University of Detroit Press.

Rapp, F., and Melnick, J. L., 1966. "The Footprints of Tumor Viruses." *Scientific American 214* (March): 34–41.

Reed, W. A., and Fawcett, E., 1964. "High-Field Galvanomagnetic Properties of Metals," *Science 146:* 603–610.

Rhodin, J. A. G., 1963. *An Atlas of Ultrastructure.* Philadelphia: Saunders.

Roberts, B. W., 1960. "Magnetoacoustic Oscillations and the Fermi Surface in Aluminum." *Physical Review 119:* 1889–1896.

Rogers, B. A., 1965. *The Nature of Metals.* Cambridge, Mass: MIT Press.

Roland, C., 1966. "Frei Otto's Pneumatic Structures." *Architectural Design 36* (July): 340–360.

Rudofsky, B., 1965. *Architecture without Architects.* New York: Museum of Modern Art.

Runnels, L. K., 1966. "Ice." *Scientific American 215* (December): 118–126.

Salvadori, M., and Heller, R., 1963. *Structure in Architecture.* Englewood Cliffs, N.J.: Prentice-Hall.

Sanderson, R. T., 1962. *Teaching Chemistry with Models.* Princeton: Van Nostrand.

Savory, T. H., 1960. "Spider Webs." *Scientific American 202* (April): 114–124.

Schoen, A. H., 1967. "Homogeneous Nets and Their Fundamental Regions." *Notices of the American Mathematical Society. 14:* 661.

—— 1968. "Infinite Regular Warped Polyhedra and Periodic Minimal Surfaces." *Notices 15:* 727.

—— 1968a. "Regular Saddle Polyhedra." *Notices 15:* 929.

—— 1969. "A Fifth Intersection-Free Infinite Periodic Minimal Surface of Cubic Symmetry." *Notices 16:* 519.

—— 1969a. "Infinite Periodic Minimal Surfaces without Self-Intersections." *NASA Technical Note C-98* (September).

—— 1970. "Infinite Periodic Minimal Surfaces without Self-Intersections." *NASA Technical Note TN D-5541* (May).

Schulze-Fielitz, E., 1962. "Une Théorie pour L'Occupation de L'Espace." *L'Architecture D'Aujourd'hui 102* (July): 78–85.

Schwarz, H. A., 1890. *Gesammelte Mathematische Abhandlungen. Vol. 1.* Berlin: Springer.

Sebera, D. K., 1964. *Electronic Structure and Chemical Bonding.* Waltham, Mass.: Blaisdell.

Shanthaveerappa, T. R., and Bourne, G. H., 1966. "Perineural Epithelium: A New Concept of its Role in the Integrity of the Peripheral Nervous System. *Science 154:* 1464–1467.

Skeist, I., 1966. *Plastics in Building.* New York: Reinhold.

*Smith, C. S., 1948. "Grains, Phases and Interfaces: An Interpretation of Microstructure." *Transactions, American Institute of Mining and Metallurgical Engineers 175:* 15–51.

—— 1952. "Grain Shapes and Other Metallurgical Applications of Topology," in *Metal Interfaces.* Cleveland: American Society of Metals, pp. 65–113.

—— 1953. "Further Notes on the Shape of Metal Grains: Space-Filling Polyhedra with Unlimited Shaving of Corners and Faces." *Acta Metallurgica 1:* 295–300.

*—— 1953a. "Microstructure," *Transactions of the American Society for Metals 45:* 533–573.

*—— 1954. "The Shape of Things." *Scientific American 190* (January): 58–64.

—— 1965. *A History of Metallography.* Chicago: University of Chicago Press.

*—— 1965a. "Structure, Substructure, Superstructure," in *Structure in Art and in Science,* Gyorgy Kepes, editor. New York: Braziller.

—— 1967. "Materials." *Scientific American 217* (September): 66–79.

*—— 1968. "Simplicity and Complexity." *Science and Technology.* No. 77 (May), pp. 60–65.

Snelson, K., 1963. "A Design for the Atom." *Industrial Design 10* (February): 48–57.

Sommerville, D. M. Y., 1958. *The Elements of Non-Euclidean Geometry.* New York: Dover.

Staff Report, 1959. "Dome Structures." *Consulting Engineer 13* (December): 89–122.

Steinhaus, H., 1960. *Mathematical Snapshots.* New York: Oxford University Press.

Stessman, B., 1934. "Periodische Minimalflachen." *Mathematische Zeitschrift 33:* 417–442.

Stevens, P. S., 1966. "A Geometric Analogue of the Electron Cloud." *Proceedings of the National Academy of Sciences 56:* 789–793.

Stix, H., Stix, M., and Abbott, R. T., 1969. *The Shell: Five Hundred Million Years of Inspired Design.* New York: Abrams.

Stuart, D. R., 1955. "On the Orderly Subdivision of Spheres." *Student Publications of the School of Design, North Carolina State College 5:* 23–33.

—— 1961. "Polyhedral and Mosaic Transformation." *Student Publications of the School of Design, North Carolina State College 12:* 3–28.

Sullenger, D. B., and Kenar, C. H. L., 1966. "Boron Crystals." *Scientific American 215* (July): 96–107.

Sutor, D. J., and Wooley, S. E., 1968. "Gallstone of Unusual Composition: Calcite, Aragonite, and Vaterite." *Science 159:* 1113–1114.

Temperley, H. N. V., 1967. "How Liquids Behave." *Science Journal 3:* 74–79.

*Thompson, D'Arcy Wentworth, 1963. *On Growth and Form.* Vols. I, II. (Cited in this work as Thompson I, II.) London: Cambridge University Press.

—— Abridged Edition, 1961. J. T. Bonner, editor. London: Cambridge University Press.

*Toth, L. F., 1964. *Regular Figures.* New York: Pergamon Press Book, Macmillan.

—— 1964a. "What the Bees Know and What They Do Not Know," *Bulletin of the American Mathematical Society* 70: 468–481.

Tsuruta, T., and Inoue, S., 1967. "Well-Ordered Polymers," *Science and Technology*, No. 71 (November), pp. 66–76.

Turnbull, D., 1965. "The Undercooling of Liquids." *Scientific American* 212 (January): 38–56.

Vanders, I., and Kerr, P., 1967. *Mineral Recognition*. New York: Wiley.

*Wachsmann, K., 1961. *The Turning Point of Building*. New York: Reinhold.

Waegell, B., 1965. "Molecular Mechanics." *International Science and Technology*, No. 48 (December), pp. 60–70.

Wannier, G. H., 1952. "The Nature of Solids." *Scientific American* 187 (December): 39–58.

Warmke, J. R., 1967. Aucuba Strain of Tobacco Mosaic Virus: An Unusual Aggregate." *Science* 156: 262–263.

Wasserman, E., 1962. "Chemical Topology." *Scientific American* 207 (November): 94–102.

Watson, J. D., 1965. *Molecular Biology of the Gene*. New York: Benjamin.

Weibel, E. R. 1963. *Morphometry of the Human Lung*. Berlin: Springer-Verlag.

Wells, A. F., 1954. "The Geometrical Basis of Crystal Chemistry. Part 1." *Acta Crystallographica* 7: 535–544.

—— 1954a. "Geometrical Basis. . . . Part 2." *Acta Cryst.* 7: 545–554.

—— 1954b. "Geometrical Basis. . . . Part 3." *Acta Cryst.* 7: 842–848.

—— 1954c. "Geometrical Basis. . . . Part 4." *Acta Cryst.* 7: 849–853.

—— 1955. "Geometrical Basis. . . . Part 5." *Acta Cryst.* 8: 32–36.

—— 1956. "Geometrical Basis. . . . Part 6." *Acta Cryst.* 9: 23–28.

*—— 1962. *The Third Dimension in Chemistry*. London: Oxford University Press.

*—— 1962a. *Structural Inorganic Chemistry*. London: Oxford University Press.

—— 1965. "Geometrical Basis. . . . Part 8." *Acta Cryst.* 18: 894–899.

—— 1968. "Geometrical Basis. . . . Part 9." *Acta Cryst.*, Ser. B, 24: 50–57.

—— 1969. "Geometrical Basis. . . . Part 10." *Acta Cryst.*, Ser. B, 25: 1711–1719.

*—— 1970. *Models in Structural Inorganic Chemistry*. London: Oxford University Press.

—— and Sharpe, R. R., 1963. "Geometrical Basis . . . . Part 7." *Acta Cryst.* 16: 857–871.

Weyl, H., 1952. *Symmetry*. Princeton: Princeton University Press.

Wheeler, G. E., 1958. "Cell Face Correlations and Geometrical Necessity." *American Journal of Botany* 45: 439–448.

Whyte, L. L., 1949. *The Unitary Principle in Physics and Biology*. New York: Holt.

*—— 1954. *Accent on Form*. New York: Harper.

*—— 1961. *Aspects of Form*. Bloomington, Indiana: Indiana University Press.

*—— 1961a. *Essay on Atomism*. Middletown, Conn.: Wesleyan University Press.

*—— 1965. "Atomism, Structure and Form," in *Structure in Art and in Science*, Gyorgy Kepes, editor. New York: Braziller.

*—— 1968. "The End of the Age of Separatism." *Saturday Review*, May 18, pp. 23–65.

Williams, R. W., 1968. "Space Filling Polyhedron: Its Relation to Aggregates of Soap Bubbles, Plant Cells, and Metal Crystallites," *Science* 161, 276–277.

Williams, M. W., and Smith, C. S., 1952. "A Study of Grain Shape in an Aluminum Alloy and Other Applications of Stereoscopic Microradiography." *Journal of Metals* 4: 755–765.

Wildy, P., and Horne, R. W., 1963. "Structure of Animal Virus Particles." *Progressive Medical Virology* 5: 1–42.

Wollaston, W. H., 1813. "On the Elementary Particles of Certain Crystals." Reprinted in *Classical Scientific Papers* (Knight).

Wood, D. G. *Space Enclosure Systems*. Columbus, Ohio: Ohio State University, Engineering Experiment Station, Bulletin 203.

Wood, E. A., 1964. *Crystals and Light*. Princeton: Van Nostrand.

Wood, W. B., and Edgar, R. S., 1967. "Building a Bacterial Virus." *Scientific American* 217 (July): 60–74.

Wunderlich, B., 1964. "The Solid State of Polyethylene." *Scientific American* 211 (November): 80–94.

Photo and Picture Credits